T0271068

HIMSS Dictionary of Health Information and Technology Terms, Acronyms, and Organizations

This significantly expanded and newest edition of the bestselling *HIMSS Dictionary of Health Information Technology Terms, Acronyms, and Organizations* has been developed and extensively reviewed by more than 50 industry experts. The sixth edition of this dictionary serves as a quick reference for students, health information technology professionals, and healthcare executives to better navigate the ever-growing health IT field and includes new terms used as a result of the COVID-19 pandemic and will serve as a resource for HIMSS' new certification based on digital health transformation as well as for those taking the CPHIMS and CAHIMS certification exams.

This valuable resource includes more than 3,000 definitions, 30 organizations, and numerous new references. Definitions of terms for the information technology and clinical, medical, and nursing informatics fields are updated and included. This sixth edition also includes an acronym list with cross-references to current definitions, new word-search capability, and a list of health IT-related associations and organizations, including contact information, mission statements, and web addresses. Academic and certification credentials are also included.

HIMSS Dictionary of Health Information and Technology Terms, Acronyms, and Organizations

Sixth Edition

A PRODUCTIVITY PRESS BOOK

First published 2025
by Routledge
605 Third Avenue, New York, NY 10158

and by Routledge
4 Park Square, Milton Park, Abingdon, Oxon, OX14 4RN

Routledge is an imprint of the Taylor & Francis Group, an informa business

© 2025 HIMSS

ISBN: 978-1-032-25997-0 (hbk)
ISBN: 978-1-032-25994-9 (pbk)
ISBN: 978-1-003-28602-8 (ebk)

DOI: 10.4324/9781003286028

Typeset in ITC Garamond Std
by Apex CoVantage, LLC

Contents

About HIMSS

HIMSS (Healthcare Information and Management Systems Society) is a global advisor, thought leader, and member-based society committed to reforming the global health ecosystem through the power of information and technology. As a mission-driven nonprofit, HIMSS offers a unique depth and breadth of expertise in health innovation, public policy, workforce development, research, and digital health transformation to advise leaders, stakeholders, and influencers across the global health ecosystem on best practices. With a community-centric approach, our innovation engine delivers key insights, education, and engaging events to healthcare providers, payers, governments, startups, life sciences, and other health services organizations, ensuring they have the right information at the point of decision.

HIMSS has served the global health community for more than 60 years, with focused operations across North America, Europe, the United Kingdom, the Middle East, and the Asia-Pacific.

HIMSS Vision

To realize the full health potential of every human, everywhere.

HIMSS Mission

Reform the global health ecosystem through the power of information and technology.

Foreword

Constant change continues to impact the ecosystem of health and healthcare as we experience consolidation, expansion, and disruption all at the same time. HIMSS' focus is evolving as well with a renewed intent to enhance value for our members while advancing the content direction of the industry through our thought leadership. What has not changed, however, is the importance of staying informed and remaining credible.

The sixth edition of *HIMSS Dictionary of Health Information and Technology Terms, Acronyms, and Organizations* is an essential resource. It reflects HIMSS' acknowledgment of the value of combining the best use of information and technology. New organizations are forming, terms are evolving, technologies are being disrupted, and much of that innovation is reflected in this new edition.

Innovation will continue to identify opportunities to improve everything from cost efficiency to the patient experience and clinical outcomes. Organizations of the future must have a vision capable of fluid change in a dynamic environment. New roles will be created as a result of the evolution of care models and services, which may or may not be accurate. This is the re-imagined becoming reality through asking, trying, and measuring the "what if" of tomorrow. We invite you to leverage this trusted resource to equip you with the knowledge needed to embark on this journey toward a value-driven health landscape.

Joyce Sensmeier, MS, RN-BC, CPHIMS, FHIMSS, FAAN
Joyce Sensmeier is a former advisor and also served as vice president of Informatics at HIMSS.

Introduction

Welcome to the sixth edition of the *HIMSS Dictionary of Health Information and Technology Terms, Acronyms, and Organizations*, which follows the anniversary of the dictionary's first publication in June 2006 through its fifth edition in 2019.

This sixth edition encompasses many terms found in the previous five editions but also includes updates to reflect the continuing evolution occurring within the health information and technology (HIT) industry. As new technologies and stakeholders emerge, the list of terms included in the dictionary has changed. The current terminology included in this sixth edition reflects, to the best of our efforts, the current state of healthcare, health information technology, and information technology.

The changes made in this edition reflect a careful process of collection, review, refinement, and, finally, compilation and include input from stakeholders from across the HIT industry. The book includes an appropriate reference for each term. We have endeavored to attach permalinks to web sites and digital object identifiers (DOIs) to journal articles. We have removed terms no longer relevant to our practice and added terms that mirror the current state of our profession.

This sixth edition contains almost 4,000 entries. Professional credentialing and organizational terms are separated from the main terms of the dictionary via appendices. Acronyms are incorporated into the alphabetical organization of the main terms to simplify searches. A separate acronym reference list is included should the user need to conduct a quick search for the acronym's full form. We hope our audience of HIT professionals, students, and others who are engaged in HIT activities will find this edition to be a useful tool.

We would like to thank HIMSS for undertaking the 2024 revision and publication of this valuable resource. Thank you to the individuals who collaborated with us, gave us new ideas on content, and suggested improvements to this edition. Thank you also to those who purchased and used previous editions of this book. Your past and continued support will ensure that future editions are accessible to the industry. Without your support, this edition would not have happened.

Christine A. Hudak, PhD, CPHIMS, FHIMSS, FAMIA
Editor

Acknowledgments

HIMSS sincerely thanks Christine A. Hudak, SAGES Fellow in Society & Technology, Case Western Reserve University, and HIMSS subject matter expert for the time and effort dedicated to the development of the sixth edition of this dictionary. Without her leadership, expertise, and consideration, this dictionary would not have become a reality.

A

AA (Attribute Authority)

A directory or database in which systems can securely add, modify, and save attributes. An attribute authority is a trusted source of data for Attribute-Based Access Control (ABAC) decisions.[21]

AAA (Authentication, Authorization, and Accounting)

A principle that is the cornerstone of security, whether IT or otherwise, and is comprised of access control, authentication, and accounting.[422] *See* **Authentication, Authorization, and Accounting**.

ABAC (Attribute-Based Access Control)

A logical access control model that is distinguishable because it controls access to objects by evaluating rules against the attributes of the entities (subject and object) actions and the environment relevant to a request.[1]

ABC (Activity-Based Costing)

An accounting technique that allows an organization to determine the actual cost associated with each product and service produced by the organization, without regard to organizational structure. A cost accounting approach concerned with matching costs with activities (called cost drivers) that cause those costs. It is a more sophisticated kind of absorption-costing and replaces labor-based costing systems. ABC states that (1) products consume activities; (2) it is the activities (and not the products) that consume resources; (3) activities are the cost drivers; and (4) activities are not necessarily based on the volume of production. Instead of allocating costs to cost centers (such as manufacturing, marketing, and finance), ABC allocates direct and indirect costs to activities such as processing an order, attending to a customer complaint, or setting up a machine.[4]

DOI: 10.4324/9781003286028-1

ABC codes (Alternative billing codes)

Terminology to describe alternative medicine, nursing, and other integrative healthcare interventions that include relative value units and legal scope of practice information. ABC codes are five-digit Health Insurance Portability and Accountability Act (HIPAA)-compliant alpha codes (e.g., AAAAA) used by licensed and non-licensed healthcare practitioners on standard healthcare claim forms (e.g., CMS 1500 Form) to describe services, remedies, and/or supply items provided and/or used during patient visits.[40]

Abend

Abnormal termination of software. **1.** A type of system error in which a task or program fails to execute properly (i.e., "abnormally ends"). The term is also used as the name for a type of error message that indicates such a failure has occurred. **2.** ABnormal END or ABortive END. System crash or other abnormal termination of a computer program caused by memory conflict or some other (usually unidentifiable) glitch.[6,4]

Abort

In data transmission, an *abort* is a function invoked by a sending station to cause the recipient to discard or ignore all bit sequences transmitted by the sender since the preceding flag sequence. To terminate a program or process abnormally and usually suddenly, with or without diagnostic information.[8,135]

Abstract message

The basic level of definition within HL7 is that of the abstract message associated with a particular trigger event. The abstract message includes the data fields that will be sent within a message, the valid response messages, and the treatment of application-level errors or the failure of the underlying communications system. An HL7 abstract message is defined in terms of HL7 segments and fields.[9]

Abstract syntax

A form of representation of data that is independent of machine-oriented structures and encodings and also of the physical representation of the data. Abstract syntax is used to give a high-level description of programs being compiled or messages passing over a communications link.[8]

A

Abstract Syntax Notation

See **ASN**.

Abstracting

An application that facilitates the collection and maintenance of coded patient information with selected patient demographic, clinical, and admissions data from the medical record, usually post-discharge. This information can be used for internal control, analysis, regulatory reports, and research.[2]

Abstraction

1. The process of extracting essential properties while omitting unessential details. **2.** The process of taking away or removing characteristics from something in order to reduce it to a set of essential characteristics. In object-oriented programming, abstraction is one of three central principles (along with encapsulation and inheritance). Through the process of abstraction, a programmer hides all but the relevant data about an object in order to reduce complexity and increase efficiency.[11,2] *See* **Encapsulation** and **Inheritance**.

ACA (Affordable Care Act)

On March 23, 2010, President Obama signed the Patient Protection and Affordable Care Act, which sought to extend healthcare coverage to more individuals and makes coverage more affordable for many others. Section 1561 requested the U.S. Department of Health and Human Services (HHS), in consultation with the Health Information Technology (HIT) Policy Committee and the HIT Standards Committee (the Committees), to develop interoperable and secure standards and protocols that facilitate electronic enrollment of individuals in federal and state health and human services programs.[12]

Acceptable downtime

See **Maximum tolerable period of disruption** and **MAO**.

Acceptable risk

Level of risk at which, given the costs and benefits associated with risk reduction measures, no action is deemed to be warranted at a given point in time.[13]

A

Acceptable Use Policy

See **AUP**.

Acceptance testing

A user-run testing event that demonstrates an application's ability to meet business objectives and system requirements. Also known as beta testing.[2]

Access

The ability and means to communicate with or otherwise interact with a system, to use system resources to handle information, to gain knowledge of the information the system contains, or to control system components and functions.[15]

Access control

The process of granting or denying specific requests for or attempts to (1) obtain and use information and related information processing services and (2) enter specific physical facilities.[15]

Access control Decision Function

See **ADF**.

Access control Enforcement Function

See **AEF**.

Access Control Information

See **ACI**.

Access Control List

See **ACL**.

Access control policy

The way an organization will manage access control and under which rules users have access to specific systems and information. It also defines the access control model that an organization may use.[423]

Access level

A category within a given security classification limiting entry or system connectivity to only authorized persons.[1]

Access mode

A distinct operation recognized by the protection mechanisms as a possible operation on an object. Read, write, and append are possible modes of access to a file, while execute is an additional mode of access to a program.[16]

Access point

A device that allows wireless devices to connect to a wired network using Wi-Fi or related standards.[1]

Access provider

See **ISP**.

Access to Radiology Information

See **ARI**.

Accountability

Refers to identifying the healthcare party (i.e., individuals, organizations, and business units) or agent (e.g., software, device, instrument, and monitor) that is responsible for data origination, amendment, verification, translation, stewardship, access and use, disclosure, and transmission and receipt.[17]

Accountable Care Organization

See **ACO**.

Accounting

Systematic and comprehensive recording of financial transactions pertaining to a business. Also refers to the process of summarizing, analyzing, and reporting these transactions to oversight agencies and tax collection entities.[18]

A

Accounting of disclosures

Individuals have a right to receive an accounting of disclosures of protected health information made by a covered entity in the six years prior to the date on which the accounting is required, subject to certain exceptions as set forth in 45 CFR (Code of Federal Regulations) 164.528.[424]

Accreditation

1. Formal declaration by a designated approving authority that an information system is approved to operate in a particular security mode using a prescribed set of safeguards at an acceptable level of risk. **2.** A process of review that healthcare organizations participate in to demonstrate their ability to meet predetermined criteria and standards established by a professional accrediting agency. Accreditation represents agencies as credible and reputable organizations dedicated to ongoing and continuous compliance with the highest standard of quality.[100,22]

ACDF (Access Control Decision Function) or ADF

A specialized function that makes access control decisions by applying access control policy rules to an access request, access control decision information (of initiators, targets, access requests, or that retained from prior decisions), and the context in which the access request is made.[16]

ACG (Ambulatory Care Group)

Also known as an *adjusted clinical group*. A method of categorizing outpatient episodes: preventive, diagnostic, therapeutic, surgical, and/or rehabilitative that are based on resource use over time and are modified by principal diagnosis, age, and sex.[23] *See* **ADG** and **APG**.

ACI (Access Control Information)

Information used for access control purposes, including contextual information. An ACI controls user access by defining the access privileges of an ITIM group or ACI principal. Members of an ITIM group or an ACI principal can view and perform operations on attributes within a target class (context) as defined by the scope of the ACI.[24,25]

ACID (Atomicity, Consistency, Isolation, and Durability)

An acronym and mnemonic device for learning and remembering the four primary attributes ensured to any transaction by a transaction manager (which is also called a transaction monitor). The ACID concept is described in ISO/IEC 10026-1 1992 Section 4. Each of these attributes can be measured against a benchmark.[2] *See* **Atomicity, Consistency, Isolation**, and **Durability**.

ACK (General acknowledgment message)

In data networking, an acknowledgment is a signal passed between communicating processes or computers to signify acknowledgment, or receipt of response, as part of a communications protocol. The ACK message is used to respond to a message where there has been an error that precludes application processing or where the application does not define a special message type for the response.[9]

ACL (Access Control List)

A list of permissions associated with an object. The list specifies who or what is allowed to access the object and what operations are allowed to be performed on the object.[1]

ACO (Accountable Care Organization)

Groups of doctors, hospitals, and other healthcare providers who come together voluntarily to give coordinated high-quality care to the patients they serve. Coordinated care helps ensure that patients, especially the chronically ill, get the right care at the right time, with the goal of avoiding unnecessary duplication of services and preventing medical errors. When an ACO succeeds in both delivering high-quality care and spending healthcare dollars more wisely, it will share in the savings it achieves.[26]

Acquisition modality

A system that acquires medical images, waveforms, or measurements while a patient or specimen is present (e.g., a computed tomography scanner, a specimen microscope, or a hemodynamic measurement system).[27]

A

Acquisition modality importer

A system that integrates a non-DICOM-ready modality into workflows.[27]

Active Directory

See **AD**.

Active Server Pages

See **ASP**.

Activity-Based Costing

See **ABC**.

Activity tracker

A device or application for monitoring and tracking fitness-related metrics such as distance walked or run, calorie consumption, heartbeat, and quality of sleep. Most often it refers to dedicated electronic monitoring devices that are synced to a computer or smartphone for long-term data tracking.[52] *See* **Wearable technology**.

Acute Physiology and Chronic Health Evaluation

See **APACHE**.

AD (Active Directory)

A system that automates network management of user data, security, and distributed resources.[2]

AD (Addendum)

New documentation used to add information to an original entry. Addenda should be timely and bear the current date and reason for the additional information being added to the health record.[28]

Addendum

See **AD**.

A

Address Resolution Protocol

See **ARP**.

ADE (Adverse Drug Event)

An injury resulting from the use of a drug. Under this definition, the term ADE includes harm caused by the drug (adverse drug reactions and over-dose) and harm from the use of the drug (including dose reductions and discontinuations of drug therapy). Adverse drug events may result from med-ication errors, but most do not. ADEs are injuries resulting from drug-related medical interventions. ADEs can occur in any healthcare setting, including inpatient, such as acute care hospitals, outpatient, and long-term care set-tings, such as nursing homes.[31, 67, 32]

ADG (Ambulatory Diagnostic Group)

A method of categorizing outpatient episodes. *See* **ACG** and **APG**.[23]

Ad hoc query

1. A query that is not determined prior to the moment it is run against a data source. **2.** A nonstandard inquiry created to obtain information as the need arises and contrasts with a query that is predefined and routinely processed.[71]

Administrative code sets

Code sets that characterize a general business situation rather than a medi-cal condition or service. Under HIPAA, these are sometimes referred to as nonclinical, or nonmedical, code sets. Compare to code sets and medical code sets.[26]

Administrative record

A record concerned with administrative matters, such as length of stay, details of accommodation, and billing.[4]

Administrative safeguards

Administrative actions, policies, and procedures to manage the selection, development, implementation, and maintenance of security measures to safeguard electronic protected health information and to manage the conduct of the covered entity's or business associate's workforce in relation to the protection of that information.[79]

Administrative Services Only

See **ASO**.

Administrator user access level

Administrator accounts are generally for users who require full access to the computer system.[425]

Admission date

The date the patient was admitted for inpatient care, outpatient service, or start of care.[26]

ADPAC (Automated Data Processing Application Coordinator)

The person responsible for implementing a set of computer programs (application package) developed to support a specific functional area such as Immunology Case Registry, PIMS, etc.[37]

ADR (Adverse Drug Reaction)

An unwanted response to a therapeutic drug. Health professionals must report all adverse reactions related to drugs or medical devices to the manufacturer and the FDA to aid in monitoring the safety of marketed medical products.[38] *See also* **ADE**.

ADR (ADT response message)

Admission, discharge, and transfer response message.[9]

ADSL (Asymmetric Digital Subscriber Line)

A type of DSL broadband communications technology used for transmitting digital information at a high bandwidth on existing phone lines to homes and businesses. Unlike dial-up phone services, ADSL provides continuously

A

available, "always on" connection. ADSL is asymmetric in that it uses most of the channel to transmit downstream to the user and only a small part to receive information from the user. ADSL simultaneously accommodates analog (voice) information on the same line.[2] With ADSL, telephone service providers compete with Internet service providers and varied Internet connection methods, such as modems, Wi-Fi routers, and fiber optic cable providers.

ADT (Admission, Discharge, and Transfer)

Admission, discharge, and transfer message for patients in a healthcare facility.[9]

ADT response message

See **ADR**.

Advance directive

A document by which a person makes provision for healthcare decisions in the event that he or she becomes unable to make those decisions. There are two main types of advance directive—the "Living Will" and the "Durable Power of Attorney for Health Care." There are also hybrid documents that combine elements of the Living Will with those of the Durable Power of Attorney.[81]

Advanced analytics

The autonomous or semi-autonomous examination of data or content using sophisticated techniques and tools, typically beyond those of traditional business intelligence, to discover deeper insights, make predictions, or generate recommendations. Advanced analytic techniques include those such as data/text mining, machine learning, pattern matching, forecasting, visualization, semantic analysis, sentiment analysis, network and cluster analysis, multivariate statistics, graph analysis, simulation, complex event processing, and neural networks.[142]

Advanced APM (Advanced Alternative Payment Model)

A track in the CMS Quality Payment Program where Eligible Clinicians (ECs) can earn a 5 percent incentive payment for achieving a threshold level of payments or patients that are achieved through a specific, designated APM. If ECs achieve these thresholds, they become a Qualifying APM Participant

A

(QP) and are excluded from the Merit-based Incentive Payment Systems (MIPS) reporting requirements and payment adjustment under QPP.[26]

Advanced Persistent Threat
See **APT**.

Advanced Technology Attachment
See **ATA**.

Adverse Drug Event
See **ADE**.

Adverse Drug Reaction
See **ADR**.

Adverse Event
See **AE**.

AE (Adverse Event/Adverse Experience)

Any untoward medical occurrence associated with the use of a drug or a medical product in humans, whether or not considered drug related. Pre-marketing: Any untoward medical occurrence in a patient or clinical investigation subject administered a pharmaceutical product that does not necessarily have a causal relationship with this treatment. Post-marketing/United States: Any adverse event associated with the use of a drug in humans, whether or not considered drug related, including the following: An adverse event occurring in the course of the use of a drug product in professional practice; an adverse event occurring from drug overdose; an adverse event occurring from drug withdrawal; and any failure of expected pharmacologic action. Post-marketing/European Union: Any undesirable experience occurring to a patient treated with a pharmaceutical product whether or not considered related to the medicinal product.[9, 41]

AE Title (Application Entity title)

An identifier utilized by Picture Archiving and Communication Systems (PACS) to uniquely name devices that can send and/or receive information to the imaging/PACS system.[42]

AEF (Access control enforcement function)

A specialized function that is part of the access path between an initiator and a target on each access request and enforces the decision made by the access control decision function.[16]

Affinity domain policy

Clearly defines the appropriate uses of the Integrating the Healthcare Enterprise (IHE) Cross-Enterprise Document Sharing (XDS) affinity domain. Within this policy is a defined set of acceptable privacy consent policies that are published and understood.[27]

Affordable Care Act

See **ACA**.

Aggregate

The collection or gathering of elements into a mass or whole.[29]

Aggregate data

1. Data elements assembled into a logical format to facilitate comparisons or to elicit evidence of patterns. **2**. A data type composed of multiple elements. An aggregate can be homogeneous (all elements have the same type), e.g., an array, a list in a functional language, a string of characters, and a file; or it can be heterogeneous (elements can have different types), e.g., a structure. In most languages, aggregates can contain elements which are themselves aggregates, e.g., a list of lists.[43,44]

Aggregation logics

Logic for aggregating detailed data into categories.[45]

A

AHT (Average Handling Time/Average Handle Time)

The average duration of a call handled by a customer service associate.[2]

AI (Artificial Intelligence)

The theory and development of computer systems able to perform tasks normally requiring human intelligence, such as visual perception, speech recognition, decision-making, and translation between languages.[107]

AIDC (Automatic Identification and Data Capture)

A broad category of technologies used to collect information from an individual, object, image, or sound without manual data entry. AIDC systems are used to manage inventory, delivery, assets, security, and documents. Sectors that use AIDC systems include distribution, manufacturing, transportation, medicine, government, and retail, among many others. AIDC applications typically fall into one of a few categories: identification and validation at the source, tracking, and interfaces to other systems. The actual technologies involved, the information obtained, and the purpose of collection vary widely. Current AIDC technologies include barcodes, 2D barcodes, magnetic strips, smart cards, optical character recognition, radio frequency identification, biometrics applications including finger scanning, and voice recognition.[2]

AIMS (Anesthesia Information Management System)

An information system that allows integrated communication with other hospital and provider systems throughout the perioperative period (such as clinical information systems used by nurses, clinical data repositories used by hospitals, and professional billing systems). AIMS are a specialized form of Electronic Health Record (EHR) systems that allow the automatic and reliable collection, storage, and presentation of patient data during the perioperative period. In addition to providing basic record-keeping functions, most AIMS also allow end users to access information for management, quality assurance, and research purposes. AIMS typically consist of a combination of hardware and software that interface with intraoperative monitors and in many cases hospital clinical data repositories or EHRs. Although the primary role of an AIMS is to capture data during the intraoperative phase, most systems can also incorporate pre- and postoperative patient information.[47]

AIS (Automated Information System)

An assembly of computer hardware, software, firmware, or any combination of these, configured to automatically accomplish specific information handling operations, such as communication, computation, dissemination, processing, and storage of information. Included are computers, word processing systems, networks, or other electronic information handling systems, and associated equipment.[109]

Alert

Written or acoustic signal to announce the arrival of messages and results and to avoid possible undesirable situations, such as contradictions, conflicts, erroneous entry, tasks that are not performed in time, or an exceptional result. A passive alert will appear on the screen in the form of a message. An active alert calls for immediate attention, and the appropriate person is immediately notified (e.g., by electronic pager).[34] *See* **Decision support system**.

Alert fatigue

Multiple false alarms by smart technology or computer programs that cause workers to ignore or respond slowly to them.[48]

Algorithm

Step-by-step procedure for problem-solving or calculating; a set of rules for problem-solving. In data mining, it defines the parameters of the data mining model.[2]

ALOS (Average Length of Stay)

Refers to the average number of days that patients spend in hospital. It is generally measured by dividing the total number of days stayed by all inpatients during a year by the total number of admissions or discharges. Day cases, such as same-day surgeries, are excluded.[49]

Alpha/beta testing

A pre-production development stage comprised of an initial trial (alpha test) by a select set of users. This initial test is to ensure that the system is stable enough for a rigorous trial (beta test) by additional users or in a variety of settings.[50, 51] *See* **Beta testing**.

16 ■ *Alternative Payment Models*

A

Alternative Payment Models

See **APMs**.

ALU (Arithmetic Logic Unit)

A major component of the Central Processing Unit (CPU) of a computer system. It does all processes related to arithmetic and logic operations that need to be done on instruction words. In some microprocessor architectures, the ALU is divided into the arithmetic unit and the logic unit.[2]

Ambulatory care

Clinical care, including diagnosis, observation, treatment, and rehabilitation, that is provided on an outpatient basis. Ambulatory care is given to persons who are able to ambulate or walk about.[96]

Ambulatory Care Group

See **ACG**.

Ambulatory care information system

Information systems used to improve the quality of care and promote business systems integration in the ambulatory care setting.[53]

Ambulatory EHR

The Electronic Health Record (EHR) that supports the ambulatory/clinic/physician office environments. Provides all of the functions of an EHR, which may include clinical documentation, order entry, clinical data repository, practitioner order entry, physician or nurse clinical documentation, etc.[2]

Ambulatory Medical Record

See **AMR**.

Amendments and corrections

Documentation meant to clarify health information within a health record. An amendment is made after the original documentation has been completed by the provider. All amendments should be timely and bear the current date of documentation. A correction is a change in the information meant to clarify inaccuracies after the original electronic document has been signed or rendered complete.[28]

American Recovery and Reinvestment Act of 2009

See **ARRA**.

American Standard Code for Information Interchange

See **ASCII**.

AMR (Ambulatory Medical Record)

An electronic or paper-based medical record used in the outpatient or ambulatory care setting.[53]

Analog

Representing data by measurement of a continuous physical variable, as voltage or pressure, as opposed to digital, which represents data as discrete units.[39]

Analog signal

In telecommunications, an analog signal is one in which a base carrier's alternating current frequency is modified in some way, such as by amplifying the strength of the signal or varying the frequency, in order to add information to the signal.[2] *See* **Digital signal**.

Analog-to-digital conversion

An electronic process in which a continuously variable (analog) signal is changed, without altering its essential content, into a multi-level (digital) signal.[2]

Analytics

A process that uses mathematics, statistics, predictive modeling, and machine learning techniques to find meaningful patterns and knowledge in recorded data.[116]

Analytics Competency Center

A cross-functional organizational team that has defined tasks, roles, responsibilities, and processes for supporting and promoting the effective use of business intelligence and/or analytics across an organization.[7]

Analytics strategy

A formal document presenting an organizational plan that outlines the goals, methods, and responsibilities for achieving analytics maturation.[10]

Ancillary care

Refers to the wide range of healthcare services. These services can be classified into three categories: diagnostic, therapeutic, and custodial. Diagnostic services include laboratory tests, radiology, genetic testing, diagnostic imaging, and more. Therapeutic services range from rehabilitation to physical and occupational therapy, as well as massage, chiropractic services, and speech therapy. Custodial services include hospice care, Long-Term Past Acute Care (LTPAC), urgent care, and nursing facility care.[54]

Anesthesia Information Management System

See **AIMS**.

ANN (Artificial Neuron Network)

An Artificial Neuron Network (ANN) is a computational model based on the structure and functions of biological neural networks. Information that flows through the network affects the structure of the ANN because a neural network changes—or learns, in a sense—based on that input and output. ANNs are considered nonlinear statistical data modeling tools where the complex relationships between inputs and outputs are modeled or patterns are found, and are among the main tools used in machine learning.[52]

Anonymization

A process that removes or replaces identity information from a communication or record. Communications and records may be made pseudonymous (see definition), in which case the same subject will always have the same replacement identity but cannot be identified as an individual.[56]

Anti-tearing

The process or processes that prevent data loss when a smartcard is withdrawn during a data operation.[2]

Anti-virus software

A program specifically designed to detect many forms of malware and prevent them from infecting computers, as well as cleaning computers that have already been infected.[1]

APACHE (Acute Physiology and Chronic Health Evaluation)

1. A severity-of-disease classification scoring system widely used in the United States. APACHE II is the most widely studied version of this instrument (a more recent version, APACHE IV, is proprietary but gaining increased usage due to its increased sensitivity), whereas APACHE II is publicly available); it derives a severity score from such factors as underlying disease and chronic health status. Other points are added for 12 physiologic variables (e.g., hematocrit, creatinine, Glasgow Coma Score, and mean arterial pressure) measured within 24 hours of admission to the ICU. The APACHE II score has been validated in several studies involving tens of thousands of ICU patients. **2.** A widely used web server platform written by the Apache Software Foundation (ASF). The Apache web server browser had a key role in the initial growth of the World Wide Web.[58]

APC (Ambulatory Payment Class)

A payment type for outpatient Prospective Payment System (PPS) claims.[59]

APG (Ambulatory Patient Group)

A reimbursement methodology developed by 3M Health Information Systems for the Health Care Financing Administration (HCFA); APGs are to outpatient procedures as DRGs are to inpatient days; APGs provide for a fixed reimbursement to an institution for outpatient procedures or visits and incorporate data regarding the reason for the visit and patient data; APGs prevent unbundling of ancillary services; *see also* **ACG** and **ADG**.[60]

A

API (Application Program Interface)

1. A set of standard software interrupts, calls, functions, and data formats that can be used by an application program to access network services, devices, applications, or operating systems. **2.** A set of pre-made functions used to build programs. APIs ask the operating system or another application to perform specific tasks. A variety of types of APIs exist, including messaging APIs for e-mail, telephony APIs for calling systems, Java APIs, and graphics APIs, such as DirectX.[2] *See* **Socket** and **SSL**.

APMs (Alternative Payment Models)

Models that offer healthcare providers added incentive payments to deliver high-quality and cost-efficient care. APMs are outlined in MACRA as a path for participation in MACRA's Quality Payment Program (QPP). Accountable Care Organizations (ACOs), Patient-Centered Medical Homes (PCMH), and bundled payment models are some examples of APMs.[26] *See* **MACRA** and **ACO**.

Application

A software program or set of related programs that provide some useful healthcare capability or functionality.[132]

Application architecture

Defines how applications are designed and how they cooperate; promotes common presentation standards to facilitate rapid training and implementation of new applications and functions. Good application architecture enables a high level of system integration, reuse of components, and rapid deployment of applications in response to changing business requirements.[57]

Application Entity title

See **AE title**.

Application integration

Sometimes called *enterprise application integration* or EAI; the process of bringing data or a function from one application program together with that of another application program. Where these programs already exist, the process is sometimes realized by using middleware, either packaged by a vendor

A

or written on a custom basis. A common challenge for an enterprise is to integrate an existing (or legacy) program with a new program or with a web service program of another company. In general, for new applications, the use of object-oriented programming and actual or de facto standard development tools and interfaces (such as Java or .NET) will help ensure that new application programs can be easily integrated with those that may be needed in the future. The Extensible Markup Language (XML) promises to serve as a tool for exchanging data among disparate programs in a standard way.[2]

Application layer

See **OSI**. Layer 7 of the OSI (Open Systems Interconnection) model. Responsible for information transfer between two network applications. This involves such functions as security checks, identification of the two participants, availability checks, negotiating exchange mechanisms, and most importantly initiating the exchanges themselves.[52]

Application metadata

See **Metadata**.

Application Program Interface

See **API**.

Application protocol services

These are services supporting application-level protocols. Simple Object Access Protocol (SOAP) will be supported. Other remoting protocols, such as remote method invocation, and DICOM, can be plugged into the application protocol service.[57]

Application role

A characteristic of an application that defines a portion of its interfaces. It is defined in terms of the interactions (messages) that the role sends or receives in response to trigger events. Thus, it is a role played by a health-care information system component when sending or receiving health information technology messages; a set of responsibilities with respect to an interaction.[9]

A

Application server

1. Program on a distributed network that provides business logic and server-side execution environment for application programs. **2.** A computer that handles all operations between a company's back-end applications or databases and the users' computers' graphical user interface or web browsers. **3.** The device that facilitates the hosting and delivery of applications, used by multiple and simultaneously connected local and remote users.[2, 10, 52]

Appointment

An appointment represents a booked slot or group of slots on a schedule, relating to one or more services or resources. Two examples might include a patient visit scheduled at a clinic and a reservation for a piece of equipment.[9]

Appropriate Use Criteria

See **AUC**.

APT (Advanced Persistent Threat)

An adversary that possesses sophisticated levels of expertise and significant resources which allow it to create opportunities to achieve its objectives by using multiple attack vectors (e.g., cyber, physical, and deception). These objectives typically include establishing and extending footholds within the information technology infrastructure of the targeted organizations for purposes of exfiltrating information; undermining or impeding critical aspects of a mission, program, or organization; or positioning itself to carry out these objectives in the future. The advanced persistent threat (1) pursues its objectives repeatedly over an extended period of time; (2) adapts to defenders' efforts to resist it; and (3) is determined to maintain the level of interaction needed to execute its objectives.[1]

Archetype

1. A named content type specification with attribute declarations. **2.** Model (or pattern) for the capture of clinical information—a machine-readable specification of how to store patient data.[61, 62]

A

Archetype instance

Metadata class instance of an archetype model, specifying the clinical concept and the value constraints that apply to one class of record component instances in an electronic health record extract.[63]

Archetype model

Information model of the metadata to represent the domain-specific characteristics of electronic health record entries by specifying values or value constraints for classes and attributes in the electronic health record reference model.[63]

Archetype repository

Persistent repository of archetype definitions accessed by a client authoring tool or by a run-time component within an electronic health record service.[63]

Architecture

1. A term applied to both the process and the outcome of specifying the overall structure, logical components, and logical interrelationships of a computer, its operating system, a network, or other conception. **2.** A framework from which applications, databases, and workstations can be developed in a coherent manner and in which every part fits together without containing a mass of design details. Normally used to describe how a piece of hardware or software is constructed and which protocols and interfaces are required for communications. Network architecture specifies the function and data transmission needed to convey information across a network.[134]

Archive

Long-term, physically or digitally separate storage.[64]

Archiving

Data archiving is the process of moving data that are no longer actively used to a separate storage device for long-term retention. Archive data consist of older data that are still important to the organization and may be needed for future reference, as well as data that must be retained for regulatory compliance. Data archives are indexed and have search capabilities so files and parts of files can be easily located and retrieved.[2]

A

Arden syntax

A language created to encode actions within a clinical protocol into a set of situation-action rules for computer interpretation and to facilitate exchange between different institutions.[65]

Argonaut Project

A private sector initiative to advance industry adoption of modern, open interoperability standards. The purpose of the Argonaut Project is to rapidly develop a first-generation FHIR-based API and Core Data Services specification to enable expanded information sharing for electronic health records and other health information technology based on Internet standards and architectural patterns and styles.[138]

ARI (Access to Radiology Information)

Specifies a number of query transactions providing access to radiology information, including images and related reports, in a DICOM format, as they were acquired or created. Such access is useful, both to the radiology department and to other departments, such as pathology, surgery, and oncology.[27]

Arithmetic Logic Unit

See **ALU**.

ARP (Address Resolution Protocol)

Performs a required function in IP routing. ARP finds the hardware address, also known as Media Access Control (MAC) address with its associated IP address.[2]

ARRA (American Recovery and Reinvestment Act of 2009)

An economic stimulus bill enacted by the 111th United States Congress and signed into law by President Barack Obama created the Health Information Technology for Economic and Clinical Health (HITECH) Act, which provided $30 billion for various health information technology investments, including funding incentives for acute care hospitals and physicians in private practice to adopt certified EHRs.[139]

Array

A set of sequentially indexed elements having the same intrinsic data type. Each element of an array has a unique identifying index number.[68]

Artificial Intelligence

See **AI**.

Artificial Neuron Network

See **ANN**.

ASA (Average Speed of Answer)

The average amount of time (measured in seconds) from when a caller calls customer service (enters the customer service queue) to when the caller begins speaking to a customer service associate.[155]

ASCII (American Standard Code for Information Interchange)

Bit standard information processing code that represents 128 possible standard characters used by PCs. In an ASCII file, each alphabetic, numeric, or special character is represented with a 7-bit number (a string of seven 0s or 1s), which yields the 128 possible characters.[2]

ASN (Abstract Syntax Notation)

The International Organization of Standardization (ISO), the International Electrotechnical Commission (IEC), and the International Telecommunications Union-Telecommunications Sector (ITU-T) (formerly known as the International Telegraph and Telephone Consultative Committee [CCITT]) have established Abstract Syntax Notation One (ASN.1) and its encoding rules as a standard for describing and encoding messages. ASN.1 is a formal notation for abstractly describing data to be exchanged between distributed computer systems. Encoding rules are sets of rules used to transform data specified in the ASN.1 notation into a standard format that can be decoded by any system that has a decoder based on the same set of rules.[2]

ASO (Administrative Services Only)

Sometimes referred to as an Administrative Services Contract (ASC), a contract between an insurance company and a self-funded plan where the insurance company performs administrative services only and does not assume any risk; services usually include claims processing but may include other services such as actuarial analysis and utilization review.[23] An arrangement in which an organization funds its own employee benefit plan such as a pension plan or health insurance program but hires an outside firm to perform specific administrative services.[18]

ASP (Active Server Pages)

Server-side scripting environment for creating dynamic and interactive web pages and applications.[68]

Assembly services

A business request may include calls to various components providing multiple result sets. These result sets will be assembled together in the appropriate output format by the assembly service. This service will use assembly templates to carry out its function.[57]

Association

Linking a document with the program that created it so that both can be opened with a single command (e.g., double-clicking a ".doc" file opens Microsoft® Word and loads the selected document).[9]

Assurance

The grounds for confidence that the set of intended security controls in an information system are effective in their application.[1]

Asymmetric cryptographic algorithm

Algorithm for performing encryption or the corresponding decryption in which the keys used for encryption and decryption differ.[72, 170]

Asymmetric Digital Subscriber Line

See **ADSL**.

Asymmetric keys

A combination of public and private keys used to encrypt and decrypt data. The public key is shared with others, and the complementary private key is kept secret. The public key may be used to encrypt the data, and the associated private key may be used to decrypt the data. Also known as public key cryptography.[2]

Asymmetric multiprocessing

This technique involves a master–slave relationship among the processors. There is one master processor that controls remaining slave processors. The master processor allots processes to slave processors, or they may have some predefined task to perform.[69]

Asynchronous communication

Communication in which the reply is not made immediately after the message is sent but when the recipient is available. E-mail is an example of asynchronous communication.[66]

Asynchronous Transfer Mode

See **ATM**.

ATCB (Authorized Testing and Certification Body)

An entity that tests and certifies that certain types of Electronic Health Record (EHR) technology (base EHRs and EHR modules) are compliant with the standards, implementation specifications, and certification criteria adopted by the U.S. Department of Health and Human Services Secretary and meet the definition of certified EHR technology.[26]

ATM (Asynchronous Transfer Mode)

A high-performance, cell-oriented, switching, and multiplexing technology that utilizes fixed-length packets to carry different types of traffic.[74] *See* **Frame relay** and **SONET**.

Atomic concept

1. Primitive concept. **2.** Concept in a formal system whose definition is not a compositional definition.[75,76]

Atomic data (atomic level data)

Data elements that represent the lowest level of possible detail in a data warehouse. The elemental, precise data captured at the source in the course of clinical care can be manipulated in a variety of ways. These data are collected once but used many times.[2]

Atomicity

Atomicity is a feature of database systems dictating where a transaction must be all-or-nothing. That is, the transaction must either fully happen or not happen at all. It must not be completed partially. Atomicity is part of the ACID model (Atomicity, Consistency, Isolation, Durability), which is a set of principles used to guarantee the reliability of database transactions. Atomicity is usually achieved by complex mechanisms, such as journaling or logging, or via operating system calls. The definition of what constitutes an atomic transaction is decided by its context or the environment in which it is being implemented.[52] *See* **ACID**.

Attachment Unit Interface

See **AUI**.

Attack vectors

Means by which an unauthorized person or entity gains access to a target (e.g., system, network, or otherwise).[2]

Attenuation

The measurement of how much a signal weakens over distance on a transmission medium. The longer the medium, the more attenuation becomes a problem without the regeneration of the signal.[2]

Attribute

An attribute expresses the characteristics of a basic elemental concept. Attributes are also known as *roles* or *relationship types*. Semantic concepts form relationships with each other through attributes. Attributes are abstractions of the data captured about classes. Attributes capture separate aspects of the class and take their values independent of one another. Attributes assume data values that are passed in HL7 messages.[9,77]

Attribute Authority

See **AA**.

Attribute certificate

1. Data structure, digitally signed by an attribute authority, which binds some attribute values with identification about its holder. **2.** A digital document containing attributes associated to the holder by the issuer.[72]

Attribute relationship

Consists of two semantic concepts related to each other through an attribute. When an attribute-value pair has been assigned to a concept, that relationship becomes part of the concept's logical definition. For this reason, attribute relationships are called "defining characteristics" of semantic concepts.[77]

Attribute type

The last part of an attribute name (suffix). Attribute-type suffixes are rough classifiers for the meaning of the attribute.[9] *See* **Data type** for contrast in definition.

Attribute-value pair

The combination of an attribute with a value that is appropriate for that attribute. Assigning attribute-value pairs to semantic concepts is known as "authoring" or "modeling" and is part of the process of semantic content development. Attributes and values are always used together as attribute-value pairs. Sometimes the entire relationship is referred to as an object-attribute-value triple, or "OAV" triple.[77]

AUC (Appropriate Use Criteria)

Criteria that are evidence based (to the extent feasible) and assist professionals who order and furnish applicable imaging services to make the most appropriate treatment decisions for a specific clinical condition. The AUC Program is established under CMS to promote the use of AUC for advanced diagnostic imaging services, as directed by Section 218(b) of the Protecting Access to Medicare Act of 2014 Title XVIII of the Social Security Act.[26]

Audit

Independent review and examination of records and activities to assess the adequacy of system controls; to ensure compliance with established policies and operational procedures; and to recommend necessary changes in controls, policies, or procedures.[132]

Audit repository

Stores audit events.[27]

Audit trail

1. Chronological record of system activity which enables the reconstruction of information regarding the creation, distribution, modification, and deletion of data. **2.** Documentary evidence of monitoring each operation of individuals on health information. May be comprehensive or specific to the individual and information. Audit trails are commonly used to search for unauthorized access by authorized users.[132]

Auditing

Specific activities that make up an audit. This can be manual, automated, or a combination.[20]

AUI (Attachment Unit Interface)

The AUI is the 15-pin physical connector interface between a computer's Network Interface Card (NIC) and an Ethernet cable.[2]

AUP (Acceptable Use Policy)

Provides guidance to employees and other workforce members regarding the appropriate use of a healthcare organization's information technology resources and data.[53]

Authentication

Security measure, such as the use of digital signatures, to establish the validity of a transmission, message, or originator, or a means of verifying an individual's authorization to receive specific categories of information. The

A

process of proving that a user or system is really who or what it claims to be. It protects against the fraudulent use of a system or the fraudulent transmission of information.[2]

Authenticity

Assurance that a message, transaction, or other exchange of information is from the source it claims to be from. Authenticity involves proof of identity.[78]

Authority certificate

Certificate issued to a certification authority or to an attribute authority. A Certificate Authority (CA) is a trusted entity that issues electronic documents that verify a digital entity's identity on the Internet. The electronic documents, which are called digital certificates, are an essential part of secure communication and play an important part in the Public Key Infrastructure (PKI).[2,72]

Authorization

A security mechanism used to determine user/client privileges or access levels related to system resources, including computer programs, files, services, data, and application features. Authorization is normally preceded by authentication for user identity verification.[52]

Authorized Testing and Certification Body

See **ATCB**.

Automated Data Processing Application Coordinator

See **ADPAC**.

Availability

Timely, reliable access to data and information services for authorized users.[1]

Average Handling Time

See **AHT**.

A

Average Length of Stay

See **ALOS**.

Average Speed of Answer

See **ASA**.

AVR (Analysis, Visualization, and Reporting)

Ability to analyze, display, report, and map accumulated data, and share data and technologies for analysis and visualization with other public health partners.[80]

B

B2B (Business-to-business)

On the Internet, B2B, also known as e-biz, is the exchange of products, services, or information (aka e-commerce) between businesses rather than between businesses and consumers.[2]

B2B2C (Business-to-business-to-consumer)

An emerging e-commerce model that combines business-to-business (B2B) and business-to-consumer (B2C) for a complete product or service transaction. B2B2C is a collaboration process that, in theory, creates mutually beneficial service and product delivery channels.[2]

B2C (Business-to-consumer)

An Internet and electronic commerce (e-commerce) model that denotes a financial transaction or online sale between a business and a consumer. B2C involves a service or product exchange from a business to a consumer, whereby merchants sell products to consumers.[2]

BA (Business Associate)

As set forth in 45 CFR 160.103, on behalf of such covered entity or of an organized healthcare arrangement in which the covered entity participates, but other than in the capacity of a member of the workforce of such covered entity or arrangement, creates, receives, maintains, or transmits protected health information for a HIPAA function or activity regulated by this subchapter, including claims processing or administration, data analysis, processing, or administration, utilization review, quality assurance, patient safety activities listed at 42 CFR 3.20, billing, benefit management, practice management, and repricing; or performs, or assists in the performance of (1) a function or activity involving the use or disclosure of individually identifiable health information, including claims processing or administration, data analysis, processing or administration, utilization review, quality assurance, billing, benefit management, practice management, and repricing; or (2) any other function or activity regulated by this subchapter; or (3) provides, other than in the capacity of a member of the workforce of such covered entity, legal, actuarial, accounting, consulting, data aggregation, management, administrative, accreditation, or financial services to or for such covered entity, or to or for an organized healthcare arrangement in which the covered entity participates, where the provision of the service involves the disclosure of individually identifiable protected health information from such covered entity or arrangement, or from another business associate of such covered entity or arrangement, to the person.[35] *See* **Covered entity** and **BAA**.

BAA (Business Associate Agreement)

Also known as HIPAA Business Associate Agreement (BAA). Identified under the U.S. Health Insurance Portability and Accountability Act, a contract between a HIPAA-covered entity and a HIPAA Ausiness Associate (BA). The contract safeguards Protected Health Information (PHI) in accordance with HIPAA guidelines.[2,35] *See* **Covered entity**.

Backbone

The high-speed, high-performance main transmission path in a network; a set of paths that local or regional networks connect to as a node for interconnection. The top level in a hierarchical network. Stub networks and transit networks which connect to the same backbone are guaranteed to be interconnected.[8]

Backdoor

1. Unauthorized hidden software or hardware mechanism used to circumvent security controls. **2.** An undocumented way of gaining access to a computer system. A backdoor is a potential security risk.[1]

Background

A task running in the background (a background task) is detached from the terminal where it was started (and often running at a lower priority); opposite of foreground. This means that the task's input and output must be from/to files (or other processes).[8]

Background process

A program that is running without user input. A number of background processes can be running on a multitasking operating system, such as Linux, while the user is interacting with the foreground process. Some background processes, such as daemons, for example, never require user input. Others are merely in the background temporarily while the user is busy with the program presently running in the foreground so that other processes can be sleeping and taking up swap space, until activated, which thus makes it currently a background process.[33]

Backup

A copy of files and programs made to facilitate recovery, if necessary.[1]

BAN (Body Area Network)

The interconnection of multiple computing devices worn on, affixed to, or implanted in a person's body. A BAN typically includes a smartphone in a pocket or bag that serves as a mobile data hub, acquiring user data and transmitting it to a remote database or other system.[2]

Bandwidth

The difference between the highest and lowest frequencies of a transmission channel (the width of its allocated band of frequencies). The term is often erroneously used to mean data rate or capacity.[8]

Bar code

A printed horizontal strip of vertical bars of varying widths, groups of which represent decimal digits and are used for identifying products, parts, or patients. Bar codes are read by a bar code reader, and the code is interpreted either through software or through a hardware decoder.[8]

Bar Code Medication Administration

See **BCMA**.

B

Bar coding

Using barcode symbols to identify an item. Bar coding is the most common form of automatic identification used in automatic data capture technologies. Bar codes track virtually everything: from retail goods to medical records, and machinery to human beings.[4]

Baseband

A transmission medium through which digital signals are sent without frequency shifting. In general, only one communication channel is available at any given time.[8]

Baseline

Hardware, software, and relevant documentation for an information system at a given point in time.[1]

Baseline configuration

A set of specifications for a system, or Configuration Item (CI) within a system, that has been formally reviewed and agreed on at a given point in time and which can be changed only through change control procedures. The baseline configuration is used as a basis for future builds, releases, and/or changes.[1]

Basic Input Output System

See **BIOS**.

Batch file

A text file containing operating system commands which are executed automatically by the command-line interpreter. Batch files can be used as a simple way to combine existing commands into new commands.[60]

Batch job

A batch job in SAP (Systems, Applications, and Products) is a scheduled background program that usually runs on a regular basis without any user intervention. Batch jobs are provided with more allocated memory than the ones that are done in the foreground. They are used to process high volumes of data that would normally consume long-term memory if run in the foreground, as well as for running programs that require less user interaction.[52]

Batch processing

A system that takes a sequence (a "batch") of commands or jobs, executes them, and returns the results, all without human intervention. This contrasts with an interactive system where the user's commands and the computer's responses are interleaved during a single run.[8]

BCMA (Bar Code Medication Administration)

An inventory control system that uses barcodes to prevent human errors in the distribution of prescription medications. The goal of BCMA is to make sure that patients are receiving the correct medications at the correct time by electronically validating and documenting medication administration. The information encoded in barcodes allows for the comparison of the medication being administered with what was ordered for the patient.[2]

BCP (Business Continuity Plan)

The documentation of a predetermined set of instructions or procedures that describe how an organization's mission/business functions will be sustained during and after a significant disruption.[1]

BEC (Business e-mail Compromise)

A sophisticated scam targeting businesses working with foreign suppliers and/or businesses that regularly perform wire transfer payments.[426]

Behavioral Health

See **BH**.

Behavioral Health Outcome Management

See **BHOM**.

Behavioral Risk Factor Surveillance System

See **BRFSS**.

Benchmarking

Refers to testing a product or service against a reference point to quantify how much better or worse it is compared to other products. Benchmarking is the standard way of comparing one product to another. With technology in particular, benchmarking against competing products is often the only way to get an objective measure of quality. This is because many technology products increase rapidly in measures such as speed and storage size when compared to the previous version from the same company, making comparisons between the versions virtually useless.[52]

Best-of-breed system

The best system in its referenced niche or category. Although it performs specialized functions better than an integrated system, this type of system is limited by its specialty area. To fulfill varying requirements, organizations often use best-of-breed systems from separate vendors. However, maintaining multiple systems provides little cross-connectivity, which creates maintenance and integration challenges.[52]

Best practice

A technique or methodology that, through experience and research, has proven to reliably lead to a desired result.[52]

Beta testing

The final stage in the testing of new software before its commercial release, conducted by testers other than its developers.[84]

BH (Behavioral Health)

Behavioral health generally refers to mental health and substance use disorders, life stressors and crises, and stress-related physical symptoms. Behavioral healthcare refers to the prevention, diagnosis, and treatment of those conditions.[85]

BHOM (Behavioral Health Outcome Management)

Involves the use of behavioral health outcome measurement data to help guide and inform the treatment of each individual patient.[7]

B

BIA (Business Impact Analysis)

An analysis of an information system's requirements, functions, and inter-dependencies used to characterize system contingency requirements and priorities in the event of a significant disruption.[1]

Big data

Any voluminous amount of structured, semi-structured, and unstructured data that can be mined for information. Big data can be characterized by the volume of data, the variety of types of data, and the velocity at which the data must be processed.[2]

Big data storage

A storage infrastructure that is designed specifically to store, manage, and retrieve massive amounts of data or big data. Big data storage enables the storage and sorting of big data in such a way that it can easily be accessed, used, and processed by applications and services working on big data. Big data storage is also able to flexibly scale as required.[52]

Binary base two

A numeric system that only uses two digits—zero and one. Computers oper-ate in binary, meaning they store data and perform calculations using only zeros and ones.[73]

Binding

Process of associating two related elements of information. An acknowl-edgment by a trusted third party that associates an entity's identity with its public key.[1]

BinHex

A Macintosh format for representing a binary file using only printable char-acters. The file is converted to lines of letters, numbers, and punctuation. Because BinHex files are simply text, they can be sent through most elec-tronic mail systems and stored on most computers. However, the conversion to text makes the file larger, so it takes longer to transmit a file in BinHex format than if the file was represented some other way.[8]

Bioinformatics

The use of computer science, statistical modeling, and algorithmic processing to understand biological data.[52]

Biomedical informatics

The interdisciplinary field that studies and pursues the effective uses of
biomedical data, information, and knowledge for scientific inquiry, problem-solving, and decision-making, motivated by efforts to improve human
health.[175]

Biomedical Translational Research Information System

See **BTRIS**.

Biometric authentication

A user identity verification process that involves biological input, or the scanning or analysis of some part of the body, such as fingerprints or iris scans.
Biometric authentication methods are used to protect different kinds of
systems—from logical systems facilitated through hardware access points to
physical systems protected by physical barriers, such as secure facilities and
protected research sites.[52]

Biometric identifier

Biologically unique data that identify a person. Under the provisions of the
Health Insurance Portability and Accountability Act, biometric identifiers
are protected health information that must be held in strict confidence by
healthcare agencies and professionals.[123]

Biometric system

A technological system that uses information about a person (or other
biological organism) to identify that person. Biometric systems rely on
specific data about unique biological traits in order to work effectively.
A biometric system will involve running data through algorithms for a
particular result, usually related to a positive identification of a user or
other individual.[52]

Biometric verification

An identity authentication process used to confirm a claimed identity through uniquely identifiable biological traits, such as fingerprints and hand geometry. Designed to allow a user to prove his or her identity by supplying a biometric sample and associated unique identification code in order to gain access to a secure environment.[52]

Biometrics

1. A physical or behavioral characteristic of a human being. **2.** Pertaining to the use of specific attributes that reflect unique personal characteristics, such as a fingerprint, an eye blood-vessel print, or a voice print, to validate the identity of a person. **3.** Biometrics is a technological and scientific authentication method based on biology and used in information assurance. Biometric identification authenticates secure entry, data, or access via human biological information such as DNA or fingerprints. Biometric systems include several linked components for effective functionality. The biometric system connects an event to a single person, whereas other ID forms, such as a Personal Identification Number (PIN), may be used by anyone.[1, 36, 52]

BIOS (Basic Input Output System)

BIOS (basic input/output system) is the program a computer's microprocessor uses to start the computer system after it is powered on. It also manages data flow between the computer's Operating System (OS) and attached devices, such as the hard disk, video adapter, keyboard, mouse, and printer.[107]

BioSense Platform

At the core of the Centers for Disease Control and Prevention's (CDC's) National Syndromic Surveillance Program (NSSP) is its BioSense Platform. It provides public health officials a common cloud-based health information system with standardized tools and procedures to rapidly collect, evaluate, share, and store information. Health officials can use the BioSense Platform to analyze and exchange syndromic data—improving their common awareness of health threats over time and across regional boundaries. They can exchange information faster and better coordinate community actions to protect the public's health. The BioSense Platform was developed through an active collaboration of the CDC and other federal agencies, state and local health departments, and public health partners. The platform hosts an array of user-selected tools and has features that are continually being enhanced to reflect their needs.[80]

Biosurveillance

The process of gathering, integrating, interpreting, and communicating essential information that might relate to disease activity and threats to human, animal, or plant health. Activities range from standard epidemiological practices to advanced technological systems, utilizing complex algorithms.[176]

Bit

A contraction of the term Binary Digit. The smallest unit of information in a binary system of notation.[1]

Bit depth

The number of bits used to represent each pixel in an image, determining its color or tonal range.[7]

Bitcoin

Virtual currency that has an equivalent value in real currency, or that acts as a substitute for real currency, is referred to as "convertible" virtual currency. Bitcoin is one example of a convertible virtual currency. Bitcoin can be digitally traded between users and can be purchased for, or exchanged into, U.S. dollars, euros, and other real or virtual currencies.[427]

Bitmap

A data file or structure which corresponds bit-for-bit with an image displayed on a screen, probably in the same format as it would be stored in the display's video memory or maybe as a device-independent bitmap. A bitmap is characterized by the width and height of the image in pixels and the number of bits per pixel which determines the number of shades of gray or colors it can represent. A bitmap representing a colored image (a "pixmap") will usually have pixels with between one and eight bits for each of the red, green, and blue components, though other color encodings are also used.

The green component sometimes has more bits than the other two to cater to the human eye's greater discrimination in this component.[8]

Bits Per Second

See **BPS**.

Blacklisting

The process of the system invalidating a user ID based on the user's inappropriate actions. A blacklisted user ID cannot be used to log on to the system, even with the correct authenticator. Blacklisting and lifting of a blacklisting are both security-relevant events. A control to prevent unwanted applications and programs from gaining access to an organization's computing resources. Blacklisted users can refer to a process, application, or human user associated with an ID.[1,2]

Blanket Purchasing Agreement

See **BPA**.

BLE (Bluetooth Low Energy)

A power-conserving variant of Bluetooth personal-area network technology, designed for use by Internet-connected machines and appliances.[2]

Blockchain

A technology for transactional applications that can be used to share a ledger across a business network. This ledger is the source of all transactions across the business network and is shared among all participants in a secure, encrypted environment. This technology grew out of the Bitcoin technological innovation. Blocks, or transaction records, are added to the chain in a linear, chronological order. Each node (or participant connected to the network) gets a copy of the blockchain, which gets downloaded automatically upon joining.[89, 18]

Blockchain node

A device on a blockchain network, which is in essence the foundation of the technology, allowing it to function and survive. Nodes are distributed across a widespread network and carry out a variety of tasks. The role of a node is to support the network by maintaining a copy of a blockchain and, in some cases, to process transactions. Nodes are often arranged in the structure of trees, known as binary trees. Nodes are the individual parts of the larger data structure that is a blockchain.[178]

Bluetooth

A specification for radio links between mobile devices, mobile phones, digital cameras, and other portable devices.[8]

Bluetooth Low Energy

See **BLE**.

Body Area Network

See **BAN**.

Boolean logic/Boolean algebra

Form of logic seen in computer applications in which all values are expressed either as true or as false. Symbols used to designate this are often called Boolean operators. They consist of equal to (=), more than (>), less than (<), and any combination of these, plus the use of "AND," "OR," and "NOT."[8]

Boot partition

Partition that contains the operating system files.[2]

Born in the cloud

Refers to a specific type of cloud service that does not involve legacy systems but was designed only for cloud delivery. This category of cloud services is instructive in changing how companies view reliance on cloud vendors.[52]

Bot

Software that performs an automated task over the Internet. More specifically, it is an automated application used to perform simple and repetitive tasks that are time-consuming, mundane, or impossible for a human to perform. Bots are also frequently used for malicious purposes.[52]

B

Bounce

An electronic mail message that is undeliverable and returns an error notification (a "bounce message") to the sender is said to "bounce."[8]

Bourne shell

A shell command-line interpreter for Unix or Unix-like operating systems.[8]

BPA (Blanket Purchase Agreement)

A method of acquiring a variety of goods and services under an agreement when an order is issued. It is not a contract; BPAs are used by government agencies and organizations for simplifying the government purchasing process.[161]

BPM (Business Process Management)

A systematic approach to making an organization's workflow more effective, more efficient, and more capable of adapting to an ever-changing environment.[2]

BPS (Bits Per Second)

The basic unit of speed associated with data transmission.[2]

BRE (Business Rules Engine)

A software component that allows non-programmers to add or change business logic in a Business Process Management (BPM) system.[2]

Breach of security

The acquisition, access, use, or disclosure of protected health information in a manner not permitted or compromises the security or privacy of the protected health information as set forth in 45 CFR 164.402.[35]

BRFSS (Behavioral Risk Factor Surveillance System)

The nation's premier system of health-related telephone surveys that collect state data about U.S. residents regarding their health-related risk behaviors, chronic health conditions, and use of preventive services. Established in

B

1984 with 15 states, BRFSS now collects data in all 50 states as well as the District of Columbia and three U.S. territories.[80]

Bridge

A device which forwards traffic between network segments based on data link layer information. These segments would have a common network layer address. Every network should only have one root bridge.[8]

Bridging router

See **Brouter**.

Bring Your Own Cloud

See **BYOC**.

Bring Your Own Device

See **BYOD**.

Broadband

A class of communication channels capable of supporting a wide range of frequencies, typically from audio up to video frequencies. A broadband channel can carry multiple signals by dividing the total capacity into multiple, independent bandwidth channels, where each channel operates only on a specific range of frequencies.[8]

Broadcast

A transmission to multiple, unspecified recipients. On Ethernet, a broadcast packet is a special type of multicast packet which all nodes on the network are always willing to receive.[8]

Broadcast storm

Result of the number of broadcast messages on the network reaching or surpassing the bandwidth capability of the network. A broadcast on a network that causes multiple hosts to respond by broadcasting themselves, causing the storm to grow exponentially in severity.[8]

Brouter (Bridging router)

A device that bridges some packets (i.e., forward based on data link layer information) and routes other packets (i.e., forward based on network layer information). The bridge/route decision is based on configuration information.[8]

Browser

A program that allows a person to read hypertext. The browser gives some means of viewing the contents of nodes (or "pages") and of navigating from one node to another.[8]

Browsing

Act of searching through information system storage or active content to locate or acquire information without necessarily knowing the existence or format of information being sought.[1]

Brute force attack

In this attack, the adversary tries every possible value for a password until they succeed. A brute force attack, if feasible computationally, will always be successful because it will essentially go through all possible passwords given the alphabet used (lowercase letters, uppercase letters, numbers, symbols, etc.) and the maximum length of the password.[429]

BTRIS (Biomedical Translational Research Information System)

A resource available to the U.S. Department of Health and Human Services' National Institutes of Health (NIH) intramural community that brings together clinical research data from the Clinical Center and other NIH Institutes and Centers. BTRIS provides clinical investigators with access to identifiable data for subjects on their own active protocols while providing all NIH investigators with access to data without personal identifiers across all protocols. Data are available from 1976 to the present.[183]

Buffer

An area of memory used for storing messages. Typically, a buffer will have other attributes such as an input pointer (where new data will be written

B

into the buffer), an output pointer (where the next item will be read from) and/or a count of the space used or free. Buffers are used to decouple processes so that the reader and writer may operate at different speeds or on different-sized blocks of data.[8]

Bug

An unwanted and/or unintended property of a program, other software or operating system component, or piece of hardware. In addition, a bug may be an operational bug or a security bug.[8]

Bus

1. A structure that is used for connecting processors and peripherals, either within a system or in a Local Area Network (LAN). **2.** The internal wiring between and within the Central Processing Unit (CPU) and other motherboard subsystems. **3.** A set of electrical conductors (wires, PCB tracks, or connections in an integrated circuit) connecting various "stations," which can be functional units in a computer or nodes in a network. A bus is a broadcast channel, meaning that each station receives every other station's transmissions and all stations have equal access to the bus.[8]

Business Associate

See **BA**.

Business Continuity Plan

See **BCP**.

Business Impact Analysis

See **BIA**.

Business intelligence

Represents the tools and systems that play a key role in the strategic planning process of the corporation. These systems allow a company to gather, store, access, and analyze corporate data to aid in decision-making.[39] *See* **Decision support system**.

Business interruption

Anticipated interruption to normal business, functions, operations, or processes due to a strike or unanticipated interruption due to a power failure.[4]

Business Process Management

See **BPM**.

Business Rules Engine

See **BRE**.

Business-to-business

See **B2B**.

Business-to-business-to-consumer

See **B2B2C**.

Business-to-consumer

See **B2C**.

BYOC (Bring Your Own Cloud)

A concept/trend in which employees are allowed to use public or private third-party cloud services to perform certain job roles. BYOC often involves the piecing together of enterprise and consumer software—both in the cloud and on the premises—to get the job done.[52]

BYOD (Bring Your Own Device)

An enterprise policy used to permit partial or full integration of user-owned mobile devices for business purposes.[52]

Byte

A component in the machine data hierarchy larger than a bit and usually smaller than a word; now nearly always eight bits and the smallest addressable unit of storage. A byte typically holds one character.[8]

C

CA (Certificate Authority)

An independent licensing agency that vouches for a patient/person's identity in encrypted electronic communication. Acting as a type of electronic notary public, a certified authority verifies and stores a sender's public and private encryption keys and issues a digital certificate, or seal of authenticity, to the recipient.[57] Also referred to as certification authority.

CA (Corrective Action)

Identification and elimination of the causes of a problem, thus preventing their recurrence.[4]

Cache

1. An area of temporary computer memory storage space that is reserved for data recently read from a disk, which allows the processor to quickly retrieve it if it is needed again. A part of Random Access Memory (RAM). **2.** A small, fast memory holding recently accessed data, designed to speed up access.[52]

Cache server

A dedicated network server or service acting as a server that saves Web pages or other Internet content locally. By placing previously requested information in temporary storage, or cache, a cache server both speeds up access to data and reduces demand on an enterprise's bandwidth. Cache servers also allow users to access content offline, including rich media files or other documents. A cache server is sometimes called a "cache engine."[2]

CAD (Computer-Aided Detection)

Combining elements of artificial intelligence and digital image processing with radiological image processing to assist in the interpretation of medical images. Designed to decrease observational oversights, thus reducing false-negative rates.[91] Also known as Computer-Aided Diagnosis (CADx).

DOI: 10.4324/9781003286028-3

C

CAH (Critical-Access Hospital)

Rural community hospitals that receive cost-based reimbursement. To be designated a CAH, a rural hospital must meet defined criteria that were outlined in the Conditions of Participation 42 CFR 485 and subsequent legislative refinements to the program through the Balanced Budget Refinement Act of 1999 (BBRA), Benefits Improvement and Protection Act (BIPA, 2000), the Medicare Modernization Act, the Medicare Improvements for Patients and Providers Act (MIPPA, 2008), and the Patient Protection and Affordable Care Act (ACA, 2010).[92]

CAL (Computer-Assisted Learning)

Any use of computers to aid or support the education or training of people. CAL can test attainment at any point, can provide faster or slower routes through the material for people of different aptitudes, and can maintain a progress record for the instructor.[56] *See* **CBL**.

Canadian Health Outcomes for Better Information and Care

See **C-HOBIC**.

Canary Test

Also known as a canary deployment or canary release is a form of A/B testing used in Agile software development. In a canary test, software releases are first deployed to a small group of end users referred to as canaries. If the canary group experiences problems after the release, the DevOps team knows the code is not ready to be deployed.[52]

CAP (Common Alerting Protocol)

A digital format for exchanging emergency alerts with a single, consistent message that are simultaneously delivered over many different communications systems.[93]

CAP (Corrective Action Plan)

A step-by-step plan of action that is developed to achieve targeted outcomes for resolution of identified errors.[4]

C

Capability

Conceptual elements that define what a technology can do and are used to understand whether two types of technology are fundamentally doing the same thing and to identify duplication in a technology portfolio.[219]

Capacity

1. The ability to run a number of jobs per unit of time. **2.** The maximum amount or number that can be received or contained.[44]

Capacitor

A passive electronic component that stores energy in the form of an electro-static field.[2]

Capitation

Pre-established payment of a set dollar amount to a provider on a per member basis for certain contracted services for a given period of time. Amount of money paid to provider depends on the number of individuals registered on their patient list, not on the volume or type of service provided.[46]

Capture

Input of data, not as a direct result of data entry but instead as a result of performing a different but related activity. Barcode-reader-equipped supermarket checkout counters, for example, capture inventory-related data while recording a sale.[4]

Card reader

The generic term for an input device that reads flash memory cards. It can be a stand-alone device that connects to a computer via USB, or it may be integrated into a computer, printer, or multifunction device. Most multifunction printer/scanner/copiers now have built-in card readers.[73]

Cardinality

1. The number of rows in a table or the number of indexed entries in a defined index. **2.** The number of elements in a set. **3.** A minimum number of required appearances and a maximum number. These numbers

C

specify the number of times the attribute may appear in any instance of the resource type.[9] *See* **Multiplicity**.

Care coordination

The deliberate organization of patient care activities between two or more participants (including the patient) involved in a patient's care to facilitate the appropriate delivery of healthcare services. Organizing care involves the marshaling of personnel and other resources needed to carry out all required patient care activities and is often managed by the exchange of information among participants responsible for different aspects of care.[94]

Care management

A set of activities that assures that every person served by the treatment system has a single approved care (service) plan that is coordinated, not duplicative, and designed to assure cost-effective and good outcomes. Care managers will oversee a patient's journey through treatment.[95]

Care plan

See **Plan of care**.

Care transitions

The various points where a patient moves to or returns from a particular physical location or makes contact with a healthcare professional for the purposes of receiving healthcare. This includes transitions between home, hospital, residential care settings, and consultations with different healthcare providers in outpatient facilities. Every change from provider or setting is another care transition.[184]

Carrier Sense Multiple Access with Collision Detection

See **CSMA/CD**.

CASE (Computer-Assisted Software Engineering)

A computer-assisted method to organize and control the development of software. CASE allows developers to share a common view, allows check-point process, and serves as a repository.[2]

Case mix

The relative numbers of various types of patients being treated as categorized by Disease-Related Groups (DRG's), severity of illness, rate of consumption of resources, and other indicators; used as a tool for managing and planning healthcare services.[123]

CAT (Computed Axial Tomography)

An x-ray procedure that combines multiple x-ray images with the aid of a computer to generate cross-sectional views and, if needed, three-dimensional images of the internal organs and structures of the body.[96] Also known as CT.

Categorization

The process by which an individual information product can be associated with other products, using vocabularies designed to help individuals locate and access information. There can be multiple attributes assigned to a product (e.g., multiple categorizations). Categorization is used to provide context to a specific product and to define relationships across a group of information products.[97] *See* **Classification**.

Cause and effect diagram

A display of the factors that are thought to affect a particular problem or system outcome. The tool is often used in a quality improvement program or in brainstorming to group people's ideas about the causes of a particular problem in an orderly way. Also known as the fishbone diagram because of the shape it takes when illustrating the primary and secondary causes.[99]

CCC (Clinical Care Classification)

Standardized, coded nursing terminology system that identifies the discrete elements of nursing practice. CCC provides a unique framework and coding structure for capturing the essence of patient care in all healthcare settings.[101]

CCD (Continuity of Care Document)

An implementation guide for sharing Continuity of Care Record (CCR) patient summary data using the HL7 Version 3 Clinical Document Architecture (CDA), Release 2. CCD establishes a rich set of templates representing the typical sections of a summary record and expresses these

C

templates as constraints on CDA. These same templates for vital signs, family history, plan of care, and so on can then be reused in other CDA document types, establishing interoperability across a wide range of clinical use cases. CCD is an XML-based markup standard intended to specify the encoding, structure, and semantics of a patient summary clinical document for exchange, used for sharing patient summary data.[9]

C-CDA (Consolidated Clinical Document Architecture)

Implementation guide developed through joint efforts of Health Level Seven (HL7), Integrating the Healthcare Enterprise (IHE), the Health Story Project, and the Office of the National Coordinator (ONC) in order to consolidate CDA implementation guides from various Standards Development Organizations (SDOs) conflicting information. C-CDA specifies a library of templates and prescribes their use for a set of specific document types. CCD is an example of a C-CDA document template.[9] *See* **CDA** and **CCD**.

CCDS (Common Clinical Data Set)

A set of data elements specified in 2014 and 2015 Edition EHR Certification Criteria, which focuses on the representation of clinical data during exchange. It specifies a list of data elements and the standards for expressing those data. In 2017, this data set was absorbed into the U.S. Core Data for Interoperability (USCDI).[12]

CCM (Chronic Care Management)

The non-face-to-face services provided to Medicare beneficiaries who have multiple (two or more), significant chronic conditions.[430]

CCMM (Continuity of Care Maturity Model)

A HIMSS Analytics Eight-Stage (0–7) Maturity Model created to demonstrate the evolution of communication between clinicians in different settings, with limited or no electronic communication to an advanced, multi-organizational, knowledge-driven community of care.[10]

CCO (Chief Compliance Officer)

Role responsible for legal processes and procedures, maintaining industry standards, and ensuring compliance with healthcare regulations.

CCR (Continuity of Care Record)

1. A standard specification developed jointly by ASTM International, the Massachusetts Medical Society (MMS), the Healthcare Information and Management Systems Society (HIMSS), the American Academy of Family Physicians (AAFP), and the American Academy of Pediatrics (AAP). It was intended to foster and improve continuity of patient care, reduce medical errors, and assure at least a minimum standard of health information transportability when a patient is referred or transferred to, or is otherwise seen by another provider. **2.** An XML document standard for a summary of personal health information that clinicians can send when a patient is referred and that patients can carry with them to promote continuity, quality, and safety of care.[103]

CDA (Clinical Document Architecture)

1. An XML-based document markup standard that specifies the structure and semantics of clinical documents for the purpose of exchange. **2.** Known previously as the patient record architecture, CDA provides an exchange model for clinical documents, such as discharge summaries and progress notes, and brings the healthcare industry closer to the realization of an electronic medical record. By leveraging the use of XML, the HL7 Reference Information Model (RIM), and coded vocabularies, the CDA makes documents both machine readable (so documents are easily parsed and processed electronically) and human readable so documents can be easily retrieved and used by the people who need them.[9, 10]

CDMA (Code Division Multiple Access)

A spread spectrum technology for cellular networks. Unlike the GSM and TDMA technologies, CDMA transmits over the entire frequency range available. It does not assign a specific frequency to each user on the communications network. Because CDMA does not limit each user's frequency range, there is more bandwidth available.[73]

CDPD (Cellular Digital Packet Data)

A specification for supporting wireless access to the Internet and other public packet-switched networks. Cellular telephone and modem providers that offer CDPD support make it possible for mobile users to get access to the Internet at up to 19.2 kbps. Because CDPD is an open specification that adheres to the layered structure of the Open Systems Interconnection (OSI)

C

model, it has the ability to be extended in the future. CDPD supports both the Internet Protocol and the ISO Connectionless Network Protocol (CLNP).[2]

CDR (Clinical Data Repository)

1. A structured, systematically collected store house of patient-specific clinical data. **2.** A centralized database that allows organizations to collect, store, access, and report on clinical, administrative, and financial information collected from various applications within or across the healthcare organization that provides an open environment for accessing/viewing, managing, and reporting enterprise information.[68]

CDS (Clinical Decision Support)

The use of automated rules based on clinical evidence to provide alerts, reminders, clinical guidelines, and other knowledge to assist users in healthcare delivery.[43]

CDS (Core Data Services)

An infrastructure layer introduced by SAP for defining semantically rich data models, which are represented as CDS views. CDS allows developers to define entity types (such as orders, business partners, or products) and the semantic relationships between them, which correspond to foreign key relationships in traditional Entity Relationship (ER) models. CDS is defined using an SQL-based Data Definition Language (DDL) that is based on standard SQL with some additional concepts, such as associations, which define the relationships between CDS views and annotations, which direct the domain-specific use of CDS artifacts.[431]

CDSS (Clinical Decision Support System)

An application that uses pre-established rules and guidelines that can be created and edited by the healthcare organization and integrates clinical data from several sources to generate alerts and treatment suggestions.[432]

CDT (Current Dental Terminology)

Official coding system for dentists to report professional services and procedures to third parties for payment. CDT is produced by the American Dental Association (ADA).

CDW (Clinical Data Warehouse)

Grouping of data accessible by a single data management system, possibly of diverse sources, pertaining to a health system or subsystem and enabling secondary data analysis for questions relevant to understanding the functioning of that health system, which can hence support proper maintenance and improvement of that health system.[104]

CE (Coded Element)

A data type that transmits codes and the text associated with the code.[9]

CEHRT (Certified EHR Technology)

Technology that meets the standards and criteria for structured data, established by the U.S. Centers for Medicare & Medicaid Services (CMS) and the Office of the National Coordinator for Health Information Technology (ONC), to qualify for use in CMS Promoting Interoperability (PI) programs. CEHRT gives assurance that an EHR system or module offers the necessary technological capability, functionality, and security to help users meet the meaningful use criteria. Certification also helps healthcare providers and patients be confident that the electronic health IT products and systems they use are secure, can maintain data confidentially, and can work with other systems to share information.[26]

Cellular Digital Packet Data

See **CDPD**.

CEN (European Committee for Standardization)

Major provider of European standards and technical specifications. CEN is the only recognized European organization for the planning, drafting, and adoption of European standards in all areas of economic activity with the exception of electrotechnology (CENELEC) and telecommunication (ETSI).[105]

Centers for Medicare & Medicaid Services (CMS) Promoting Interoperability Programs

Programs that provide Medicare incentive payments to eligible clinicians, eligible hospitals, and Critical-Access Hospitals (CAHs) as they adopt, implement, upgrade, or demonstrate meaningful use of certified EHR technology as well as payment adjustments for providers that fail to meet the criteria.[26]

Central Processing Unit

See **CPU** and **Microprocessor**.

Centralized computing

A type of computing architecture where all or most of the processing/computing is performed on a central server. Centralized computing enables the deployment of all of a central server's computing resources, administration, and management. The central server, in turn, is responsible for delivering application logic, processing, and providing computing resources (both basic and complex) to the attached client machines.[52]

CERT (Computer Emergency Response Team)

A trusted authority and team of system specialists and other professionals who are dedicated to improving the security and resilience of computer systems and networks and are a national asset in the field of cybersecurity.[106]

Certificate

An electronic document that allows a person, system, or organization to exchange information securely in an electronic format using Public Key Infrastructure (PKI) to verify identity and ownership of a public key.[2] Also known as digital certificate or identity certificate. See **Public key certificate**.

Certificate Authority

See **CA**.

Certificate distribution

Act of publishing certificates and transferring certificates to security subjects.[72]

Certificate extension

Extension fields (known as extensions) in X.509 certificates that provide methods for associating additional attributes with users or public keys and for managing the certification hierarchy. Note: Certificate extensions may be either critical (i.e., a certificate-using system has to reject the certificate if it

C

encounters a critical extension it does not recognize) or noncritical (i.e., it may be ignored if the extension is not recognized).[72]

Certificate generation

Act of creating certificates.[72]

Certificate issuer

Authority trusted by one or more relying parties to create and assign certificates and which may, optionally, create the relying parties' keys.[72] Note 1: Adapted from ISO 9594-8:2001. Note 2: "Authority" in the Certificate Authority (CA) term does not imply any government authorization; it only denotes that the certificate authority is trusted. Note 3: *CA* is more widely used.

Certificate management

Procedures relating to certificates (i.e., certificate generation, certificate distribution, certificate archiving, and revocation).[72]

Certificate Policy

See **CP**.

Certification

1. Comprehensive evaluation of the technical and nontechnical security features of an IT system and other safeguards, made in support of the accreditation process, to establish the extent that a particular design and implementation meets a set of specified requirements. **2.** Procedure by which a third party gives assurance that all or part of a data processing system conforms to specified requirements. **3.** A defined process to ensure that EHR technologies meet the adopted standards, certification criteria, and other technical requirements to achieve meaningful use of those records in systems.[1,72]

Certification Practices Statement

See **CPS**.

Certification profile

Specification of the structure and permissible content of a certificate type.[72]

Certification revocation

Act of removing any unreliable link between a certificate and its related owner (or security subject owner) because the certificate is not trusted any more, even though it is unexpired.[72]

Certified EHR Technology

See **CEHRT**.

Certified Health IT Product List

See **CHPL**.

CF (Conditional Formatting/Coded Formatted element)

1. A tool that allows a user to apply formats to dynamically style a cell or range of cells and have that formatting change, depending on the value of the cell or the value of a formula. **2.** Coded element with formatted values data type. This data type, outlined in HL7, transmits codes and the formatted text associated with the code.[108,9]

CGI (Common Gateway Interface)

A standard or protocol for external gateway programs to interface with information servers, such as HTTP servers. Part of the overall HTTP protocol.[73]

Chain of trust

A linked path of verification and validation to ensure SSL/TLS certificates utilize a chain of trust. The trust anchor for the digital certificate is the root Certificate Authority (CA). An ordered list of certificates containing an end-user subscriber certificate and intermediate certificates that enables the receiver to verify that the sender and all intermediate certificates are trustworthy.[188]

Channel

A path for the transmission of signals between a transmitting and receiving device.[2]

Channel Sharing Unit/Data Service Unit

See **CSU/DSU**.

CHAP (Challenge Handshake Authentication Protocol)

An authentication protocol used to log in a user to an Internet access provider.[7]

Character

A member of a set of elements that is used for representation, organization, or control of data.[36]

Character-based terminal

A type of computer terminal and system that supports only alphabetical or numeric characters, with the visual displays and "mouse"-driven, bitmap software that most systems now utilize; the opposite of Graphical User Interface (GUI).[7]

Characteristic

Abstraction of a property of an object or a set of objects.[75]

ChatBot

An Artificial Intelligence (AI) program that simulates interactive human conversation by using key pre-calculated user phrases and auditory or text-based signals. Chatbots are frequently used by organizations to provide 24-hour Customer Relationship Management (CRM) services. This type of software bot can also be used as an intelligent virtual assistant.[52]

ChatGPT

ChatGPT (Chat Generative Pre-trained Transformer) is a complex machine learning model that is able to carry out Natural Language Generation (NLG)

C

tasks with such a high level of accuracy that the model can pass a Turing test. ChatGPT was trained on massive amounts of unlabeled data scraped from the Internet before 2022. The model is continually being monitored and fine-tuned for specific language-oriented tasks with additional data sets labeled by humans.[52]

Check digit

Number added to a code (such as a bar code or account number) to derive a further number as a means of verifying the accuracy or validity of the code as it is printed or transmitted. A code consisting of three digits, for example, such as 135 may include 9 (sum of 1, 3, and 5) as the last digit and be communicated as 1359.[4]

Chief Compliance Officer

See **CCO**.

Chief Experience Officer

See **CXO**.

Chief Health Informatics Officer

See **CHIO**.

Chief Information/Informatics Officer

See **CIO**.

Chief Information Security Officer

See **CISO**

Chief Medical Information/Informatics Officer

See **CMIO**.

Chief Nursing Informatics/Information Officer

See **CNIO**.

Chief Security Officer

See **CSO**.

Chief Technology and Innovation Officer

See **CTIO**.

Chief Technology Officer

See **CTO**.

Child document

Subordinate to another, such as a parent document.[9]

Children's Health Insurance Program

See **CHIP**.

CHIO (Chief Health Informatics Officer)

A strategic, executive-level position responsible for managing health informatics and Information Management (IT) strategies. Organizations hiring a CHIO typically look for a physician who can combine health IT expertise with strong leadership skills to transform a healthcare organization by using data to improve health outcomes, drive down costs, and empower patients. The Chief Health Informatics officer is an evolution of the Chief Medical Information Officer (CMIO). The CMIO oversees the adoption and management of health IT systems, such as Electronic Health Records (EHR) and Computerized Physician Order Entry (CPOE). Now that the deployment of EHR is complete at most hospitals, the CMIO role is evolving from operational to strategic, with a focus on innovation.[2]

CHIP (Children's Health Insurance Program)

An insurance program under the Centers for Medicare & Medicaid Services (CMS), CHIP provides low-cost health coverage to children in families that earn too much money to qualify for Medicaid. In some states, CHIP covers pregnant women. Each state offers CHIP coverage and works closely with its state Medicaid program.[218]

C-HOBIC (Canadian Health Outcomes for Better Information and Care)

Joint project between the Canadian Nurses Association (CNA) and Canada Health Infoway to begin the process of collecting standardized clinical outcomes that are reflective of nursing practice for inclusion in electronic health records.[110]

CHPL (Certified Health IT Product List)

The comprehensive and authoritative listing of all certified Health Information Technology which has been successfully tested and certified by the ONC Health IT Certification program. All products listed on the CHPL have been tested by an ONC-Authorized Testing Labs (ONC-ATLs) and certified by an ONC-Authorized Certification Body (ONC-ACB) to meet criteria adopted by the U.S. Secretary of the Department of Health and Human Services (HHS).[88]

Chronic Care Management

See **CCM**.

Chronic care model

Model developed by Edward Wagner and colleagues that provides a solid foundation from which healthcare teams can operate. The model has six dimensions: community resources and policies; health system organization of healthcare; patient self-management supports; delivery system redesign; decision support; and clinical information system. The ultimate goal is to have activated patients interact in a productive way with well-prepared healthcare teams. Three components that are particularly critical to this goal are adequate decision support, which includes systems that encourage providers to use evidence-based protocols; delivery system redesign, such as using group visits and same-day appointments; and use of clinical information systems, such as disease registries, which allow providers to exchange information and follow patients over time.[111]

Chronic disease

An illness that is long-lasting or recurrent. Examples include diabetes, asthma, heart disease, kidney disease, and chronic lung disease.[111]

C

CHV (Consumer Health Vocabulary initiative)

Open-access, collaborative initiative that links everyday words and phrases about health to technical terms or jargon used by healthcare professionals.[112]

CIA (Confidentiality/Integrity/Availability)

The *CIA triad* is a model designed to guide policies for information security within an organization. The model is also sometimes referred to as the AIC triad (availability, integrity, and confidentiality) to avoid confusion with the acronym for the Central Intelligence Agency. The elements of the triad are considered the three most crucial components of security.[2]

CIO (Chief Information Officer/Chief Informatics Officer)

Executive responsible for overseeing people, processes, and technologies within a company's IT organization to ensure they deliver outcomes that support the goals of the business. The CIO plays a key leadership role in the critical strategic, technical, and management initiatives that mitigate threats and drive business growth.[142]

Cipher text

Data produced through the use of encipherment, the semantic content of which is not available.[72]

Circuit switched

A type of network in which a physical path is obtained for and dedicated to a single connection between two end points in the network for the duration of the connection.[2] *See* **Packet switching**.

CIS (Clinical Information System)

A system dedicated to collecting, storing, manipulating, and making available clinical information important to the delivery of healthcare. Clinical information systems may be limited in scope to a single area (e.g., lab system, ECG management system) or they may be comprehensive and cover virtually all facets of clinical information (e.g., electronic patient; the original discharge summary residing in the chart, with a copy of the report sent to the admitting physician and another copy existing on the transcriptionist's machine).[458]

CISC (Complex Instruction Set Computer or Computing)

Computers designed with a full set of computer instructions that were intended to provide needed capabilities in the most efficient way. Later, it was discovered that by reducing the full set to only the most frequently used instructions, the computer would get more work done in a shorter amount of time for most applications. Since this was called Reduced Instruction Set Computing (RISC), there was a need to have something to call full-set instruction computers, which resulted in the term CISC.[2]

CISO (Chief Information Security Officer)

Controls information security issues in an organization and is responsible for securing anything related to digital information. The CISO and Chief Security Officer (CSO) roles may be interchangeable, but CISOs may also handle a company's physical security.[52]

CISSP (Certified Information Systems Security Professional)

A vendor-neutral, independent certification offered by the International Information System Security Certification Consortium, otherwise known as (ISC)[2]. This globally recognized certification is designed to show an employer that a job candidate has the knowledge and experience necessary to effectively design, implement, and manage an organization's cybersecurity.[52]

Claim attachment

Any variety of hardcopy forms or electronic records needed to process a claim in addition to the claim itself.[113]

Claim status category codes

A national administrative code set that indicates the general category of the status of healthcare claims. This code set is used in the Accredited Standards Committee (ASC) X12 248 claim status notification transaction and is maintained by the healthcare code maintenance committee.[113]

Claim status codes

A national administrative code set that identifies the status of healthcare claims. This code set is used in the Accredited Standards Committee (ASC)

X12 277 claim status notification transaction and is maintained by the health-care code maintenance committee.[113]

Class

A term used in programs written in the object-oriented paradigm. A blueprint, template, or set of instructions to build a specific type of object. It is a basic concept of object-oriented programming which revolves around real-life entities.[192]

Classification

The systematic placement of things or concepts into categories that share some common attribute, quality, or property. A classification structure is a listing of terms that depicts hierarchical structures. In data management, classification enables the separation and sorting of data according to set requirements for various business or personal objectives. In Machine Learning (ML), classification is used in predictive modeling to assign input data with a class label. For example, an e-mail security program tasked with identifying spam might use Natural Language Processing (NLP) to classify e-mails as being "spam" or "not spam."[52]

Clear text

See **Plain text**.

Client

The receiving end of a service or the requestor of a service in a client/server model type of system. The client is most often located on another system or computer, which can be accessed via a network. This term was first used for devices that could not run their own programs and were connected to remote computers that could via a network. These were called dumb terminals, and they were served by time-sharing mainframe computers.[52]

Client application

A system entity, usually a computer process acting on behalf of a human user, which makes use of a service provided by a server.[459]

C

Client records

All personal information that has been collected, compiled, or created about clients, which may be maintained in one or more locations and in various forms, reports, or documents, including information that is stored or transmitted by electronic media.[459]

Client registry

The area where a patient/person's information (i.e., name, date of birth, Social Security number, and health access number) is securely stored and maintained.[460]

Client/server model

A distributed communication framework of network processes among service requestors, clients, and service providers. The client-server connection is established through a network or the Internet. Web technologies and protocols built around the client-server model include Hypertext Transfer Protocol (HTTP), Domain Name System (DNS), and Simple Mail Transfer Protocol (SMTP).[52]

Clinical algorithm

Flow charts to which a diagnostician or therapist can refer for a decision on how to manage a patient with a specific clinical program.[461]

Clinical Care Classification

See **CCC**.

Clinical data

All relevant clinical and socioeconomic data disclosed by the patient and others, as well as observations, findings, therapeutic interventions, and prognostic statements, generated by the members of the healthcare team.[459]

Clinical Data Repository

See **CDR**.

C

Clinical Data Warehouse
See **CDW**.

Clinical Decision Support
See **CDS**.

Clinical Decision Support System
See **CDSS**.

Clinical Document Architecture
See **CDA**.

Clinical documentation system

An application that allows clinicians to chart treatment, therapy, and/or health assessment results for a patient. This application provides the flow sheets and care plan documentation for a patient's course of therapy.[459]

Clinical informaticist/Clinical informaticians

Transform healthcare by analyzing, designing, implementing, and evaluating information and communication systems that enhance individual and population health outcomes, improve patient care, and strengthen the clinician–patient relationship. Clinical informaticians use their knowledge of patient care combined with their understanding of informatics concepts, methods, and tools (1) to assess information and knowledge needs of healthcare professionals and patients; (2) characterize, evaluate, and refine clinical processes; (3) develop, implement, and refine clinical decision support systems; and (4) lead or participate in the procurement, customization, development, implementation, management, evaluation, and continuous improvement of clinical information systems such as electronic health records and order entry systems.[462]

Clinical informatics

1. Promotes the understanding, integration, and application of information technology in healthcare settings to ensure adequate and qualified support of clinician objectives and industry best practices. **2.** The application

C

of informatics and information technology to deliver healthcare services. Clinical informatics is concerned with information use in healthcare by clinicians. It includes a wide range of topics ranging from clinical decision support to visual images (e.g., radiological, pathological, dermatological, and ophthalmological); from clinical documentation to provider order entry systems; and from system design to system implementation, adoption, and optimization issues.[86]

Clinical Laboratory Information System

See **LIS**.

Clinical observation

1. The act of measuring, questioning, evaluating, or otherwise observing a patient or a specimen from a patient in healthcare; the act of making a clinical judgment. **2.** The result, answer, judgment, or knowledge gained from the act of observing a patient or a specimen from a patient in healthcare.[463]

Clinical Observation Access Service

See **COAS**.

Clinical Pathways (CPWs)

Tools used to guide evidence-based healthcare that translate clinical practice guideline recommendations into clinical processes of care within a healthcare venue. A CPW is a structured multidisciplinary care plan. It (1) details the steps in a course of treatment or care in a plan, pathway, algorithm, guideline, protocol, or other "inventory of actions" and (2) aims to standardize care for a specific clinical problem, procedure, or episode in a specific population.[464]

Clinical performance measure

At a high level, clinical performance measures are indicators of the quality of care rendered by clinicians. The National Quality Forum (NQF) describes performance measures as a way to calculate whether and how often a healthcare system does what it should. Measures are based on scientific evidence about processes, outcomes, perceptions, or systems that relate to high-quality care. (1) The Centers for Medicare & Medicaid Services (CMS)

C

considers high-quality care to include effective, safe, efficient, patient-centered, equitable, and timely care. (2) Performance measures are also used by health payers, such as CMS, to incentivize providers to improve quality of care.[465]

Clinical practice guidelines

A set of systematically developed statements, usually based on scientific evidence, to assist practitioners and patients in decision-making about appropriate healthcare for specific clinical circumstances.[208]

Clinical protocol

A set of rules defining a standardized treatment program or behavior in certain circumstances.[222]

Clinical Quality Language

See **CQL**.

Clinical Quality Measures

See **CQM**.

Clinical Record

See **EHR**.

Cloud

A general metaphor that is used to refer to the Internet. Initially, the Internet was seen as a distributed network, and then, with the invention of the World Wide Web, as a tangle of interlinked media. As the Internet continued to grow in both size and the range of activities it encompassed, it came to be known as "the cloud."[52]

CMET (Common Message Element Type)

Common, reusable, standardized model fragments produced by a particular work group within HL7 that are intended to be building blocks that domains can use or include in their design. The use of CMETs can reduce the effort to produce a domain-specific design while maintaining similar content across several domains.[9]

CMIO (Chief Medical Information Officer/ Chief Medical Informatics Officer)

A person that provides overall leadership in the ongoing development, implementation, advancement, and optimization of electronic information systems that impact patient care. Works in partnership with the organization's IT leadership to translate clinician requirements into specifications for clinical and research systems.[459]

CNIO (Chief Nursing Information Officer/ Chief Nursing Informatics Officer)

Leads the strategy, development, and implementation of information technology to support nursing, nursing practice, and clinical applications, collaborating with the chief nursing officer on the clinical and administration decision-making process.[459]

COAS (Clinical Observations Access Service)

Standardizes access to clinical observations in multiple formats, including numerical data stored by instruments or entered from observations.[118]

COB (Coordination of Benefits)

1. The process by which a payer handles claims that may involve other insurance companies (i.e., situations in which an insured individual is covered by more than one insurance plan). **2.** Process of determining which health plan or insurance policy will pay first and/or determining the payment obligations of each health plan, medical insurance policy, or third-party resource when two or more health plans, insurance policies, or third-party resources cover the same benefits.[466]

Code

1. Concept identifier that is unique within a coding system. **2.** A representation assigned to a term so that the term may more readily be electronically processed.[2]

Code 128

A one-dimensional bar code symbology, using four different bar widths, used in blood banking and other healthcare and non-healthcare applications.[199] *See* **ISBT 128**.

Code Division Multiple Access

See **CDMA**.

Code meaning

In a general sense, the language understood by the computer. Computers don't understand natural language. As such, the human language has to be converted into a set of "words" that are understood by the computer. The words that initiate a standard action when used in a program are called keywords. The arrangement of keywords for successful execution of a desired computation is called syntax. The set of keywords and syntax form a programming language.[52]

Code set

1. A set of elements which is mapped onto another set according to a coding scheme. **2.** Clinical or medical code sets identify medical conditions and the procedures, services, equipment, and supplies used to deal with them. Nonclinical or nonmedical or administrative code sets identify, or characterize, entities and events in a manner that facilitates an administrative process.[121]

Code set maintaining organization

Under the Health Insurance Portability and Accountability Act (HIPAA), this is an organization that creates and maintains the code sets adopted by the HHS Secretary for use in the transactions for which standards are adopted.[113, 121]

Code Signing

A technology for verifying the authenticity of the publisher of a download to avoid a computer virus or malware. Software signed with a digital signature is considered safe to download. Unsafe or unrecognized software publishers may be identified by a pop-up indicating that the publisher or author is

C

not recognized and cautioning the user to be certain the download is from a worthy source.[52]

Code value

Result of applying a coding scheme to a code meaning.[121]

Codec (Compression/decompression)

An algorithm or specialized computer program that reduces the number of bytes consumed by large files and programs.[117]

Coded Element

See **CE**.

Coded Formatted elements

See **CF**.

Coded with Exceptions

See **CWE**.

Codex

An Artificial Intelligence (AI) system developed by OpenAI that allows users to input natural language (text) and receive code as a response. Using machine learning, Codex, can assemble code instantly—helping streamline the coding process for beginners and professionals. Codex can generate code in multiple programming languages. This code can be used to build snippets, functions, or even entire programs.[52]

Coding

The creation of computer programming code. More generally, the act of assigning a classification to something.[52]

Coding scheme

Any text-based data is stored by the computer in the form of bits and follows the specified coding scheme. The coding scheme is a standard that tells the computer which character represents which set of bytes. Specifying the coding scheme is important because the computer could interpret the given bytes as a different character than intended since bytes may look the same but can be interpreted differently in different coding schemes.[467]

Coding system

Combination of a set of concepts (coded concepts), a set of code values, and at least one coding scheme mapping code values to coded concepts.[77]

Cognitive computing

Type of computing that addresses human kinds of problems that are complex, ambiguous, and uncertain. In these situations, the data are dynamic, information-rich, shifting and changing frequently, and can be conflicting. This type of computing allows for the synthesis of information sources, influences, contexts, and insights and allows the systems to make decisions that are the "best" for a given situation versus "right." Cognitive computing allows for the system to compute the context of a situation and make a decision based on the information available at a given time and/or place. Cognitive computing may serve as an assistant or coach for the user (e.g., Amazon Alexa) and may act autonomously in some or many problem-solving situations.[223] *See* **Artificial intelligence**.

Cold Server

A disaster recovery backup server that operates only if the main server is interrupted or fails. A cold server holds all main server files and programs and remains in an unpowered state until a backup is required.

Cold Site

A business location that is used for backup in the event of a disruptive operational disaster at the normal business site. A cold site is an office, but it does not always have the necessary equipment to resume prompt operations. The business paying for the cold site provides and installs this equipment.[52]

Cold Standby

A redundancy method that involves having one system as a backup for another identical primary system. The cold standby system is called upon only on failure of the primary system.[52]

C

Collect and communicate audit trails

Means to define and identify security-relevant events and the data to be collected and communicated, as determined by policy, regulation, or risk analysis.[1]

Collect/collection

The assembling of information through interviews, forms, reports, or other information sources.[1]

Collision Detection

See **CSMA/CD**.

Command

A specific action assigned to a program to perform a specific task.[52]

Committee Draft

See **CD**.

Common Alerting Protocol

See **CAP**.

Common Clinical Data Set

See **CCDS**.

Common Criteria

An international set of guidelines and specifications developed for evaluating information security products, specifically to ensure they meet an agreed-upon security standard for government deployments. Common Criteria is more formally called "Common Criteria for Information Technology Security Evaluation."[52]

Common Gateway Interface

See **CGI**.

Common Message Element Type

See **CMET**.

Common Object Request Broker Architecture

See **CORBA**.

Common services

A type of software service that can be shared across multiple applications. These include services such as messaging, security, logging, auditing, and mapping. Common services are part of the health information access layer.[224]

Common Vulnerabilities and Exposures

See **CVE**.

Common Weakness Enumeration

See **CWE**.

Communication bus

Part of the health information access layer that allows applications to communicate according to standard messages and protocols.[468]

Communication network

Configuration of hardware, software, and transmission facilities for transmission and routing of data-carrying signals between electronic devices.[469]

Communities of interest

Inclusive term to describe collaborative groups of users who must exchange information in pursuit of shared goals, interests, missions, or business process and must have a shared vocabulary for the information exchanged. Communities provide an organization and maintenance construct for data.[122]

Community Health Information Network

See **CHIN**.

C

Comparability

Comparability of data values **over populations** is the degree to which data values representing two or more populations have the same definition and are measured in the same way.[470]

Compatibility

Suitability of products, processes, or services for use together under specific conditions to fulfill relevant requirements without causing unacceptable interactions.[226] *See* **Forward compatibility**.

Compiler

1. Programs written in high-level languages are translated into assembly language or machine language by a compiler. Assembly language programs are translated into machine language by a program called an assembler. Every CPU has its own unique machine language. Programs must be rewritten or recompiled, therefore, to run on different types of computers. **2.** A software that translates a program written in a high-level programming language to a machine-language program, which can then be executed.[39,52,226] *See* **Assembler**.

Complex Instruction Set Computer Processor

See **CISC**.

Compliance

Adherence to those policies, procedures, guidelines, laws, regulations, and contractual arrangements to which the business process is subject.[13]

Compliance date

Under the Health Insurance Portability and Accountability Act (HIPAA), this is the date by which a covered entity must comply with a standard, an implementation specification, or a modification. This is usually 24 months after the effective date of the associated final rule for most entities, and 36 months for small health plans. For future changes in the standards, the compliance date would be at least 180 days after the effective date but can be longer for small health plans or for complex changes.[113]

Component

An object-oriented term used to describe a reusable building block of GUI applications. A software object that contains data and code. A component may or may not be visible.[2]

Component object model

Used by developers to create reusable software components, link components together to build applications, and take advantage of Windows® services.[52]

Composite Message

See **CM**.

Comprehensive Primary Care Initiative

See **CPC**.

Comprehensive Primary Care Plus Initiative

See **CPC+**.

Compression/decompression

See **Codec**.

Compromise

Disclosure of information to unauthorized persons or a violation of the security policy of a system in which unauthorized intentional or unintentional disclosure, modification, destruction, or loss of an object may have occurred.[459]

Computer-Aided Detection

See **CAD**.

Computer-assisted coding

Software solutions using Natural Language Processing (NLP), which is an exclusive patented algorithmic software to electronically analyze entire medical charts to pre-code with both CPT procedure and ICD diagnostic nomenclatures.[471]

Computer-Assisted Learning

See **CAL**.

Computer-assisted medicine

Use of computers directly in diagnostic or therapeutic interventions (e.g., computer-assisted surgery).[123]

Computer-Assisted Software Engineering

See **CASE**.

Computer Emergency Response Team

See **CERT**.

Computer Ethics

Deals with the procedures, values, and practices that govern the process of consuming computing technology and its related disciplines without damaging or violating the moral values and beliefs of any individual, organization, or entity. Computer ethics is a concept in ethics that addresses the ethical issues and constraints that arise from the use of computers and how they can be mitigated or prevented.[52]

Computer-on-Wheels

See **COW**.

Computer security

COMPUter SECurity (COMPUSEC) is a military term used in reference to the security of computer system information. Today, it can relate to either the military or civilian community. COMPUSEC also concerns preventing unauthorized users from gaining entry to a computer system.[52]

Computer Security Incident Response Team

See **CSIRT**.

C

Computer system

An integrated arrangement of computer hardware and software operated by users to perform prescribed tasks.[52]

Computer Telephony Integration

See **CTI**.

Computer Vision

A technology that enables computers, smart phones, and other digital devices to identify objects visually. Artificial intelligence and machine learning technologies are the base for computer vision technology. It has multiple use cases like medical imaging, autonomous vehicle, and agriculture. Concerns are also being raised about the data privacy, confidentiality, and misuse of personal user data.[52]

Computerized Axial Tomography

See **CAT**.

Computerized Practitioner Order Entry

See **CPOE**.

Computing environment

The total environment in which an automated information system, a network, or a component operates. The environment includes physical, administrative, and personnel procedures, as well as communication and networking relationships with other information systems.[1]

Concentrator

Network device where networked nodes are connected. Used to divide a data channel into two or more channels of lower bandwidth.[2] *See* **Hub**.

Concept

1. An abstraction or a general notation that may serve as a unit of thought or a theory. In terminology work, the distinction is made between a concept and the terms that reference the concept. Where the concept is identified as abstract from the language and the term is a symbol that is part of the language. **2.** A clinical idea to which a unique concept has been assigned. Each concept is represented by a row in the concepts table. Concept equivalence occurs when a post-coordinated expression has the same meaning as a pre-coordinated concept or another post-coordinated expression.[459]

Concept harmonization

Activity for reducing or eliminating minor differences between two or more concepts that are closely related to each other. Note: Concept harmonization is an integral part of standardization.[472]

Concept identifier

Concept name, code, or symbol which uniquely identifies a concept.[472]

Concept status

A field in the concepts table that specifies whether a concept is in current use. Values include "current," "duplicate," "erroneous," "ambiguous," and "limited."[472]

Concept Unique Identifier

See **CUI**.

Concepts table

A data table consisting of rows, each of which represents a concept.[472]

Concurrent Versioning System

See **CVS**.

Conditional Formatting

See **CF**.

Confidential Computing

An emerging approach to cybersecurity that runs computational workloads in isolated, hardware-encrypted environments. In a confidential computing architecture, all computations are carried out in an encrypted, hardware-based environment in the CPU called a Trusted Execution Environment (TEE). Data and code cannot be viewed, added, removed, or modified when they are within the TEE.[52]

Confidentiality

1. Obligation of an entity that receives identifiable information about an individual as part of providing a service to that individual to protect that data or information, including not disclosing the identifiable information to unauthorized persons or through unauthorized processes. **2.** A property by which information relating to an entity or party is not made available or disclosed to unauthorized individuals, entities, or processes.[1, 20, 36]

Confidentiality/Integrity/Availability

See **CIA**.

Configuration

The manner in which components are arranged to make up the computer system. Configuration consists of both hardware and software components. Sometimes, people specifically point to hardware arrangement as hardware configuration and to software components as software configuration. Understanding of computer configuration is important as for certain hardware or software applications, a minimum configuration is required.[52]

Configuration control

Process of controlling modifications to an IT system's hardware, firmware, software, and documentation to ensure the system is protected against improper modifications prior to, during, and after system implementation.[472]

Configuration management

Management of security features and assurances through control of changes made to hardware, software, firmware, documentation, test, test fixtures, and test documentation throughout the lifecycle of the IT.[472]

Configuration manager

The individual or organization responsible for configuration control or configuration management.[472]

C

Configuration services

This service is used to configure an Electronic Health Record (EHR). This includes configuration of the EHR data repository, the system, the metadata, the service components, EHR indexes, schema support, security, session, caching mechanism, etc.[472]

Conformance

The precise set of conditions for the use of options which must be implemented in a standard. There are two types of conformance: dynamic and static. Dynamic conformance requirements of a standard are all those requirements (including options) which determine the possible behavior permitted by the standard. Static conformance is a statement of what conforming implementation should be capable of doing (i.e., what is implemented).[36]

Conformance assessment process

The complete process of accomplishing all conformance testing activities necessary to enable the conformance of an implementation or system to one or more standards to be assessed.[472]

Conformance testing

Testing to determine whether a system meets some specified standard. To aid in this, many test procedures and test setups have been developed, either by the standard's maintainers or by external organizations, specifically for testing conformance to standards. Conformance testing is often performed by external organizations, sometimes the standards body itself, to give greater guarantees of compliance. Products tested in such a manner are then advertised as being certified by that external organization as complying with the standard.[248]

Connected health

The use of technology to connect the various pieces of the healthcare system (people, tools, facilities, and so on) in a way that enables delivery of ongoing, virtual care as needed across a patient population.[247]

Connectivity

The process of connecting various parts of a network to one another through the use of routers, switches, and gateways.[2]

Consensus

General agreement, characterized by the absence of sustained opposition to substantial issues by any important part of the concerned interests and by a process that involves seeking to take into account the views of all parties concerned and to reconcile any conflicting arguments.[255, 52]

Consensus algorithm

A process in computer science used to achieve agreement on a single data value among distributed processes or systems. Consensus algorithms are designed to achieve reliability in a network involving multiple nodes.[2] Blockchain technology and cryptocurrencies have introduced a revolutionary way to exchange and store monetary value. A consensus algorithm, also known as the **consensus** mechanism, lies at the heart of this technology. The consensus algorithm is the process where blockchain nodes (computers validating and recording transactions) reach an agreement on the state of the ledger.[52]

Consensus standards

These are standards developed or adopted by consensus standards bodies, both domestic and international. Such work and the resultant standards are usually voluntary.[36]

Consent

Under the HIPAA Privacy Rule, consent is made by an individual for the covered entity to use or disclose identifiable health information for treatment, payment, and healthcare operations purposes only. This is different from consent for treatment, which many providers use and which should not be confused with the consent for use or disclosure of identifiable health information. Consent for use and/or disclosure of identifiable health information is optional under the HIPAA Privacy Rule, although it may be required by state law and may be combined with consent for treatment unless prohibited by other law.[20]

Consent directive

The record of a healthcare consumer's privacy policy that grants or withholds consent for: one or more principals (identified entity or role);

C

performing one or more operations (e.g., collect, access, use, disclose, amend, or delete); purposes, such as treatment, payment, operations, research, public health, quality measures, health status evaluation by third parties, or marketing; certain conditions (e.g., when unconscious); specified time period (e.g., effective and expiry dates); and certain context (e.g., in an emergency).[20]

Consenter

An author of a consent directive; and may be the healthcare consumer or patient, a delegate of the healthcare consumer (e.g., a representative with healthcare power of attorney), or a provider with legal authority to either override a healthcare consumer's consent directive or create a directive that prevents a patient's access to Protected Health Information (PHI) until the provider has had an opportunity to review the PHI with the patient.[20]

Consistency

1. The transaction takes the resources from one consistent state to another.[7]
2. In the context of databases, it states that data cannot be written that would violate the database's own rules for valid data. If a certain transaction occurs that attempts to introduce inconsistent data, the entire transaction is rolled back and an error is returned to the user.[52] *See* **ACID**.

Consistent Presentation of Images

See **CPI**.

Consistent Time

See **CT**.

Consumer Health Vocabulary initiative

See **CHV**.

Content profile

An Integrating the Healthcare Enterprise (IHE) content profile specifies a coordinated set of standards-based information content exchanged between the functional components of communicating healthcare IT systems and devices. An IHE content profile specifies a specific element of content (e.g., a document) that may be conveyed through the transactions of one or more associated integration profiles.[124]

Contingency Plan

An alternative Information Systems Security (INFOSEC) plan that is implemented when normal business operations are interrupted by emergency, failover, or disaster. Contingency plans ensure continuous on-site and off-site business operations, customer satisfaction, and on-time product and service delivery.[52]

Continua Design Guidelines

Open implementation framework for authentic, end-to-end interoperability of personal connected health devices and systems. The Continua Design Guidelines are based on common international standards defined by recognized standards development organizations.[255]

Continuity

Strategic and tactical capability, preapproved by management, of an organization to plan for and respond to conditions, situations, and events in order to continue operations at an acceptable predefined level.[459]

Continuity of Care Document

See **CCD**.

Continuity of Care Maturation Model

See **CCMM**.

Continuity of Care Record

See **CCR**.

Continuity of Operations Plan (COOP)

Part of a principle called continuity of operations that helps to ensure trouble-free operations through unanticipated events. Many attribute this term and idea to the U.S. Federal government which has mandated that agencies need to provide for continuity of operations in many different crises.[52]

Continuity strategy

Approach by an organization intended to ensure continuity and ability to recover in the face of a disruptive event, emergency, crisis, or other major outage.[459]

Control

Means of managing risk, including policies, procedures, guidelines, practices, or organizational structures, which can be of an administrative, technical, management, or legal nature.[459]

Control chart

A graphic display of the results of a process over time and against established control limits. The dispersion of data points on the chart is used to determine whether the process is performing within prescribed limits and whether variations taking place are random or systematic.[98]

Control Unit

See **CU**.

Controlled medical vocabulary

An approved list of terms coded in a fashion that facilitates the use of the computer. Controlled vocabularies are essential if clinical applications are to function as intended. Widely used systems include the American College of Radiology (ACR) Code, Current Procedural Terminology (CPT), Diagnostic and Statistical Manual of Mental Disorders (DSM-IV), and the International Classification of Diseases, Ninth Revision (ICD-9).[142]

Convergence

The end point of any algorithm that uses iteration or recursion to guide a series of data processing steps. An algorithm is usually said to have reached convergence when the difference between the computed and observed steps falls below a predefined threshold. Convergence alludes to a process's

C

limit and may be a valuable analytical tool for assessing an optimization algorithm's predicted performance. It may be a valuable empirical tool for investigating the optimization algorithms' learning dynamics and machine learning algorithms taught using optimization algorithms. This encourages researchers to look at approaches and learning curves like early quitting. While optimization is a method for generating candidate solutions, convergence occurs when the process comes to a halt and no more modifications are needed or expected.[127]

Cookies

A small amount of data generated by a web site and saved to the web browser or in another location. The purpose is to remember information about the web session, similar to a preference file created by a software application. This data may be persistent or temporary.[73]

Cookie Theft

Occurs when a third party copies unencrypted session data and uses it to impersonate the real user. Cookie theft most often occurs when a user accesses trusted sites over an unprotected or public Wi-Fi network. Although the username and password for a given site will be encrypted, the session data traveling back and forth (the cookie) is not.[52]

Coordination of Benefits

See **COB**.

Coprocessor

A supplementary processor unit or an entirely different circuitry that is designed to complement the Central Processing Unit (CPU) of a computer. Its basic functionality is to offload other processor-intensive tasks from the CPU in order to achieve accelerated system performance by allowing the CPU to focus on tasks essential to the system.[52]

CORBA (Common Object Request Broker Architecture)

A standard developed by the Object Management Group (OMG) to provide interoperability among distributed objects. It is a design specification for

C

an Object Request Broker (ORB), where an ORB provides the mechanism required for distributed objects to communicate with one another, whether locally or on remote devices, written in different languages, or at different locations on a network.[257]

Core-Based Statistical Area

See **CBSA**.

Core Data Services

See **CDS**.

Corporate executives or C-level

See **CxO**.

Corrective action plan

See **CAP**.

Cost-Benefit Analysis (CBA)

A process that is used to estimate the costs and benefits of projects or investments to determine their profitability for an organization. A CBA is a versatile method that is often used for business administration, project management and public policy decision.[273]

Cost containment

The process of planning in order to keep costs within certain constraints.[4]

Cost-effectiveness

A system contributing to cost savings in healthcare by efficiently collecting, storing, and aggregating data and by providing decision support and augmented practices with appropriate and timely information.[4]

Countermeasure Response Administration

See **CRA**.

Covered entity

Health plans, healthcare clearinghouses, and healthcare providers who transmit any health information in electronic form, in connection with a transaction that is subject to Health Insurance Portability and Accountability Act (HIPAA) requirements, as those terms are defined and used in the HIPAA regulations, 45 CFR Parts 160 and 164.[262]

Covered function

Functions that make an entity a health plan, a healthcare provider, or a healthcare clearing house.[113]

COW (Computer-on-Wheels)

Allows a single computer to operate in multiple places around the hospital or other healthcare setting. This method is used to save space as there is minimal space to accommodate a computer in every patient room.[128]

CP (Certificate Policy)

Named set of rules that indicates the applicability of a certificate to a particular community and/or class of application with common security requirements.[72]

CPC (Comprehensive Primary Care Initiative)

A four-year multi-payer Centers for Medicare & Medicaid Services (CMS) initiative designed to strengthen primary care. CMS collaborates with commercial and State health insurance plans in U.S. regions to offer population-based care management fees and shared savings opportunities to participating primary care practices to support the provision of a core set of five "Comprehensive" primary care functions. These five functions are (1) Risk-stratified Care Management; (2) Access and Continuity; (3) Planned Care for Chronic Conditions and Preventive Care; (4) Patient and Caregiver Engagement; and (5) Coordination of Care across the Medical Neighborhood. CPC serves as the foundation for Comprehensive Primary Care Plus (CPC+). *See* **CPC+**.[26]

CPC+ (Comprehensive Primary Care Plus Initiative)

A five-year advanced primary care medical home model launched in January 2017. CPC+ integrates many lessons learned from CPC, including insights on practice readiness, the progression of care delivery redesign, actionable performance-based incentives, necessary health information technology, and claims data sharing with practices. *See* **CPC**.[26]

CPOE (Computerized Practitioner Order Entry)

1. An order entry application specifically designed to assist practitioners in creating and managing medical orders for patient services and medications. This application has special electronic signature, workflow, and rules engine functions that reduce or eliminate medical errors associated with practitioner ordering processes. **2.** A computer application that accepts the provider's orders for diagnostic and treatment services electronically instead of the clinician recording them on an order sheet or prescription pad. Also known as computerized physician order entry, computerized patient order entry, and computerized provider order entry.[11]

CPR (Computer-based Patient Record)

See **EHR**.

CPRS (Computer-based Patient Record System)

See **EHR**.

CPS (Certification Practices Statement)

Statement of the practices that a certification authority employs in issuing certificates.[72]

CPT (Current Procedural Terminology)

1. The official coding system for physicians to report professional services and procedures to third parties for payment. It is published by the American Medical Association.[46] **2.** A medical code set, maintained and copyrighted by the AMA, that has been selected for use under HIPAA for non-institutional and non-dental professional transactions.[121, 268]

CPU (Central Processing Unit)

Main system board (motherboard) integrated chip that directs computer operations. The component in a digital computer that interprets and executes the instructions and data contained in software. Microprocessors are CPUs that are manufactured on integrated circuits, often as a single-chip package. Performs the arithmetic, logic, and control operations in the computer.[52]

CQL (Clinical Quality Language)

A Health Level Seven International (HL7) authoring language standard that is intended to be human readable. It is part of the effort to harmonize standards used for electronic clinical quality measures (eCQMs) and clinical Decision Support (CDS). CQL provides the ability to express logic that is human readable yet structured enough for processing a query electronically.[474]

CQM (Clinical Quality Measures)

Tools that measure and track the quality of healthcare services provided by eligible clinicians, eligible hospitals, and critical-access hospitals (CAHs) within the U.S. healthcare system.[26]

CRA (Countermeasure Response Administration)

Systems that manage and track measures taken to contain an outbreak or event and to provide protection against a possible outbreak or event. This Public Health Information Network (PHIN) functional area also includes multiple dose delivery of countermeasures: anthrax vaccine and antibiotics; adverse events monitoring; follow-up of patients; isolation and quarantine; and links to distribution vehicles (such as the Strategic National Stockpile).[80]

Crash

An event wherein the operating system or computer application stops functioning properly. It typically occurs when hardware fails in a non-recoverable fashion, operating system data are corrupted or recovery from an error is not possible without loss of data. An application crash can result in an unexpected exit from the applications, whereas a system crash can result in the freezing of the computer.[52]

Crawler

See **Web crawler**.

C

Credential

Evidence attesting to one's right to credit or authority; in this standard, the data elements associated with an individual that authoritatively binds an identity (and, optionally, additional attributes) to that individual.[64]

Crippleware

A software program or hardware device with limited functionality and services that is released by its developer or vendor. Crippleware is a technique employed by software and hardware vendors to give prospective buyers/users a sneak peek or test drive of new software or hardware without providing the full version. In the case of software, crippleware is generally provided for free; users must then buy the full software package to enjoy all the features available. In hardware, crippleware often refers to hardware that is designed to underperform in order to inspire consumers to purchase an upgrade to make it work better.[52]

Crisis management team

Group of individuals functionally responsible for directing the development and execution of the response and operational continuity plan, declaring an operational disruption or emergency/crisis situation, and providing direction during the recovery process, both pre- and post-disruptive incidents. The crisis management team may include individuals from the organization as well as immediate and first responders, stakeholders, and other interested parties.[87]

Critical-Access Hospital

See **CAH**.

Critical Error

A serious computer error that forces the program to stop and it becomes impossible for the running program, operating system, or software to continue working normally. This error might cause the computer to reboot or freeze.[52]

Critical pathway

A tool that supports collaborative, coordinated practices. It provides for multidisciplinary communication, treatment and care planning, and documentation of caregiver's evaluations and assessments.[475]

Critical Security Parameter

Data using a cryptography module to process encryption functions. Data include passwords, security codes, cryptographic keys, Personal Identification Numbers (PIN), and any other unprotected security information.[52]

Criticality assessment

A process designed to systematically identify and evaluate an organization's assets based on the importance of its mission or function, the group of people at risk, or the significance of a disruption to the continuity of the organization.[87] *See* **Risk assessment**.

CRM (Customer relationship management)

1. A computerized system for identifying, targeting, acquiring, and retaining the best mix of customers. **2.** In healthcare, CRM is an organization-wide strategy for managing an organization's interactions with its patients and their supporting infrastructure, suppliers, providers, and/or employees using CRM technologies. IT seeks to optimize the way we establish and nurture meaningful and sustainable relationships in efforts to enhance patient experience, improve population health, reduce costs, and improve the work life of healthcare providers—ultimately leading to increased trust in and loyalty to the organization.[4, 456]

Cross-enterprise Document Sharing

See **XDS**.

Cross map

A reference from one concept in one terminology to another in a different terminology. A concept may have a single cross map or a set of alternative cross maps.[77]

Cross-platform

A product or system that can work across multiple types of platforms or operating environments. Different kinds of cross-platform systems include both hardware and software systems, as well as systems that involve separate builds for each platform, as well as other broader systems that are designed to work the same way across multiple platforms.[52]

C

Crosstalk

A disturbance caused by the electric or magnetic fields of one telecommunication signal affecting a signal in an adjacent circuit.[2]

Crosswalk

See **Data mapping**.

CRUD (Create, Read, Update, and Delete)

The basic processes that are applied to data.[2, 52, 60]

Cryptocurrency

See **Bitcoin**.

Cryptographic algorithm cipher

Method for the transformation of data in order to hide its information content, prevent its undetected modification, and/or prevent its unauthorized use.[72]

Cryptography

The act of creating written or generated codes that allow information to be kept secret. Cryptography converts data into a format that is unreadable for an unauthorized user, allowing it to be transmitted without unauthorized entities decoding it back into a readable format, thus compromising the data.[52]

CSIRT (Computer Security Incident Response Team)

See **CERT**.

CSMA/CD (Carrier Sense Multiple Access with Collision Detection)

1. A network control protocol in which a carrier-sensing scheme is used; and a transmitting data station that detects another signal while transmitting a frame stops transmitting that frame, transmits a jam signal, and then waits for a random time interval (known as "backoff delay" and determined using

C

the truncated binary exponential backoff algorithm) before trying to send that frame again. Ethernet is the classic CSMA/CD protocol. **2.** A protocol for carrier transmission access in Ethernet networks. On Ethernet, any device can try to send a frame at any time. Each device senses whether the line is idle and therefore available to be used. If it is, the device begins to transmit its first frame. If another device has tried to send at the same time, a collision is said to occur, and the frames are discarded. Each device then waits a random amount of time and retries until successful in getting its transmission sent.[2, 7, 52]

CSO (Chief Security Officer)

The person in an organization with the responsibility for the security of the paper-based and electronic information, as well as the physical and electronic means of managing and storing that information.[129]

CSU/DSU (Channel Sharing Unit/Data Service Unit)

A channel service unit (CSU) is a device that connects a terminal to a digital line. A Data Service Unit (DSU) is a device that performs protective and diagnostic functions for a telecommunications line. Typically, the two devices are packaged as a single unit, CSU/DSU.[2]

CTI (Computer Telephony Integration)

Systems that enable a computer to act as a call center, accepting incoming calls and routing them to the appropriate device or person.[2]

CTIO (Chief Technology and Innovation Officer)

A person in a company who is primarily responsible for managing the process of innovation and change management in an organization, as well as being in some cases the person who originates new ideas and/or recognizes innovative ideas generated by others.[7]

CTO (Chief Technology Officer)

1. Executive with overall responsibility for managing technical vendor relationships and performance, as well as the physical and personnel technology infrastructure, including technology deployment, network and systems management, integration testing, and developing technical operations personnel.

2. Develops technical standards and ensures compatibility for the enterprise-wide computer environment.[52]

CTS (Common Terminology Services)

Specification developed as an alternative to a common data structure.[9]

CU (Control Unit)

Portion of the CPU that handles all processor control signals. It directs all input and output flow, fetches code for instructions from microprograms, and directs other units and models by providing control and timing signals.[52]

CUI (Concept Unique Identifier)

An identifier leveraged by the Unified Medical Language System (UMLS) to uniquely represent a meaning or sense.[270]

Cure letter

A letter sent by one party to another proposing or agreeing to actions that a party will take to correct legal errors or defects that have occurred under a contract between the parties or other legal requirement.[13]

Current Procedural Terminology

See **CPT**.

Custom, customized

Software that is designed or modified for a specific user or organization; may refer to all or part of a system.[7]

Customer-centric

Placing the customer at the center or focus of design or service.[4]

Customer-driven

Strategies, offerings, or systems focused on user acceptance; focused on customer demands or requirements.[4]

Customer Relationship Dashboard

A CRM dashboard is an Enterprise Application (EA) interface used for the monitoring of business and sales opportunities, processes, and performance. A CRM dashboard provides real-time business event snapshots, which are used to measure and develop analytics for business reporting.[52]

Customer Relationship Management

See **CRM**.

CVE (Common vulnerabilities and exposures)

A list of standardized names for vulnerabilities and other information security exposures. CVE aims to standardize the names of all publicly known vulnerabilities and security exposures.[24]

CVS (Concurrent Versioning System)

Concurrent versions system (CVS) is an open-source software configuration management utility designed to manage different versions of the same software project in a specialized repository.[52]

CWE (Coded with Exceptions)

Specifies a coded element and its associated detail. The CWE data type is used (1) when more than one table may be applicable, or (2) when the specified HL7 or externally defined table may be extended with local values, or (3) when the text is in place, the code may be omitted.[130]

CWE (Common Weakness Enumeration)

A community-developed formal list of software weaknesses, idiosyncrasies, faults, and flaws.[24]

CXO (Chief Experience Officer)

An individual primarily responsible for maintaining good interactions between a brand and its customer base. This is a role that has been created within many large companies in order to more effectively manage the ways that customers experience a company and its products or services.[52]

CxO (Corporate executives or C-level or C-Suite)

A short way to refer, collectively, to corporate executives at what is some-times called the C-level, whose job titles typically start with "Chief" and end with "Officer."[2]

Cyberattack

An attack, via cyberspace, targeting an enterprise's use of cyberspace for the purpose of disrupting, disabling, destroying, or maliciously controlling a computing environment/infrastructure; or destroying the integrity of the data or stealing controlled information.[1]

Cyberdefense

A computer network defense mechanism which includes response to actions, critical infrastructure protection, and information assurance for orga-nizations, government entities, and other possible networks. Cyberdefense focuses on preventing, detecting, and providing timely responses to attacks or threats so that no infrastructure or information is tampered with. With the growth in volume as well as complexity of cyberattacks, cyber defense is essential for most entities in order to protect sensitive information as well as to safeguard assets.[52]

Cybersecurity

The practice of keeping computers and electronic information safe and secure by preventing, detecting, and responding to attacks or unauthorized access against a computer system and its information.[12]

Cyberspace

Refers to the virtual computer world and, more specifically, an electronic medium that is used to facilitate online communication. Cyberspace typically involves a large computer network made up of many worldwide computer subnetworks that employ TCP/IP protocol to aid in communication and data exchange activities. The realm of communications and computation. A term used to refer to the electronic or virtual universe of information.[52,73]

D

DaaS (Data as a Service)

A cloud strategy used to facilitate the accessibility of business-critical data in a well-timed, protected, and affordable manner. DaaS depends on the principle that specified, useful data can be supplied to users on-demand, irrespective of any organizational or geographical separation between consumers and providers.[52]

Daemon

A long-running background process that answers requests for services. The term originated with Unix, but most operating systems use daemons in some form or another. In Unix, the names of daemons conventionally end in "d." Some examples include inetd, httpd, nfsd, sshd, named, and lpd.[437]

DAF (Data Access Framework)

HL7 initiative that identifies and recommends standards for the interoperable representation and transmission of data using the notion of a Query Stack which modularizes the various layers of the Data Access Framework. The DAF FHIR Implementation Guide provides requirements and implementation guidance for the various layers of the DAF Query Stack which includes Queries including structure, vocabularies, and value sets; Query Results including structure, vocabularies, and value sets; Transport Requirements; and Security and Privacy controls required for data access.[9]

DAG (Directed Acyclic Graph)

In mathematics, a graph that travels in one direction without cycles connecting the other edges, meaning that it is impossible to traverse the entire graph by starting at one edge. It is a form of distributed ledger technology in which transactions are represented as a node in a graph. These transactions are "directed" (the links point in the same direction) and "acyclic" (a transaction cannot loop back on itself after linking to another transaction).[438]

DOI: 10.4324/9781003286028-4

DAM (Domain Analysis Model)

An abstract representation of a subject area of interest, complete enough to allow instantiation of all necessary concrete classes needed to develop child design artifacts.[9]

DApp (Decentralized Application)

Application that runs on a P2P (peer-to-peer) network of computers rather than a single computer. A type of software program designed to exist on the Internet in a way that is not controlled by a single entity. DApps can be defined by four characteristics: decentralized (all records of operation and app transactions are stored on a public ledger and run on blockchain or blockchain-like cryptographic networks with no central server or network hierarchy); incentivized (consists of a reward system to encourage network nodes to participate and collectively perform the duties of a central server); open source (source codes are available to the public); and consensus mechanism (a working protocol is required for achieving the consensus with the DApp blockchain. Any and every decision within the DApp is subject to such a protocol and it is usually implemented in the form of cryptographic hashing protocol).[271,272] Also known as dApp, Dapp.

Dashboard

A user interface or web page that gives a current summary, usually in graphic, easy-to-read form, of key information relating to progress and performance, especially for a business or website.[44] An executive dashboard is a visual software tool that helps company executives to handle their daily affairs. In general, the "dashboard" is a tool that visually represents data for use. Executive dashboards are crafted according to the needs of the typical business executive.[52]

Data

1. Factual information used as a basis for reasoning, discussion, or calculation. **2.** Discrete entities that are described objectively without interpretation.[2,29]

D

Data access

Refers to a user's ability to access or retrieve data stored within a database or other repository. Users who have data access can store, retrieve, move, or manipulate stored data, which can be stored on a wide range of hard drives and external devices.[2]

Data Access Framework

See **DAF**.

Data aggregation

1. A process by which information is collected, manipulated, and expressed in summary form. **2.** Combining protected health information by a business associate, on behalf of more covered entities than one, to permit data analysis related to the healthcare operations of the participating covered entities.[20, 131]

Data analytics

The systematic use of data to drive fact-based decision-making for planning, management, measurement, and learning. Analytics may be descriptive, predictive, or prescriptive. In healthcare, data analytics is being used to drive clinical and operational improvements to meet business challenges. Data analytics focuses on inference, the process of deriving a conclusion based solely on what is already known by the researcher.[89] *See* **Analytics**.

Data architecture

A set of rules, policies, standards, and models that govern and define the type of data collected and how data are used, stored, managed, and integrated within an organization and its database systems. It provides a formal approach to creating and managing the flow of data and how data are processed across an organization's IT systems and applications.[211]

Data as a Service

See **DaaS**.

D

Data capture

The retrieval of information from a document using methods other than data entry. The utility of data capture is the ability to automate this information retrieval where data entry would be inefficient, costly, or inapplicable.[133]

Data center

1. A centralized repository, either physical or virtual, for the storage, management, and dissemination of data and information organized around a particular body of knowledge or pertaining to a particular business. **2.** Computer facility designed for continuous use by several users and well-equipped with hardware, software, peripherals, power conditioning, backup, communication equipment, security systems, etc.[2,4]

Data classification

1. Conscious decision to assign a level of sensitivity to data as they are being created, amended, enhanced, stored, or transmitted. The classification of the data, whether established by federal or state law or by the entity holding the data, will determine the extent the data need to be protected, controlled, and/or secured and is indicative of its value in terms of information assets. **2.** The process of separating and organizing data into relevant groups ("classes") based on their shared characteristics, such as their level of sensitivity, the risks they present, and the compliance regulations that protect them. To protect sensitive data, it must be located, classified according to its level of sensitivity, and accurately tagged. Then, enterprises must handle each group of data in ways that ensure only authorized people can gain access, both internally and externally, and that the data are always handled in full compliance with all relevant regulations.[20,473]

Data cleaning/cleansing

Also known as data scrubbing. **1.** A process of amending or removing data that are incorrect, incomplete, improperly formatted, or duplicated. **2.** The process of altering data in a given storage resource to make sure that it is accurate and correct. There are many ways to pursue data cleansing in various software and data storage architectures; most of them center on the

D

careful review of data sets and the protocols associated with any particular data storage technology.[2, 52]

Data collection

1. A systematic approach to gathering information from a variety of sources to get a complete and accurate picture of an area of interest. **2.** The process of gathering and measuring data, information, or any variables of interest in a standardized and established manner that enables the collector to answer or test hypothesis and evaluate outcomes of the particular collection. This is an integral, usually initial, component of any research done in any field of study, such as the physical and social sciences, business, humanities and others.[2, 52]

Data compression

A reduction in the number of bits needed to represent data. Compressing data can save storage capacity, speed file transfer, and decrease costs for storage hardware and network bandwidth.[2]

Data condition

The rule that describes the circumstances under which a covered entity must use a particular data element or segment.[20]

Data content

All the data elements and code sets inherent to a transaction and not related to the format of the transaction.[113]

Data corruption

A deliberate or accidental violation of data integrity.[1]

Data Definition Language

See **DDL**.

Data dictionary

A collection of descriptions of the data objects or items in a data model for the benefit of programmers and others who need to refer to them.[2]

D

Data De-identification

Data de-identification is a computing standard in which sensitive medical information contained in Electronic Health Records (EHR) can be de-identified so that unauthorized users are unable to read the actual content since it is no longer in its original state. There are two types of data de-identification and they are the statistical method which makes the EHR disconnected to the individual. The second type is deletion of the 18 most common identifiers. Some of these include names, cities, street numbers, birth date, discharge date, phone numbers, Social Security numbers, Medical record numbers, and e-mail addresses.[52]

Data diddling

A cybercrime where a person intentionally enters wrong information into a computer, system, or document. It is often used when businesses and individuals want to hide part of their profits for tax evasion purposes. It could also be used to do the opposite—fabricate the average order value or the number of sales to make it look like the business has more customers than it really does. This is done to get a better loan proposal from the bank. If a business owner wants to bring their competitors down, they can also use this technique to cause damage to someone's company or its reputation. Data diddling can be performed by someone whose job it is to enter the data or remotely by hacking the system or using malware to automatically change input data. While most cybercrime involves compromising or stealing data that has already been entered, data diddling refers to compromising raw data at the entry point, just before it is processed by a computer or a system.[477]

Data element

1. The smallest named unit of information in a transaction or database. **2.** A unit of data for which the definition, identification, representation, and permissible values are specified by means of a set of attributes.[36, 113]

Data Elements for Emergency Department Systems

See **DEEDS**.

D

Data Encapsulation

Refers to sending data where the data is augmented with successive layers of control information before transmission across a network. The reverse of data encapsulation is decapsulation, which refers to the successive layers of data being removed (essentially unwrapped) at the receiving end of a network.[52]

Data entry

Direct input of data in the appropriate data fields of a database, through the use of a human data-input device such as a keyboard, mouse, stylus, or touch screen, or through speech recognition software. *See* **Data capture** and **Data logging**.[4, 52]

Data exchange

The sharing of data between systems, organizations, and individuals. During this process, the information content or meaning assigned to the data is not altered during transmission.[2]

Data field

In the structure of a database, the smallest component under which data are entered through data capture or data entry. All data fields in the same database have unique names; several data fields make up a data record; several data records make up a data file; and several data files make up a database.[4]

Data Flow Diagram

See **DFD**.

Data governance

The overall management of the availability, usability, integrity, and security of the data employed in an enterprise. A sound data governance program includes a governing body or council, a defined set of procedures, and a plan to execute those procedures.[2, 52]

Data granularity

See **Granularity**.

Data integration

A process in which heterogeneous data are retrieved and combined as an incorporated form and structure. Data integration allows different data types (such as data sets, documents, and tables) to be merged by users, organizations, and applications for use as personal or business processes and/or functions.[52]

Data integrity

1. Assurance of the accuracy, correctness, or validity of data using a set of validation criteria against which data are compared or screened. **2.** The property that data have not been altered or destroyed in an unauthorized manner or by authorized users; it is a security principle that protects information from being modified or otherwise corrupted, either maliciously or accidentally.[52]

Data interchange

The process of transferring data from an originating system to a receiving system.[52] *See* **EDI**.

Data leakage

The unauthorized transfer of classified, sensitive, proprietary, or otherwise private information from a computer, device, or datacenter to the outside world.[150]

Data linkage

1. The merging of information from two or more sources of data with the object of consolidating facts. **2.** A complex technique for connecting data records within and between data sets using demographic data (e.g., name, date of birth, address, sex, and medical record number). Also known as "Record Linkage" or "Linkage."[436]

Data link layer

Second layer in the Open Systems Interconnection (OSI) architecture model. It is the protocol layer in a program that handles the moving of data into and out of a physical link in a network. Consists of Logical Link Control (LLC) and Media Access Control (MAC) sublayers. Handles data flow control, the packaging of raw data in its frames, or frames into raw data bits, and retransmits frames as needed.[2]

Data logging

1. The process of using a computer to collect data through sensors, analyze the data, save, and output the results of the collection and analysis. Data logging also implies control over how the computer collects and analyzes the data. **2.** The process of collecting and storing data over a period of time in order to analyze specific trends or record the data-based events/actions of a system, network, or IT environment. It enables the tracking of all interactions through which data, files, or applications are stored, accessed, or modified on a storage device or application.[39, 52]

Data Manipulation Language

See **DML**.

Data mapping

A process used in data warehousing by which different data models are linked to each other using a defined set of methods to characterize the data in a specific definition. This data linking follows a set of standards, which depend on the domain value of the data model used.[52]

Data mart

1. A repository of data that serves a particular community of knowledge workers. The data may come from an enterprise-wide database or a data warehouse. **2.** Collection of data focusing on a specific topic or organization unit or department created to facilitate strategic business decisions. **3.** The access layer of the data warehouse environment that is used to get data out to users. It is a subset of the data warehouse, usually oriented to a specific business line or team. **4.** A subject-oriented archive that stores data and uses the retrieved set of information to assist and support the requirements involved within a particular business function or department. Data marts exist within a single organizational data warehouse repository.[2, 136, 7, 52]

Data messaging

See **Messaging**.

D

Data migration

1. The process of transferring data between data storage systems, data formats, or computer systems. **2.** The process of transporting data between computers, storage devices, or formats. It is a key consideration for any system implementation, upgrade, or consolidation. During data migration, software programs or scripts are used to map system data for automated migration.[2, 52]

Data mining

1. The process of finding anomalies, patterns, and correlations within large data sets to predict outcomes and solve outcomes through data analysis. **2.** The process of analyzing hidden patterns of data according to different perspectives in order to turn that data into useful and often actionable information. Data are collected and assembled in common areas, such as data warehouses, and data-mining algorithms look for patterns that businesses can use to make better decisions, such as decisions that help cut costs, increase revenue, or better serve customers or clients.[2, 116, 52]

Data model

1. A conceptual model of the information needed to support a business function or process. **2.** Describes the organization of data in an automated system. The data model includes the subjects of interest in the system (or entities) and the attributes (data elements) of those entities. It defines how the entities are related to each other (cardinality) and establishes the identifiers needed to relate entities to each other. A data model can be expressed as a conceptual, logical, or physical model. **3.** Refers to the logical interrelationships and data flow between different data elements involved in the information world. It also documents the way data are stored and retrieved. Data models facilitate communication business and technical development by accurately representing the requirements of the information system and by designing the responses needed for those requirements. Data models help represent what data are required and what format is to be used for different business processes.[113, 52]

Data modeling

1. A method used to define and analyze data requirements needed to support the business functions of an enterprise. Data modeling defines the data elements, their relationships, and their physical structure in preparation for creating a database. **2.** A representation of the data structures in a table for a company's database and is a very powerful expression of the company's business requirements. This data model is the guide used by functional and technical analysts in the design and implementation of a database.[7, 52]

Data Obfuscation

A form of data masking where data are purposely scrambled to prevent unauthorized access to sensitive materials. This form of encryption results in unintelligible or confusing data. There are two types of DO encryption: (1) Cryptographic DO, input data encoding prior to being transferred to another encryption schema and (2) network security DO, payload attack methods are purposely enlisted to avoid detection by network protection systems. DO is also known as data scrambling and privacy preservation.[252]

Data object

1. A data object is a collection of one or more data points that create meaning as a whole. In other words, "data object" is an alternate way of saying "this group of data should be thought of as standalone." The most common example of a data object is a *data table* but others include arrays, pointers, records, files, sets, and scalar types. Values in a data object may have their own unique IDs, data types, and attributes. In this way, data objects vary across database structures and different programming languages. **2.** A collection of data that has a natural grouping and may be identified as a complete entity.[478, 120]

Data origin authentication

Corroboration that the source of data is received as is claimed.[1]

Data originator

1. The creating entity for each information element that identifies the source of the information captured in the electronic case report form for a clinical investigation. The source could be a person, computer system, device, or instrument (FDA). **2.** The person, organization, or system that generates data, such as the patient for symptoms, the physician for examination and decisions, the nurse for patient care, medical devices, and EHRs.[52, 41]

D

Data Perturbation

A form of privacy-preserving data mining for Electronic Health Records (EHR). There are two main types of data perturbation appropriate for EHR data protection. The first type is known as the probability distribution approach and the second type is called the value distortion approach. Data perturbation is considered a relatively easy and effective technique for protecting sensitive electronic data from unauthorized use.[52]

Data processing

1. The end-to-end process of collecting raw data and turning it into useful and actionable knowledge. It also includes data reporting and data storage. Data can be collected manually or automatically. Processing transforms big data into useful information. Once processing is complete, we must store the data. **2.** The process of converting of raw data into machine-readable form and its subsequent processing (as storing, updating, rearranging, or printing out) by a computer.[479, 29]

Data Profiling

A technique used to examine data for different purposes, like determining accuracy and completeness. This process examines a data source, such as a database, to uncover the erroneous areas in data organization. Deployment of this technique improves data quality. Data profiling is also referred to as data discovery.[52]

Data provenance

1. The ability to trace and verify the creation of data, how it has been used or moved among different databases, as well as altered throughout its life cycle. **2.** Information about the source of the data and processing/transitions the data have undergone.[137, 12]

Data quality

1. Perception or assessment of data's ability to serve its purpose in a given context, determined by factors such as accuracy, completeness, reliability, relevance, and how up to date it is. **2.** The features and characteristics that ensure data are accurate, complete, and convey the intended meaning.

3. The degree to which a given data set meets a user's needs. Data quality is an important criteria for ensuring that data-driven decisions are made as accurately as possible.[2, 43, 52]

Data registry

An information resource by a registration authority that describes the meaning and representational form (metadata) of data units, including data element identifiers, definitions, units, allowed value domains, etc. A **clinical** data registry is an interactive database that collects, organizes, and displays healthcare information. The purpose of a data registry is the same: to evaluate and improve outcomes for a population defined by a particular condition, disease, or exposure. Registries use observational study methods to collect and harmonize data about the treatment, outcomes, and well-being of patients who receive care over time. They aggregate large data sets and analyze trends or patterns in treatments and outcomes. Clinical data registries are also sometimes called patient registries and disease registries.[480]

Data repository

See **Repository** and **Data warehouse**.

Data Segmentation for Privacy

See **DS4P**.

Data Service Unit

See **DSU**.

Data set

A collection of discrete items of related data that may be accessed individually or in combination or managed as a whole entity such as Uniform Hospital Discharge Data Set (UHDDS). Analyzing data sets during data mining can help discover patterns and use those patterns to forecast or predict the likelihood of future events.[2, 52] *See* **PNDS, NMDS**, and **NMMDS**.

Data standards

Consensual specifications for the representation of data from different sources and settings; necessary for the sharing, portability, and reusability of data.[140]

D

Data structure

Interrelationships among data elements that determine how data are recorded, manipulated, stored, and presented by a database. Methods of organizing units of data within larger data sets. Achieving and maintaining specific data structures help improve data access and value. Data structures also help programmers implement various programming tasks.[4, 52]

Data subject

The person whose information is collected, stored, or processed. Any person formally residing in the EU who has their data collected, held, or processed by a controller or processor.[273]

Data synchronization

The process of maintaining the consistency and uniformity of data instances across all consuming applications and storing devices. It ensures that the same copy or version of data is used in all devices—from source to destination.[52]

Data tagging

A formatted word that represents a wrapper for a stored value. The data tag is a small piece of scripting code, typically JavaScript, that transmits page-specific information via query string parameters. The process begins when a page containing a data tag is requested from the server. The tag is a piece of scripting code executed when the page is loaded into the browser. The data tag constructs the query string by scanning the document source for HTML, beginning with a specific identifier.[141]

Data Terminal Ready

See **DTR**.

Data transformation

The process of converting data or information from one format to another, usually from the format of a source system into the required format of a new destination system. The usual process involves converting documents, but data conversions sometimes involve the conversion of a program from one computer language to another to enable the program to run on a different platform. The usual reason for this data migration is the adoption of a new system that is totally different from the previous one.[52]

Data type

1. A category of data. The broadest data types are alphanumeric and numeric. Programming languages allow for the creation of several data types, such as integer (whole numbers), floating point, date, string (text), logical (true/false), and binary. Data type usually specifies the range of values, how the values are processed by the computer, and how the data type is stored. **2.** The categories of data that will persist in the EHR. They include voice, wave forms, clinical notes, and summaries, diagnostic imaging, lab, and pharmacy information. **3.** The data type of a value (or variable in some contexts) is an attribute that tells what kind of data that value can have. Most often the term is used in connection with static typing of variables in programming languages like C/C++, Java, and C#, where the type of a variable is known at compilation time. Data types include storage classifications like integers, floating point values, strings, characters, etc.[273,57,52]

Data Use Agreement

See **DUA**.

Data validation

Data validation means checking the accuracy and quality of source data before using, importing, or otherwise processing data. Different types of validation can be performed depending on the destination constraints or objectives. Data validation is a form of data cleansing. When moving and merging data, it is important to make sure data from different sources and repositories will conform to business rules and not become corrupted due to inconsistencies in type or context. The goal is to create data that are consistent, accurate, and complete to prevent data loss and errors during a move.[481]

Data visualization

The presentation of data in a pictorial or graphical format. It enables decision-makers to see analytics presented visually, so they can grasp difficult concepts or identify new patterns or trends.[116]

Data warehouse

A storage architecture designed to hold data extracted from transaction systems, operational data stores, and external sources. The warehouse then combines that data in an aggregate, summary form suitable for enterprise-wide data analysis and reporting for predefined business needs. The five components of a data warehouse are Production data sources, Data extraction and conversion, Data warehouse database management system, Data warehouse administration, and Business Intelligence (BI) tools.[482]

Database

A collection of information that is organized to be easily accessed, managed, and updated. The basic database contains fields, records, and files; a field is a single piece of information, a record is one complete set of fields, and a file is a collection of records. In this electronic system, data are easily accessed, manipulated, and updated.[2, 52]

Database Administrator

See **DBA**.

Database Authentication

The process or act of confirming that a user who is attempting to log in to a database is authorized to do so and is only accorded the rights to perform activities that he or she has been authorized to do.[52]

Database design

This includes logical (entity relationship) and physical (table, column, and key) design tools for data. Physical data modeling is becoming almost mandatory for applications using Relational Database Management Systems (RDBMS).[142]

Database Management System

See **DBMS**.

D

Database schema

The organization of data as a blueprint of how the database is constructed (divided into database tables in the case of relational databases). Refers to the logical and visual configuration of the entire relational database. The database objects are often grouped and displayed as tables, functions, and relations. A schema describes the organization and storage of data in a database and defines the relationship between various tables. A database schema includes descriptive details of the database that can be depicted through schema diagrams.[10, 480]

Datum

Any single observation or fact. A medical datum generally can be regarded as the value of a specific parameter (e.g., a patient and at a specific time).[274]

Daughterboard

A circuit board that attaches to another board, such as the motherboard or an expansion card.[2]

DaVinci Project

Initiative working to accelerate the adoption of HL7 Fast Healthcare Interoperability Resources (FHIR) as the standard to support and integrate Value-Based Care (VBC) data exchange across communities. Initial use cases focus on exchange between payer and provider trading partners.[9]

DBA (Database Administrator)

The person responsible for the creation, maintenance, backup, querying, security, and user rights assignment of a database system.[52]

DBMS (Database Management System)

1. A program that lets one or more computer users create and access data in a database. On personal computers, Microsoft® Access® is a popular example of a single or small group user DBMS. Microsoft's SQL server is an example of a DBMS that serves database requests from a larger number of users. **2.** A set of programs used to define, administer, store, modify, process, and extract information from a database. **3.** A Database Management System

(DBMS) is a middle ware that allows programmers, Database Administrators (DBAs), software applications, and end users to store, organize, access, query, and manipulate data in a database.[10, 52]

DCM (Detailed Clinical Models)

An information model designed to express one or more clinical concept(s) and their context in a standardized and reusable manner, specifying the requirements for clinical information as a discrete set of logical clinical data elements.[70]

DCM (Dynamic case management)

The handling of case-related work through the use of technologies that automate and streamline aspects of each case. In this context, a case is a collection of information about a particular instance of something, such as a person, company, incident, or problem.[459]

DDL (Data Definition Language)

A language used to define data structures and modify data. For example, DDL commands can be used to add, remove, or modify tables within a database. DDLs used in database applications are considered a subset of SQL, the Structured Query Language. However, a DDL may also define other types of data, such as XML.[73, 52]Also known as data description language.

Debugging

The process of discovering and eliminating abnormalities errors and defects, or bugs, in program code.[52]

Decision support (analytics)

Recommendations for intervention based on computerized care protocols.[48]

Decision tree

1. A schematic, tree-shaped diagram used to determine a course of action or show a statistical probability. Each branch represents a possible decision, occurrence of reaction. **2.** A flowchart-like representation of data that graphically resembles a tree that has been drawn upside down. In this analogy, the root of the tree is a decision that has to be made; the tree's branches are actions that can be taken; and the tree's leaves are potential decision outcomes. The purpose of a decision tree is to partition a large data set into subsets that contain instances with similar values in order to understand the likely outcomes of specific options.[18, 52]

Decompression

The expansion of compressed image files.[2] *See* **Lossless compression** and **Lossy compression**.

Decryption

The process of transforming encrypted data back to its original, unencrypted form. A system of extracting and converting garbled data and transforming them into text and/or images that are human and/or machine readable.[52]

Dedicated line

A telephone or data line that is always available. This line is not used by other computers or individuals, is available 24 hours a day, and is never disconnected. In IT, a dedicated line is a particular fiber optic cable, twisted-pair cable line, coaxial cable, or other physical cable line that is available at all times for a specific service.[276, 52]

DEEDS (Data Elements For Emergency Department Systems)

The recommended data set for use in emergency departments; it is published by the Centers for Disease Control and Prevention (CDC). Subsequently, Health Level Seven (HL7) DEEDS was created to improve interoperability of emergency care data.[80, 9, 481]

Deep learning

An iterative approach to Artificial Intelligence (AI) that stacks machine learning algorithms in a hierarchy of increasing complexity and abstraction. Each deep learning level is created with knowledge gained from the preceding layer of the hierarchy. The first layer of a deep image recognition algorithm, for example, might focus on learning about color patterns in training data, while the next layer focuses on shapes. Eventually, the hierarchy will have layers that focus on various combinations of colors and shapes, with the top layer focusing on the actual object being recognized. Deep learning is currently the most sophisticated AI architecture in use today.[52, 278]

Default gateway

An access point or IP router that a networked computer uses to send information to a computer in another network or the Internet. Default simply means that this gateway is used by default, unless an application specifies another gateway.[52] *See* **Gateway**.

Default route

The route that takes effect when no other route is available for an IP destination address. A default route, also known as the gateway of last resort, is the route used by the router when the IP destination address of a certain packet is unknown.[52, 482]

Definition

Statement that describes a concept and permits differentiation from other concepts within a system.[36]

Degaussing

Exposure to high magnetic fields. One method of destroying data on a hard drive, USB thumb drive, smartphone, or floppy disk. Also commonly used to improve the picture resolution on electronic displays. Many display manufacturers include an internal coil that will degauss the display when it is turned on. Display monitors and televisions with Cathode Ray Tube (CRT) technology are particularly subject to the buildup of magnetic fields.[2]

De-identified health information

Removal of individual identifiers so that the corresponding information cannot be used to identify an individual. De-identified health information is not protected by HIPAA. Health information that meets the standard and implementation specifications for de-identification under 45 CFR § 164.514(a) and (b) is considered not to be individually identifiable health information, i.e., de-identified.[20]

D

Deliverable

Any tangible outcome that is produced by the project. These can be documents, plans, computer systems, buildings, aircraft, etc. Internal deliverables are produced as a consequence of executing the project and are usually only needed by the project team. External deliverables are those that are created for clients and stakeholders.[459]

Delivery System Reform Incentive Payment

See **DSRIP**.

Demodulation

Reverse of modulation. The act of extracting the original information-bearing signal from a modulated carrier wave or signal. The conversion from analog signals to digital signals occurring in a modem at a receiving site. Analog signals are used to transfer data over phone lines. Digital signals are in a format that can be used by a computer.[459]

Demographic data

Data that describe the characteristics of enrollee populations such as within a managed care entity. Demographic data include, but are not limited to, age, sex, race/ethnicity, and primary language.[26]

Denial-of-service attack

An attack in which a user or a program attempts to prevent legitimate users from accessing the service by increasing traffic or taking up so much of a shared resource that the network or server is busy or none of the resource is left for other users or uses.[52]

Derivative

Any reuse of information at the application level. Captures the notion of "collect once, use many times." For example, detailed data information from an accounting system can be used for financial planning. Loosely adapted from mathematics, investing.[4]

D

Derivative file

Often called *service, access, delivery, viewing,* or *output* files; derivative files are by their nature secondary items and generally are not considered to be permanent parts of an archival collection.[489]

Description logics

A family of knowledge representation languages that can be used to represent the terminological knowledge of an application domain in a structured and formally well-understood way. The name *description logic* refers, on the one hand, to concept descriptions used to describe a domain and, on the other hand, to the logic-based semantics which can be given by a translation into first-order predicate logic.[143]

Descriptor

1. The text defining a code in a code set. **2.** In an information retrieval system, a descriptor is a word or a characteristic feature used to identify an item (as a subject or document). In computer vision, visual descriptors present the descriptions of the visual features of the images or video contents. They describe, under invariance conditions, the elementary characteristics such as shape, color, or texture.[459,484]

Design

1. Phase of software development following analysis and concerned with how the problem is to be solved. **2.** The process and result of describing how a system or process is to be automated. Design must thoroughly describe the function of a component and its interaction with other components. Design usually also identifies areas of commonality in systems and optimizes reusability.[488]

Designated approval authority

Official with the authority to formally assume the responsibility for operating a system or network at an acceptable level of risk. This term is synonymous with authorizing official, designated accrediting authority, and delegated accrediting authority. Rationale: This term has been replaced by the term "authorizing official."[1]

D

Designated code set

A medical code set or an administrative code set that is required to be used by the adopted implementation specification for a standard transaction.[26]

Designated record set

A group of records maintained by or for a covered entity that comprises the medical records and billing records about individuals maintained by or for a covered healthcare provider; enrollment, payment, claims adjudication, and case or medical management record systems maintained by or for a health plan; or other records that are used, in whole or in part, by or for the covered entity to make decisions about individuals.[35]

Designated Standard Maintenance Organization

See **DSMO**.

DFD (Data Flow Diagram)

A two-dimensional diagram that explains how data are processed and transferred in a system. The graphical depiction identifies each source of data and how it interacts with other data sources to reach a common output. This type of diagram helps business development and design teams visualize how data are processed and identify or help improve certain aspects.[4]

DHCP (Dynamic Host Configuration Protocol)

A network management protocol used to dynamically assign an IP address to any new node entering the network. DHCP permits a node to be configured automatically, thereby avoiding the necessity of involvement by a network administrator.[52]

DI (Diagnostic Imaging)

Also called medical imaging. The use of digital images and textual reports prepared as a result of performing diagnostic studies, such as x-rays, CT scans, and MRIs.[144]

Diagnostic and Statistical Manual

See **DSM**.

DICOM (Digital Imaging and Communications in Medicine)

1. A standard for the electronic communication of medical images and associated information. DICOM relies on explicit and detailed models of how patients, images, and reports involved in radiology operations are described and how the above are related. The DICOM standards contain information object definitions, data structure, data dictionary, media storage, file format, communications formats, and print formats. **2.** An ANSI-accredited standards development organization that has created a standard protocol for exchanging medical images among computer systems.[459] *See* **RIS**.

Dictionary

In computer science programming languages, a dictionary is an abstract data type storing items or values. A value is accessed by an associated key. Basic operations are new, insert, find, and delete.[145]

Digital

Data are in terms of two states: positive and nonpositive. Positive is expressed or represented by the number 1 and nonpositive by the number 0. Thus, data transmitted or stored with digital technology are expressed as a string of 0's and 1's. Each of these state digits is referred to as a bit, and a string of bits that a computer can address individually as a group is a byte.[2]

Digital certificate

An electronic "passport" that allows a person, computer, or organization to exchange information securely over the Internet using the Public Key Infrastructure (PKI). A digital certificate may also be referred to as a public key certificate. Just like a passport, a digital certificate provides identifying information, is forgery resistant, and can be verified because it was issued by an official, trusted agency. The certificate contains the name of the certificate holder, a serial number, expiration dates, a copy of the certificate holder's public key (used for encrypting messages and digital signatures), and the digital signature of the Certificate Authority (CA) so that a recipient can verify that the certificate is real.[2]

Digital envelope

Data appended to a message that allow the intended recipient to verify the integrity of the content of the message.[36]

Digital health

According to Paul Sonnier, digital health is defined as the "convergence of the digital and genomic revolutions with health, healthcare, living, and society. The essential elements of digital health include wireless devices, hardware sensors and software sensing technologies, microprocessors and integrated circuits, the Internet, social networking, mobile and body area networks, health information technology, genomics, and personal genetic information."[490]

Digital Health Collaborative

An open-source initiative whose goal is to use the power of the community to accelerate the adoption and implementation of innovative health solutions.

Digital Health Literacy

Also known as e-Health literacy; it is the use of digital literacy skills in health. It has been defined as the ability to seek, find, understand, and appraise health information from electronic resources and apply such knowledge to addressing or solving a health problem.[491]

Digital Imaging and Communications in Medicine

See **DICOM**.

Digital radiography

A form of radiography, using a digital x-ray detector to automatically acquire images and transfer them to a computer for viewing. This system is additionally capable of fixed or mobile use. Given its high-volume capabilities, it is often the choice for larger or busier clinics or health systems.[280]

Digital signal

Transmission signal that carries information in the discrete value form of 0 and 1.[69]

Digital signature

A mathematical technique used to validate the authenticity and integrity of a message, software, or digital document.[2] *See* **Private key** and **Public key**.

Digital signature standard

Specifies algorithms for applications requiring a digital signature rather than a written signature. A digital signature is represented in a computer as a string of bits. A digital signature is computed using a set of rules and a set of parameters that allow the identity of the signatory and the integrity of the data to be verified. Digital signatures may be generated on both stored and transmitted data. Signature generation uses a private key to generate a digital signature; signature verification uses a public key that corresponds to, but is not the same as, the private key. Each signatory possesses a private and public key pair. Public keys may be known by the public; private keys are kept secret. Anyone can verify the signature by employing the signatory's public key. Only the user that possesses the private key can perform signature generation.[146]

Digital Subscriber Line

See **DSL**.

Digital Subscriber Line Access Multiplexer

See **DSLAM**.

Digital therapeutics

A class of digital tools that helps people make positive and sustainable behavior changes that can be as effective as taking a medication or in some cases more effective.[281]

D

Digital Twin

A virtual representation of an entity or system that exists in the physical world. Digital twins can be either static or dynamic. Static twins, which are also referred to as simulations, represent an entity or system at a specific point in time. Dynamic twins are linked to the physical entity or system they represent in order to accurately depict the state of the entity or system in real or near-real time. Popular uses for digital twins include forecasting the health of an entity or system under specific conditions; training staff how to use/manage a physical entity or system; capturing requirements for a new entity or system; predicting how a change will affect a real-world entity or system; comparing two different lifecycle plans for an entity or system; understanding an entity or system's dependencies prior to building it in the real world; testing dangerous scenarios without involving people; assessing risk without causing a serious impact; and simultaneously running simulations for different "what if" scenarios.

Today, digital twins play an important role in many industries—especially those industries that rely on or use complex physical entities that are both valuable and unique.[52]

Digitize

To convert something, such as data or an image to digital form.[29]

Digitized signature

See **Electronic Signature**.

Dimension table

A building block of a star schema data model; it contains the descriptive data regarding the objects in a fact table.[2]

Direct address

A direct address is similar to a typical e-mail address which can be issued to an individual, organization, or machine. It is different because a direct address serves as a secure messaging system that provides for identity management and message encryption. This enables the secure sending and receiving of personal health information and other sensitive communication exchange.[492]

D

Direct connection

A situation where one computer is directly linked to another computer by a cable instead of via a network connection.[52]

Direct exchange

Describes the push of health information from a sender to a known receiver, similar to how an e-mail or fax is pushed from one endpoint to another.[492]

Direct Memory Access

See **DMA**.

Direct messaging

One type of secure messaging that is generally recognized as an effective, secure, encrypted communication mechanism for use in the point-to-point exchange of sensitive clinical and administrative data.[492]

DIRECT Project

Launched in March 2010 as a part of the Nationwide Health Information Network, the DIRECT Project was created to specify a simple, secure, scalable, standards-based way for participants to send authenticated, encrypted health information directly to known, trusted recipients over the Internet. Participants include EHR and PHR vendors, medical organizations, systems integrators, integrated delivery networks, federal organizations, state, and regional health information organizations, organizations that provide health information exchange capabilities, and health information technology consultants. Two primary DIRECT project specifications are the Applicability Statement for Secure Health Transport and the XDR and XDM for Direct Messaging.[12]

Direct Sequence Spread Spectrum

See **DSSS**.

Directed Acyclic Graph

See **DAG**.

D

Directory

An organizing unit in a computer's file system for storing and locating files.[459]

Directory Services Markup Language

See **DSML**.

Disaster Recovery Plan (DRP)

A business plan that describes how work can be resumed quickly and effectively after a disaster. Disaster recovery planning is just part of business continuity planning and is applied to aspects of an organization that rely on an IT infrastructure to function. The overall idea is to develop a plan that will allow the IT department to recover enough data and system functionality to allow a business or organization to operate—even possibly at a minimal level. The creation of a DRP begins with a DRP proposal to achieve upper level management support. Then a Business Impact Analysis (BIA) is needed to determine which business functions are the most critical and the requirements to get the IT components of those functions operational again after a disaster, either on-site or off-site.[52]

Disclosure history

Under the Health Insurance Portability and Accountability Act (HIPAA), this is a list of any entity that has received personally identifiable healthcare information for uses unrelated to treatment and payment.[35]

Disclosure/disclose

The release, transfer, provision of, access to, or divulging in any other manner of information outside the entity holding the information.[20]

Discovery/e-discovery

Electronic discovery, or e-discovery, is a type of cyber forensics (also referred to as computer or digital forensics) and describes the process whereby law enforcement or attorneys can obtain, secure, search, and process any electronic data for use as evidence in a legal proceeding or investigation. Electronic discovery may be limited to a single computer or a network-wide search.[39]

Discrete data

Information that can be categorized into a classification. Discrete data are based on counts. Only a finite number of values are possible, and the values cannot be subdivided meaningfully. For example, the number of parts damaged in shipment.[148]

Disease registry

A large collection or registry that contains information on different chronic health problems affecting patients within the system. A disease registry helps to manage and log data on chronic illnesses and diseases. All data contained within the disease registry are logged by healthcare providers and are available to providers to perform benchmarking measures on healthcare systems.[12]

Disease staging

A classification system that uses diagnostic findings to produce clusters of patients based on etiology, pathophysiology, and severity. It can serve as the basis for clustering clinically homogeneous patients to assess quality of care, analysis of clinical outcomes, utilization of resources, efficacy of alternative treatments, and assignment of credentials for hospital privileges. Staging was also designed as a quality assurance tool for evaluating ambulatory care by comparing levels of severity at the time of hospitalization for patients receiving their health benefits from government and private insurers.[149] *See* **Severity system**.

Disk striping

The process of dividing a body of data into blocks and separating the data blocks across multiple storage devices.[2]

Disk striping with parity

Fault-tolerant storage technique that distributes data and parity across three or more physical disks. Storage technique that stripes data and parity in 64K

D

blocks across all disks in the array. Striping provides fast data transfer and protection from a single-disk failure by regenerating data for a failed disk through the stored parity. Minimum of three physical disks are required for disk striping with parity.[1] Also known as RAID 5.

Disk striping without parity

Storage technique that distributes data across two or more physical disks in 64K blocks across all disks in the array. Striping provides fast data transfer. Minimum of two physical disks are required for disk striping without parity. This technique is not fault-tolerant.[2] Also known as RAID 0.

Distinguished name

A name given to a person, company, or element within a computer system or network that uniquely identifies it from everything else.[150]

Distributed computing environment

Technology for setting up and managing computing and data exchange in a system of distributed computers.[2]

Distributed database

A database in which portions are stored in more than one physical location, and processing is distributed among multiple database nodes.[2] *See* **Federated Database**.

Distributed ledger

A database held and updated independently by each participant (or node) in a large network. Records are not communicated to various nodes by a central authority but instead are independently constructed and held by each node. Every node on the network processes every transaction, coming to consensus with all nodes on the conclusions related to that transaction. Also known as **Distributed Ledger Technology** or **DLT**. [281]

Distributed processing

1. The distribution of computer processing work among multiple computers to run an application. Often refers to Local Area Networks (LANs) designed so a single program can run simultaneously at various sites. **2**. A setup in which multiple individual Central Processing Units (CPU) work on the same programs, functions, or systems to provide more capability for a computer or other device.[39, 52]

DLC (Data Link Control)

A service that ensures reliable network data communication by managing frame error detection and flow control. DLC is based on the Data Link layer of the Open Systems Interconnection (OSI) model.[52]

DLL (Dynamic Link Library)

A collection of small programs that can be loaded when needed by larger programs and used at the same time. The small program lets the larger program communicate with a specific device, such as a printer or scanner. It is often packaged as a DLL program, which is usually referred to as a DLL file.[2]

DLT (Distributed Ledger Technology)

See **Distributed ledger**.

DMA (Direct Memory Access)

Method that allows an input/output device to send or receive data directly to/from the main memory, bypassing the CPU to speed up memory operations. The process is managed by an integrated computer chip, known as the DMA controller.[52]

DME (Durable Medical Equipment)

Equipment and supplies ordered by a healthcare provider for everyday or extended use. Coverage for DME may include oxygen equipment, wheelchairs, crutches, or blood testing strips for diabetics.[493]

DML (Data Manipulation Language)

A family of computer languages, including commands permitting users to manipulate data in a database. This manipulation involves inserting data into database tables, retrieving existing data, deleting data from existing tables, and modifying existing data. DML is most often incorporated into Structured Query Language (SQL) databases.[52]

DNS (Domain Name Server)

A database of public IP addresses and their associated host names. It serves to resolve or translate those common host names to IP addresses as requested. This server allows for the translation of host names to IP addresses and vice versa to allow for mapping between human-readable names and machine-readable IP addresses to access websites.[203,456]

DNSSEC (Domain Name System Security Extension)

A set of Internet Engineering Task Force (IETF) standards created to address vulnerabilities in the Domain Name System (DNS) and protect it from online threats. The purpose of DNSSEC is to increase the security of the Internet as a whole by addressing DNS security weaknesses. Essentially, DNSSEC adds authentication to DNS to make the system more secure.[2]

Document management

1. The process of storing, locating, updating, and sharing data for the purpose of workflow progression and business outcomes. Centralized sharing and data storage within specific servers help organizations access information efficiently and effectively, along with securing protected data. Programs and servers are used in the process of document management. Important metadata is centralized, as opposed to decentralized or difficult to locate. **2.** Software systems allowing organizations to control the production, storage, management, and distribution of electronic documents, yielding greater efficiencies in the ability to reuse information and to control the flow of the documents, from creation to archiving.[52]

Document Type Definition

See **DTD**.

Documentation and procedures test

A testing event that evaluates the accuracy of user and operations documentation and determines whether the manual procedure will work correctly as an integral part of the system.[459]

Documentation integrity

The accuracy of the complete health record. It encompasses information governance, patient identification, authorship validation, amendments, and record corrections. It also includes auditing the record for documentation validity when submitting reimbursement claims.[459]

Domain

A domain contains a group of computers that may be accessed and administered with a common set of rules.[73]

Domain Analysis Model

See **DAM**.

Domain information model

The model provides a view of an entire domain, commonly constructed in diagrams to represent the semantics of an entire domain using language that subject matter experts understand.[283]

Domain Name Server

See **DNS**.

Dongle

A piece of hardware used for software protection that is connected to a computer's I/O port to ensure that software is executed securely. The dongle must be present for the software to run. The dongle's main purpose is to prevent piracy or unauthorized execution of software, and its use is generally limited to high-end software with a small core market, such as audio mixing or computer-assisted design software. Other terms for dongle include hardware key, hardware token, or security device.[52]

Dot pitch

A measurement (in millimeters) of the distance between dots on a monitor. The lower the number, the higher the clarity of the display.[2]

D

Dots Per square Inch

See **DPI**.

Download (D/L)

The process of receiving data from a central server to a user's computer. The source can be a Web server, FTP server, e-mail server, or other similar system. The term download technically means receiving information from the Internet to an individual local computer. The information could be in the form of a text file, upgrade, movie, music, freeware, shareware or sounds, etc. Download refers to receiving and saving rather than just receiving, because the information received from a remote server is saved to a local computer but can only be used when data have been fully received in its entirety. The term is most often mistaken and confused with the term "transferring," which is the sending and receiving of data between storage devices—completely different from downloading.[52]

DPI (Dots per square inch)

A measure of the resolution of a printer, scanner, or monitor. It refers to the number of dots per inch. The more dots per inch, the higher the resolution.[73]

Draft Standard for Trial Use

See **DSTU**.

Draft supplement for public comment

A specification candidate for addition to an IHE Domain Technical Framework (e.g., a new profile) that is issued for comment by an interested party.[124,456]

Draft Technical Report

See **DTR**.

DRAM (Dynamic Random Access Memory)

A type of memory used for data or program code that a processor needs to function. A common type of random access memory (RAM) that must

D

refresh every few milliseconds, by rewriting the data to the module. It accesses memory directly, holds memory for a short period, and loses its data when power is shut off.[52]

DRG (Diagnosis Related Group)

A classification system that groups patients according to diagnosis, type of treatment, age, and other relevant criteria. Under the prospective payment system, hospitals are paid a set fee for treating patients in a single DRG category, regardless of the actual cost of care for the individual.[494]

Drilldown

Exploration of multidimensional data allows moving down from one level of detail to the next, depending on the granularity of data at that level.[459]

Driver

A piece of software that enables an external device, such as a printer, hard disk, CD-ROM drive, or scanner to work with a computer's operating system.[73]

Drop-down list (or menu)

A menu of commands or options that appears when you select an item with a mouse. The item you select is generally at the top of the display screen, and the menu appears just below it, as if you had it dropped down or you had pulled it down.[29,73]

Drug information system

A computer-based system that maintains drug-related information, such as information concerning appropriate dosages and side effects, and may access a drug interaction database. A drug information system may provide, by way of a directed consultation, specific advice on the usage of various drugs.[459]

Drug interaction database

Database containing information on drug interactions.[459]

D

Drug reference terminology

A collection of drug concepts and information such as definitions, hierarchies, and other kinds of knowledge and relationships related to the drug concepts.[459]

Drug therapy

The use of drugs to cure a medical problem, to improve a patient's condition, or to otherwise produce a therapeutic effect.[459]

DS4P (Data Segmentation for Privacy)

Standard that allows a provider to tag a Consolidated-Clinical Document Architecture (CCDA) document with privacy metadata that expresses the data classification and possible re-disclosure restrictions placed on the data by applicable law. This aids in the electronic exchange of this type of health information.[12]

DSA (Digital Signature Algorithm)

See **Digital signature**.

DSG (Document Digital Signature)

See **Digital signature**.

DSL (Digital Subscriber Line)

A communications medium used to transfer digital signals over standard telephone lines. Along with cable Internet, DSL is one of the most popular ways ISPs provide broadband Internet access.[73]

DSL (Domain-Specific Language)

A small expressive programming language custom designed for specific tasks. Unlike a General-Purpose Language (GPL) such as C# or UML, DSL is designed to express statements in a particular problem space or domain. Well-known DSLs include regular expressions and SQL.[30]

DSLAM (Digital Subscriber Line Access Multiplexer)

A device used by Internet Service Providers (ISPs) to route incoming DSL connections to the Internet. Since a "multiplexer" combines multiple signals into one, a DSLAM combines a group of subscribers' connections into one aggregate Internet connection.[73]

DSM (Diagnostic and Statistical Manual of Mental Disorders)

Manual produced by the American Psychiatric Association. Used by clinicians and researchers to diagnose and classify mental disorders. The criteria are concise and explicit, intended to facilitate an objective assessment of symptom presentations in a variety of clinical settings—inpatient, outpatient, partial hospital, consultation-liaison, clinical, private practice, and primary care.[151]

DSML (Directory Services Markup Language)

A proposed set of rules for using Extensible Markup Language (XML) to define the data content and structure of a directory and maintain it in distributed directories. It permits XML and directories to work together, enabling applications to use directories efficiently.[52]

DSMO (Designated Standard Maintenance Organization)

An organization, designated by the Secretary of the U.S. Department of Health and Human Services, to maintain standards adopted under Subpart I of 45 CFR Part 162. A DSMO may receive and process requests for adopting a new standard or modifying an adopted standard.[495]

DSRIP (Delivery System Reform Incentive Payment)

A Medicaid delivery system reform program providing states with funding that can be used to support hospitals and other providers in changing how they provide care to Medicaid beneficiaries.[459]

DSSS (Direct Sequence Spread Spectrum)

Also known as Direct Sequence Code Division Multiple Access (DS-CDMA), one of two approaches to spread spectrum modulation for digital signal

D

transmission over the airwaves. In direct sequence spread spectrum, the stream of information to be transmitted is divided into small pieces, each of which is allocated to a frequency channel across the spectrum. A data signal at the point of transmission is combined with a higher data-rate bit sequence (also known as a chipping code) that divides the data according to a spreading ratio. The redundant chipping code helps the signal resist interference and also enables the original data to be recovered if data bits are damaged during transmission.[2]

DSTU (Draft Standard for Trial Use)

A standard or implementation specification released to allow implementers to test the standard. At the end of the trial period, the standard may be balloted, revised, or withdrawn.[2, 152]

DSU (Data Service Unit)

A device used for interfacing Data Terminal Equipment (DTE) to the public telephone network.[459]

DSU/CSU (Data Service Unit/Channel Service Unit)

A hardware device about the size of an external modem that converts a digital data frame from the communications technology used on a Local Area Network (LAN) into a frame appropriate to a Wide Area Network (WAN) and vice versa. For example, if you have a web business from your own home and have leased a digital line (perhaps a T-1 or fractional T-1 line) to a phone company or a gateway at an Internet service provider, you have a CSU/DSU at your end, and the phone company or gateway host has a CSU/DSU at its end.[2]

DT (Date data Type) (YYYY-MM-DD)

International format defined by ISO (ISO 8601) to define a numerical date system as follows: YYYY-MM-DD, where YYYY is the year (all the digits, i.e., 2012), MM is the month (01 [January] to 12 [December]), and DD is the day (01 to 31).[459]

DTD (Document Type Definition)

A specific document defining and constraining definition or set of statements that follow the rules of the Standard Generalized Markup Language (SGML)

D

or of the Extensible Markup Language (XML), a subset of SGML. A DTD is a specification that accompanies a document and identifies what the markup codes are that, in the case of a text document, separate paragraphs, identify topic headings, and so forth, and how each is to be processed. By mailing a DTD with a document, any location that has a DTD "reader" (or "SGML compiler") will be able to process the document and display or print it as intended. This means that a single standard SGML compiler can serve different kinds of documents that use a range of different markup codes and related meanings. The compiler looks at the DTD and then prints or displays the document accordingly.[2]

DTE (Data Terminal Equipment)

An end instrument that converts user information into signals for transmission or reconverts the received signals into user information.[459]

DTR (Draft Technical Report)

Standards that are in the process of review but are implementable in their current form.[459]

DUA (Data Use Agreement)

Contractual, confidentiality agreement between a covered entity and the recipient of health information in a limited data set.[20, 456]

Dual-use technology

Technology that has both civilian and military applications (e.g., cryptography).[459]

Dumb terminal

Device that consists of a keyboard and a monitor and a connection to a server PC, minicomputer, or a mainframe computer. Dumb terminals have no "intelligence" (data processing or number crunching power) and depend entirely on the computer to which they are connected for computations, data storage, and retrieval. Dumb terminals are used by airlines, banks, and other such firms for inputting data to, and recalling it from, the connected computer.[4]

D

Durability

A database property that ensures transactions are saved permanently and do not accidentally disappear or get erased, even during a database crash. This is usually achieved by saving all transactions to a nonvolatile storage medium. Durability is part of the ACID acronym, which stands for atomicity, consistency, isolation, and durability. ACID is a set of properties guaranteeing the reliability of all database transactions.[52] *See* **ACID**.

Durable Medical Equipment

See **DME**.

DVD (Digital Video Disk or Digital Versatile Disk)

A type of optical media used for storing digital data. It is the same physical size as a CD but has a larger storage capacity. Some DVDs are formatted specifically for video playback, while others may contain different types of data, such as software programs and computer files.[73]

Dynamic Host Configuration Protocol

See **DHCP**.

Dynamic Link Control

See **DLC**.

Dynamic Link Library

See **DLL**.

Dynamic RAM

See **DRAM**.

E

e-[text] or e-text

Short for "electronic," e-[text] is used as a prefix to indicate that something is Internet-based, not just electronic. The trend began with e-mail in the 1990s and now includes e-Commerce, eHealth, e-GOV, etc.[29]

E-1 (European digital signal)

Digital transmission format devised by the ITU-TS and given the name by the Conference of European Postal and Telecommunication Administration (CEPT). It is the equivalent of the North American T-carrier system format. E2 through E5 are carriers in increasing multiples of the E1 format.[2]

EAI (Enterprise Application Integration)

1. The use of software and architectural principles to bring together (integrate) a set of enterprise computer applications. It is an area of computer systems architecture that gained wide recognition from about 2004 onward. EAI is related to middleware technologies, such as Message-Oriented Middleware (MOM), and data representation technologies, such as eXtensible Markup Language (HTML and XML). Newer EAI technologies involve using web services as part of service-oriented architecture as a means of integration. **2.** A presentation-level integration technology that provides a single point of access to conduct business transactions that utilize data from multiple disparate applications.[52] *See* **System integration**.

EAP (Extensible Authentication Protocol)

A general protocol for authentication that also supports multiple authentication methods, such as token cards, one-time passwords, certificates, public key authentication, and smartcards.[2]

DOI: 10.4324/9781003286028-5

E

Early Event Detection

See **EED**.

EAV (Entity-Attribute-Value) model

The EAV database model, also known as "open schema" or "vertical model," describes entities where the number of all attributes is unknown and potentially significant. An entity could be another name for an object. An attribute could be an object property. Value is the value of attribute. The EAV model is a vertical model because the database table usually consists of a few columns but a large number of rows. Developers sometimes use EAV in early design, where business requirements are not precise or one of the stakeholders wants to have a generic flexible approach that would fit everything he or she might need (or not) in the future. When developers have a tight schedule or want to handle the unknown, the EAV model is very tempting.[496]

EBCDIC (Extended Binary Coded Decimal Interchange Code)

A character set coding scheme that represents 256 standard characters. IBM mainframes use EBCDIC coding, while personal computers use American Standard Coding for Information Interchange (ASCII) coding. Networks that link personal computers to IBM mainframes must include a translating device to mediate between the two systems. It is an 8-bit binary code for numeric and alphanumeric characters. It was developed and used by IBM. It is a coding representation in which symbols, letters, and numbers are presented in binary language.[52]

EC (Eligible Clinician)

According to the Centers for Medicare & Medicaid Services (CMS), an individual physician or healthcare practitioner that is eligible to participate in, or is subject to, mandatory participation in a payment incentive adjustment or quality reporting program. For the purposes of the Merit-based Incentive Payment System (MIPS), an MIPS-eligible clinician includes physicians, physician assistants, nurse practitioners, clinical nurse specialists, and certified registered nurse anesthetists.[459]

E

EC (Electronic Commerce)

Consists of the buying and selling of products or services over electronic systems such as the Internet and other computer networks.[156] Also known as *e-Commerce*.

ECN (Explicit Congestion Notification)

An extension to the Transmission Control Protocol (TCP) packet that notifies networks about congestion with the goal of reducing packet loss and delay by making the sending device decrease the transmission rate until the congestion clears without dropping packets.[279]

eCQI (Electronic Clinical Quality Improvement)

The use of common standards and shared technologies to monitor and analyze the quality of healthcare provided to patients and patient outcomes.[88]

eCQM (Electronic Clinical Quality Measures)

The use of data from electronic health records (EHR) and/or health information technology systems to measure healthcare quality. The Centers for Medicare & Medicaid Services (CMS) use eCQMs in a variety of quality reporting and incentive programs. eCQMS are seen as an improvement over traditional quality measure collection because if the EHRs are not used, the work to gather the data from medical charts, e.g., "chart-abstracted data," is very resource intensive and subject to human error.[88]

ED (Encapsulated Data)

The coupling or encapsulation of the data with a select group of functions that defines everything that can be done with the data.[52]

EDC (Electronic Data Capture System)

A computerized system designed for the collection of clinical data in electronic format for use mainly in human clinical trials.[286]

EDDS (Electronic Document Digital Storage)

Document management systems available online.[29]

E

EDI (Electronic Data Interchange)

1. Even before HIPAA, the American National Standards Institute (ANSI) approved the process for developing a set of EDI standards known as the X12. EDI is a collection of standard message formats that allows businesses to exchange data via any electronic messaging service. **2.** The electronic transfer of data between companies using networks to include the Internet. Secure communications are needed in healthcare to exchange eligibility information, referrals, authorization, claims, encounters, and other payment data needed to manage contracts and remittance.[19] *See* **X12 Standard**.

EDI Gateway (Electronic Data Interchange gateway)

An electronic process to send data (claims, membership, and benefits) back and forth between providers and insurance companies.[46]

EDIT

In the Centers for Medicare & Medicaid Services, the logic within the Standard Claims Processing System (or PSC Supplemental Edit Software) that selects certain claims, evaluates or compares information on the selected claims or other accessible source, and, depending on the evaluation, takes action on the claims, such as pay in full, pay in part, or suspend for manual review.[13,456]

EDXL (Emergency Data Exchange Language)

A standard message distribution framework for data sharing among emergency information systems.[157,456]

EDXL–HAVE (Emergency Data Exchange Language–Hospital Availability Exchange)

Describes a standard message for data sharing among emergency information systems using the XML-based Emergency Data Exchange Language (EDXL).[157,456]

EED (Early Event Detection)

This component of the www.cdc.gov (PHIN) preparedness uses case and suspect case reporting, along with statistical surveillance of health-related data, to support the earliest possible detection of events that may signal a public health emergency.[80,456]

EEPROM (Electronically Erasable Programmable Read-Only Memory)

A reprogrammable memory chip that can be electronically erased and reprogrammed through the application of higher than normal electronic voltage without having to remove the chip from the computer for modification.[2]

Effective date

This is the date that a federal agency final rule is effective, which is usually 60 days after it is published in the *Federal Register*.[113,456]

E-GOV

The E-Government Act of 2002 was signed into law by President George W. Bush in July 2002. It aims to enhance the management and promotion of electronic Government services and processes by establishing a Federal Chief Information Officer within the Office of Management and Budget and by establishing a broad framework of measures that require using Internet-based information technology to enhance citizen access to Government information and services, and for other purposes.[283]

eHealth (also written e-health)

A broadly defined term for healthcare practice which is supported by information and communication technologies; the term eHealth encompasses a whole range of services that is at the edge of medicine/healthcare and information technology, including electronic medical records, telemedicine, and evidence-based medicine.[7,456]

EHR (Electronic Health Record)

1. A longitudinal electronic record of patient health information generated by one or more encounters in any care delivery setting. Included in this information are patient demographics, progress notes, problems, medications, vital signs, past medical history, immunizations, laboratory data, and radiology reports and images. The EHR automates and streamlines the clinician's workflow. The EHR has the ability to generate a complete record of a clinical patient encounter, as well as supporting other care-related activities directly or indirectly via interface, including evidence-based decision support, quality management, and outcomes reporting. **2.** Health-related information on an individual that conforms to nationally recognized interoperability standards and that can be created, managed, and consulted by authorized clinicians and staff from more than one healthcare organization. *See* **EMR**.[12,456]

EIDE (Enhanced or Extended Integrated Drive Electronics)

A standard interface for high-speed disk drives that operates at speeds faster than the standard Integrated Drive Electronics (IDE) interface. It has since been replaced by other standards that offer faster transfer rates.[52]

EIN (Employer Identification Number)

1. Employers, as sponsors of health insurance for their employees, often need to be identified in healthcare transactions, and a standard identifier for employers would be beneficial for electronically exchanged transactions. Healthcare providers may need to identify the employer of the participant on claims submitted electronically to health plans. **2.** The HIPAA standard is the EIN, the taxpayer-identifying number for employers that is assigned by the Internal Revenue Service. This identifier has nine digits with the first two digits separated by a hyphen as follows: 00-000000.[113]

EIP (Enterprise Information Portal)

1. A framework for integrating information, people, and processes across organization boundaries. Provides a secure unified access point. **2.** An Internet-based approach to consolidate and present an organization's business intelligence and information resources through a single access point via an intranet.[2] Also known as an Internet portal enterprise portal.

EIS (Enterprise Information System)

Any kind of information system that improves the functions of enterprise business processes by integration. This means typically offering high-quality service, dealing with large volumes of data, and being capable of supporting some large and possibly complex organization or enterprise. An EIS is capable of being used by all parts and all levels of an enterprise. The word enterprise can have various connotations. Frequently, the term is used only to refer to very large organizations such as multi-national companies or public sector organizations. However, the term may be used to mean virtually anything, since it has become the latest corporate-speak buzzword. Enterprise information systems provide a technological platform that enables organizations to integrate and coordinate their business processes on a robust foundation. An EIS is currently used in conjunction with customer relationship management and supply chain management systems to automate business processes. An enterprise information system provides a single system that is central to the organization that ensures information can be shared across all functional levels and management hierarchies. An EIS can be used to increase business productivity and reduce service cycles, product development cycles, and marketing life cycles. It may be used to amalgamate existing applications. Other outcomes include higher operational and cost savings. Financial value is not usually a direct outcome of the implementation of an enterprise information system.[497]

Electromagnetic Interference

See **EMI**.

Electronic Audit Trail

An electronic audit trail; in the context of Electronic Medical Records (EMR), it is used for the following reasons: security purposes to gauge who has logged into patient records; medical billing purposes; and data gathering for public health reporting and medical research. EMRs should be protected and secure due to their online status. Not only is it imperative to protect EMRs from unauthorized outside access but data trails are necessary in order to make sure that they are accessed only on a need-to-know basis in-house. Laws such as the Health Insurance Portability and Accountability Act (HIPAA) demand that only authorized users access medical records.[52]

Electronic certificate

See **Digital certificate**.

Electronic claim

Any claim submitted for payment to a health plan by a central processing unit, tape diskette, direct data entry, direct wire, dial-in telephone, digital fax, or personal computer download or upload.[46] *See* **EDI Gateway**.

E

Electronic Clinical Quality Improvement

See **eCQI**.

Electronic Clinical Quality Measures

See **eCQM**.

Electronic Commerce

See **EC**.

Electronic data

Recorded or transmitted electronically, while non-electronic data would be everything else. Special cases would be data transmitted by fax and audio systems, which are, in principle, transmitted electronically but which lack the underlying structure usually needed to support automated interpretation of its contents.[113]

Electronic Data Capture System

See **EDC**.

Electronic Data Interchange

See **EDI**.

Electronic Data Interchange Gateway

See **EDI Gateway**.

Electronic forms management

A software system that automatically generates forms and can be populated by importing data from another system and/or can export data that have been entered into another system.[459]

Electronic Health Record

See **EHR**.

E

Electronic health record provider

Entity in legitimate possession of electronic health record data and in a position to communicate that data to another appropriate entity.[63]

Electronic Long-Term Services and Supports

See **eLTSS**.

Electronic media

1. Electronic storage media, including memory devices in computers (hard drives) and any removable/transportable digital memory media, such as magnetic tapes or disks, optical disks, or digital memory cards. **2.** Transmission media used to exchange information already in electronic storage media, including, for example, the Internet (wide open), extranet (using Internet technology to link a business with information accessible only to collaborating parties), leased lines, dial-up lines, private networks, and the physical movement of removable/transportable electronic storage media. Certain transmissions, including paper via facsimile and voice via telephone, are not considered to be transmissions via electronic media because the information being exchanged did not exist in electronic form before the transmission.[498]

Electronic Media Claims

See **EMC**.

Electronic Medical Record

See **EMR**.

Electronic Medical Record Adoption Model

See **EMRAM**.

Electronic Medication Administration Record

See **eMAR**.

Electronic Patient Record

See **EHR**.

Electronic Patient Release of Information

Electronic patient release of information forms include patient signatures that authorize treating health entities to release Protected Health Information (PHI) to other health entities. In the digital age, electronic signatures are increasingly required. Electronic patient release of information forms are not all-out information release consents but rather specific consents providing patient authorization to divulge their Electronic Health Records (EHR) to designated agencies on an as-needed basis. These forms also designate what information can be released.[52]

Electronic Personal Health Record

See **ePHR** and **PHR**.

Electronic prescribing

See **E-prescribing**.

Electronic Prescriptions for Controlled Substances

See **EPCS**.

Electronic Prior Authorization

See **ePA**.

Electronic Protected Health Information

See **ePHI**.

Electronic Remittance Advice

See **ERA**.

Electronic signature

Also known as e-signature. **1.** An electronic indication of a person's intent to agree to the content of a document or a set of data to which the signature

E

relates. Like its handwritten counterpart in the offline world, an electronic signature is a legal concept capturing the signatory's intent to be bound by the terms of the signed document. **2.** A digital version of a traditional pen and ink signature, often providing the same legal commitment as a handwritten signature. The terms e-signature and digital signature are often confused and used incorrectly as synonyms by laymen. A digital signature is a type of e-signature that uses mathematics to validate the authenticity and integrity of a message, software, or digital document.[285]

Electronic text

See **e-[text]** or **e-text**.

Electronic Waste (e-Waste)

Electronic waste (e-waste) refers to the disposal of broken or obsolete electronic components and materials. E-waste materials may be valuable and recyclable, such as random access memory and reusable laptops. However, hazardous materials, such as cathode ray tube monitors, require special handling in disposal. Common discarded electronic products include computers, televisions, stereos, copiers, and fax machines.[52]

Electronically Erasable Programmable Read-Only Memory

See **EEPROM**.

Eligible Clinician

See **EC**.

eLTSS (Electronic Long-Term Services and Supports)

Initiative within the U.S. Office of the National Coordinator for Health IT (ONC) to facilitate the development of basic elements for inclusion in electronic standards. These standards will enable the creation, exchange, and reuse of interoperable service plans by beneficiaries, community-based long-term services and support providers, payers, healthcare providers, and the individuals they serve.[12]

E-mail (Electronic mail)

The exchange of computer-stored messages via telecommunication. These messages are usually encoded in ASCII text but can include non-text files, such as graphic images and sound files.[2]

E-mail spoofing

A fraudulent e-mail activity hiding e-mail origins. The act of e-mail spoofing occurs when impostors are able to deliver e-mails by altering e-mails' sender information. Although this is usually done by spammers and through phishing e-mails for advertising purposes, e-mail spoofing can have malicious motives such as virus spreading or attempts to gain personal banking information. Simple Mail Transfer Protocol (SMTP) does not provide any type of authentication process for people sending e-mails. Yet, it is the primary e-mail system for most people, facilitating e-mail spoofing. Today, most e-mail servers can provide further security. Also many digital software vendors have created products remedying this problem.[52]

E-Mail train

Refers to the long trail of previous messages that is formed when the people in the e-mail reply without deleting the previous replies. In some cases, an e-mail train can be useful to track the progression of a conversation, much like discussion boards do. However, the creation of e-mail trains is usually frowned upon as poor e-mail etiquette.[52]

eMAR (Electronic Medication Administration Record)

An electronic record-keeping system that documents when medications are given to a patient during a hospital stay. This application supports the five rights of medication administration (right patient, right medication, right dose, right time, and right route of administration) and can be used with bar coding functionality, although bar coding is not required. eMAR functionality is normally found within a nursing documentation application.[52,456]

EMC (Electronic Media Claims)

This term usually refers to a flat file format used to transmit or transport claims.[113]

E

Emergency

Sudden demand for action; a condition that poses an immediate threat to the health of the patient.[66]

Emergency access

Granting of user rights and authorizations to permit access to protected health information and applications in emergency conditions outside of normal workflows. Emergency room access is considered to be a normal workflow.[20,456]

Emergency care system

An application that assists emergency department clinicians and staff in the critical task of managing patients quickly and efficiently; directs each step of the patient management/patient flow and patient documentation process, including triage, tracking, nursing and physician charting, disposition, charge capture, and management reporting.[66]

Emergency Data Exchange Language

See **EDXL**.

Emergency permission

Permission granted to certain caregivers in advance that allows self-declaration of an emergency and assumption of an emergency role. Emergency permissions defined in standard ways, compliant with appropriate ANSI standards and Health Level Seven (HL7) healthcare permission definitions, are suitable for federated circumstances, where the person declaring the emergency is not a member of the organization possessing the requested information.[20]

Emergency Repair Disk

See **ERD**.

Emergency Respond Data Architecture

See **ERDA**.

E

Emergency Responder Electronic Health Record

A specific electronic form designed for first responders and other emergency care personnel who assist in natural disasters and other widespread disasters such as bio-terrorism attacks in the U.S. The IT surrounding these records has been developed through the Office of Public Health Emergency Preparedness (OPHEP). ER-EHR provides the standards required to allow emergency personnel, medical examiners, fatality managers, and public health practitioners to keep track of information about the treatment, care, or other investigation of emergency incident victims. A key feature of this standard is its interoperability between the systems of the various organizations involved in ER-EHR. The standard has definition and structure for the exchange of information on local, regional, and national-scale emergencies and covers on-site, emergency, and definitive care.[52]

EMI (Electromagnetic Interference)

Any disruption of operation of an electronic device caused by electromagnetic waves.[2]

Emissions security

See **EMSEC**.

Emoticons

A combination word for "emotional icon," it is a small picture created with the normal keys on a keyboard meant to denote the writer's mood in a message.[459]

EMPI (Enterprise Master Patient Index)

A system that maintains consistent and accurate information about each patient registered by a healthcare organization. It may link several smaller MPIs together, such as those from outpatient clinics and rehabilitation facilities. It can also aggregate patient data from separate systems within one facility.[2]

Employee Retirement Income and Security Act

See **ERISA**.

E

Employee welfare benefit plan

A plan, fund, or a program maintained by an employer or an employee organization that provides medical, surgical, or hospital care.[459]

Employer Identification Number

See **EIN**.

EMR (Electronic Medical Record)

1. An application environment that is composed of the clinical data repository, clinical decision support, controlled medical vocabulary, order entry, computerized practitioner order entry, and clinical documentation applications. This environment supports the patient's electronic medical record across inpatient and outpatient environments and is used by healthcare practitioners to document, monitor, and manage healthcare delivery. **2.** Health-related information on an individual that can be created, gathered, managed, and consulted by authorized clinicians and staff within one healthcare organization.[12,456] *See* **EHR.**

EMRAM (Electronic Medical Record Adoption Model)

A tool developed by HIMSS Analytics guiding hospitals to improved clinical outcomes.[10]

EMSEC (Emanations Security)

Measures taken to deny unauthorized persons information derived from intercept and analysis of compromising emanations from crypto-equipment of an IT system.[1]

Emulation

A software program that allows a computer to imitate another computer with a differing operating system.[2]

EN (European standard)

Developed by the European Committee for Standardization (CEN). CEN is a major provider of European standards and technical specifications.[286]

EN 46000 Medical Device Quality Management Systems Standard

The Medical Device Quality Management Systems Standard addresses the particular concerns of the medical devices industry in interpreting and implementing ISO 9000. Published in 1994, the standard provides medical device manufacturers, distributors, importers, assemblers, component manufacturers, and service organizations with an industry-specific quality management system. EN 46000 must be used in combination with ISO 9001. EN 46000 embraces the principles of good manufacturing practice commonly used in medical device manufacture. It offers its users an auditing process similar to a quality management systems audit. The standard also helps users market their products throughout the EU because its conformity assessment process under the Medical Device Directive 93/42/EEC permits CE marking. Conversely, if a company wants to be CE compliant, it must also comply with EN 46000. EN 46000 is technically equivalent to ISO 13485 1996, an international medical device standard. So few differences exist between the two that if an organization is prepared to comply with one, it may easily comply with the other as well.[499]

Encapsulated Data type

See **ED**.

Encapsulation

In object-oriented programming, the inclusion within a program object of all the resources needed for the object to function—basically, the methods and the data. The object is said to "publish its interfaces." Other objects adhere to these interfaces to use the object without having to be concerned with how the object accomplishes it. An object can be thought of as a self-contained atom. The object interface consists of public methods and instantiated data.[2]

Encoded data

Data represented by some identification of classification scheme, such as a provider identifier or a procedure code.[459]

Encoder

This application enables health information management personnel to find and use complete and accurate codes and code modifiers for procedures

E

and diagnosis to optimize billing and reimbursement. For example, 1234 is bronchitis, whereas 1235 is bronchitis with asthma, and 1236 is bronchitis with stomach flu.[459]

Encoding-decoding services

This service will encode and/or decode messages from and to different coding formats, such as Unicode, UTF-8, and Base64.[459]

Encounter

1. An instance of direct provider/practitioner to patient interaction, regardless of the setting, between a patient and practitioner vested with primary responsibility for diagnosing, evaluating, or treating the patient's condition, or both, or providing social worker services. **2.** A contact between a patient and practitioner who has the primary responsibility for assessing and treating the patient at a given contact, exercising independent judgment. Encounter serves as a focal point linking clinical, administrative, and financial information. Encounters occur in many different settings—ambulatory care, inpatient care, emergency care, home healthcare, field, and virtual (telemedicine).[102,456]

Encounter data

Detailed data about individual services provided by a capitated managed care entity. The level of detail about each service reported is similar to that of a standard claim form. Encounter data are also sometimes referred to as "shadow claims."[26,456]

Encryption

1. An application/technology that provides the translation of data into a secret code. Encryption is the most effective way to achieve data security. To read an encrypted file, you must have access to a secret key or password that enables you to decrypt it. Unencrypted data are called plain text; encrypted data are referred to as cipher text. **2.** Means of securing data by transforming/generating them into apparently meaningless random characters between source and destination. A process by which a message is encoded so that its meaning is not obvious. It is transformed into a second message using a complex function and a special encryption key.[1]

E

Encryption-decryption services

This encrypts and decrypts messages. It could use X.509 certificates and other cryptography mechanisms.[57]

End point authentication

Endpoint authentication is a security mechanism designed to ensure that only authorized devices can connect to a given network, site, or service. The approach is also known as device authentication. In this context, the endpoint most often considered is a mobile computing device, like a laptop, smart phone, or tablet, but it could be any connected hardware device on a TCP/IP network. The possibilities include desktop computers, printers, servers, and specialized hardware such as POS terminals, Smart meters, and other smart devices.[2]

End user

In information technology, the person for whom a hardware or software product is designed by the developers, installers, and servicers of the product.[2]

End-User License Agreement

See **EULA**.

Enhanced or Extended Integrated Drive Electronics

See **EIDE**.

Enhanced Oversight Accountability Rule

See **EOA**.

Enterprise

A business organization.[29]

Enterprise Application Integration

See **EAI**.

E

Enterprise architecture

1. A strategic resource that aligns business and technology, leverages shared assets, builds internal and external partnerships, and optimizes the value of information technology services. **2.** A business-focused framework developed in accordance with the Clinger-Cohen Act of 1996 that identifies the business processes, systems that support processes, and guidelines and standards by which systems must operate. **3.** A comprehensive operational framework that explores all of an organization's functional areas while defining how technology benefits and serves the organization's overall mission. The technological aspect of EA defines the hardware, operating systems, programming, and networking solutions a business employs and how those may be used to achieve its current and future objectives.[52, 497]

Enterprise architecture integration

Tools and techniques that promote, enable, and manage the exchange of information and distribution of business processes across multiple application systems, typically within a sizable electronic landscape, such as large corporations, collaborating companies, and administrative regions.[459]

Enterprise Information Portal

See **EIP**.

Enterprise Information System

See **EIS**.

Enterprise Master Patient Index

See **EMPI**.

Enterprise Master Person Index

A system that coordinates client identification across multiple systems, namely, by collecting and storing IDs and person-identifying demographic information from the source system (track new persons and track changes to existing persons). These systems also take on several other tasks and responsibilities associated with client ID management.[459]

E

Enterprise network

An enterprise's communications backbone that helps connect computers and related devices across departments and workgroup networks, facilitating insight and data accessibility. An enterprise network reduces communication protocols, facilitating system and device interoperability, as well as improved internal and external enterprise data management.[52]

Enterprise Resource Planning

See **ERP**.

Enterprise scheduling

Ability to schedule procedures, exams, and appointments across multiple systems and/or locations spanning an entire jurisdiction.[459]

Entity

Something that has a distinct, separate existence, though an entity need not be a material existence. In some usages, an entity is close in meaning to "object."[2]

Entity identity assertion

Ensures that an entity is the person or application that claims the identity provided.[20]

Entity Relationship Diagram

See **ERD**.

Entries

Health record data in general (clinical observations, statements, reasoning, intentions, plans, or actions) without particular specification of their formal representation, hierarchical organization, or of the particular record component class(es) that might be used to represent them.[63]

EOA (Enhanced Oversight Accountability Rule)

This rule finalizes modifications and new requirements under the ONC Health IT Certification Program, including provisions related to the Office of the National Coordinator for Health Information Technology (ONC)'s role. The final rule creates a regulatory framework for ONC's direct review of health information technology (health IT) certified under the Program, including, when necessary, requiring the correction of non-conformities found in health IT certified under the Program and suspending and terminating certifications issued to Complete EHRs and Health IT Modules. The final rule also sets forth processes for ONC to authorize and oversee accredited testing laboratories under the Program. In addition, it includes provisions for expanded public availability of certified health IT surveillance results.[12]

EOB (Explanation of Benefits)

A document detailing how a claim was processed according to the insured's benefits.[46]

EOP (Explanation of Payment)

Generated to the provider in reply to a claim submission.[46]

ePA (Electronic Prior Authorization)

An electronic process established in the National Council for Prescription Drug Programs (NCPDP) SCRIPT Standard that enables patient and drug-specific prior authorization criteria and a real-time approval for medication prior authorization.[289]

EPCS (Electronic Prescriptions for Controlled Substances)

A technology solution to help address prescription drug abuse in the United States. The rule "Electronic Prescriptions for Controlled Substances" provides practitioners with the option of writing and transmitting prescriptions for controlled substances electronically. The regulations also permit pharmacies to receive, dispense, and archive these electronic prescriptions. The technology addresses the problem of forged or stolen prescriptions by requiring authentication of prescribers, improving security standards, and auditing activity on EPCS platforms.[289, 456]

ePHI (Electronic Protected Health Information)

Any Protected Health Information (PHI) that is created, stored, transmitted, or received electronically.[20]

E

ePHR (Electronic Personal Health Record)

A universally accessible, layperson-comprehensible lifelong tool for managing relevant health information, promoting health maintenance, and assisting with chronic disease management via an interactive, common data set of electronic health information and eHealth tools. The ePHR is owned, managed, and shared by the individual or his or her legal proxy(s) and must be secure to protect the privacy and confidentiality of the health information it contains. It is not a legal record unless so defined and is subject to various legal limitations.[459] *See* **PHR**.

Episode of care

Services provided by a healthcare facility or provider for a specific medical problem, or condition, or specific illness during a set time period. An episode of care can be given either for a short period or on a continuous basis or it may consist of a series of intervals marked by one or more brief separations from care.[459]

E-prescribing (Electronic prescribing)

A prescriber's ability to electronically send an accurate, error-free, and understandable prescription directly to a pharmacy from the point-of-care and is an important element in improving the quality of patient care. The inclusion of electronic prescribing in the Medicare Modernization Act (MMA) of 2003 gave momentum to the movement, and the July 2006 Institute of Medicine report on the role of e-prescribing in reducing medication errors received widespread publicity, helping to build awareness of e-prescribing's role in enhancing patient safety. Adopting the standards to facilitate e-prescribing is one of the key action items in the Federal government's plan to expedite the adoption of electronic medical records and build a national electronic health information infrastructure in the United States. The computer-based electronic generation, transmission, and filling of a prescription.[501]

ERA (Electronic Remittance Advice)

Any of several electronic formats for explaining the payments of healthcare claims.[459]

E

ERD (Entity Relationship Diagram)

A type of diagram that illustrates how entities, such as people, objects, or concepts, relate to each other within a system. Also known as ER diagrams.[290]

ERDA (Emergency Respond Data Architecture)

A data architecture developed to support real-time information sharing and interoperability during emergency situations of all types.[459]

ERISA (Employee Retirement Income and Security Act of 1975)

Most group health plans covered by ERISA are also health plans under the Health Insurance Portability and Accountability Act.[20]

ERP (Enterprise Resource Planning)

Management information systems that integrate and automate many of the business functions associated with the operations or production aspects of an enterprise, such as general ledger, budgeting, materials management, purchasing, payroll, and human resources.[18]

Error chain

Generally, refers to the series of events that led to a disastrous outcome, typically uncovered by a root cause analysis. A more specific meaning of error chain, especially when used in the phrase "break the error chain," relates to the common themes or categories of causes that emerge from root cause analyses. These categories go by different names in different settings, but they generally include (1) failure to follow standard operating procedures; (2) poor leadership; (3) breakdowns in communication or teamwork; (4) overlooking or ignoring individual fallibility; and (5) losing track of objectives. Used in this way, "break the error chain" is shorthand for an approach in which team members continually address these links as a crisis or routine situation unfolds; the checklists that are included in teamwork training programs have categories corresponding to these common links in the error chain (e.g., establish a team leader, assign roles and responsibilities, and monitor your teammates).[459]

E

Error proofing

Error proofing or mistake proofing or fail-safing is also called as "Poka-Yoke" (pronounced as Po-kaa-Yo-kay) in Japanese. Error proofing was previously called fool-proofing or idiot proofing. Error proofing involves the use of any automatic device or method that makes it impossible to make an error or at least detect it as soon as possible in order to correct it. It can be a simple process as to draw a picture of a TV remote on the table and hence help everybody at home in reminding to keep the remote in the same place every time or a washing machine not turning ON till the water is turned on and machine is shut properly.[502]

eRX

See **e-prescribing**.

ESS (Executive Support System)

A class of decision support systems that provide predefined data presentation and exploration functionality to top-level executives. The system is intended to facilitate and support the information and decision-making needs of senior executives by providing ready access to both internal and external information relevant to meeting the strategic goals of the organization. Commonly considered a specialized form of Decision Support Systems (DSS). The emphasis of ESS is on graphical displays with reporting and drill-down capabilities. In general, an ESS is an enterprise-wide DSS that allows executives to analyze, compare, and highlight trends and important variables as well as monitor performance and identify opportunities and problems.[52]

Ethereum

A decentralized blockchain application platform that runs smart contracts, applications that run exactly as programmed without the possibility of downtime, censorship, fraud, or third-party interference. These applications run on a custom-built blockchain, creating an environment for developers to create markets, store registries, move funds, etc., without a middleman or counterparty risk.[292]

Ethernet

1. The most common type of connection computers use within a Local Area Network (LAN). An Ethernet port looks much like a regular phone jack,

E

but it is slightly wider. This port can be used to connect the computer to another computer, a local network, or an external DSL or cable modem. **2.** A family of computer networking technologies and protocols for Local Area Networks (LANs) commercially introduced in 1980. **3.** A frame-based computer networking technology for LANs. The name comes from the physical concept of ether. It defines wiring and signaling for the physical layer and frame formats and protocols for the Media Access Control (MAC)/data link layer of the Open Systems Interconnection (OSI) model. Ethernet is mostly standardized as IEEEs 802. It has become the most widespread LAN technology in use during the 1990s to the present.[459, 52]

Ethical Hacker

An individual hired to hack into a system to identify and repair potential vulnerabilities, effectively preventing exploitation by malicious hackers. They are security experts that specialize in the penetration testing (pen-testing) of computer and software systems for the purpose of evaluating, strengthening, and improving security. An ethical hacker is also known as a white hat hacker, red team, tiger team, or sneaker.[52]

ETL (Extraction, Transformation, Loading)

Short for **e**xtract, **t**ransform, **l**oad, three database functions that are combined into one tool to pull data out of one database and place it into another database. Extract is the process of reading data from a database. Transform is the process of converting the extracted data from its previous form into the form it needs to be in so that it can be placed into another database. Transformation occurs by using rules or lookup tables or by combining the data with other data. Load is the process of writing the data into the target database. ETL is used to migrate data from one database to another, to form data marts and data warehouses, and also to convert databases from one format or type to another.[39]

EULA (End-User License Agreement)

An agreement between a software application licensor and the end user of the application. Also referred to as a software license.[2]

European committee for standardization

See **CEN**.

European digital signal

See **E-1**.

European standard

See **EN**.

Event

Action or activity that occurs within a system and/or network scope, inclusive of its boundaries.[20,456]

Event aggregation

Identifies the sum total of actions performed by a user that are initiated outside of a computer program but are used in conjunction with that program. An aggregate event usually occurs after a series of events of another type has occurred, and it is that series of events that it represents. An event is initiated either by the user or by device hardware, such as a device that sets off a timer. Aggregate events are typically related and occur on one or more configuration items contained within the same logical group. Aggregate events serve as a feasible platform for complicated, demonstrational, end-user programming and work to match up event histories to the user's intentions.[52]

Event correlation

Relationships between two or more log entries.[459]

Event filtering

Suppression of log entries from analysis, reporting, or long-term storage because their characteristics indicate that they are unlikely to contain information of interest.[459]

Event reduction

Removal of unneeded data fields from all log entries to create a new log that is smaller.[459]

E

Evidence Documents

See **ED**.

Evidence-based medicine

1. The conscientious, explicit, judicious, and reasonable use of modern, best evidence in making decisions about the care of an individual. It integrates clinical experience and patient values with the best available research information. **2.** Evidence-based medicine follows four steps: formulate a clear clinical question from a patient's problem; search the literature for relevant clinical articles; evaluate (critically appraise) the evidence for its validity and usefulness; and implement useful findings in clinical practice.[295,456]

Evidence-based practice

See **Evidence-based medicine**.

Evil Twin

In the context of network security, it is a rogue or fake Wireless Access Point (WAP) that appears as a genuine hotspot offered by a legitimate provider. In an evil twin attack, an eavesdropper or hacker fraudulently creates this rogue hotspot to collect the personal data of unsuspecting users. Sensitive data can be stolen by spying on a connection or using a phishing technique.[52]

Exceeds authorized access

Defined in the Computer Fraud and Abuse Act (CFAA), this means to access a computer with authorization and to use such access to obtain or alter information in the computer that the accessor is not entitled to obtain or alter.[16]

Exception

In programming, an unplanned event, such as invalid input or a loss of connectivity, that occurs while a program is executing and disrupts the flow of its instructions.[2]

E

Exchange format

The first instance of a data interchange format was released in the early 1980s, when a software firm delivered the specifications in copies of their widely popular spreadsheet program and simultaneously published them in a leading computer magazine. Data Information Format (DIF) was initially used as a text file format for the import/export transfer of single spreadsheet files between various spreadsheet programs from many platforms. A similar interchange format was released, called the Lightweight Directory Access Protocol (LDAP) Data Interchange Format, in the 1990s, and this could transfer not only text-form data but also directory data in text form and allowed modifications of the directory data.[503]

Exclusive branching

Splits a process in several branches, only one of which can be selected based on the fulfillment of a condition associated with a given branch.[459]

Exclusive choice

The divergence of a branch into two or more branches such that when the incoming branch is enabled, the thread of control is immediately passed to precisely one of the outgoing branches, based on a mechanism that can select one of the outgoing branches.[459] *See* **Simple merge**.

Executive Information System

See **EIS**.

Expert system

Artificial intelligence-based system that converts the knowledge of an expert in a specific subject into a software code. This code can be merged with other such codes (based on the knowledge of other experts) and used for answering questions (queries) submitted through a computer. Expert systems typically consist of three parts: (1) a knowledge base which contains the information acquired by interviewing experts and logic rules that govern how that information is applied; (2) an inference engine that interprets the submitted problem against the rules and logic of information stored in the knowledge base; and (3) an interface that allows the user to express the problem in a human language such as English.[4,456]

E

Explanation of Benefits

See **EOB**.

Explanation of Payment

See **EOP**.

Explicit Congestion Notification

See **ECN**.

Expression

The textual means to convey a concept to the user. It can be a major concept, a synonym, or a lexical variant.[29]

Extended ASCII (Extended American Standard Code for Information Interchange)

Extensively used 8-bit standard information processing code with 256 characters.[39]

Extended Binary Coded Decimal Interchange Code

See **EBCDIC**.

Extensibility

1. System design feature that allows for future expansion without the need for changes to the basic infrastructure. **2.** The ability to economically modify or add functionality.[459, 501]

Extensible Authentication Protocol

See **EAP**.

Extensible Markup Language

See **XML**.

E

Extensible Stylesheet Language

See **XSL**.

External customer

A person or organization that receives a product, service, or information; not part of the organization supplying the product, service, or information.[60]

Extraction, Transformation, Loading

See **ETL**.

Extranet

Restricted network of computers that allows controlled access to a firm's internal information to authorized outsiders (customers, suppliers, joint venture partners, etc.) by connecting them (usually via the Internet) to the firm's intranet.[4]

F

Fact table

In data warehousing, a fact table is the primary table that contains quantitative or factual data of a business. It may also contain textual attributes to limit the usage of dimension tables. In a dimensional database, there can be multiple business processes that are used, which can warrant the use of many fact tables.[296, 297]

Failback

The process of restoring operations to a primary machine or facility after it has been shifted to a secondary machine or facility during a failover.[2]

Failover

A backup operational mode in which the functions of a system component (such as a processor, server, network, or database) are assumed by secondary system components when the primary component becomes unavailable through either failure or scheduled downtime. Used to make systems more fault-tolerant, failover is typically an integral part of mission-critical systems that must be constantly available.[2]

Failsafe

Incorporating some feature for automatically counteracting the effect of an anticipated possible source of failure.[29]

Failure Modes and Effect Analysis (FMEA)

A systematic, proactive method for evaluating a process to identify where and how it might fail and to assess the relative impact of different failures in order to identify the parts of the process that are most in need of change.[445]

F

False Acceptance

False acceptance is an error in biometrics that causes an unauthorized person to be authenticated. Biometrics uses distinguishing human characteristics as a mode of authentication, such as fingerprints or voice. False acceptance is the most serious biometric security problem, as it permits unauthorized users to access sensitive systems.[52]

Family set

Group of backup tapes consisting of a single run of backup information.[36]

FAR (False Acceptance Ration)

The false acceptance ratio (FAR) is a unit used to measure the average number of false acceptances within a biometric security system. It measures and evaluates the efficiency and accuracy of a biometric system by determining the rate at which unauthorized or illegitimate users are verified on a particular system. A statistic used to measure biometric performance when operating in the verification task. The percentage of times a system produces a false accept, which occurs when an individual is incorrectly matched to another individual's existing biometric. FAR is also known as false acceptance rate or type II error rate/ratio.[52, 14]

Fast Healthcare Interoperability Resources

See **FHIR**.

FAT Client

A networked computer with most resources installed locally rather than distributed over a network as is the case with a thin client. Also called thick, heavy, or rich client.[2]

Fat protocol

A network protocol that uses commands and identifiers that are typically text based and rather wordy and consume more bandwidth than a "thin" protocol. For example, SOAP, which is used to invoke processing on a remote server, is considered fat compared to CORBA or DCOM. While the

F

Internet stack is composed of thin protocols, blockchain application stack is composed of fat protocols.[150, 298]

Fatal Error

A fatal error is an error that causes a program to terminate without any warning or saving its state. A fatal error, upon occurring, aborts the application currently running and may cause the user to lose any unsaved changes made in the program. Exact reasons for fatal errors are very difficult to determine.[52]

Fault Management

Fault management is a network management component that deals with the detection, isolation, and resolution of network problems. The proper implementation of a fault management system can help ensure that networks function optimally.[52]

FCoE (Fiber Channel over Ethernet)

Fiber Channel over Ethernet (FCoE) is a protocol that encapsulates Fiber Channel (FC) frames over Ethernet networks. FCoE relies on Storage Area Network (SAN) mapping without Ethernet forwarding dependence for robust and reliable SAN performance. FCoE utilizes 10 gigabit (Gb) Ethernet networks and fully adheres to FC protocol requirements. FCoE links to networks via converged FC host bus adapters and/or Ethernet Network Interface Cards (NIC). FCoE provides FC-2 layer transfer for upper FC-3 and FC-4 layer transmission and replaces FC0 and FC1 Ethernet stack layers. FCoE does not function in routed Internet Protocol (IP) networks. Many storage and network vendors support FCoE, which is a standard component of the International Committee for Information Technology Standards (INCITS) T11 FC-BB-5.[52]

FDDI (Fiber-Distributed Data Interface)

A set of ANSI and ISO standards for data transmission on fiber optic lines in a Local Area Network (LAN) that can extend in range up to 200 km (124 miles). The FDDI protocol is based on the token-ring protocol. In addition to being large geographically, an FDDI local area network can support thousands of users. FDDI is frequently used on the backbone of a Wide Area

Network (WAN). FDDI is a type of physical network based on fiber optics. It is supported by the Digital Imaging and Communications in Medicine (DICOM) standard.[2]

Federal Financial Participation (FFP)

See **FFP**.

Federal Health Architecture (FHA)

It is a U.S. initiative designed to coordinate and manage health IT under-takings within more than 20 federal health agencies. The FHA focuses on Health Information Exchange (HIE) and interoperability in Electronic Health Records (EHR) so that they are ultimately far-reaching within common regions and organizations in order to provide quality patient care. The FHA is an e-government line-of-business initiative.[52]

Federal Information Security Management Act

See **FISMA**.

Federated database

A system in which several databases appear to function as a single entity. Each component database in the system is completely self-sustained and functional. When an application queries the federated database, the sys-tem figures out which of its component databases contains the data being requested and passes the request to it.[2]

Feeder systems

Operational systems that will feed patient/person data to the EHR in the form of real-time single messages, multiple messages, or batch file uploads.[57] *See* **Source systems**. These systems may also be known as legacy systems and are often involved in extract-transform-load processes.[50] *See* **ETL**.

Fee-For-Service

See **FFS**.

F

FFP (Federal Financial Participation)

The U.S. Federal Government's share of a state's expenditures under the Medicaid program. This funding can be provided through different funding methods including 90/10, 50/50, and 75/25.[299]

FFS (Fee-for-Service)

A type of payment in which a person or a system pays a specific amount of money for medical treatment according to the type of treatment received regardless of the outcome achieved. Federal payment systems are continuing to attempt to shift providers toward value-based care delivery and away from the FFS reimbursement model.[26, 135]

FHIR (Fast Healthcare Interoperability Resources)

A next-generation standards framework created by HL7®, FHIR combines the best features of HL7's V2, HL7 V3, and CDA product lines that leverage emerging web standards which apply a tight focus on ease of implementation. Furthermore, it defines a set of resources for health that represent granular clinical concepts that can be exchanged to quickly and effectively solve problems in healthcare and related processes. The resources cover the basic elements of healthcare—patients, admissions, diagnostic reports, medications, and problem lists, with their typical participants. In addition, the resources support a range of richer and more complex clinical models. The simple direct definitions of the resources are based on thorough requirements gathering, formal analysis, and extensive cross-mapping to other relevant standards.[9]

FHIR resource

The basic building block in the FHIR standard. All exchangeable content is defined as a resource. Resources all share the following set of characteristics: a common way to define and represent them, building them from data types that define common reusable patterns of elements, a common set of metadata, and a human-readable part.[9]

Fiber Channel (FC)

1. FC is a computer networking technology that is used to transfer data between one or more computers at very high speeds. It was initially

F

designed for supercomputers but is now commonly implemented in storage networking server environments as a replacement to Small Computer System Interface (SCSI) and other serial storage technologies. **2.** A gigabit-speed network technology primarily used for storage networking.[52]

Fiber Channel over Ethernet

See **FCoE**.

Fiber-Distributed Data Interface

See **FDDI**.

Fiber optic cable

A pure glass cable used for the high-speed transmission of digital signals. Data are transmitted through the cable via rapid pulses of light. The receiving end translates the light pulses into binary values. The cables are less susceptible to noise and interference compared to copper wires or telephone lines.[73]

Fiber optic transceiver

Device that converts fiber optic signals to digital signals and vice versa. Usually used to make a connection from a fiber run to an Ethernet segment.[52]

Fiber optics

High-speed communications technology that uses glass or plastic medium to transmit light pulses produced by LEDs or ILDs to represent data. Fiber optics are immune to electronic magnetic interference but susceptible to chromatic dispersion. Information is transmitted through the fiber as pulsating light. The light pulses represent bits of information. Fiber optics gives users of telecommunications added capacity, better transmission quality, and increased clarity.[2, 300]

Field

The smallest component under which data are entered through data capture or data entry.[4]

F

Field components

Makes up the discernible parts or components of a field entry. For example, the patient's name is recorded as the last name, first name, and middle initial, each of which is a distinct entity separated by a component delimiter.[9]

Field level security

Data protection and/or authorization of specified fields or data elements within files rather than of entire files.[301]

FIFO (First In, First Out)

A data buffer approach to handling program requests from queues or stacks so that the oldest request is handled next.[2]

File

A collection of data stored in one unit. Files have unique names and entities that allow them to be stored, moved, and edited. Types of files include documents, pictures, audio, video, data library, or application. Often, a file's extension describes its type, such as a Microsoft document file (.doc) or an audio file (MP3, WAV, etc.).[73]

File extension

A file extension is an identifier used as a suffix to the name of the computer file in an operating system such as Microsoft Windows®. It can be categorized as a type of metadata. A file extension helps the operating system to understand the characteristics of the file and to some extent, its intended use.[52]

File server

A networked computer that provides file handling and storage for users with network access. A computer that each computer on a network can use to access and retrieve files that can be shared among the attached computers. Access to a file is usually controlled by the file server software rather than by the operating system of the computer that accesses the file.[2]

File Transfer Protocol

See **FTP**.

Filmless radiology

Use of devices that replace film by acquiring digital images and related patient information and transmit, store, retrieve, and display them electronically.[167]

Filter

A program that accepts a certain type of data as input, transforms the data in some manner, and then outputs the transformed data. Also defined as a pattern through which data are passed. Only data that match the pattern are allowed to pass through the filter.[39]

FIPS (Federal Information Processing Standard)

Under the Information Technology Management Reform Act (Public Law 104-106), the Secretary of Commerce approves standards and guidelines that are developed by the National Institute of Standards and Technology (NIST) for federal computer systems. These standards and guidelines are issued by NIST as Federal Information Processing Standards (FIPS) for use government wide. NIST develops FIPS when there are compelling federal government requirements, such as for security and interoperability, and there are no acceptable industry standards or solutions.[168]

Firewall

A system designed to prevent unauthorized access to or from a network. Firewalls can be implemented in both hardware and software or a combination of both.[1]

Firmware

Software programs or computer instructions written to a hardware device on how the device communicates with various hardware components. It is typically stored in the flash ROM of a hardware device, meaning it can be erased and rewritten because it is a type of flash memory.[18]

First In, First Out

See **FIFO**.

FISMA (Federal Information Security Management Act)

U.S. legislation that defines a comprehensive framework to protect government information, operations, and assets against natural or man-made threats. FISMA was signed into law as part of the Electronic Government Act of 2002.[2]

Fixed wireless

The point-to-point transmission over the air between stationary devices. Fixed wireless is typically used for "last-mile" connectivity to buildings, and it implies high-speed (broadband) transmission. Contrast with mobile wireless.[150]

Flash drive

A small, ultra-portable storage device which, unlike an optical drive or a traditional hard drive, has no moving parts. Flash drives connect to computers and other devices via a built-in USB Type-A plug, making a flash drive a kind of combination USB device and cable.[203]

Flash memory

Nonvolatile, rewritable storage chip. Comprised of cells that hold a charge without power, flash memory is extremely durable and used in just about every electronic device, including cameras, smartphones, tablets, music players, and USB drives.[150]

Flat files

1. Files in which each record has the same length, whether or not all the space is used. Empty parts of the record are padded with a blank, or zero, depending on the data type of each field. **2.** Refers to a file that consists of a series of fixed-length records that include some sort of record type code.[113]

Flat table

A flat database is a simple database system in which each database is repre-sented as a single table in which all of the records are stored as single rows of data, which are separated by delimiters such as tabs or commas. The table is usually stored and physically represented as a simple text file.[50, 52]

Flexibility

The ability to support architectural and hardware configuration changes.[57]

Flip-flop

An electronic circuit that maintains its 0 or 1 state and is used in static memories and hardware registers.[150]

Flow chart

A diagram that combines symbols and abbreviated narratives to describe a sequence of operations and/or a process. The flow chart is a tool typically associated with the waterfall methodology of software development.[2]

Flow sheet

A tabular summary of information that is arranged to display the values of variables as changed over time.[302]

Foreground

Contains the applications the user is working on.[150] *See* **Background**.

Foreign key

A column or group of columns in a relational database table that provides a link between data in two tables. It acts as a cross-reference between tables because it references the primary key of another table, thereby establishing a link between them. The majority of tables in a relational database system adhere to the foreign key concept. In complex databases and data ware-houses, data in a domain must be added across multiple tables, thus main-taining a relationship between them. The concept of referential integrity is derived from foreign key theory. Foreign keys and their implementation are more complex than primary keys.[52, 150] *See* **Primary key**.

F

Formal system

In a concept representation, a set of machine-processable definitions in a subject field.[169]

Format

(disk formatting). The configuring process of a data storage media such as a hard disk drive, floppy disk, or flash drive for initial usage. Any existing files on the drive would be erased with disk formatting. Disk formatting is usually done before initial installation or before installation of a new operating system. Disk formatting is also done if there is a requirement for additional storage in the computer. Specifications of how data or files are to be characterized.[52]

Forward compatibility

Ability of an IT system to be compatible with or to support a similar version of itself in the future. Also known as upward compatibility, future-time compatibility, or newer-version compatibility.[52]

Foundation Model AI

A foundation model is a deep learning algorithm that has been pre-trained with extremely large data sets scraped from the public Internet. Unlike narrow Artificial Intelligence (narrow AI) models that are trained to perform a single task, foundation models are trained with a wide variety of data and can transfer knowledge from one task to another. This type of large-scale neural network can be trained once and then fine-tuned to complete different types of tasks. Foundation models can cost millions of dollars to create because they contain hundreds of billions of hyperparameters that have been trained with hundreds of gigabytes of data. Once completed, however, each foundation model can be modified an unlimited number of times to automate a wide variety of discrete tasks.[52]

Foundational interoperability

Refers the building blocks of information exchange between disparate systems by establishing the interconnectivity requirements needed for one system or application to share data with and receive data from another. It does not outline the ability of the receiving information technology system to interpret the data without interventions from the end user or other technologies.[53] *See* **Interoperability**

FQDN (Fully Qualified Domain Name)

A phrase that describes a concept uniquely and in a manner that is intended to be unambiguous. In the context of networking, the term fully qualified domain name may be used similarly. A Fully Qualified Domain Name (FQDN) is the complete domain name for a specific computer, or host, on the Internet. Also known as fully specified name. A FQDN is a domain name that specifies not only its top-level domain and parent domain name but also its local host. These more specific domain names reveal additional information about the origin of a Web page in the actual Uniform Resource Locater (URL).[52]

FQHC (Federally Qualified Health Centers)

Community-based healthcare providers that receive funds from the Health Resources and Services Administration (HRSA) Health Center Program to provide primary care services in underserved areas. They must meet a stringent set of requirements, including providing care on a sliding fee scale based on ability to pay and operating under a governing board that includes patients. FQHCs may be Community Health Centers, Migrant Health Centers, Health Care for the Homeless, and Health Centers for Residents of Public Housing.[181]

Frame

A unit of data. A frame works to help identify data packets used in networking and telecommunications structures. Frames also help to determine how data receivers interpret a stream of data from a source. Frame is a term used to refer to the existence of data at the Data Link Layer of the OSI Model.[39, 52] *See* **OSI**.

Frame relay

A high-speed packet switching protocol used in Wide Area Networks (WANs). Providing a granular service of up to DS3 speed (45 Mbps), it has become popular for LAN to LAN connections across remote distances, and services are offered by most major carriers.[150] *See* **ATM** and **SONET**.

Framework

1. A structured description of a topic of interest, including a detailed statement of the problem(s) to be solved and the goals to be achieved. An annotated outline of all the issues that must be addressed while developing acceptable solutions to the problem(s). A description and analysis of the constraints that must be satisfied by an acceptable solution and detailed specifications of acceptable approaches to solving the problem(s). **2.** The ideas, information, and principles that form the structure of an organization or plan.[135]

Free text

Unstructured, uncoded representations of information in text format (e.g., sentences describing the results of a patient's physical condition).[302]

FTP (File Transfer Protocol)

A standard high-level protocol for transferring files between computers over a TCP/IP network. FTP is a client-server protocol that relies on two communications channels between client and server: a command channel for controlling the conversation and a data channel for transmitting file content. Clients initiate conversations with servers by requesting to download a file. Using FTP, a client can upload, download, delete, rename, move, and copy files on a server.[2]

Full duplex

Data transmission that occurs in both directions on a signal carrier at the same time.[2]

Fully Qualified Domain Name

See **FQDN**.

Functional requirements

A declaration of intended function of a system and its components. Based on the functional requirements, an engineer determines the behavior or output that a device or software is expected to exhibit given a certain input.[52]

G

Gantt chart

A type of bar chart used in process or project planning, and control to display planned work targets for completion of work in relation to time. Typically, a Gantt chart shows the week, month, or quarter in which each activity will be completed, and the person or persons responsible for carrying out each activity.[304]

Gap analysis

The comparison of a current condition to the desired state. Gap analysis is a term also used within process analysis to describe the variance between current and future state processes.[159]

Garbage In, Garbage Out

See **GIGO**.

Gateway

1. A computer or a network that allows access to another computer or network. **2.** A phrase used by web masters and search engine optimizers to describe a web page designed to attract visitors and search engines to a particular web site. A typical gateway page is small, simple, and highly optimized. **3.** A technical term for the software interface between a web-based shopping cart (or order form) and a merchant account.[305] *See* **Electronic commerce**.

GB (Gigabyte)

Approximately one billion (1,024 megabytes) bytes. Unit of computer storage capacity.[2]

GBps (Gigabits per second)

Transmission of a billion bits per second.[73]

DOI: 10.4324/9781003286028-7

GDPR (General Data Protection Regulation)

European Union (EU) regulation designed to harmonize data privacy laws across the EU, to protect and empower all EU citizen data privacy, and to reshape the way organizations approach data privacy. It replaces the Data Protection Directive 95/46/EC. The regulation applies to all companies processing the personal data of data subjects residing in the EU, regardless of the company's location.[306]

GELLO (Guideline Expression Language, Object Oriented)

An object-oriented query and expression language for clinical decision support.[102] Note: GELLO is an HL7 standard.[172]

General Data Protection Regulation

See **GDPR**.

General order message

The function of this message is to initiate the transmission of information about an order. This includes placing new orders, cancellation of existing orders, discontinuation, holding, etc. Messages can originate with a placer, filler, or interested third party.[15] Also known as ORM messages.

Genomics

The study of all of a person's genes (the genome), including interactions of those genes with each other and with the person's environment. Genomics includes the scientific study of complex diseases that are typically caused more by a combination of genetic and environmental factors than by individual genes.[173] *See* **Precision medicine**.

Geographic Information Science (GISci)

This is the field that studies, researches, analyzes, and processes geographical data and information. It is the science of understanding geographic data and using mathematical and computational tools and technologies to analyze and process that data into meaningful information.

G

GIF (Graphics Interchange Format)

An image file format used for images on the web and graphics in software programs. Unlike JPEG, GIF uses lossless compression that does not degrade the image quality.[73]

GIG (Global Information Grid)

A globally interconnected, end-to-end set of information capabilities, associated processes, and personnel for collecting, processing, storing, disseminating, and managing information on-demand.[160]

Gigabit

One billion bits; commonly used for measuring the amount of data transferred in a second between two telecommunication points.[2]

Gigabits per second

See **Gbps**.

Gigabyte

See **GB**.

Gigahertz

One billion cycles per second, commonly used to measure computer processing speeds.[73]

GIGO (Garbage In, Garbage Out)

Synonymous with the entry of inaccurate or useless data and processed output of worthless/useless information. A concept common to computer science and mathematics: the quality of output is determined by the quality of the input.[2]

Global Information Grid

See **GIG**.

G

Global System for Mobile Communications
See **GSM**.

Global Unique Device Identification Database
See **GUDID**.

Global Unique Identifier
See **GUID**.

Governance Plan

A governance plan refers to roles and processes in an enterprise that serve as a guideline for fulfilling, sustaining, and extending IT planning. A governance plan crosses all organizational layers, including stakeholders, administration, maintenance, strategy, policy, and support.[52]

Graduated security

Refers to a model or architecture in which information security is implemented in multiple layers based on the requirements, threats, and vulnerabilities of the system or environment. It enables securing a system in several different protection modes that work on par with the base requirement of the underlying IT system, environment, or infrastructure.[52]

Granular data

Detailed data or the lowest level that data can be in a target set. It refers to the size that data fields are divided into, in short how detail-oriented a single field is. A good example of data granularity is how a name field is subdivided, whether it is contained in a single field or subdivided into its constituents such as first name, middle name, and last name. As the data become more subdivided and specific, it is also considered more granular.[52]

Granularity

The level of depth represented by the data in a fact or dimension table in a data warehouse. High granularity means a minute, sometimes atomic grade of detail, often at the level of the transaction. Low granularity zooms out

G

into a summary view of data and transactions. In computer science, granularity refers to a ratio of computation to communication—and also, in the classical sense, to the breaking down of larger holistic tasks into smaller, more finely delegated tasks. Granularity can inform development practices and direct design for technologies by bringing attention to how computing tasks work in the context of an entire project [52]

Graphical User Interface

See **GUI**.

Grid computing

Uses the resources of many separate computers connected by a network (usually the Internet) to solve large-scale computation problems. Also known as Beowulf computing.[307]

GS1 standards

Set of standards that provide a common language and help to create seamless work processes that allow businesses to identify, capture, and share information the same way all over the world. A common standard from the GS1 organization is the UPC barcode.[308]

GSM (Global System for Mobile Communications)

1. A worldwide digital mobile telephony system widely used in Europe and other parts of the world. GSM uses a variation of Time Division Multiple Access (TDMA). It digitizes and compresses data, then sends it down a channel with two other streams of user data, each in its own time slot. GSM typically operates in either the 900 MHz or 1800 MHz frequency band.[2]

GUDID (Global Unique Device Identification Database)

A Food and Drug Administration (FDA) publicly accessible database that would hold information about each medical device marketed in the United States.[41]

GUI (Graphical User Interface)

G

User interface that employs graphical elements such as windows, icons, and buttons as opposed to text-based command-line entry to execute programs, commands, or resources.[73]

GUID (Global Unique Identifier)

A Microsoft® term for a number that its programming generates to create a unique identity for each entity. GUIDs are widely used in Microsoft products to identify interfaces, replica sets, records, and other objects.[309]

Guideline Expression Language, Object Oriented

See **GELLO**.

H

Hackathon

A gathering where programmers collaboratively code in an extreme manner over a short period of time. Hackathons are at least a few days—or over a weekend—and generally no longer than a week. While working on a particular project, the idea is for each developer to have the ability and freedom to work on whatever he or she wants.[52]

Hacker

Unauthorized user who attempts to or gains access to an information system. Hacking actions are differentiated as illegal and unacceptable (black/gray hat hacking), or legal and acceptable (white hat hacking).[1,52]

Hacking Tool

A hacking tool is a program or utility designed to assist a hacker with hacking. It can also be proactively utilized to protect a network or computer from hackers.[52]

Hacktivist/hacktivism

Hacktivism is the act of hacking a website or computer network in an effort to convey a social or political message. The person who carries out the act of hacktivism is known as a hacktivist. In contrast to a malicious hacker who hacks a computer with the intent to steal private information or cause other harm, hacktivists engage in similar forms of disruptive activities to highlight political or social causes. For the hacktivist, hacktivism is an Internet-enabled strategy to exercise civil disobedience. Acts of hacktivism may include website defacement, denial-of-service attacks (DoS), redirects, website parodies, information theft, virtual sabotage, and virtual sit-ins.[52]

Hadoop

An open-source software framework for storing data and running applications on clusters of commodity hardware. It provides massive storage for

DOI: 10.4324/9781003286028-8

H

any kind of data, large processing power, and the ability to handle virtually limitless concurrent tasks or jobs.[116]

Half duplex

The transmission of data in both directions, but only one direction at a time. For example, two-way radio (push-to-talk phones) use half-duplex communications. When one party speaks, the other party listens.[150]

HAN (Health Alert Network)

To ensure that each community has rapid and timely access to emergent health information; a cadre of highly trained professional personnel; and evidence-based practices and procedures for effective public health preparedness, response, and service on a 24/7 basis.[80]

Handheld

A portable computer that is small enough to hold in one's hand. Used to refer to a variety of devices ranging from personal data assistance, such as smartphones, to more powerful devices that offer many of the capabilities of desktop or laptop computers. Handhelds are used in clinical practice for such tasks as ordering prescriptions, accessing patients' medical records, and documenting patient encounters.[52]

Hard copy

Printed output.[150]

Hard disk

Part of a unit, often called a "disk drive" or "hard disk drive," that stores and provides relatively quick access to large amounts of data on an electromagnetically charged surface or set of surfaces.[2]

Hardware

The physical equipment of a computer system, including the central processing unit, data storage devices, terminals, and printers.[52]

H

Harmonization

The prevention or elimination of differences in the technical content of standards having the same scope, particularly differences that may cause hindrances to trade. The coordination processes used by standard development organizations to make standards work together. Processes to achieve harmonization include convergence, modeling, mapping, translation, and other techniques.[446]

Hash function

A type of cryptography algorithm in which a fixed-length hash value is computed based on the plaintext, making it impossible for either the contents or length of the plaintext to be recovered.[311]

Hash value

A numeric value of fixed length that uniquely identifies data or the contents of a file. It serves as a digital fingerprint of a message's contents, which ensures that the message has not been altered by an intruder, virus, or other means. If the data or contents are modified in any way, the hash value will also change significantly.[311]

Hashing

Iterative process that computes a hash value from a particular data unit using a mathematical function. It enables security during the process of message transmission. A formula generates a hash value to protect against tampering.[52] *See* **Hash function**.

Hashtag

A type of label or metadata tag used on social network and blogging services to make it easier for users to find messages with a specific theme, or content, or community.[6] Users create and use hashtags by placing the hash character "#" in front of a word or un-spaced phrase. Hashtags tie public conversation from different users into a single stream that can be found by searching for a hashtag, clicking on one, or using a third-party monitoring tool.[174]

H

HCPCS (Healthcare Common Procedure Coding System)

For Medicare and other health insurance programs to ensure that health-care claims are processed in an orderly and consistent manner, standardized coding systems are essential. The HCPCS Level II Code Set is one of the standard code sets used for this purpose. The HCPCS is divided into two principal subsystems, referred to as level I and level II of the HCPCS.[447]

hData

A specification for lightweight, scalable information exchange. hData creates network-facing interfaces based on REST and Atom that can enable interactions with existing health data systems.[9]

Heads-Up Display

See **HUD**.

Health Alert Network

See **HAN**.

Health informatics

The intersection of clinical informatics and public health informatics. It is one of several fields which compose the interdisciplinary field known as biomedical informatics. Health informatics is the interdisciplinary study of the design, development, adoption, and application of IT-based innovations in healthcare services delivery, management, and planning. Health Informatics (HI) is the design, development, and execution of IT resources, specifically for medical health business processes. It is the coupling and alignment of IT and health sciences to build comprehensive health information systems, providing specialized IT services for the healthcare industry.[86, 52]

Health information

Information, whether oral or recorded in any form or medium, that
(1) is created or received by a healthcare provider, health plan, public health authority, employer, life insurer, school or university, or healthcare

clearinghouse; and (2) relates to the past, present, or future physical or mental health or condition of an individual; the provision of healthcare to an individual; or the past, present, or future payment for the provision of healthcare to an individual.[20]

Health Information Exchange

See **HIE**.

Health Information Organization

See **HIO**.

Health Information Privacy

An individual's right to control the acquisition, uses, or disclosures of his or her identifiable health data.[20] *See* **HIPAA**.

Health information security

Refers to physical, technological, or administrative safeguards or tools used to protect identifiable health data from unwarranted access or disclosure.[20]

Health Information Service Provider

See **HISP**.

Health information system

Computer systems that capture, store, process, communicate, and present any healthcare information, including Patient Medical Record Information (PMRI).[448]

Health Information Technology

See **HIT**.

Health Information Technology Advisory Committee

See **HITAC**.

H

Health Information Technology for Economic and Clinical Health Act

See **HITECH Act**.

Health Insurance Exchange

See **HIEx**.

Health Insurance Portability and Accountability Act of 1996

See **HIPAA**.

Health interoperability ecosystem

Comprises individuals, systems, and processes that want to share, exchange, and access all forms of health information, including discrete, narrative, and multimedia. Individuals, patients, providers, hospitals/health systems, researchers, payers, suppliers, and systems are potential stakeholders within this ecosystem. Each is involved in the creation, exchange and use of health information and/or data. An efficient health interoperability ecosystem provides an information infrastructure that uses technical standards, policies, and protocols to enable seamless and secure capture, discovery, exchange, and utilization of health information.[53]

Health IT

See **HIT**.

Health Literacy

The degree to which individuals have the capacity to obtain, process, and understand basic health information needed to make appropriate health decisions.[449,447]

Health Quality Measure Format

See **HQMF**.

Healthcare Clearinghouse

Organization that processes health information received from another entity in a nonstandard format or containing nonstandard data content into standard data elements or a standard transaction, or vice versa.[1]

Healthcare Common Procedure Coding System

See **HCPCS**.

Healthcare data card

A machine-readable card conformant to ISO 7810 intended for use within the healthcare domain.[120]

Healthcare Data Encryption

Healthcare data encryption is a form of data security whereby Electronic Medical Records (EHR) are disguised so that unauthorized users may not read or make sense of them. Personal Health Information (PHI), including medical diagnoses, surgeries, and other sensitive health data, needs to be secured to guard against malicious motives as well as confidentiality breaches that can result in huge fines.[52]

Healthcare Effectiveness Data and Information Set

See **HEDIS**.

Healthcare evaluation

Critical assessment, through rigorous processes, of an aspect of healthcare to assess whether it fulfills its objectives.[313]

Healthcare terminology

A collective term used to describe the continuum of code set, classification, and nomenclature (or vocabulary). A code is a representation assigned to a term so that it may more readily be processed. A classification arranges or organizes like or related terms for easy retrieval. A nomenclature, or vocabulary, is a set of specialized terms that facilitates precise communication by eliminating ambiguity. The term *controlled vocabulary* suggests only the set of individual terms in the vocabulary. A *structured vocabulary*, or *reference terminology*, relates terms to one another (with a set of relationships) that qualifies them (with a set of attributes) to promote precise and accurate interpretation.[43, 52]

HealthKit

Apple's software platform for collecting data from various health and fitness apps and then making that data easily available to Apple users through the company's new Health app.[178]

HEDIS (Healthcare Effectiveness Data and Information Set)

The HEDIS is a tool used by more than 90 percent of U.S. health plans to measure performance on important dimensions of care and service. More than 190 million people are enrolled in health plans that report quality results using HEDIS. Since 2008, HEDIS has also been available for use by medical providers and practices. Because so many health plans use HEDIS and because the measures are so specifically defined, HEDIS can be used to make comparisons among plans. To ensure that HEDIS stays current, the National Committee for Quality Assurance (NCQA) has established a process to evolve the measurement set each year through its Committee on Performance Measurement.[451]

Heuristics

An approach to problem-solving in which the objective is to produce a working solution within a reasonable time frame. Instead of looking for a perfect solution, heuristic strategies look for a quick solution that falls within an acceptable range of accuracy. Heuristics are used in Machine Learning (ML) and Artificial Intelligence (AI) when it is impractical to solve a particular problem with a step-by-step algorithm. Because a heuristic approach emphasizes speed over accuracy, it is often combined with optimization algorithms to improve results. Successive iterations are interdependent, and each level of a deep neural network decides which avenues to choose and discard, based on their proximity to the desired solution.[52]

Hexadecimal

Base 16 numbering system where 4 bits are used to represent each digit. Uses the 0–9 digits and A–F letters for the representations of the 10–15 digits.[314]

HIE (Health Information Exchange)

1. The sharing action between any two or more organizations with an executed business/legal arrangement that have deployed commonly agreed-upon technology with applied standards for the purpose of electronically exchanging health-related data between the organizations. **2.** A catch-all phrase for all health information exchanges, including RHIOs, QIOs, AHRQ-funded communities, and private exchanges. **3.** A concept evolved from the community health information exchanges of the mid-1990s. HIE provides the capability to electronically move clinical information among disparate healthcare information systems and maintain the meaning of the information being exchanged. The goal of HIE is to facilitate access to and retrieval of clinical data to provide safer, more timely, efficient, effective, and equitable patient-centered care. HIE is also used by public health authorities to assist in the analysis of the health of populations.[452]

HIEx (Health Insurance Exchange)

A set of state-regulated and standardized healthcare plans in the United States from which individuals may purchase health insurance eligible for federal subsidies. All exchanges must be fully certified and operational by January 1, 2014, under federal law outlined in the Affordable Care Act (ACA).[315] Also referred to as a health insurance marketplace.

Hijacking

1. A type of network security attack in which the attacker takes control of communication. **2.** An attack in which the Attacker is able to insert himself or herself between a Claimant and a Verifier subsequent to a successful authentication exchange between the latter two parties. The Attacker is able to pose as a Subscriber to the Verifier or vice versa to control session data exchange. Sessions between the Claimant and the Relying Party can also be similarly compromised.[2,1]

HIO (Health Information Organization)

An organization that oversees and governs the exchange of health-related information among organizations according to nationally recognized standards. The purpose of an HIO is to perform oversight and governance functions for Health Information Exchanges (HIEs).[12]

HIPAA (Health Insurance Portability and Accountability Act of 1996)

Title I of HIPAA protects health insurance coverage for workers and their families when they change or lose their jobs. Title II of HIPAA, the Administrative Simplification (AS) provisions, requires the establishment of national standards for electronic healthcare transactions and national identifiers for providers, health insurance plans, and employers. The AS provisions also address the security and privacy of health data. The standards are meant to improve the efficiency and effectiveness of the nation's healthcare system by encouraging the widespread use of electronic data interchange in healthcare. Also known as the Kennedy-Kassebaum Bill, K2, Public Law 104-91.[20]

HIPAA administrative code sets

Code sets that characterize a general business situation, rather than a medical condition or service.[20] Also called nonmedical code sets.

HIPAA administrative simplification

HIPAA, Title II, Subtitle F, gives the U.S. Department of Health and Human Services the authority to mandate the use of standards for the electronic exchange of healthcare data; specify what medical and administrative code sets should be used within those standards; require the use of national identification systems for healthcare patients, providers, payers (or plans), and employers (or sponsors); and specify the types of measures required to protect the security and privacy of personally identifiable healthcare information.[20]

HIPAA clearinghouse (or healthcare clearinghouse)

Under HIPAA, this is a public or private entity that reformats health information, especially billing transactions, from a nonstandard format into a standard and approved format.[20]

HIPAA data dictionary

A data dictionary that defines and cross-references the contents of all X12 transactions included in the HIPAA mandate. The dictionary is maintained by the X12N/TG3.[20]

HIPAA Privacy Rule

Establishes national standards to protect individuals' medical records and other personal health information and applies to health plans, healthcare clearinghouses, and those healthcare providers that conduct certain healthcare transactions electronically. The Rule requires appropriate safeguards to protect the privacy of personal health information and sets limits and conditions on the uses and disclosures that may be made of such information without patient authorization. The Rule also gives patients' rights over their health information, including the right to examine and obtain a copy of their health records, and to request corrections. The Privacy Rule is located at 45 CFR Part 160 and Subparts A and E of Part 164.[35]

HIPAA Security Rule

Establishes national standards to protect individuals' electronic personal health information that is created, received, used, or maintained by a covered entity. The Security Rule requires appropriate administrative, physical, and technical safeguards to ensure the confidentiality, integrity, and security of electronic protected health information. The Security Rule is located at 45 CFR Part 160 and Subparts A and C of Part 164.[35]

HIPAA standard

Any data element or transaction that meets each of the standards and implementation specifications adopted or established by the Secretary of the U.S. Department of Health and Human Services.[20]

HIPAA standard setting organization

An organization accredited by the American National Standards Institute (ANSI) to develop information transactions or data elements for health plans, clearinghouses, and/or providers.[20]

HIPAA unique identifier

A standard unique health identifier for each employer, health plan, and healthcare provider for use in the healthcare system.[26]

HIS (Health Information System)

Any system that captures, stores, manages, or transmits information related to the health of individuals or activities of organizations that work within the health sector.[448]

HISP (Health Information Service Provider)

Term used by the DIRECT project to describe both a function (the management of security and transport for directed exchange) and an organizational model (an organization that performs HISP functions on behalf of the sending or receiving organization or individual).[453]

HIT (Health Information Technology)

An area of Information Technology (IT) that involves the design, development, creation, use, and maintenance of information systems for the health and healthcare markets.[2] It involves the application of information processing with both computer hardware and software that deals with the storage, retrieval, sharing, and use of health and healthcare data, information, and knowledge for communication and decision-making. As an industry, it has gained prominence in the last several years as healthcare has modernized to adopt IT. Enterprise resource planning, revenue cycle management, and other business applications have been joined by Electronic Health Records (EHRs), population health platforms, personal health devices, and other health-oriented applications to represent health IT.[454]

HITAC (Health Information Technology Advisory Committee)

Group that was established in the 21st Century Cures Act (P.L. 114-255) and is governed by the provisions of the Federal Advisory Committee Act (FACA), P.L. 92-463, as amended, 5 U.S.C. App. 2, which sets forth standards for the formation and use of federal advisory committees. HITAC will recommend to the National Coordinator for Health Information Technology, policies, standards, implementation specifications, and certification criteria, relating to the implementation of a health information technology infrastructure, nationally and locally, that advances the electronic access, exchange, and use of health information. HITAC unifies the roles of, and replaces, the Health Information Technology Policy Committee and the Health Information Technology Standards Committee, as in existence before the date of the enactment of the 21st Century Cures Act.[12]

HITECH Act (Health Information Technology for Economic and Clinical Health Act)

Part of the American Recovery and Reinvestment Act of 2009 (ARRA) that addresses privacy and security concerns related to the transmission of electronic health information. The HITECH Act broadened the scope of privacy and security measures for Personal Health Records (PHRs) under the Health Insurance Portability and Accountability Act (HIPAA) and also increased certain legal liabilities for noncompliance.[35,452]

HL7 V2

A messaging standard for electronic data exchange that is widely implemented in healthcare globally. The standard allows the exchange of clinical data between systems. It is designed to support a central patient care system as well as a more distributed environment where data resides in departmental systems.[9]

Hospital Availability Exchange

See **EDXL–HAVE**.

Host

For companies or individuals with a web site, a host is a computer with a web server that serves the pages for one or more web sites. A host can also be the company that provides that service, which is known as hosting.[2]

Hot Site

An off-premises location where a company's work can resume during a disaster. A hot site has all the equipment necessary for a business to resume regular activities, including jacks for phones, backup data, computers, and related peripherals.[52]

H

HQMF (Health Quality Measure Format)

A standards-based representation of quality measures as electronic documents. It is developed by Health Level Seven International (HL7). HQMF defines the information necessary to compute a quality measure and result value.[456]

HTML (Hypertext Markup Language)

1. American Standard Code for Information Exchange (ASCII)-based language used for creating files to display documents or web pages to web browsers. **2.** Hypertext markup language is the standard provided by the World Wide Web Consortium (W3G) used for web pages on the Internet.[2,52]

HTTP (Hypertext Transfer Protocol)

1. Communication link protocol used by web servers and browsers to transfer/exchange HTML documents or files (text, graphic images, sound, video, and other multimedia files) over the Internet. **2.** Protocol with lightness and speed necessary for a distributed collaborative hypermedia information system. It is a generic, stateless, object-oriented protocol, which may be used for many similar tasks, such as name servers and distributed object-oriented systems, by extending the commands or "methods" used.[2,52] *See* **HTTPS**.

HTTPS (HTTP Secure or HTTP over SSL)

The use of Secure Socket Layer (SSL) or Transport Layer Security (TLS) as a sublayer of regular HTTP application layering. HTTPS is a web protocol developed by Netscape and built into its and other browsers, which encrypts and decrypts user page requests as well as the pages that are returned by the web server.[2,52]

Hub

Electronic network device to which multiple networked computers are attached. Divides a data channel into two or more channels of lower bandwidth. Hubs function at the physical layer (first layer) of the Open Systems Interconnection (OSI) model. These devices have long since been replaced by switches, but it is possible to see variants (e.g., switching hubs/intelligent hubs).[39] *See* **Concentrator**.

H

HUD (Heads-Up Display)

A computer-augmented display that presents information, data, or other visual elements to a user's focal viewpoint. HUD imaging, or display technology, enables visual data viewing on a transparent glass screen without requiring head/neck shifting or scrolling.[52, 2]

Human Augmentation (Human2.0).

Generally used to refer to technologies that enhance human productivity or capability or that somehow add to the human body. Modern advancements in many areas of IT have led to a greater variety of implants and other technologies that could be classed as human augmentation.[52]

Human–Computer Interaction

The study and planned design of human and computer activities. HCI uses productivity, safety, and entertainment to support and fulfill human-computer activities and is applied to various types of computer systems, including air traffic control, nuclear processing, offices, and computer gaming. HCI systems are easy, safe, effective, and enjoyable.[52]

Human Interface Device

A method by which a human interacts with an electronic information system either by inputting data or by providing output. A myriad of HID devices exist. The most common are keyboards, mice, computer speakers, webcams, and headsets. All devices providing an interface between the user and computer machines are considered HIDs.[52]

Hybrid network

A communications network comprising public and private transports.[150]

Hybrid smartcard

A card that has two chips: one with a contact interface and one with a contactless interface. The chips are not interconnected.[318]

H

Hype cycle

Hype Cycle of Emerging Technology (Gartner Group), a five-stage progression concerning "the visibility" of an emerging technology (e.g., in the popular press): (1) technology trigger; (2) peak of inflated expectations; (3) trough of disillusionment; (4) slope of enlightenment; and (5) plateau of productivity. Relative values on a 0–10 scale: 0, 9, 2, 3, and 4. Used to convey the sense that new technologies are always oversold at first. Though they eventually are useful, they seldom live up to initial expectations.[142]

Hyperconverged Infrastructure

An infrastructure model that utilizes a software-centric architecture and has tight integration with the storage, networking, computing, and virtualization software and hardware resources. A hyperconverged infrastructure enables the management of all the integrated resources from a single common toolset. A hyperconverged infrastructure is an improvement over a converged infrastructure, where the vendor provides a preconfigured bundle of software and hardware as a single unit. This type of infrastructure reduces complexity and helps simplify management of resources.[52]

Hyperledger

An open-source collaborative effort to advance cross-industry blockchain technologies, hosted by the Linux Foundation. Hyperledger offers a number of tools, frameworks, and platforms for developers looking to implement blockchain and distributed ledger technologies.[317]

Hypertext Markup Language

See **HTML**.

Hypertext Transfer Protocol

See **HTTP**.

Hypervisor

A function which abstracts operating systems and applications from the underlying computer hardware. This abstraction allows the underlying host machine hardware to independently operate one or more virtual machines as guests, allowing multiple guest VMs to effectively share the system's physical compute resources, such as processor cycles, memory space, network bandwidth, and so on. A hypervisor is sometimes also called a virtual machine monitor.[2, 454]

Hz (Hertz)

One cycle per second. Processing speeds for CPUs are measured in GHz.[73]

I

I/O (Input/output device)

A hardware device that has the ability to accept input, output, or other processed data.[52]

I/O bus

A signal route to which a number of input and output devices can be connected in parallel.[56]

IAM (Identity and Access Management)

Set of services to include authentication, User Provisioning (UP), password management, role matrix management, enterprise single sign-on, enterprise access management, federation, virtual and meta-directory services, and auditing. Identity and Access Management (IAM) is the process used in businesses and organizations to grant or deny employees and others authorization to secure systems. IAM is an integration of work flow systems that involves organizational think tanks who analyze and make security systems work effectively. Policies, procedures, protocols, and processes are all linked to IAM. Identity and security applications are also important considerations. IAM verifies user access requests and either grants or denies permission to protect company materials. It also deals with various administrative functions including password problems and helps oversee employee identity management. Standards and applications of IAM include the maintenance of user life cycles, various application accesses, and singular logons.[52]

ICC (Integrated Circuit Chip)

A small chip that can function as an amplifier, oscillator, timer, microprocessor, or even computer memory. An ICC is a small wafer, usually made of silicon, that can hold billions of transistors, resistors, and capacitors. These extremely small electronics can perform calculations and store data using either digital or analog technology.[2]

ICD (International Classification of Diseases)

The standard diagnostic tool for epidemiology, health management, and clinical purposes, including the analysis of the general health situation of population groups. Also used to monitor the incidence and prevalence of diseases and other health programs and to classify diseases and other health problem records on the many types of health and vital records, including death certificates and health records. It may also be used for reimbursement and resource allocation decision-making by countries. It is published by the World Health Organization. The latest edition currently in practice in the United States is ICD-10, endorsed in 1990 by the World Health Assembly but not implemented within the U.S. healthcare system until 2015.[507]

ICIDH (International Classification of Improvements, Disability, and Health)

Classification that promotes a common framework and definitions of disability-related issues. The ICIDH was published in 1980 by the World Health Organization, Geneva. The ICIDH distinguishes three dimensions that can be studied to monitor the situation of people with disabilities: impairment (organ and body dimension), disability (individual dimension), and handicap (social dimension).[508]

ICMP (Internet Control Message Protocol)

An extension to the Internet protocol, or IP, that supports packets containing error, control, and information messages. The PING command uses ICMP to test an Internet connection.[73]

ICO (Initial Coin Offering)

An unregulated means by which funds are raised for a new cryptocurrency venture. An ICO is used by startups to bypass the rigorous and regulated capital-raising process required by venture capitalists or banks. In an ICO campaign, a percentage of the cryptocurrency is sold to early backers of the project in exchange for legal tender or other cryptocurrencies.[18]

Icon

A picture or symbol that graphically represents an object or a concept.[29]

ICON

An informational tool to describe nursing practice and provide data representing nursing practice in comprehensive health information systems. A combinatorial terminology for nursing practice that includes nursing phenomena, nursing actions, and nursing outcomes and facilitates cross-mapping of local terms and existing vocabularies and classifications.[459]

ICR (Intelligent Call Routing)

Capability that automatically routes each call, based on caller profile, to the best available agent to handle the need, anywhere in the network.[73] *See* **PING**.

ICR (Intelligent Character Recognition)

The computer translation of manually entered text characters into machine-readable characters.[73]

Identification

The ability to identify uniquely a user of a system or an application that is running in the system.[64]

Identification and authentication

1. Identification is the ability to identify uniquely a user of a system or an application that is running in the system. Authentication is the ability to prove that a user or application is genuinely who that person or what that application claims to be. Authentication can occur through a variety of mechanisms, including challenge/response, time-based code sequences, biometric comparison, or other techniques. **2.** Use of a password, or some other form of identification, to screen users and to check their authorization.[64]

Identifier

Unique data used to represent a person's identity and associated attributes. A name or a card number are examples of identifiers.[64]

Identity

The set of physical and behavioral characteristics by which an individual is uniquely recognizable.[64]

Identity Access Management

See **IAM**.

Identity Digital Management

See **IDM**.

Identity Management System

See **IDMS**.

Identity proofing

The process of providing sufficient information (e.g., identity history, credentials, and documents) to a Personal Identity Verification (PIV) registrar when attempting to establish an identity.[64]

Identity verification

The process of confirming or denying that a claimed identity is correct by comparing the credentials of the person requesting access with those previously proven and stored in the Personal Identity Verification (PIV) card/system and associated with the identity being claimed.[64]

IDM (Identity Digital Management)

Composed of the set of business processes and a supporting infrastructure for the creation, maintenance, and use of digital identities within a legal and policy context.[459]

IDMS (Identity Management System)

1. Composed of one or more systems or applications that manage identity verification, validation, and issuance process. **2.** Software that is used to automate administrative tasks such as resetting user passwords. It enables users to reset their own passwords. There is also identity management "password synchronization" software that enables users to access resources across the system with a single password or single sign-on. In an enterprise setting, identity management is used to increase security and productivity while decreasing cost and redundant effort.[509]

IDN (Integrated Delivery Network)

A formal system of providers and sites of care that provides both healthcare services and a health insurance plan to patients in a particular geographic area. The functionalities included in an IDN vary but can include acute care, long-term health, specialty clinics, primary care, and home care services—all supporting an owned health plan.[183]

IDR (Intelligent Document Recognition)

1. Based on intelligent character recognition, the IT system automatically identifies structural features of a document to allow for a more rapid creation of the document text. **2.** Provides the ability to make sense of and help manage the unstructured, untagged information that is coming into the corporation or organization. It can provide the front-end understanding needed to feed Business Process Management (BPM) and Business Intelligence (BI) applications, as well as traditional accounting and document or records management systems.[184]

IDS (Integrated Delivery System)

See **IDN**.

IGP (Interior Gateway Protocol)

A protocol for exchanging routing information between gateways (hosts with routers) within an autonomous network.[2]

IHE (Integrating the Healthcare Enterprise)

An initiative by healthcare professionals and industry to improve the way computer systems in healthcare share information. IHE promotes the coordinated use of established standards such as DICOM and HL7 to address specific clinical needs in support of optimal patient care. Systems developed in accordance with IHE communicate with one another better, are easier to

I

implement, and enable care providers to use information more effectively.[27] *See* **Appendix B**.

IHE profile

Provides a common language for purchasers and vendors to discuss the integration needs of healthcare sites and the integration capabilities of healthcare IT products. IHE profiles offer developers a clear implementation path for communication standards supported by industry partners and are carefully documented, reviewed, and tested. They give purchasers a tool that reduces the complexity, cost, and anxiety of implementing operating systems.[27]

IIF (Information in Identifiable Form)

Any representation of information that permits the identity of an individual to whom the information applies to be reasonably inferred by either direct or indirect means.[1]

IIS (Immunization Information Systems)

Confidential, population-based, computerized databases that record all immunization doses and related information as administered by participating providers to persons residing within a given geopolitical area.[80]

IIS (Internet Information Systems)

A flexible, general-purpose web server from Microsoft that runs on Windows® systems to serve requested HTML pages or files.[2]

IKE (Internet Key Exchange)

A key management protocol standard that is used in conjunction with the IPSec standard. IPSec is an IP security feature that provides robust authentication and encryption of IP packets.[52]

ILD (Injection Laser Diode)

Also known as an injection laser or diode laser, it is a semiconductor device that produces coherent radiation (in which the waves are all at the same frequency and phase) in the visible or Infrared (IR) spectrum when current passes through it. Laser diodes are used in optical fiber systems, Compact Disk (CD) players, laser printers, remote control devices, and intrusion detection systems.[2]

Image compression

The process of encoding or converting an image file in such a way that it consumes less space than the original file.[52]

Imaging

In medicine, the use of a variety of technologies to view the human body in order to diagnose, monitor, or treat medical conditions. Each type of technology gives different information about the area of the body being studied or treated, related to possible disease, injury, or the effectiveness of medical treatment.[459]

Immunization Information Systems

See **IIS**.

Immutable object

In computer science, an object whose state, or data, cannot change after it is constructed. Maximum reliance on immutable objects is widely accepted as a sound strategy for creating simple, reliable code. Immutable objects are particularly useful in concurrent applications. Since they cannot change state, they cannot be corrupted by thread interference or observed in an inconsistent state.[459]

Impact analysis

Process of analyzing all operational functions and the effect that an operational interruption might have upon them.[459]

Implementation

In an IT context, software or hardware implementation refers to the process of installing and maintaining a new system and making sure it operates correctly in its new business environment.[2]

I

Implementation guide

1. A document explaining the proper use of a standard for a specific purpose. **2.** Method for standardized installation and maintenance of computer software and hardware. The implementation guidelines include recommended administrative processes and span the devices' lifecycle.[2, 113]

Implementation specification

Specific instructions for implementing a standard.[113]

In-band

Communications that occur together in a common communications method or channel. For example, a privacy label that applies to a clinical document will be sent in-band with the document.[113]

Incident

Event that has the capacity to lead to human, intangible, or physical loss, or a disruption of an organization's operations, services, or functions—which, if not managed, can escalate into an emergency, crisis, or disaster.[87]

Independent Practice Association

See **IPA**.

Indicator

A measurable variable (or characteristic) that can be used to determine the degree of adherence to a standard or the level of quality achieved.[2]

Individual

Person who is the subject of information collected, used, or disclosed by the entity holding the information.[20]

Individually identifiable data

Data that are a part of health information, including demographic information collected from an individual that is individually identifying.[317]

Individually identifiable health information

Information that is a subset of health information, including demographic information collected from an individual: (1) created or received by a healthcare provider, health plan, employer, or healthcare clearinghouse and (2) relates to the past, present, or future physical or mental health or condition of an individual; the provision of healthcare to an individual; or the past, present, or future payment for the provision of healthcare to an individual. Information that (1) identifies the individual or (2) with respect to which there is a reasonable basis to believe the information can be used to identify the individual.[20]

Individually identifying information

Single item or compilation of information or data that indicate or reveal the identity of an individual, either specifically (such as the individual's name or Social Security number) or that do not specifically identify the individual but from which the individual's identity can reasonably be ascertained.[20]

Infobutton

The HL7 Context-Aware Knowledge Retrieval Standard provides a standard mechanism for EHR systems and knowledge resources to communicate, implementing infobutton capabilities. The Infobutton Standard consists of the following specifications:

- Context-Aware Knowledge Retrieval Application ("Infobutton"), Knowledge Request—normative specification that includes a domain analysis model and a message information model. By itself, this specification is not implementable.
- URL-Based Implementation Guide, Release 4—specifies infobutton knowledge requests in a URL format.
- Infobutton Service-Oriented Architecture (SOA) Implementation Guide, Release 1—RESTful specification an knowledge response in XML and JSON formats.[510]

Infographics

A representation of information in a graphic format designed to make the data easily understandable at a glance. The ability to package more information in a smaller space makes infographics an attractive tool for instruction and marketing.[2, 52]

Informatics

The study of the behavior and structure of any system that generates, stores, processes, and then presents information; it is basically the science of information. The field takes into consideration the interaction between the information systems and the user, as well as the construction of the interfaces between the two, such as the user interface.[52]

Information

Data that have been processed, organized, structured, or presented in a given context to make them meaningful or useful.[318]

Information asset

Refers to any information in any form (e.g., written, verbal, oral, or electronic) upon which the organization places a measurable value. This includes information created by the entity holding the information, gathered for the entity, or stored by the entity for external parties.[20]

Information compromise

An intentional or accidental disclosure or surrender of clinical data to an unauthorized receiver.[73]

Information exchange initiative

Efforts by two or more independent Healthcare Organizations (HCOs) in a geographic area to collaborate to share common patient information for the improvement of community health status, patient care, or viability of the HCOs.[452]

Information flow model

A diagrammatic representation of the flow and exchange of information within a system. Data flow models are used to graphically represent the flow of data in an information system by describing the processes involved in transferring data from input to file storage and reports generation.[52]

Information infrastructure

1. The combination of computers and an information system. **2.** The standards, laws, regulations, business practices, and technologies needed to facilitate unauthorized sharing of comparable data in a safe and secure manner.[284]

Information in Identifiable Form

See **IIF**.

Information interchange

(American Standard Code) A code for information exchange between computers made by different companies; a string of seven binary digits represents each character; used in most microcomputers.[73]

Information model

1. A conceptual model of the information needed to support a business function or process. **2.** A representation of concepts, relationships, constraints, rules, and operations to specify data semantics for a chosen domain.[459]

Information modeling

The building of abstract models for the purpose of developing an abstract system.[459]

Information privacy

The ability an organization or individual has to determine what data in a computer system can be shared with third parties.[2]

Information Resource Management

See **IRM**.

Information security

A set of strategies for managing the processes, tools, and policies necessary to prevent, detect, document, and counter threats to digital and non-digital information. Information security responsibilities include establishing a set of business processes that will protect information assets regardless of how the information is formatted or whether it is in transit, is being processed, or is at rest in storage.[2]

Information system

An integrated set of components for collecting, storing, and processing data and for providing information, knowledge, and digital products.[319]

Information system architecture

A framework from which applications, system software, and hardware can be developed in a coherent manner and in which every part fits together without containing a mass of design details.[459]

Information technology

The hardware, firmware, and software used as part of the information system to perform information functions. This definition includes computers, telecommunications, automated information systems, and automatic data processing equipment. Information Technology (IT) includes any assembly of computer hardware, software, and/or firmware configured to collect, create, communicate, compute, disseminate, process, store, and/or control data or information.[1]

Information Technology Management Reform Act of 1996

See **ITMRA**.

Information warfare

The tactical and strategic use of information to gain an advantage.[52]

Infrared Data Association

See **IrDA**.

Infrastructure-centric

A security management approach that considers information systems and their computing environment as a single entity.[459]

Inheritance

In object-oriented programming, the concept that when a class of objects is defined, any subclass that is defined can inherit the definitions of one or more general classes. For the programmer, this means that an object in a subclass need not carry its own definition of data and methods that are generic to the class (or classes) of which it is a part. This not only speeds up program development, it also ensures an inherent validity to the defined subclass object (what works and is consistent about the class will also work for the subclass).[2]

Initiator

An (authenticated) entity (e.g., human user or computer-based entity) that attempts to access other entities.[24] Also known as claimant or principal.

Injection Laser Diode

See **ILD**.

Inpatient

Patient in the hospital who receives lodging and food as well as treatment.[26]

Inpatient record

Healthcare record of a hospitalized patient.[26]

Inputs

The resources needed to carry out a process or provide a service. Inputs required in healthcare are usually financial and physical structures, such as buildings, supplies and equipment, personnel, and clients.[2]

Integrated care

The systematic coordination of general and behavioral healthcare. Integrating mental health, substance abuse, and primary care services produces the best outcomes and proves the most effective approach to caring for people with multiple healthcare needs.[511]

Integrated Circuit Chip

See **ICC**.

Integrated client

Existing applications in hospitals and other medical facilities that will provide EHR functionality by integrating with the EHR using specified HL7 v3 messages.[9]

Integrated Delivery Network

See **IDN**.

Integrated Delivery System

See **IDS**.

Integrated network

A network of providers that share information via EHRs to improve the quality of patient care, reduce costs, and demonstrate value in the healthcare marketplace. Typically physician-led, CINs can be composed of employed and/or independent physicians and can also include partnerships with healthcare systems. Leadership within a CIN will establish clear goals and objectives, as well as participation guidelines for members to meet the demands of the ever-changing healthcare landscape.

Integrated Service Digital Network

See **ISDN**.

Integrating the Healthcare Enterprise

See **IHE**.

Integration

1. The process of bringing together related parts into a single system. To make various components function as a connected system. **2.** Combining separately developed parts into a whole so that they work together. The means of integration may vary, from simply mating the parts together at an interface to radically altering the parts or providing something to mediate between them.[2]

Integration layer

Software component that presents a single, consolidated point of access to several systems and/or services.[2]

Integration profile

A precise description of how standards are to be implemented to address a specific clinical or operational integration need. Each integration profile includes definition of the use case, the information and workflow involved, and the set of actors and transactions that address that need. Integration profiles reference the fully detailed implementation specifications defined in the IHE technical framework in a form that is convenient to use in requests for proposals and product descriptions.[27]

Integration services

This group of services is made up of services that manage the integration, message brokering, and service catalog functions.[2]

Integration testing

A testing event that seeks to uncover errors in the interactions and interfaces among application software components when they are combined to form larger parts of a system.[51]

Integrity

1. Quality of an IT system reflecting the logical correctness and reliability of the operating system; the logical completeness of the hardware and software implementing the protection mechanisms; and the consistency of the data structures and occurrence of the stored data. It is composed of data integrity and system integrity. **2.** Knowledge that a message has not been modified while in transit. May be done with digitally signed message digest codes. Data integrity, the accuracy and completeness of the data, program integrity, system integrity, and network integrity are all components of computer and system security.[2]

Intelligent agent

A type of software application that searches, retrieves, and presents information from the Internet. This application automates the process of extracting data from the Internet, such as information selected based on a predefined criterion, keywords, or any specified information/entity to be searched.[52]

Intelligent Call Routing

See **ICR**.

Intelligent Character Recognition

See **ICR**.

Intelligent Document Recognition

See **IDR**.

Intended Use/Intended Purpose

Use for which a product, process, or service is intended according to the specifications, instructions, and information provided by the manufacturer.[2]

Interaction model

Logical diagram or narrative describing the exchange of data and sequence of method invocation between objects to perform a specific task within a use case.[2]

Interactive services detection

A feature for legacy applications that detects if a service is trying to interact with the Windows® desktop.[512]

Interactive Voice Response

See **IVR**.

Interface

Computer hardware or software that is designed to communicate information between devices, programs, or a computer and a user.[52]

Interface engine

Tool that translates functions from different systems and protocols into a common format to facilitate information sharing. It is a translator for data or files to pass between systems.[52]

Interface terminology

Support interactions between healthcare providers and computer-based applications. They aid practitioners in converting clinical "free text" thoughts into the structured, formal data representations, used internally by application programs.[111]

Interior Gateway Protocol

See **IGP**.

International standard

Standard that is adopted by an international standardizing/standards organization and made available to the public.[52]

Internet

The global communication network that allows almost all computers worldwide to connect and exchange information.[44]

Internet Control Message Protocol

See **ICMP**.

Internet Information Server

See **IIS**.

Internet Key Exchange

See **IKE**.

Internet of Things

See **IoT**.

Internet Protocol

See **IP**.

Internet Protocol address

See **IP address**.

Internet Protocol datagram

See **IPsec**.

Internet Protocol security

See **IPsec**.

Internet Relay Chat

See **IRC**.

Internet Service Provider

See **ISP**.

Internetwork Packet Exchange/Sequence Packet Exchange

See **IPX/SPX**.

Interoperability

It is the ability of different information systems, devices, and applications (systems) to access, exchange, integrate, and cooperatively use data in a coordinated manner, within and across organizational, regional, and national boundaries, to provide timely and seamless portability of information and optimize the health of individuals and populations globally. Health data exchange architectures, application interfaces, and standards enable data to be accessed and shared appropriately and securely across the complete spectrum of care, within all applicable settings and with relevant stakeholders, including the individual. There are four levels of interoperability

- **Foundational (Level 1):** Establishes the interconnectivity requirements needed for one system or application to securely communicate data to and receive data from another.

- **Structural (Level 2):** Defines the format, syntax, and organization of data exchange including at the data field level for interpretation.
- **Semantic (Level 3):** Provides for common underlying models and codification of the data including the use of data elements with standardized definitions from publicly available value sets and coding vocabularies, providing shared understanding and meaning to the user.
- **Organizational (Level 4):** Includes governance, policy, social, legal, and organizational considerations to facilitate the secure, seamless and timely communication, and use of data both within and between organizations, entities, and individuals. These components enable shared consent, trust, and integrated end-user processes and workflows.[53]

Interoperability Standards Advisory

See **ISA**.

Interpreted language

In programming language, code that is saved in the same format that it is entered. Code that is not compiled.[322]

Interrupt

A signal from a device attached to a computer or from a program within the computer that requires the operating system to stop and figure out next steps.[2]

Interrupt Request

See **IRQ**.

Intranet

Private computer network that uses Internet protocols and Internet-derived technologies, including web browsers, web servers, and web languages, to facilitate collaborative data sharing within an enterprise.[52]

Intrusion detection

The act of detecting actions that attempt to compromise the confidentiality, integrity, or availability of a resource.[2]

I

iOS (formerly iPhone OS)

A mobile operating system created and developed by Apple Inc. exclusively for its hardware and devices, including the iPhone, iPad, and iPod Touch. The iOS user interface is based upon direct manipulation using multi-touch gestures. Interface control elements consist of sliders, switches, and buttons. Interaction with the OS includes gestures such as swipe, tap, pinch, and reverse pinch, all of which have specific definitions within the context of the iOS operating system and its multi-touch interface. Internal accelerometers are used by some applications to respond to shaking the device (one common result is the undo command) or rotating it in three dimensions (one common result is switching between portrait and landscape mode).[73]

IoT (Internet of Things)

1. The ever-growing network of physical objects that feature an IP address for Internet connectivity, and the communication that occurs between these objects and other Internet-enabled devices and systems. IoT extends Internet connectivity beyond traditional devices like desktop and laptop computers, smartphones, and tablets to a diverse range of devices and everyday items, such as kitchen appliances, with embedded technology to communicate and interact with the external environment via the Internet.[39] **2.** A system of interrelated computing devices, mechanical and digital machines, objects, animals, or people that are provided with unique identifiers and the ability to transfer data over a network without requiring human-to-human or human-to-computer interaction.[2]

IP (Internet Protocol)

The method or protocol by which data are sent from one computer to another on the Internet. Each computer (known as a host) on the Internet has at least one IP address that uniquely identifies it from all other computers on the Internet.[2]

IP address (Internet protocol address)

The equivalent of an Internet mailing address, which identifies the network, the subnet, and the host, such as 168.100.209.246. A specific 32-bit (4 octet) unique address assigned to each networked device.[2]

IP datagram (Internet Protocol datagram)

Format of data that can be recognized by IP. It consists of two components, namely, the header and data, which need to be transmitted.[323]

IPA (Independent Practice Association)

An Independent Physician Association (IPA) is a business entity organized and owned by a network of independent physician practices for the purpose of reducing overhead or pursuing business ventures such as contracts with employers, Accountable Care Organizations (ACO), and/or Managed Care Organizations (MCOs). There are substantial opportunities for innovation in delivery system modeling and benefit design in the creation of physician networks. Specifically, the creation of practice networks involving medical homes may accelerate important and necessary changes in healthcare delivery.[196]

iPhone Operating System

See **iOS**.

IPsec (Internet Protocol security)

1. A developing low-level protocol for encrypting the Internet protocol packet layer of a transmission instead of the application layer to provide improved confidentiality, authentication, and integrity. IPsec can be handled without requiring changes to individual user computers. **2.** IPSec Virtual Private Network (VPN) is a compilation of standards created by the Internet Engineering Task Force to help the user filter the encrypted data packet.[2]

IPv4 and IPv6 (Internet Protocols versions 4 and 6)

Used to identify computers on the Internet.[324]

IPX/SPX (Internetwork Packet Exchange/ Sequence Packet Exchange)

A set of network protocols that provide packet switching and sequencing for small and large networks. IPX works at layer three of the Open Systems Interconnection (OSI) model and SPX works at layer 4.[52]

IRC (Internet Relay Chat)

An application-layer protocol that facilitates real-time communication using a client-server platform.[2]

IrDA (Infrared Data Association)

A group of device manufacturers that developed a standard for transmitting data via infrared light waves. Increasingly, computers and other devices (such as printers) come with *IrDA* ports. This enables you to transfer data from one device to another without any cables.[39]

IRM (Information Resource Management)

A philosophical and practical approach to managing information. Information is regarded as a valuable resource that should be managed like other resources and should contribute directly to accomplishing organizational goals and objectives. IRM provides an integrated view for managing the entire life cycle of information, from generation to dissemination to archiving and/or destruction, for maximizing the overall usefulness of information, and for improving service delivery and program management. IRM views information and information technology as an integrating factor in the organization, that is, the various organizational positions that manage information are coordinated and work together toward common ends. Further, IRM looks for ways in which the management of information and the management of information technology are interrelated and fosters that interrelationship and organizational integration. IRM includes the management of (1) the broad range of information resources, e.g., printed materials, electronic information, and microforms; (2) the various technologies and equipment that manipulate these resources; and (3) the people who generate, organize, and disseminate those resources.[459]

IRQ (Interrupt Request Line)

Hardware lines over which devices can send interrupt signals to the microprocessor.[39]

ISA (Interoperability Standards Advisory)

The model by which the Office of the National Coordinator for Health Information Technology (ONC) coordinates the identification, assessment, and determination of "recognized" interoperability standards and implementation specifications for industry use to fulfill specific clinical health IT interoperability needs.[11]

ISBT 128

The global standard for the terminology, identification, coding, and labeling of medical products of human origin (including blood, cell, tissue, milk, and organ products). It is used in more than 77 countries across six continents and disparate healthcare systems. It is widely endorsed by the professional community. The standard has been designed to ensure the highest levels of accuracy, safety, and efficiency for the benefit of donors and patients worldwide. ISBT 128 provides international consistency to support the transfer, traceability, and transfusion/transplantation of blood, cells, tissues, and organs.[195]

ISDN (Integrated Service Digital Network)

A data transfer technology that can transfer data significantly faster than a dial-up modem. ISDN enables wider bandwidth digital transmission over the public telephone network, which means more data can be sent at one time.[459]

ISO/IEEE 11073 Standards

Health Informatics and Medical Devices Communication Standards that provide the interconnection and interoperation of medical devices with computerized healthcare information systems in a way that is suitable for a clinical environment. This family of standards provides real-time plug-and-play interoperability and facilitates the efficient exchange of vital signs and medical device data acquired at the point-of-care.[325]

ISO/TC 215 International Organization for Standardization (ISO) Technical Committee for Health Informatics

Committee that focuses on standardization in the field of information for health, and Health Information and Communications Technology (ICT). Promotes interoperability between independent systems to enable compatibility and consistency for health information and data as well as to reduce duplication of effort and redundancies.[36]

I

Isolation

1. A transaction's effect is not visible to other transactions until the transaction is committed. **2.** Transaction isolation levels specify what data are visible to statements within a transaction. These levels directly impact the level of concurrent access by defining what interaction is possible between transactions against the same target data source.[459,89] *See* **ACID**.

ISP (Internet Service Provider)

Company that provides Internet connectivity and Internet-related services, online computer access, web site hosting, and domain name registration.[18]

ITIM Group

Group that administers user access to the Tivoli Identity Manager system. An ITIM group is a generic user group for the Tivoli Identity Manager Server; it is used to grant access to ITIM users through the use of Access Control Information (ACIs). You can structure the system access and administration with ITIM groups. Before a person entity can be assigned to an ITIM group as an ITIM user, the entity must be provisioned with a Tivoli Identity Manager account. ITIM groups have four basic properties: Name, Description, Access option, and User list.[459]

ITMRA (Information Technology Management Reform Act)

Division E of the 1996 National Defense Authorization Act (NDAA). It repealed the Brooks Act, defined information technology and National Security Systems (NSS), established the requirement to designate a Chief Information Officer (CIO) for each major federal agency, assigned the responsibility for management of IT to the Director, Office of Management and Budget (OMB), and moved procurement protest authority from the General Services Administration (GSA) to the Government Accountability Office (GAO). Frequently, but erroneously, referred to as the Clinger-Cohen Act (CCA).[513]

IVR (Interactive Voice Response)

Ability to access information over the phone (claim payments, claim status, and a patient's eligibility).[46]

J

JAD (Joint Application Development)

A development methodology that involves continuous interaction with users and designers of the system in development. JAD centers on workshop sessions that are structured and focused to improve the quality of the final product by focusing on the up-front portion of the development lifecycle, thus reducing the likelihood of errors that are expensive to correct later.[39]

JASON

An independent federal scientific advisory group that provides consulting services to the U.S. government on matters of defense, science, and technology. It was established in 1960. In 2014, the group published a Robust Health Data Infrastructure, which focuses on a joint task force of HIT standards and Policy Committees.[268, 327, 12]

Jasper AI

An Artificial Intelligence (AI) platform that allows users to instantly produce human-like copy for blog posts, social media ads, e-mails, landing pages, and more. The platform uses GPT-3 technology to create this copy, which is best known for being a cornerstone of ChatGPT.[52]

JavaScript Object Notation

See **JSON**.

J-codes

A subset of the Healthcare Common Procedure Coding System (HCPCS) level II code set with a high-order value of "J" that has been used to identify certain drugs and other items. The final HIPAA transactions and code sets rule states that these J-codes will be dropped from the HCPCS and that NDC codes will be used to identify the associated pharmaceuticals and supplies.[113]

DOI: 10.4324/9781003286028-10

233

J

JCR (Joint Commission Resources)

Consulting division of The Joint Commission whose mission is to continuously improve the safety and quality of healthcare in the United States and in the international community through the provision of education, publications, consultation, and evaluation services.[328]

JFS (Journaling File System)

A fault-resilient file system in which data integrity is ensured because updates to directories and bitmaps are constantly written to a serial log-on disk before the original disk log is updated. In the event of a system failure, a full journaling file system ensures that the data on the disk have been restored to its pre-crash configuration. It also recovers unsaved data and stores it in the location where it would have gone if the computer had not crashed, making it an important feature for mission-critical applications.[2]

JIRA

Issue tracking system used by organizations, including the Office of the National Coordinator for Health Information Technology (ONC). JIRA is a commercial software program developed by Atlassian that is used for issue tracking and project management.[12, 329]

Joins

A data query operation performed on data tables in a relational Database Management System (DBMS), in which the data from two or more tables are combined using common data elements into a single table. Typically performed using Structured Query Language (SQL).[330]

Joint Application Development

See **JAD**.

Joint Commission

An independent, not-for-profit organization, The Joint Commission accredits and certifies nearly 21,000 healthcare organizations and programs in the United States. Joint Commission accreditation and certification are recognized nationwide as a symbol of quality that reflects an organization's commitment to meeting certain performance standards.[229]

Joint Commission Resources

See **JCR**.

Joint Photographic Experts Group

See **JPEG**.

Journaling File System

See **JFS**.

JPEG (Joint Photographic Experts Group)

An image file format. It is commonly used by digital cameras to store photos since it supports 16,777,216 colors. The format also supports varying levels of compression, which makes it ideal for web graphics.[2] Also referred to as JPG.

JPEG compression

A process to reduce the size of a JPEG image file.[2]

JPG

See **JPEG**.

JSON (JavaScript Object Notation)

A lightweight data interchange format that is easy for humans to read and write and easy for machines to parse and generate. It is based on the subject of JavaScript Programming Language, Standard ECMA-262, 3rd Edition. JSON is a text format that is completely language independent but uses conventions familiar to programmers of the C-family of languages, including C, C++, C#, Java, JavaScript, Perl, Python, and others. JSON is built on two structures: (1) a collection of name/value pairs, also known as an object and (2) an ordered list of values, also known as an array.[201]

JTC (Joint Technical Committee)

A standards body straddling the International Organization for Standardization (ISO) and International Electrotechnical Commission (IEC).[60]

K

KAS (Clinical Decision Support (CDS) Knowledge Artifact Specification)

Provides guidance on how to specify and implement shareable CDS knowledge artifacts using XML. The scope of the specification includes event-condition-action rules, order sets, and documentation templates.[9]

KB (Kilobyte)

Equal to 1024 bytes of digital data.[73]

Kbps (Kilobits per second)

Transmission of a thousand bits per second.[2]

Kerberos

A protocol for authenticating service requests between trusted hosts across an untrusted network, such as the Internet.[2]

Kernel

The central module of an Operating System (OS). It is the part of the operating system that loads first, and it remains in main memory. The kernel is responsible for memory management, process and task management, and disk management. The kernel connects the system hardware to the application software.[39]

Key

1. A field or combination of fields in a database table used to retrieve and sort rows based on certain requirements. **2.** A value that particularizes the use of a cryptographic system. **3.** An input that controls the transformation of data by an encryption algorithm.[52]

DOI: 10.4324/9781003286028-11

K

Key management services

As data are brought in from various sources, there will be cases where certain primary source identity keys are not unique across source systems. The key management service will generate and manage keys during insert and update operations in the EHR repository.[52]

Keystroke verification

The determination of the accuracy of data entry by the re-entry of the same data through a keyboard.[36]

Keyword

In the context of search engine optimization, a particular word or phrase that describes the contents of a Web page. Keywords are intended to act as shortcuts that sum up an entire page. Keywords form part of a Web page's metadata and help search engines match a page with an appropriate search query.[52]

KHz (Kilohertz)

One thousand cycles per second.[2]

Kludge

Generally defined as a poorly set up system with mismatched parts or elements, a clumsy construction that might work but not particularly well. This term, and its spelling variant "kluge," have become ways to talk about clunky or disjointed IT systems.[52]

Knowledge

The distillation of information that has been collected, classified, organized, integrated, abstracted, and value-added. Knowledge is at a higher level of abstraction than the data and information on which it is based and can be used to deduce new information and new knowledge.[236]

Knowledge acquisition

The process of eliciting, analyzing, transforming, classifying, organizing, and integrating knowledge; representing that knowledge in a form that can be used in a computer system.[236]

K

Knowledge base

Data tables, databases, and other tools designed to assist the process of care.[43]

Knowledge-Based Authentication (KBA)

It is a security measure that identifies end users by asking them to answer specific security questions in order to provide accurate authorization for online or digital activities. Knowledge-based authentication has become prevalent in many different types of network setups and across the Internet, where companies often ask users to answer these questions in order to gain access to personal, password-protected areas of a site.[52]

Knowledge Discovery in Databases (KDD)

It is the process of discovering useful knowledge from a collection of data. This widely used data-mining technique is a process that includes data preparation and selection, data cleansing, incorporating prior knowledge of data sets, and interpreting accurate solutions from the observed results.[52]

Knowledge Engineer

A knowledge engineer is a professional engaged in the science of building advanced logic into computer systems in order to try to simulate human decision-making and high-level cognitive tasks. A knowledge engineer supplies some or all of the "knowledge" that is eventually built into the technology.[52]

Knowledge engineering

Converting knowledge, rules, relationships, heuristics, and decision-making strategies into a form understandable to the artificial software upon which an expert system is built.[2]

Knowledge Management

The process of creating, sharing, using, and managing the knowledge and information of an organization. Typically refers to a multidisciplinary approach to achieving organizational objectives by making the best use of knowledge.[2]

Knowledge representation

1. The process and results of formalization of knowledge in such a way that the knowledge can be used automatically for problem-solving. **2.** The field of knowledge representation involves considering artificial intelligence and how it presents some sort of knowledge, usually regarding a closed system. IT professionals and others may monitor and evaluate an artificial intelligence system to get a better idea of its simulation of human knowledge or its role in presenting data about focus input[236, 52]

L

Lab Results Interface

See **LRI**.

Laboratory Information Management System

See **LIS**.

Laboratory Information System

See **LIS**.

LAN (Learning and Action Network)

The U.S. Department of Health and Human Services (through CMS) launched the Health Care Payment Learning and Action Network (LAN) in March 2015 to align with public and private sector stakeholders in shifting away from the current FFS (Fee-for-Service) volume-based payment system to one that pays for high-quality care and improved health. The LAN provides a forum for generating evidence, sharing best practices, developing common approaches to the design and monitoring of APMs, and removing barriers to healthcare transformation across the U.S. healthcare system.[505]

LAN (Local Area Network)

A single network of physically interconnected computers that is localized within a small geographical area. Operates in a span of short distances (office, building, or complex of buildings). *See* **MAN, WAN**, and **WLAN**.[202]

LAN adapter

Allows access to a network, usually a wireless network.[202]

DOI: 10.4324/9781003286028-12

LASA (Look-Alike/Sound-Alike Drugs)

Care providers developed a list of look-alike/sound-alike medications they store, dispense, or administer. LASA lists are used to determine which medications require special safeguards to reduce the risk of errors and minimize harm.[229]

LAT (Local Area Transport)

A proprietary network protocol developed by Digital Equipment Corp. and used in local area networks and terminal server connections. LAT was created to provide connection between terminal servers and host computers via Ethernet cable and enable communication between these hosts and serial devices such as video terminals and printers.[52]

Latent Dirichlet Allocation

See **LDA**.

Lattice Security Model

A security model with increasing degrees of security.[45]

Layered defense

Also called overlapping controls; employing more than one control against an attack on the computer or network where one control will compensate for a failure in another.[45]

Layered trust

Concept in design of a secure operating system utilizing a layered design in which the trustworthiness and access rights of a process can be judged by the process's proximity to the center. The more trusted processes are closer to the center.[45]

Layering networks

Each layer in the OSI model reformats the transmission and exchanges information with its peer layer.[45]

L

LDA (Latent Dirichlet Allocation)

In natural language processing, a generative statistical model that allows sets of observations to be explained by unobserved groups that explain why some parts of the data are similar; used as a topic model.[332]

LDAP (Lightweight Directory Access Protocol)

A software protocol for enabling anyone to locate data about organizations, individuals, and other resources such as files and devices in a network—whether on the public Internet or a corporate intranet. LDAP is a "lightweight" version of Directory Access Protocol (DAP), which is part of X.500, a standard for directory services in a network. LDAP is considered lightweight because it uses a smaller amount of code than other protocols. A directory tells the user where in the network something is located. On TCP/IP networks—including the Internet—the Domain Name System (DNS) is the directory system used to relate the domain name to a specific network address, which is a unique location on the network. However, the user may not know the domain name. LDAP allows a user to search for an individual without knowing where they are located, although additional information will help with the search.[2]

Learning and Action Network

See **LAN**.

Least privilege

1. The principle that a security architecture should be designed so that each entity is granted the minimum system resources and authorizations that the entity needs to perform its function. **2.** A security principle that restricts the access privileges of authorized personnel (e.g., program execution privileges and file modification privileges) to the minimum necessary to perform their jobs.[1]

Ledger

A written or computerized record of all the transactions a business has completed.[330]

Left without Being Seen

See **LWBS**.

Legacy systems

Refers to outdated computer systems, programming languages, or application software that is used instead of available upgraded versions. Legacy systems also may be associated with terminology or processes that are no longer applicable to current contexts or content, thus creating confusion. Most organizations have legacy systems—to some extent. A legacy system may be problematic due to compatibility issues, obsoletion, or lack of security support. A legacy system is also known as a legacy platform. Outdated computing software and/or hardware that is still in use. The system still meets the needs it was originally designed for but does not allow for growth. What a legacy system does now for the company is all it will ever do. A legacy system's older technology would not allow it to interact with newer systems.[52]

Letter of Intent

See **LOI**.

Level of Effort

See **LOE**.

Lexicon

A group of related terms used in a particular profession, subject area, or style.[29]

Lexicon Query Service

See **LQS**.

Licensed Independent Practitioner

See **LIP**.

Life Safety Code

See **LSC**.

L

Lifecycle

All phases in the life of a medical device or system, from the initial conception to final decommissioning and disposal.[459]

LIFO (Last In, First Out)

A queue that executes last-in requests before previously queued requests. To better understand LIFO, imagine stacking a deck of cards by placing one card on top of the other, starting from the bottom. Once the deck has been fully stacked, you begin to remove the cards, starting from the top. This process is an example of the LIFO method, because the last cards to be placed on the deck are the first ones to be removed. The LIFO method is sometimes used by computers when extracting data from an array or data buffer. When a program needs to access the most recent information entered, it will use the LIFO method. When information needs to be retrieved in the order it was entered, the FIFO method is used.[73.]

Lightweight Directory Access Protocol

See **LDAP**.

Limited data set

Specifies health information from which identifiers have been removed. Information in a limited data set is protected but may be used for research, healthcare operations, and public health activities without the individual's authorization.[20]

Limited privilege

A program is allowed to access secure data, but the access is minimized and neither the access rights nor the data are passed along the other untrusted programs or back to an untrusted caller.[45]

Link

A connection between two network devices. Also known as anchors, hotlinks, and hyperlinks. A link (short for hyperlink) is an HTML object that allows you to jump to a new location when you click or tap it. Links are found on almost every webpage and provide a simple means of navigating

L

between pages on the web. Links can be attached to text, images, or other HTML elements. Most text links are blue since that is the standard color web browsers use to display links. However, links can be any color since the style of the link text may be customized using HTML or CSS styles. In the early days of the web, links were underlined by default. Today, underlining links is less common.[1,2]

LINUX

A Unix-like, open source and community-developed Operating System (OS) for computers, servers, mainframes, mobile devices, and embedded devices. It is supported on almost every major computer platform, including x86, ARM, and SPARC, making it one of the most widely supported operating systems.[2]

LIP (Licensed Independent Practitioner)

An individual, as permitted by law and regulation and also by the organization, to provide care and services without direction or supervision within the scope of the individual's license and consistent with the privileges granted by the organization. Each state has different laws as to who can practice without supervision.[226]

LIS (Laboratory Information System)

An application to streamline the process management of the laboratory for basic clinical services, such as hematology and chemistry. This application may provide general functional support for microbiology reporting but does not generally support blood bank functions. Provides an automatic interface to laboratory analytical instruments to transfer verified results to nurse stations, chart carts, and remote physician offices. The module allows the user to receive orders from any designated location, process the order and report results, and maintain technical, statistical, and account information. It eliminates tedious paperwork, calculations, and written documentation while allowing for easy retrieval of data and statistics. Also known as LIS, Laboratory Information Management System (LIMS), and Laboratory Management System (LMS).[2]

LISTSERV

A program that automatically redistributes e-mail to names on a mailing list. Users can subscribe to a mailing list by sending an e-mail note to a mailing list they learn about; listserv will automatically add the name and distribute future e-mail postings to every subscriber.[2]

LLC (Logical Link Control)

One of two sublayers that make up the Data Link Layer of the OSI Model. The logical link control layer controls frame synchronization, flow control, and error checking.[39]

Local Area Network

See **LAN**.

Local Area Transport

See **LAT**.

Local codes

Generic term for code values that are defined for specific payers, providers, or political jurisdictions.[46]

Local name space

Collection of objects to which a process has access. The local name space or domain might include some programs, files, data segments, and I/O devices such as a printer and a terminal.[459]

Lock Out/Tag Out

See **LOTO**.

LOE (Level of effort)

Any particular support type activity that customarily does not lend itself to the ultimate establishment via measure of the sum total of discrete accomplishment. The level of effort is typically denoted through and via a uniform set of work performance rates over a period of time (typically a predefined period of time) over which the activities of note took place. Level of effort can be measured via independent observation or by members of the project group.[333]

L

Log

Record of events occurring within an organization's systems and networks.[2]

Log analytics

Studying log entries to identify events of interest or suppress log entries for insignificant events.[2]

Log archival

Retaining logs for an extended period of time, typically on removable media, a Storage Area Network (SAN), or a specialized log archival appliance or server.[2]

Log clearing

Removal of all entries from a log that precede a certain date and time.[2]

Log compression

Storing a log file in a way that reduces the amount of storage space needed for the file without altering the meaning of its contents.[2]

Log conversion

The process of parsing a log in one format and storing its entries in a second format.[2]

Log entry

Individual record within a log.[2]

Log management

Process for generating, transmitting, storing, analyzing, and disposing of log data.[2]

Logic bombs

A malicious program timed to cause harm at a certain point in time but is inactive up until that point. A set trigger, such as a preprogrammed

L

date and time, activates a logic bomb. Once activated, a logic bomb implements a malicious code that causes harm to a computer. A logic bomb's application programming points may also include other variables such that the bomb is launched after a specific number of database entries. However, computer security experts believe that certain gaps in action may launch a logic bomb as well and that these types of logic bombs may actually cause the greatest harm. A logic bomb may be implemented by someone trying to sabotage a database when they are fairly certain they would not be present to experience the effects, such as full database deletion. In these instances, logic bombs are programmed to exact revenge or sabotage work.[52]

Logical access control

An automated system that controls an individual's ability to access one or more computer system resources, such as a workstation, network, application, or database.[1]

Logical Data Model

Represents the structure of the relationship of data elements and entities within an information system. The logical model is crucial to the proper function of any system within an enterprise. The logical model allows for elegance in system design so that the system is adaptable to the changing information needs of the enterprise.[459]

Logical drive

A part of a physical disk drive that has been partitioned and allocated as an independent unit and functions as a separate drive altogether. For example, one physical drive can be partitioned into drives F, G, and H, each representing a separate logical drive but still part of the one physical drive.[39]

Logical Link Control

See **LLC**.

Logical observation identifiers names and codes

See **LOINC**.

L

Logical separation

Users operate under the illusion that no other processes exist, as when an operating system constrains a program's accesses so that the program cannot access objects outside its permitted domain.[45]

Logical system design

Describes the functionality of the system and presents the vision of system performance and its features.[459]

Logical topology

A concept in networking that defines the architecture of the communication mechanism for all nodes in a network. Using network equipment such as routers and switches, the logical topology of a network can be dynamically maintained and reconfigured. Logical topologies contrast with physical topologies, which refer to the physical interconnections of all devices in the network.[52]

Logical Unit Number

See **LUN**.

Logoff/logout

To formally exit from the computer's environment.[2]

Logon

Process to get access to an operating system or application, often requiring a user ID and password.[2]

LOI (Letter of Intent)

Used in most major business transactions, a Letter of Intent (LOI) outlines the terms of a deal and serves as an "agreement to agree" between two parties.[18]

LOINC (Logical Observation Identifiers Names and Codes)

Universal identifiers for laboratory and clinical observations, measurements, and documents, including such things as vital signs, hemodynamic measures, intake/output, EKG, obstetric ultrasound, cardiac echo, urologic imaging, gastro-endoscopic procedures, pulmonary ventilator management, selected survey instruments, and other clinical observations.[203]

Longitudinal health record

A comprehensive clinical summary of a patient-based clinical experience as opposed to encounter-based or provider-based records.[334] *See* **EHR**.

Longitudinal Patient Disease Registries

See **LPDR**.

Long-Term and Post-Acute Care

See **LTPAC**.

Long-Term Care

See **LTC**.

Long-Term Care Facility

See **LTCF**.

Long-Term Services and Support

See **LTSS**.

Look Alike/Sound Alike

See **LASA**.

Loop

A programming function that iterates a statement or condition based on specified boundaries. The loop function uses almost identical logic and syntax in all programming languages. Thus, a specific statement or a group

LOTO (Lock Out/Tag Out) ■ 251

L

of instructions is continuously executed until a specific loop body or boundary condition is reached. The result of the entire loop body's first operation cycle serves as the next repetition's starting point.[52]

Loophole

An incompleteness or error in a computer code that can allow a program to be manipulated or exploited; usually referred to in relation to computer or network security.[335]

Loose lipped system

System provides too much information to an unknown user.[45]

Loosely coupled

Describes how multiple computer systems, even those with incompatible technologies, can be joined together for transactions regardless of functional components.[39]

Loss reduction

A protection risk management strategy, loss reduction focuses on a single incident or claim and requires immediate response to any adverse occurrence.[459]

Lossless compression

Method of data compression that permits reconstruction of the original data exactly, bit-for-bit. The Graphics Interchange File (GIF) is an image format used on the web that provides lossless compression.[52]

Lossy compression

Method of data compression that permits reconstruction of the original data approximately rather than exactly. JPEG is an example of lossy compression.[52]

LOTO (Lock Out/Tag Out)

Addresses the practices and procedures necessary to disable machinery or equipment, thereby preventing the release of hazardous energy while employees perform servicing and maintenance activities. This is generally done by affixing the appropriate lockout or tag out devices to energy-isolating devices and by de-energizing machines and equipment.[336]

Low-Volume Threshold

See **LVT**.

LPDR (Longitudinal Patient Disease Registries)

A secure informatics system designed to enable enhanced data collection, sharing, management, and analysis for specific conditions to improve patient outcomes.[337]

LQS (Lexicon Query Service)

Standardizes a set of read-only interfaces able to access medical terminology system definitions, ranging from sets of codes to complex hierarchical classification and categorization schemes.[459]

LRI (Lab Results Interface)

Support the electronic transmission of clinical results from a Laboratory Information System (LIS) into an Electronic Health Record (EHR). This class of interface is designed to allow the unattended transfer and real-time processing of interface messages from a remotely located trading partner system, or the EHR.[9]

LSC (Life Safety Code)

A set of fire protection requirements designed to provide a reasonable degree of safety from fire for healthcare facilities. The code covers construction, protection, and operational features designed to provide safety from fire, smoke, and panic. The Health Care Facilities Code Requirements (HCFC) is a set of requirements intended to provide minimum requirements for the installation, inspection, testing, maintenance, performance, and safe practices for facilities, material, equipment, and appliances. The LSC and HCFC, which are revised periodically, are publications of the National Fire Protection Association (NFPA), which was founded in 1896 to promote the science and improve the methods of fire protection.[506]

L

LTC (Long-Term Care)

Involves a variety of services designed to meet a person's health or personal care needs during a short or long period of time. These services help people live as independently and safely as possible when they can no longer perform everyday activities on their own. Long-term care is provided in different places by different caregivers, depending on a person's needs. Most long-term care is provided at home by unpaid family members and friends. It can also be given in a facility such as a nursing home or in the community, for example, in an adult day care center.[339]

LTCF (Long-Term Care Facility)

Nursing homes, skilled nursing facilities, and assisted living facilities, known as Long-Term Care Facilities (LTCFs), provide a variety of services, both medical and personal care, to patients who are unable to manage independently in the community.[80]

LTPAC (Long-Term and Post-Acute Care)

Segment of the healthcare continuum that works to provide comprehensive longitudinal chronic care over a long period of time. Skilled nursing facilities, home care, hospice, long-term acute care, inpatient rehabilitation, assisted living, medication management, Program of All-Inclusive Care for the Elderly (PACE), and independent care fall within this spectrum of care.[12]

LTSS (Long-Term Services and Support)

A wide array of medical and nonmedical services which are provided over a prolonged period of time for people of all ages with impaired mobility, impaired cognitive function, physical or mental disabilities, complex medical needs, or chronic disease. Caregivers provide services and support to help individuals with daily living activities—such as eating, bathing, and dressing—or other activities such as housekeeping or managing medications that help people live independently.[338]

LU (Logical Unit)

Portion of the Arithmetic Logic Unit (ALU) within the CPU that coordinates logical operations.[2]

L

Luminance brightness

The amount of light, in lumens, that is emitted by a pixel or an area of the computer screen.[459]

LUN (Logical Unit Number)

A unique identifier for designating an individual or collection of physical or virtual storage devices that execute input/output (I/O) commands with a host computer, as defined by the Small System Computer Interface (SSCI) standard.[2]

LVT (Low-Volume Threshold)

Part of the Quality Payment Program (QPP) through Medicare for Medicare Part B, established in 1977 to control the cost of payments from Medicare to Physicians, Clinicians, or Health Care Providers must meet the Low-Volume Threshold (LVT) to qualify for the Merit-based Incentive Payment System (MIPS). The LVT is less than or equal to $30,000 in Medicare Part B patients allowed charges or less than or equal to 100 Medicare patients.[459]

LWBS (Left without Being Seen)

Refers the status of a patient who left a healthcare facility without examination or treatment.[459]

MAC (Mandatory Access Control)

A security strategy that restricts the ability individual resource owners have to grant or deny access to resource objects in a file system. MAC criteria are defined by the system administrator, strictly enforced by the Operating System (OS) or security kernel, and are unable to be altered by end users.[52]

MAC (Message Authentication Code)

A cryptographic checksum that is generated on data using a cryptographic algorithm that is parameterized by a symmetric key. The message authentication code is designed to provide data origin authentication and detect both accidental errors and intentional modification of the data.[1]

MAC address (Media Access Control address)

A hardware identification number that uniquely identifies each device on a network.[18]

Machine code/machine language

The lowest-level programming language (except for computers that utilize programmable microcode).[39]

Machine learning

A subset of artificial intelligence that permits computers to learn either inductively or deductively. Inductive machine learning is the process of reasoning and making generalizations or extracting patterns and rules from huge data sets; that is, reasoning from a large number of examples to a general rule. Deductive machine learning moves from premises that are assumed to be true to conclusions that must be true if the premises are true.[2]

DOI: 10.4324/9781003286028-13

M

Machine-Readable Zone (MRZ)

A particular area in an identity document (passport specifically) that encloses the document holder's personal data. Nowadays, almost every country's official identity or travel documents have MRZ, containing confidential information encoded. Generally, MRZ has two or three lines with the OCR (optical character recognition) font text printed. The MRZ-based documents are referred to as machine-readable documents because a machine only reads the texts they contain.[340]

MACRA (Medicare Access and CHIP Reauthorization Act 2015)

A law that dictates three major changes to how Medicare reimburses those providers delivering care. These changes which created the Quality Payment Program (QPP) under MACRA include (1) ending the Sustainable Growth Rate (SGR), a formula previously used to determine Medicare payment for provider services; (2) creating a framework to reward providers for delivering better care instead of more care; and (3) aligning existing quality programs into one single program to measure provider care quality and reduce duplicative reporting. Eligible Clinicians (ECs) have two paths within QPP: (1) the Merit-Based Incentive Payment System (MIPS), which includes the merging of existing quality programs, or (2) Advanced Alternative Payment Models (Advanced APMs), which allow providers to explore new models to deliver outcomes-focused care.[544] *See* **MIPS, ECs,** and **Advanced APMs**.

Macro

An automated input sequence that imitates keystrokes or mouse actions. A macro is typically used to replace a repetitive series of keyboard and mouse actions and used often in spreadsheets and word processing applications like MS Excel and MS Word. The file extension of a macro is commonly. MAC. The concept of macros is also well-known among MMORPG gamers (Massively Multiplayer Online Role-Playing Games) and SEO (Search Engine Optimization) specialists. In the world of programming, macros are programming scripts used by developers to reuse code. The term macro stands for "macro-instruction" (long instruction). [52]

M

Mail merge

The connecting of a single form template with a data source that contains information about the recipient's name, address, or other information. Mail merge enables the automation of sending bulk mail.[52]

Mailing list

A list of people who subscribe to a periodic mailing distribution. On the Internet, these lists include each person's e-mail address instead of postal address.[2]

Malicious code

Malicious code is the language hostile parties "speak" to manipulate computer systems into dangerous behaviors. It is created by writing changes or add-ons to the existing programming of computer programs, files, and infrastructure. This threat is the foundational tool used to carry out the vast majority of cybersecurity attacks. Hackers probe and find weaknesses that are based on the languages used to program computers. They then create "phrases" known as scripts or lists of commands to abuse these vulnerabilities in these languages. These scripts can be reused and automated via macroinstructions, or macros for short. Hackers and other threat actors would move very slowly if they were restricted to manual methods of exploiting computer systems. Unfortunately, malicious code allows them to automate their attacks. Some codes can even replicate, spread, and cause damage on their own. Other types of code may need human users to download or interact with it. The consequences of malicious code may often lead to any of the following: corruption of data, distributed denial-of-service (DdoS), credential theft and private information theft, ransom and extortion, and nuisance and inconvenience.[545]

Malware

Malicious software is any program or file that is intentionally harmful to a computer, network or server. Types of malware include computer viruses, worms, Trojan horses, ransomware, and spyware. These malicious programs steal, encrypt, and delete sensitive data; alter or hijack core computing functions; and monitor end users' computer activity.[2]

M

MAN (Metropolitan-Area Network)

A computer network that is larger than a single building Local Area Network (LAN) but is located in a single geographic area that is smaller than a Wide Area Network (WAN). Generally, it is several LANs interconnected by dedicated backbone connections. It may also refer to public use networking infrastructure in a municipality or region.[2]

Manage consent directives

Ensure that protected health information is only accessed with a consumer's consent.[20]

Managed care

Managed care refers to a healthcare insurance approach that integrates the financing of healthcare and the delivery of care and related services to keep the costs to the purchaser at a minimum while delivering what is appropriate for a given patient or population of patients. The precise definition of managed care has evolved over several decades. Common to most definitions of managed care are several features or components such as a limited network of providers (professionals such as physicians and organizations such as hospitals, imaging centers, pharmacies, and laboratories) who are each credentialed and contracted, utilization management, quality management, financial incentives for the patient to use network providers, and some level of financial incentives or risk-sharing by the provider for the care provided.[546]

Management Information System (service)

See **MIS**.

Management Service Organization

See **MSO**.

Mandatory Access Control

See **MAC**.

MAO (Maximum Acceptable/Allowable Outage)

The timeframe during which a recovery must become effective before an outage compromises the ability of an organization to achieve its business objectives or its survival.[547]

Map

A relationship between a concept in a terminology and a concept in the same or another terminology, according to a mapping scheme or rules.[75]

Mapping

1. Assigning an element in one set to an element in another set through semantic correspondence. **2.** A rule of correspondence established between data sets that associates each element of a set with an element in the same or another set.[29,76] *See* **Data mapping** and **Crosswalk**.

Masking

The process of systematically removing a field or replacing it with a value in a way that does not preserve the analytic utility of the value, such as replacing a phone number with asterisks or a randomly generated pseudonym.[1]

Masquerading

A type of attack where the attacker pretends to be an authorized user in order to gain access or gain greater privileges.[2]

Massively Parallel Processing

See **MPP**.

Master browser

Computer that collects and maintains a list of available servers that have shared network resources in its domain.[459]

Master data

1. Core data that are essential to operations in a specific business or business unit and varies by industry and company. **2.** Often refers to data units that are nontransactional that an organization may reuse across a variety of software programs and technologies.[2,52] Also known as reference data.

Master Data Management
See **MDM**.

Master Patient Index
See **MPI**.

Master Services Agreement
See **MSA**.

Match/matching

The process of comparing biometric information against previously stored biometric data and scoring the level of similarity.[64]

Math coprocessor

A mathematical circuit that performs high-speed floating point operations. Also called a "Floating Point Unit" (FPU), the math coprocessor may be a stand-alone chip or circuits built into the CPU. Floating point capability is very important to computation-intensive work such as Computer-Aided Design (CAD), and many CAD programs will not operate without it.[146]

MAU (Media Access Unit)

A network hub or switch.[146] *See* **MSAU**.

Maximum Acceptable/Allowable Outage
See **MAO**.

Maximum defined data set

All of the required data elements for a particular standard based on a specific implementation specification. An entity creating a transaction is free to include whatever data any receiver might want or need. The recipient is free

M

to ignore any portion of the data that is not needed to conduct his or her part of the associated business transaction, unless the inessential data are needed for coordination of benefits.[459]

Maximum Tolerable Period of Disruption or MTPOD

See **MAO**.

Mb (Megabit)

1,048,576 bits or 1024kb.[2]

MBDS (Minimum Basic Data Set)

A set of data that are the minimum required for a healthcare record to conform to a given standard.[459]

Mbps (Megabits per second)

Transmission of a million bits per second.[2]

MDA (Model-Driven Architecture)

A type of approach to software design, development, and implementation. As the name suggests, this approach uses models as a set of guidelines used in structuring design specifications. The reason why models were selected as the central object in this design principle is because it helps designers to reason out the system design by allowing them to ignore extra details and giving them more focus on the relevant issues. Models are also used all throughout the engineering and design field to understand complex and real-world systems.[52]

MDI (Medical Device Interface)

Includes all points of interaction between the user and the device, including all elements of the device with which the user interacts. A device user interface might be used while the user sets up the device (e.g., unpacking, set up, and calibration), uses the device, or performs maintenance on the device (e.g., cleaning, replacing a battery, and repairing parts).[41]

MDI-X port (Medium-Dependent Interface Crossover)

An MDI port or uplink port is a port on a switch, router, or network hub connecting to another switch or hub using a straight-through cable rather than an Ethernet crossover cable. Generally, there are one to two ports on a switch or hub with an uplink switch, which can be used to alter between an MDI and MDI-X interface. The "X" or crossover is in reference to the transmitting wires (MDI), which must be connected to the receiving (MDI-X) wires to "crossover" signals.[52]

MDM (Master Data Management)

A comprehensive method of enabling an enterprise to link all of its critical data to one file, called a master file, which provides a common point of reference. MDM can help streamline data sharing among departments and facilitate computing in multiple system architectures, platforms, and applications. MDM tools are used in healthcare by health information organizations to maintain a high degree of confidence that patient identity information is consistent, disambiguated, and de-duplicated across multiple disparate systems.[2]

MDM (Medical Document Management Message)

The HL7 MDM message helps manage medical records by transmitting new or updated documents or by transmitting important status information and/ or updates for the record. Trigger events and messages can be one of two categories: they can either describe the status of the document or they can describe the status of the document AND contain the document contents. MDM messages can be created in relation to an order or independently of them.[459]

MDM (Mobile Device Management)

Software dealing with deploying, securing, monitoring, integrating, and managing mobile devices, such as smartphones, laptops, and tablets, in the workplace. The intent is to optimize the functionality and security of devices within the enterprise while protecting the corporate network.[2]

M

MDS (Minimum Data Set)

Part of the federally mandated process for clinical assessment of all residents in Medicare- and Medicaid-certified nursing homes. This process provides a comprehensive assessment of each resident's functional capabilities and helps nursing home staff identify health problems. Care Area Assessments (CAAs) are part of this process and provide the foundation upon which a resident's individual care plan is formulated. MDS assessments are completed for all residents in certified nursing homes, regardless of source of payment for the individual resident. MDS assessments are required for residents on admission to the nursing facility, periodically, and on discharge. All assessments are completed within specific guidelines and time frames. In most cases, participants in the assessment process are licensed healthcare professionals employed by the nursing home. MDS information is transmitted electronically by nursing homes to the national MDS database at CMS.[548]

Mean Time Between Failure

See **MTBF**.

Mean Time To Diagnose

See **MTTD**.

Mean Time To Repair

See **MTTR**.

Meaningful Use

See **MU**.

Measure

A number or quantity that records a directly observable value or performance. All measures have a unit attached to them and can be expressed as counts (45 visits), rates (10 visits/day), proportions (45 primary healthcare visits/380 total visits = .118), percentages (12 percent of the visits made), or ratios (45 visits four health workers = 11.25).[4]

M

MedDRA (Medical Dictionary for Regulatory Activities)

1. Used by regulatory agencies and drug manufacturers. **2.** A terminology developed under the auspices of the International Conference on Harmonization of Technical Requirements for Registration of Pharmaceuticals for Human Use. MedDRA is a standard international terminology for regulatory communication in the registration, documentation, and safety monitoring of medical products throughout all phases of their regulatory cycle. As a standard, MedDRA is expected to promote the harmonization of regulatory requirements and documentation for medical products in the United States, Japan, and the European Union.[549]

Media access control

Lower portion of the second layer, the data link layer, of the Open Systems Interconnection (OSI) model. Responsible for the transmission of data packets to and from the network interface card, and to and from another remotely shared channel.[52] *See* **MAC address**.

Media Access Control Address

See **MAC address**.

Media Access Unit

See **MAU**.

Medicaid Information Technology Architecture

See **MITA**.

Medicaid Management Information System

See **MMIS**.

Medical code sets

Codes that characterize a medical condition to treatment. These code sets are usually maintained by professional societies and public health organizations.[117]

Medical device

Any instrument, apparatus, implement, machine, appliance, implant, in vitro reagent or calibrator, software, material, or other similar or related article intended by the manufacturer to be used, alone or in combination, for human beings for one or more of the specific purposes of diagnosis, prevention, monitoring, treatment, or alleviation of disease; diagnosis, monitoring, treatment, alleviation of, or compensation for an injury; investigation, replacement, modification, or support of the anatomy or of a physiological process; supporting or sustaining life; control of conception; disinfection of medical devices; providing information for medical purposes by means of in vitro examination of specimens derived from the human body; and which does not achieve its primary intended action in or on the human body by pharmacological, immunological, or metabolic means but which may be assisted in its function by such means.[550]

Medical error

1. The failure of a planned action to be completed as intended or the use of a wrong plan to achieve an aim in the healthcare delivery process. **2.** A mistake that harms a patient. Adverse drug events, hospital-acquired infections, and wrong-site surgeries are examples of preventable medical errors.[343]

Medical home

1. A model of delivering primary care that is accessible, continuous, comprehensive, family-centered, coordinated, compassionate, and culturally effective. **2.** In a medical home model, primary care clinicians and allied professionals provide conventional diagnostic and therapeutic services as well as coordination of care for patients who require services not available in primary care settings. The goal is to provide a patient with a broad spectrum of care, both preventive and curative, over a period of time and to coordinate all of the care the patient receives.[551]

Medical Information BUS

See **MIB**.

M

Medical Record

See **EHR** and **EMR**.

Medical Subject Heading

See **MeSH**.

Medical terminology

A system of words that are used to describe specific medical aspects and diseases.[56]

Medication error

A medication error is any preventable event that may cause or lead to inappropriate medication use or patient harm while the medication is in the control of the healthcare professional, patient, or consumer. Such events may be related to professional practice, healthcare products, procedures, and systems, including prescribing, order communication, product labeling, packaging, and nomenclature, compounding, dispensing, distribution, administration, education, monitoring, and us[552]

Megabyte

One million bytes of data used as a measure of computer processor storage and real and virtual memory. A megabyte is actually 2 to the 20th power, or 1,048,576 bytes.[2]

Memorandum of Understanding

See **MOU**.

Memory

1. Any medium of data storage, but usually refers to random access memory, RAM. **2.** Any information or data, often in binary format, that a technology can recall or use.[73, 52] *See* **RAM** and **ROM**.

Memory ballooning

A management technique that allows a physical host to take advantage of unused memory on its guest Virtual Machines (VMs).[2]

Merit-based Incentive Payment System

See **MIPS**.

MeSH (Medical Subject Heading)

A thesaurus of concepts and terms used for the indexing of biomedical literature controlled by the National Library of Medicine (NLM). [553]

Message authentication

Ensuring that a message is genuine, has arrived exactly as was sent, and comes from the stated source.[2]

Message Authentication Code

See **MAC**.

Message format standards

Protocols that make communication between disparate systems possible. These message format standards should be universal enough that they do not require negotiation of an interface agreement between the two systems in order to make the two systems communicate.[459]

Message syntax

System of rules and definitions specifying the basic component types of messages, interrelationships, and arrangement.[459]

Message type

An identified, named, and structured set of functionally related information that fulfills a specific business purpose.[459]

Message, instant

IM or IM'ing is the exchange of near-real-time messages through a stand-alone application or embedded software. Unlike chatrooms with many users engaging in multiple and overlapping conversations, IM sessions usually take place between two users in a private, back-and-forth style of communication. A core feature of many instant messenger clients is the ability to see whether a friend or co-worker is online and connected through the selected

M

service—a capability known as *presence*. As the technology has evolved, many IM clients have added support for features such as file transfer and image sharing within an IM session. Instant messaging differs from e-mail in the immediacy of the message exchange. IM also tends to be session-based, having a start and an end. Because IM is intended to mimic in-person conversations, individual messages are often brief. E-mail, on the other hand, usually reflects a longer-form, letter writing style.[2]

Messaging

Creating, storing, exchanging, and managing data messages across a communications network. The two main messaging architectures are publish-subscribe and point-to-point.[459]

Messaging services

A group of services that handles messages. Services in this group include parsing, serialization, encryption and decryption, encoding and decoding, transformation, and routing.[459]

Meta tag

An HTML coding statement that provides information about a web page. The information in a meta tag is used by search engines to index a page.[2]

Metadata

Structured information that describes other data to help make such data easier to retrieve, use, or manage as an information resource. There are three main types of metadata: (1) descriptive metadata describes a resource for purposes of discovery and identification; (2) structural metadata indicate how compound objects are put together; and (3) administrative metadata provide information to help manage a resource, such as when or how it was created, file type, and other technical information.[148]

Metadata registry

A system that contains information that describes the origin, structure, format, and definitions of data. These registries provide an integrating resource for legacy data, acts as a lookup tool for designers of new databases, and documents each data element.[148]

M

Metadata stewards

Organizations that have the responsibility for the ongoing maintenance of a metadata item.[2]

Metathesaurus

The National Library of Medicine's Unified Medical Language System (UMLS) Metathesaurus cross-references national and international medical vocabularies.[554] *See* **UMLS**.

Metropolitan-Area Network

See **MAN**.

mHealth (Mobile health)

General term for the use of mobile phones and other wireless technology in medical care. Examples of use include patient education, remote monitoring, treatment support, epidemic outbreak tracking, and chronic disease management.[2]

MHz (Megahertz)

One million times, cycles, occurrences, alterations, or pulses per second. Used to describe a measurement of CPU or processor speed.[2]

MIB (Medical Information BUS)

1. A hardware and software standard (IEEE P11073) that enables standardized connections between medical monitoring devices and clinical information systems. **2.** Institute of Electrical and Electronics Engineers (IEEE) P11073 (standard designation) standard for data exchange in a medical environment.[555]

Microcomputer

A computer with a Central Processing Unit (CPU) as a microprocessor. Designed for individual use.[52]

M

Microprocessor

Central processing unit. A microprocessor is a computer processor on a microchip. It is the "engine" that goes into motion when you turn your computer on. Designed to perform arithmetic and logic operations that make use of small number-holding areas called *remote monitoring.*[2] *See* **CPU**.

Middleware

Software systems that function as a conversion or translation layer. Middleware is also a consolidator and integrator. Custom-programmed middleware solutions have been developed for decades to enable one application to interface with another, which either runs on a different platform or comes from a different vendor.[146]

MIME (Multipurpose Internet Mail Extensions)

A method for transmitting non-text files via Internet e-mail, which was originally designed for only ASCII text. Defined by IETF RFC 2822, MIME encodes the files using one of two encoding methods and decodes them back to their original format at the receiving end. A MIME header is added to the file which includes the type of data contained and the encoding method used. The MIME "type" (renamed "Internet media type") has become the de facto standard for describing files on the Internet.[146]

Minimum Basic Data Set

See **MBDS**.

Minimum necessary

Minimum amount of protected health information necessary to accomplish permitted use or disclosure for payment or healthcare operations.[20]

Minimum scope of disclosure

The principle that, to the extent practical, individually identifiable health information should only be disclosed to the extent needed to support the purpose of the disclosure.[20]

MIPS (Merit-based Incentive Payment System)

A program created as a result of MACRA enacted in 2015 that combines the components of existing quality and incentive programs such as the Physician Quality Reporting System (PQRS), the Value-based Payment Modifier (VM), and the Medicare Electronic Health Record Incentive Program (also known as Medicare's version of Meaningful Use). Under MIPS, Eligible Clinicians (ECs) are measured on quality, cost, improvement activities, and the Promoting Interoperability Program.[26] *See* **MACRA,** and **QPP.**

Mirror site

A website that is a replica of an already existing site, used to reduce network traffic (hits on a server) or improve the availability of the original site. Mirror sites are useful when the original site generates too much traffic for a single server to support.[39]

MIS (Management Information System)

A set of systems and procedures that gather data from a range of sources, compile them, and present them in a readable format. An MIS is used to create reports with an overview of all information needed to make management decisions.[345]

Mission critical

Activities, processing, etc., which are deemed vital to the organization's business success and, possibly, its very existence.[18]

MITA (Medicaid Information Technology Architecture)

A national framework to support improved systems development and healthcare management for the Medicaid enterprise.[556]

MMIS (Medicaid Management Information System)

An integrated group of procedures and computer processing operations (subsystems) developed at the general design level to meet the principal objectives of a state-directed program.[556]

M

Mobile app

A software application developed specifically for use on small, wireless computing devices, such as smartphones and tablets, rather than desktop or laptop computers. Mobile apps are sometimes categorized by whether they are web-based or native apps created specifically for a given platform. A third category, hybrid apps, combines elements of both web-based and native apps.[2]

Mobile computing

The use of portable computing devices, such as laptop or handheld computers, in conjunction with mobile communication technologies to enable users to access the Internet and data on their home or work computer from any location. Also known as nomadic computing.[2]

Mobile Device Management

See **MDM**.

Mobile device

A portable device that uses wireless technologies to transmit and exchange data and has a capacity for general computing.[2]

Mobile health

See **mHealth**.

Model

A very detailed description or scaled representation of one component of a larger system that can be created, operated, and analyzed to predict actual operational characteristics of the final produced component.[459]

Model-Driven Architecture

See **MDA**.

Modeling

The process of defining concepts to reflect their unique definition and meaning.[459] *See* **Data modeling**.

Modularity

The characteristic of a system that has been divided into small subsystems which interact with each other.[459]

MOLAP (Multidimensional Online Analytical Processing [OLAP])

A technical OLAP approach that uses a multidimensional data model to analyze data. MOLAP requires that information first be processed before it is indexed directly into a multidimensional database.[52]

Moore's Law

The empirical observation that at our rate of technological development, the complexity of an integrated circuit, with respect to minimum component cost, will double in about 18 months. It is attributed to Gordon E. Moore, a cofounder of Intel, and published in 1965.[557, 555]

Motion Picture Experts Group

See **MPEG**.

MOU (Memorandum of Understanding)

A nonbinding agreement between two or more parties outlining the terms and details of an understanding, including each parties' requirements and responsibilities. An MOU is often the first stage in the formation of a formal contract.[18]

MPAI (Moving Picture, Audio and Data Coding by Artificial Intelligence)

Develops standards for applications of major practical interests in human-machine communication, enhanced audio, financial data, video coding, online gaming, connected autonomous cars, mixed-reality collaborative spaces, and more.[559]

MPEG (Motion Picture Experts Group)

International standards for compression, decompression, processing, and coded representation of moving pictures, audio, and their combination. Now

M

replaced by Moving Picture, Audio and Data Coding by Artificial Intelligence (MPAI).[346]

MPI (Master Patient Index)

Facilitates the identification and linkage of patients' clinical information within a particular institution. The term "Enterprise Master Patient Index" (EMPI) is sometimes used to distinguish between an index that serves a single institution (i.e., MPI) and one that contains data from multiple institutions (EMPI). MPIs are not themselves patient identity management strategies but rather informational infrastructures within which those strategies are applied. Most MPIs use a patient matching algorithm to identify matches and then assign a unique patient identifier that is associated with that patient record going forward.[459] *See* **EMPI**.

MPP (Massively Parallel Processing)

The coordinated processing of a program by multiple processors that work on different parts of the program, with each processor using its own operating system and memory.[2]

MSA (Master Services Agreement)

An agreement between two or more parties that sets forth terms and conditions relevant to one or more services and transactions between parties. Additional terms, conditions, and other information may be incorporated by reference.[209]

MSAU (Multiple Station Access Unit)

A central device/hub used in computer networking to connect network nodes, computers, or devices with local area networks. MSAU provides a means of data sharing between different computing devices in an organization. The working mechanism of MSAU is based on a token-ring network topology in which all computers and computing devices are connected with each other in a logical circle. In this system, connectivity with other computers remains stable, and users continue to communicate with each other when one computer or computing device fails. Also known as a Media Access Unit (MAU), which is often called an Ethernet transceiver. MSAU is a stand-alone device or connector that is used to connect devices attached to a network over a token-ring network.[52]

MSO (Management Service Organizations)

These are entities designed to help with the administrative, or nonmedical, work involved in running a practice. These organizations may be owned by non-healthcare provider investors, hospitals, groups of physicians, be a joint venture between a hospital and physicians, or even owned by health plans. MSOs can assist practices with operational issues, financial management, human resources, staff training, coding, billing and collection services, office space needs, discounts on EHRs and medical equipment, regulatory compliance, contract management, credentialing, group purchasing, and risk management.[210]

MTBF (Mean Time Between Failures)

Measure of how reliable a hardware product is, indicating the amount of time before a product fails to function properly.[2] *See* **Risk tolerance**.

MTTD (Mean Time To Detect)

Mean Time To Detect (MTTD) is a measure of how long a problem exists in an IT deployment before the appropriate parties become aware of it. MTTD is also known as mean time to discover or mean time to identify. MTTD is a common Key Performance Indicator (KPI) for IT incident management. A shorter MTTD indicates that users suffer from IT disruptions for less time compared with a longer MTTD.[2] *See* **Risk tolerance**.

MTTR (Mean Time To Repair)

The time it takes to restore a device to service from a failure.[2] *See* **Risk tolerance**.

MU (Meaningful Use)

The set of standards defined by the Centers for Medicare & Medicaid Services (CMS) Incentive Programs that governs the use of electronic health records and allows eligible providers and hospitals to earn incentive payments by meeting specific criteria. MU Stage 1, data capture and sharing; MU Stage 2, advance clinical processes; and MU Stage 3, improved outcomes.[560]

M

Multicast Network Transmission

Sends IP packets to a group of hosts on a network, allowing for data to be streamed at multiple concurrent locations.[349]

Multidimensional Online Analytical Processing

See **MOLAP**.

Multi-homed host

Computer that is physically connected to multiple data links on the same or different networks. Has two IP addresses assigned to it, one for each network interface.[2]

Multimedia

Applications and technologies that manipulate text, data, images, sound, and full-motion-video objects. Given the usage of multiple formats, multimedia is capable of delivering a stronger and more engaging message than standard text. Multimedia files are typically larger than text-based information and are therefore usually stored on CD-ROMs. Games and educational software commonly use multimedia.[131]

Multiple Station Access Unit

See **MSAU**.

Multiplexing

Technique that involves taking multiple signals and combining them into one signal for transmission over a single medium, such as a telephone line. The input signals can be either analog or digital. The purpose of multiplexing is to enable signals to be transmitted more efficiently over a given communication channel, thereby decreasing transmission costs.[52]

Multiplexer, MultipleXer, or MultipleXor

See **MUX**.

M

Multipurpose Internet Mail Extensions

See **MIME**.

Multisite testing

A testing event that determines the ability of the application or its subsystems to function in multiple geographical settings.[459]

Mutual authentication

Occurs when parties at both ends of a communication activity authenticate each other.[459]

MUX (Multiplexer, MultipleXer, or MultipleXor)

A network device allowing one or more low-speed analog or digital input signals to be selected, combined, and transmitted at a higher speed on a single shared medium or within a single shared device.[52]

Mware vSphere Metro Storage Cluster (VMware vMSC)

A configuration option that allows clustered servers to be spread across geographical locations. This configuration, which is referred to as stretched clustering or distributed clustering, allows an organization to perform load balancing and nondisruptive live migrations between active data centers.[2]

MyHealthEData

An initiative to empower patients by ensuring that they control their health-care data and can decide how their data are going to be used, all while keeping the information safe and secure. The initiative is led by the U.S. Centers for Medicare & Medicaid Services (CMS), the Office of the National Coordinator for Health Information Technology (ONC), the National Institutes of Health (NIH), and the Department of Veterans Affairs (VA).[459]

N

NAC (Network Access Control/ Network Admission Control)

A method of bolstering the security of a proprietary network by restricting the availability of network resources to endpoint devices that comply with a defined security policy.[2]

Name

Designation of an object by a linguistic expression.[459]

Name resolution

See **ARP**.

Named pipes

Allows data to be exchanged from one application to another either over a network or running within the same computer.[146]

NANDA taxonomy II

A taxonomy of nursing diagnostic concepts that identify and code a patient's responses to health problems or life processes.[5]

Narrowband

Refers to data communication and telecommunications tools, technologies, and services that utilize a narrower set or band of frequencies in the communication channel. These utilize the channel frequency that is considered flat or which will use a lesser number of frequency sets.[52]

NAS (Network Attached Storage)

A file server that connects to the network. An NAS contains the file sharing components of a server and generally does not run applications like a

DOI: 10.4324/9781003286028-14

general-purpose computer. However, it is often designed to run NAS-related programs such as backup, cloud synchronization, streaming, surveillance, and other services.[146]

NAT (Network Address Translation)

The technology that maintains the privacy of the addresses of the computers in a home or business network when accessing the Internet. It converts the private addresses that are assigned to the internal computers to one or more public addresses that are visible on the Internet. NAT is an IETF standard that is implemented in a router or firewall as well as in any user's machine that is configured to share its Internet connection.[146]

National Drug Code

See **NDC**.

National Emergency Medical System (EMS) Information System

See **NEMSIS**.

National employer ID

A system for uniquely identifying all sponsors of healthcare benefits.[121]

National Health-Related Items Code

See **NHRIC**.

National Member Body

See **NMB**.

National patient identifier (ID)

A system for uniquely identifying all recipients of healthcare services. Sometimes referred to as the National Individual Identifier or as the healthcare ID.[518]

N

National payer ID

A system for uniquely identifying all organizations that pay for healthcare services.[519]

National Provider File

See **NPF**.

National Provider Identifier

See **NPI**.

National Standard Format

See **NSF**.

National standardization

Standardization that takes place at the level of a specific country.[459]

National standards body

Standards body recognized at the national level that is eligible to be the national member of the corresponding international and regional standards organization.[459]

National Standards System Network

See **NSSN**.

Native format

Default file format that an application uses to create or save files.[52]

Natural language

Spoken or written human language in contrast to a computer language.[39]

Natural Language Processing

See **NLP**.

N

Navigation tools

Allow users to find their way around a website or multimedia presentation. They can be hypertext links, clickable buttons, icons, or image maps.[350]

NCPDP Batch Standard

1. A National Council for Prescription Drug Programs (NCPDP) standard designed for use by low-volume dispensers of pharmaceuticals, such as nursing homes. Use of Version 1 of this standard has been mandated under the Health Insurance Portability and Accountability Act (HIPAA). **2.** Created to use the functionality of the NCPDP Telecommunication Standard. Uses the same syntax, formatting, data set, and rules as the Telecommunication Standard. The Batch Standard wraps the Telecommunication Standard around a detail record; then adds a batch header and trailer. This allows implementers to code one. It was intended that once an NCPDP Data Record (containing the Telecommunication Standard transaction) was built, it could then be wrapped with the Detail Data Record. Then, the Transmission Header Record and the Transmission Trailer Record are created. The Batch consisting of Header, Detail Data Records, and Trailer are formed into a batch file.[211]

NCPDP Telecommunication Standard

1. A National Council for Prescription Drug Programs (NCPDP) standard designed for use by high-volume dispensers of pharmaceuticals, such as retail pharmacies. Use of Version 5.1 of this standard has been mandated under HIPAA. **2.** Developed to provide a standard format for the electronic submission of third-party drug claims. The development of the standard was to accommodate the eligibility verification process at the point-of-sale and to provide a consistent format for electronic claims processing.[211]

NDC (National Drug Code)

The Drug Listing Act of 1972 requires registered drug establishments to provide the Food and Drug Administration (FDA) with a current list of all drugs manufactured, prepared, propagated, compounded, or processed by it for commercial distribution. (*See* Section 510 of the Federal Food, Drug, and Cosmetic Act [Act] [21 U.S.C. § 360].) Drug products are identified and reported using a unique, three-segment number, called the National Drug Code (NDC), which is a universal product identifier for human drugs.[41]

NDIS (Network Driver Interface Specification)

A Windows® specification for how communication protocol programs and network device drivers should communicate with each other. It is an Application Programming Interface (API) standard for network devices.[2, 52]

NEDSS (National Electronic Disease Surveillance System)

An initiative that promotes the use of data and information system standards to advance the development of efficient, integrated, and interoperable surveillance systems at federal, state, and local levels. It is a major component of the Public Health Information Network (PHIN).[20]

Needs assessment

A needs assessment is a systematic process that examines what criteria must be met in order to reach a desired outcome. For example, a laboratory needs assessment might be used to build a business case for replacing software the hospital uses to conduct laboratory tests. The first step in a needs assessment is to conduct a gap analysis that identifies the differences between the current state and the desired state. Once gaps have been identified, changes can be made to improve performance or fix a deficiency.[2]

NEMSIS (National EMS Information System)

Framework for collecting, storing, and sharing standardized Emergency Medical System (EMS) data from states nationwide.[212]

Nesting

Embedding one object in another object of the same type. Nesting is common in programming, where different logic structures are combined.[39]

Net-centric

Depending on the Internet to sell products, manage services or get information.[131]

Net Neutrality

Network neutrality (net neutrality) is a principle that asserts that governments and Internet service providers should not place restrictions on consumers' access

N

to networks participating in the Internet. In general, net neutrality prevents restrictions on content, platforms, sites and equipment, and modes of communication. Network neutrality may also be known as Internet neutrality.[52]

Network

A group of two or more devices, such as computers, printers, modems, servers, etc., that can communicate. Networks allow computers and/or individuals to share information and resources.[52]

Network Access Control

See **NAC**.

Network adapter

Component of a computer's internal hardware that is used for communicating over a network with another computer.[52]

Network Address Translation

See **NAT**.

Network administration

The process of managing all components of network operations. This may include WANs as well as LANs. Network administration includes the design, installation, and evaluation of the network, execution of backups, creation of technical documentation, provision for authentication to access resources, troubleshooting assistance, and administration of network security.[52]

Network architecture

Refers to how network elements are organized in a system and how tasks are allocated between and across those elements. It is the complete physical and logical design of an organization's network infrastructure often represented as a map or schematic diagram. Designed by network architects, managers, administrators, engineers, and design engineers, the network architecture is a network's functional organization and configuration, from a signal's generation to its termination. It details the interconnected physical components of a network (topology), the operational principles, procedures, and protocols governing how the network functions, and the media used for data transmission.[520]

Network Attached Storage

See **NAS**.

Network drive

A disk drive that contains files and applications that is accessible by users in the network.[146]

Network Driver Interface Specification

See **NDIS**.

Network file system

See **NFS**.

Network Information Center

See **NIC**.

Network layer

Third layer of the OSI model. Provides a routing path for network communication. Data are transferred in the form of packets via logical network paths in an ordered format controlled by the network layer.[52]

Network Operating System

See **NOS**.

Network Operation Center

See **NOC**.

Network printer

Shared printer available to network users. Can be connected to a print server, directly connected to the network, or shared from a workstation.[202]

N

Network protocol services

A network protocol is a set of established rules that specify how to format, send, and receive data so that computer network endpoints, including computers, servers, routers, and virtual machines, can communicate despite differences in their underlying infrastructures, designs, or standards.[2]

Network redirector

Software components installed on a client computer that are used for accessing files and other resources. The network redirector sends or redirects requests for file operations from local client applications to a remote server, where the requests are processed.[30]

Network server

A computer designed to act as a central repository and help in providing various resources like hardware access, disk space, and printer access to other computers in the network.[52]

Network Service Provider

See **NSP**.

Network topology

The arrangement of a network including its nodes and connecting lines. The physical topology is the actual geometric layout of workstations. Logical topology refers to the nature of the paths the signals follow between nodes.[2]

Network traffic

The amount of data moving across a network at a given point of time.[52]

Network weaving

A penetration technique in which different communication networks are used to gain access to a data processing system to avoid detection and trace back.[36]

New Work Item Proposal

See **NWIP**.

NFS (Network File System)

A client/server application that allows a computer user to view and option-ally store and update files on a remote computer as if they were on its local disks.[2]

NHRIC (National Health-Related Items Code)

A system for identification and numbering of marketed device packages that is compatible with other numbering systems such as the National Drug Code (NDC) or Universal Product Code (UPC). In the early 1970s, the Drug Listing Branch of the FDA set aside a block of numbers that could be assigned to medical device manufacturers and distributors. Those manufacturers who desire to use the NHRIC number for unique product identification may apply to the FDA for a labeler code.[41]

NIC (Network Interface Card)

A computer hardware component that allows one to access a network.[52] *See* **LAN adapter**.

NIC (Nursing Intervention Classification)

A comprehensive, research-based, standardized classification of interventions that nurses perform. NIC is useful for standardizing clinical documentation, communication of care across settings, integration of data across systems and settings, effectiveness research, productivity measurement, competency evaluation, reimbursement, and curricular design.[213]

NLP (Natural Language Processing)

A subfield of artificial intelligence that helps computers understand, interpret, and manipulate human language. NLP draws from many disciplines, includ-ing computer science and computational linguistics, in its pursuit to fill the gap between human communication and computer understanding.[52]

NMB (National Member Body)

The standards instituted in each country that is a member of the International Organization for Standardization (ISO).[36]

NMDS (Nursing Minimum Data Set)

1. The foundation for nursing languages development that identified nursing diagnosis, nursing intervention, nursing outcomes, and intensity of nursing care as unique nursing components of the Uniform Hospital Discharge Data Set (UHDDS). **2.** Essential set of information items that has uniform definitions and categories concerned with nursing. It is designed to be an abstraction tool or system for collecting uniform, standard, compatible, and minimum nursing data.[5, 48]

NMMDS (Nursing Management Minimum Data Set)

A data set used to describe the environment at unit level of service related to nursing delivery (unit/service, patient/client population, and care delivery method), as well as nursing care resources and financial resources.[5]

NOC (Network Operation Center)

A location from which the operation of a network or Internet is monitored. Additionally, this center usually serves as a clearinghouse for connectivity problems and efforts to resolve those problems.[2]

NOC (Nursing outcome classification)

A comprehensive, standardized classification of patient/client outcomes developed to evaluate the effects of nursing interventions. Standardized outcomes are necessary for documentation in electronic records, for use in clinical information systems, for the development of nursing knowledge, and the education of professional nurses.[213]

Node

1. A connection point that can receive, create, store, or send data along distributed network routes. **2.** Computer or device connected to a network. Also known as a host.[2, 39]

NOI (Notice of Intent)

A document that describes a subject area for which the federal government is considering developing regulations. It may describe the presumably relevant considerations and invite comments from interested parties. These comments can then be used in developing a Notice of Proposed Rulemaking (NPRM) or a final regulation.[113]

Nomenclature

A consistent method for assigning names to elements of a system.[50]

Nomophobia

Refers to a psychological syndrome in which a person is afraid of being out of mobile or cell phone contact. Nomophobia, coined from the term "no-mobile-phone-phobia" during a research study to find out the psychological ramifications and stress level of mobile phone usage on behavior, describes the level of fear generated when a user is unable to communicate through their cell phone.[52]

Nonconformity

Deviation from a specification, a standard, or an expectation.[4]

Non-overwriting virus

A computer virus that appends the virus code to the physical end of a program or moves the original code to another location.[1]

Nonrepudiation

Cryptographic receipts created so that an author of a message cannot falsely deny sending a message. Proof to a third party that only the signer could have created a signature.[1]

Nonuniform Memory Architecture

See **NUMA**.

Nonvolatile data

Data that persist even when power is removed.[1]

N

Normalization

1. The process of creating a uniform and agreed-upon set of standards, policies, definitions, and technical procedures to allow for interoperability. **2.** The process of organizing the fields and tables of a relational database to minimize redundancy.[352, 108]

Normalization services

This service will take various data from different sources, normalize, and store them in the EHR's internal form. This service could be extended to include normal values based on incoming and outgoing profiles.[344]

Normative document

Document that provides rules, guidelines, or characteristics for activities or results.[34]

NOS (Network Operating System)

Operating system that includes special functions for connecting computers and devices into a LAN. The term *network operating system* is generally reserved for software that enhances a basic operating system by adding networking features.[39]

NoSQL

Originally referring to not SQL or non-relational data models, an approach to databases that shifts away from traditional Relational Database Management Systems (RDBMS). NoSQL databases do not rely on the traditional structures in RDBMS (tables, columns, rows, and schemas) and use more flexible data models. It is useful for storing unstructured data, including user and session data, chat, messaging, log data, time series data, Internet of Things (IoT), and device data, etc. Unlike SQL, many NoSQL databases can be scaled horizontally across thousands of servers.[352, 353] *See* **RDBMS** and **SQL**.

Not Invented Here Syndrome (NIH)

Not Invented Here Syndrome (NIHS) is a mindset or corporate culture that favors internally developed products over externally developed products, even when the external solution is superior. NIHS is frequently used in the context of software development, where a programmer will overlook all the attributes of an existing solution simply because it was not produced in-house.[52]

Notice of Intent

See **NOI**.

NPF (National Provider File)

The database envisioned for use in maintaining a national provider registry.[113]

NPI (National Provider Identifier)

1. A system for uniquely identifying all providers of healthcare services, supplies, and equipment. **2.** A Health Insurance Portability and Accountability Act (HIPAA) Administrative Simplification Standard. The NPI is a unique identification number for covered healthcare providers. Covered healthcare providers and all health plans and healthcare clearinghouses must use the NPIs in the administrative and financial transactions adopted under HIPAA. The NPI is a 10-position, intelligence-free numeric identifier (10-digit number). This means that the numbers do not carry other information about healthcare providers, such as the state in which they live or their medical specialty. The NPI must be used in lieu of legacy provider identifiers in the HIPAA standards transactions.[26, 113]

NSF (National standard format)

Generically, this applies to any nationally standardized data format, but it is often used in a more limited way to designate the professional flat file record format used to submit professional claims.[113]

NSP (Network Service Provider)

A company providing consolidated service such as network access and bandwidth by allowing access into its backbone infrastructure or access to its network access points.[52]

N

NSSN (National Standards System Network)

A National Resource for Global Standards is a search engine that provides users with standards-related information from a wide range of developers, including organizations accredited by the American National Standards Institute (ANSI), other U.S. private sector standards bodies, government agencies, and international organizations.[19]

NUMA (Nonuniform Memory Architecture)

A method of configuring a cluster of microprocessors in a multiprocessing system so they can share memory locally, improving performance and the ability of the system to be expanded. NUMA is used in an SMP system.[2] *See* **SMP** and **MPP**.

Nursing informatics

The specialty that integrates nursing science with multiple information and analytical sciences to identify, define, manage, and communicate data, information, knowledge, and wisdom in nursing practice.[5]

Nursing information system

Part of the healthcare information system that deals with nursing documentation, particularly the maintenance of the nursing record.[459]

Nursing Intervention Classification

See **NIC**.

Nursing Management Minimum Data Set

See **NMMDS**.

Nursing Minimum Data Set

See **NMDS**.

Nursing Outcome Classification

See **NOC**.

N

Nutrition informatics

The effective retrieval, organization, storage, and optimum use of information, data, and knowledge for food- and nutrition-related problem-solving and decision-making. Informatics is supported by the use of information standards, processes, and technology.[354]

NwHIN Direct

See **Direct Project**.

NWIP (New Work Item Proposal)

First balloting phase for draft standards and draft technical specifications. During this phase, at least five experts from five participating ISO/TC 215 countries are chosen to work on the document.[36]

Nym Server

A nym server is a pseudonym server that furnishes an untraceable e-mail address. The purpose of this server is to allow users to have usernames (pseudonyms) and send and receive messages without revealing their true identities. Even the nym server operators cannot trace a user's e-mail address.[52]

O

OASIS (Outcome and Assessment Information Set)

A group of data elements that represent core items of a comprehensive assessment for an adult home care patient and form the basis for measuring patient outcomes for purposes of outcome-based quality improvement. This assessment is performed on every patient receiving services from home health agencies that are approved to participate in the Medicare and/or Medicaid programs.[514]

OAuth (Open Authorization)

An open standard for token-based authentication and authorization on the Internet. OAuth allows an end user's account information to be used by third-party services without exposing the user's password.[2]

Object

Any item that can be individually selected and manipulated. In object-oriented programming, an object is a self-contained entity that consists of both data and procedures to manipulate the data.[39]

Object Identifier

See **OID**.

Object Linking and Embedding

See **OLE**.

Object model

Conceptual representation, typically in the form of a diagram, which describes a set of objects and their relationship.[52]

O

Object-oriented

A programming language, system, or software methodology that is built on the concept of logical objects. It works through the creation, utilization, and manipulation of reusable objects to perform a specific task, process, or objective. While conventional programming focuses on functions/behaviors, object-oriented works on the interactions of one or more objects.[52]

Object-Oriented Programming

See **OOP**.

Object Request Broker

See **ORB**.

Object reuse

Reassignment and reuse of a storage medium containing one or more objects after ensuring no residual data remains on the storage medium.[1, 456]

Objective evidence

Objective medical evidence means signs, laboratory findings, or both from a medical source. Objective medical evidence does not include symptoms, diagnoses, or medical opinions.[515]

OC (Optical Carrier)

Used to specify the speed of fiber optic networks conforming to the Synchronous Optical Networking (SONET) standard.[52]

OCR (Optical Character Recognition)

Recognition of printed or written text characters by a computer using a technology that involves photo-scanning of the text, analysis of the image, and translation of the character image into character codes.[2]

OCSP (Online Certificate Status Protocol)

An Internet protocol used for obtaining the revocation status of an SSL certificate.[355]

O

Octal

Base eight numbering system where three bits are used to represent each digit. Uses the 0–7 digits for representations.[2]

Octet

Eight-bit or 1-byte unit of data. Four octets are used in an IP address.[2]

ODA (Open Document Architecture)

An internationally standardized electronic representation for document content and structure. ODA has been ratified by the International Organization of Standardization as ISO 8613. ODA is a critical standard for anyone who wants to share documents without sacrificing control over content, structure, and layout of those documents. It is designed to solve difficulties created by the variety of document formats that exist. An ODA document can be opened, changed, exchanged, stored, and reproduced by any ODA-compliant program.[356]

ODBC (Open Database Connectivity)

A standard application programming interface (API) for accessing Database Management Systems (DBMS).[30]

ODS (Operational Data Store)

A type of database that serves as an interim area for a data warehouse in order to store time-sensitive operational data that can be accessed quickly and efficiently. In contrast to a data warehouse, which contains large amounts of static data, an ODS contains small amounts of information that is updated through the course of business transactions. The general purpose of an ODS is to integrate data from disparate source systems in a single structure using data integration technologies like data virtualization, data federation, or extract, transform, and load. This will allow operational access to the data for operational reporting, master data or reference data management.[39,456]

OEID (Other Entity Identifier)

Data element adopted by the Department of Health and Human Services (HHS) and intended to function as a voluntary identifier for entities that are not health plans, healthcare providers, or individuals.[357]

Offline

Condition of being capable of but not currently connected to a network or other device.[2]

OID (Object Identifier)

A string, usually of numbers, used to uniquely name an object that is registered with the International Organization for Standardization (ISO).[1]

OLAP (Online Analytical Processing)

A high-level concept that describes a category of tools that aid in the analysis of multidimensional queries.[52]

OLE (Object Linking and Embedding)

1. A document standard developed by Microsoft® that allows for the creation of objects within one application and links them into a second application. **2.** OLE is used for compound document management as well as application data transfer via drag-and-drop and clipboard operations.[52]

OLTP (Online Transaction Processing)

A class of systems that supports or facilitates high transaction-oriented applications. OLTP's primary system features are immediate client feedback and high individual transaction volume.[52]

OM (Outbreak Management)

The capture and management of information associated with the investigation and containment of a disease outbreak or public health emergency.[80]

Omaha nursing diagnosis/intervention

See **Omaha system**.

Omaha system (Omaha nursing diagnosis/intervention)

A research-based, comprehensive, and standardized taxonomy designed to enhance practice, documentation, and information management. It consists of three relational, reliable, and valid components: The Problem

Classification Scheme, the Intervention Scheme, and the Problem Rating Scale for Outcomes. The components provide a structure to document client needs and strengths, describe multidisciplinary practitioner interventions, and measure client outcomes in a simple, yet comprehensive, manner.[214]

Ombudsman

An official appointed to investigate individuals' complaints of maladministration.[4]

On-chip applications

Applications that reside on the integrated circuit chip.[459]

Online

Condition of being connected to a network of computers or other devices.[2]

Online Analytical Processing

See **OLAP**.

Online Certificate Status Protocol

See **OCSP**.

Online service provider

Any company, organization, or group that provides an online service. These types of services may include web sites, discussion forums, chat rooms, or web mail. OSPs may also refer to a company that provides dial-up access to the Internet.[39]

Online Transaction Processing

See **OLTP**.

Ontology

1. A specification of a conceptualization of a knowledge domain. An ontology is a controlled vocabulary that describes objects and the relations between them in a formal way and has a grammar for using the vocabulary terms to express something meaningful within a specified domain of interest. The vocabulary is used to make queries and assertions. Ontological commitments are agreements to use the vocabulary in a consistent way for knowledge sharing. Ontologies can include glossaries, taxonomies, and thesauri but normally have greater expressivity and stricter rules than these tools. A formal ontology is a controlled vocabulary expressed in an ontology representation language. **2.** An information model of entities and interactions in some particular domain of knowledge and practices. It serves as a set of concepts, such as things, events, and relations, which are specified in some way in order to create an agreed-upon vocabulary for exchanging information.[516, 2]

OOA (Out of Area)

Not within the market geographic bounds.[46]

OON (Out of Network)

In healthcare, this refers to physicians, hospitals, or other providers who do not participate in an insurer's provider network.[359]

OOP (Object-Oriented Programming)

A style of programming characterized by the identification of classes of objects closely linked with the methods (functions) with which they are associated. It also includes ideas of inheritance of attributes and methods. It is a technique based on a mathematical discipline called "abstract data types" for storing data with the procedures needed to process that data. OOP offers the potential to evolve programming to a higher level of abstraction.[517] *See* **SOA**.

OOP (Out of Pocket)

Expenses for medical care that are not reimbursed by insurance. Out-of-pocket costs include deductibles, coinsurance, and copayments for covered services plus all costs for services that are not covered.[218]

Open access

The free, immediate, online availability of research outputs with the rights to use these articles fully in the digital environment, though there may be some restrictions on use in terms of licensing and copyrights.[217]

Open Authorization

See **OAuth**.

Open source

Software in which the source code is available free to users, who can read and modify the code.[82]

Open systems architecture

In telecommunications, the layered hierarchical structure, configuration, or model of a communications or distributed data processing system that (1) enables system description, design, development, installation, operation, improvement, and maintenance to be performed at a given layer or layers in the hierarchical structure; (2) allows each layer to provide a set of accessible functions that can be controlled and used by the functions in the layer above it; (3) enables each layer to be implemented without affecting the implementation of other layers; and (4) allows the alteration of system performance by the modification of one or more layers without altering the existing equipment, procedures, and protocols at the remaining layers.[459]

Open systems

A computer system that combines portability and interoperability and makes use of open software standards. It typically refers to a computer system that is interoperable between different vendors and standards, allowing for modularity so that hardware and software need not be attached to a single vendor or platform.[52]

Open Systems Interconnection

See **OSI**.

Operating System

See **OS**.

Operating system (O/S) interface layer

The software layer that allows the user to interact directly with the operating system. There are two distinct types: the text-based Command-Line Interface

O

(CLI) and icon-based Graphical User Interface (GUI). Also known as user interface.[360]

Operational Data Store

See **ODS**.

Operator

A symbol that tells the compiler or interpreter to perform specific mathematical, relational, or logical operation and produce the final result.[52]

Optical card

A form of optical storage in which the medium is in credit-card form, intended for uses similar to those of a magnetic-stripe card with higher capacity.[459]

Optical Carrier

See **OC**.

Optical Character Recognition

See **OCR**.

Optical disk

1. An electronic data storage medium that is read or recorded using a low-powered laser beam. There has been a constant succession of optical disk formats, first in CD formats, followed by a number of DVD formats. Optical disk offers a number of advantages over magnetic storage media. An optical disk holds much more data. **2.** A disk read or written by light, generally laser light, such a disk may store video, audio, or digital data.[2, 52]

Optical resolution

The built-in resolution of a scanning device. Contrast with "interpolated resolution" or "digital resolution" which enhances an image by software. Both resolutions are given as dots per inch (dpi), thus a 2400 dpi scanner can be the true resolution of the machine or a computed resolution.[459]

Optimization

An act, process, or methodology of making something (such as a design, system, or decision) as fully perfect, functional, or effective as possible.[459]

Opt-in

Mechanism that states data collection and/or use methods and provides user choice to accept such collection and/or use.[2]

Opt-out

Mechanism that states data collection and/or use methods and provides user choice to decline such collection and/or use.[2]

ORB (Object Request Broker)

A middleware application component that uses the Common Object Request Broker Architecture (CORBA) specification, enabling developers to make application calls within a computer network. ORB is an agent that transmits client/server operation invocations in a distributed environment and ensures transparent object communication.[52]

Order

Request for a certain procedure or activity to be performed.[9]

Order Entry System

See **CPOE**.

Organized healthcare arrangement

Arrangement in which participants need to share protected health information about their patients to manage and benefit the common enterprise. A key component of any organized healthcare arrangement is that the individual who obtains services from the arrangement has an expectation that the arrangement is integrated and that the participants jointly manage their operations.[28]

O

Organizational Interoperability

See **Interoperability**.

OS (Operating System)

Software that manages the computer's memory and processes, as well as all of its software and hardware.[52]

OSI (Open Systems Interconnection)

A reference model to the protocols in the seven-layer data communications networking standards model and services performed at each level. It is used by systems open to interconnection and communication with other systems. Each layer makes up a conceptual collection of services provided to the layers above and below it. The OSI standard is defined by the International Organization for Standardization (ISO). The seven layers from the bottom are physical, data link, network, transport, session, presentation, and application.[2]

Out of Area

See **OOA**.

Out of Network

See **OON**.

Out of Pocket

See **OOP**.

Outbreak Management

See **OM**.

Outcome and Assessment Information Set

See **OASIS**.

O

Outcome measure

A parameter for evaluating the results of an activity, program, system, treatment, or process and their comparison with the intended or projected results.[4]

Out-of-band

Activity that occurs outside of a telecommunications frequency band or channel.[2]

Outpatient

Patient who is not hospitalized overnight but who visits a hospital, clinic, or associated facility for diagnosis or treatment.[29]

Output

The direct result of the interaction of inputs and processes in the system; the types and qualities of goods and services produced by an activity, project, or program.[459]

OWL (Web Ontology Language)

Designed for use by applications that need to process the content of information instead of just presenting information to humans. OWL facilitates greater machine interpretability of web content than that supported by Extensible Markup Language (XML), Resource Description Framework (RDF), and RDF Schema (RDF-S) by providing additional vocabulary along with formal semantics.[61]

P

P

P2P (Peer-to-Peer) network

A network structure in which the computers share processing and storage tasks as equivalent members of the network.[2]

Packet

In computer networks, a container or box that carries data over a TCP/IP network and internetworks. A packet is the most fundamental logical arbitration of data that is passed over a network. A packet normally represents the smallest amount of data that can traverse over a network at a single time. A TCP/IP network packet contains several pieces of information, including the data it is carrying, source destination IP addresses, and other constraints required for quality of service and packet handling.[52]

Packet-filtering firewall

A technique used to control network access by monitoring outgoing and incoming packets and allowing them to pass or halt based on the source and destination Internet Protocol (IP) addresses, protocols, and ports.[52]

Packet header

A group of fields in a network packet that describes its content, all required destination addresses to reach its target, and all source information necessary to allow a response to come back.[459]

Packet Internet Groper

See **PING**.

Packet sniffing

Packet Sniffer is a hardware or software that connects to a network to monitor, analyze, log, and capture all the network traffic. Historically, packet sniffers were small portable appliances that can be plugged into the network to

DOI: 10.4324/9781003286028-16

P

sniff traffic on-demand if there is a suspected network issue. Packet sniffing can also be done using a laptop and packet sniffing software. The inspection of packets being transmitted in a network. Packet sniffing is sometimes used as a synonym for *"packet capture"* and both do the same thing—it is simply a matter of scale. Packet capture is often seen as being the "big brother" of packet sniffing. Packet sniffing is typically done on-demand, using portable packet sniffer devices, and usually only collects small volumes of traffic. Packet capture solutions, on the other hand, are usually deployed as a permanent component of network infrastructure. They are designed to record much larger volumes of traffic and at much higher speeds than packet sniffer.[561]

Packet switched

The type of network in which relatively small units of data called packets are routed through a network based on the destination address contained within each packet. Breaking communication down into packets allows the same data path to be shared among many users in the network.[2]

Packet switching

A digital network transmission process in which data are broken into suitably sized pieces or blocks for fast and efficient transfer via different network devices. When a computer attempts to send a file to another computer, the file is broken into packets so that it can be sent across the network in the most efficient way. These packets are then routed by network devices to the destination.[52]

PACS (Picture Archiving and Communication System)

Medical imaging technology used for storing, retrieving, presenting, and sharing images produced by various medical hardware modalities, such as x-ray, CT scan, MRI, and ultrasound machines. The DICOM standard is commonly used to enable the sharing of images and other medical information within PACS technologies and other information systems.[2] *See* **RIS**.

PAN (Personal-Area Network)

Interconnects technology devices, typically within the range of a single user, which is approximately 10 meters or 33 feet. This type of network is designed to enable devices in a Small Office or Home Office (SOHO)

P

environment to communicate and share resources, data, and applications, either wired or wirelessly. PANs typically consist of laptops, smartphones, tablets, wearables, printers, and entertainment devices. These devices are generally interconnected using some form of wireless technology. This kind of PAN could also be connected to the Internet or other networks without wires. The concept of a PAN was first developed by Thomas Zimmerman and other researchers at MIT's Media Lab and was later supported by IBM's Almaden research lab.[2]

PAP (Password Authentication Protocol)

User authentication protocol that does not encrypt the data and sends the password and username to the authentication server as plain text. PAP is very vulnerable to being read from the Point-to-Point Protocol (PPP) data packets exchanged between the authentication server and the user's machine.[52]

Parallel branching

Specifies that two or more tasks are executed independently of each other.[459] *See* **Exclusive branching**.

Parallel split

The divergence of a branch into two or more parallel branches, each of which executes concurrently.[459]

Parameter

A value that is used to control the operation of a function or that is used by a function to compute one or more outputs.[1]

Parameter RAM

See **PRAM**.

Parser

A routine that analyzes a continuous flow of text-based input and breaks it into its constituent parts. Program that is part of the compiler, and parsing is part of the compiling process. Parsing happens during the analysis stage

P

of compilation. In parsing, code is taken from the preprocessor, broken into smaller pieces, and analyzed so other software can understand it. The parser does this by building a data structure out of the pieces of input.[2]

Parser services

This service will parse the messages that come in through the protocol layer. The parser will provide support for input formats such as XML, flat files positional, and flat file fixed field length.[459]

Partitioning code

Applications can be broken into three logical parts: presentation, logic, and data. These are areas in which the program can be separated to facilitate execution of each logical piece on a different machine. Each segment is known as a partition. For example, the thin-client web model requires that interface presentation be handled by the browser, application logic by the web server and other application servers, and data by a database server. Developers are responsible for determining where the separation occurs.[138]

PAS (Publicly Available Specification)

Standards from the International Organization for Standardization (ISO) which are freely available for standardization purposes. PAS is protected by ISO copyright.[459]

Passive attack

An attack against an authentication protocol where the attacker intercepts data traveling along the network but does not alter the data.[1]

Password

A string of characters used to authenticate an identity or to verify access authorization.[1]

Password authentication protocol

See **PAP**.

P

Password cracking

A process of recovering passwords stored in a computer system or transmitted over a network.[1]

Patch

A software update comprised of code inserted (or patched) into the code of an executable program. Typically, a patch is installed into an existing software program. Patches are often temporary fixes between full releases of a software package. Patches may do any of the following: fix software bugs, install new drivers, address new security vulnerabilities, address software stability issues, and upgrade the software.[52]

Patent Internet Groper

See **PING**.

Patient Administration System (PAS)

Captures, stores, and manages essential patient details including name, address, date of birth, and comprehensive records of a patient's interactions with the hospital, across both outpatient and inpatient services. A contemporary PAS is expected to be user-friendly and sufficiently robust to support an array of patient management tasks such as overseeing patient admissions, transfers, and discharges. It should provide a streamlined way to monitor patient movements and manage both ward attendances and appointments.[562]

Patient Care Data Set

See **PCDS**.

Patient-Centered Data Home

See **PCDH**.

Patient-Centered Medical Home

See **PCMH**.

P

Patient-centric

1. Putting the patient first in an open and sustained engagement with the patient to respectfully and compassionately achieve the best experience and outcome for that person and their family. **2.** Technology that puts the patient at the center of the digital experience to drive patient empowerment and engagement.[364,365]

Patient Classification (PCS)

Also known as a patient acuity system, it is a tool used for managing and planning the allocation of nursing staff in accordance with nursing care needs. PCS helps determine workload requirements and staffing needs. There are different kinds of PCS available, but the three most commonly used are descriptive, checklist, and time standards.[563]

Patient identifier domain

A single system or a set of interconnected systems that all share a common identification scheme for patients. Such a scheme includes (1) a single identifier-issuing authority; (2) an assignment process of an identifier to a patient; (3) a permanent record of issued patient identifiers with associated traits; and (4) a maintenance process over time. The goal of patient identification is to reduce errors.[459]

Patient portal

A secure online website that gives patients convenient, 24-hour access to personal health information from anywhere with an Internet connection. Using a secure username and password, patients can view health information such as recent doctor visits, discharge summaries, medications, immunizations, allergies, and lab results. Some patient portals also allow you to securely message your doctor, request prescription refills, schedule non-urgent appointments, check benefits and coverage, update contact information, make payments, download and complete forms, and view educational materials.[564]

Patient Protection and Affordable Care Act

See **PPACA** and **ACA**.

P

Patient record

Systematic record of the history of the health of a patient kept by a physician, nurse, or other healthcare practitioner.[459]

Patient registry

1. A database maintained by a hospital, provider's office, or health plan that allows the identification of patients according to a condition, diagnosis, demographic characteristics, and other factors. Patient registries can help providers better coordinate care for their patients, monitor treatment and progress, and improve overall quality of care. **2.** Patient registries are also maintained by local and state governments (e.g., immunization registry), specialty societies (cardiovascular disease registry of the American College of Cardiology), and some patient support organizations.[459]

Patient-specific data

All data captured and stored in the system pertaining to a patient, such as clinical assessments, medications, and insurance information.[459]

Patient Unified Lookup System for Emergencies

See **PULSE**.

Payer

A third-party entity that pays for or underwrites coverage for healthcare expenses. A payer may be an insurance company, a health maintenance organization (HMO), a Preferred Provider Organization (PPO), an accountable care organization (ACO), a government agency, or an agency, such as a Third-Party Administrator (TPA).[459]

PC (Personal Computer)

A small computer designed for an individual user. All personal computers are based on the microprocessor technology that enables manufacturers to put an entire CPU on one chip.[39]

P

PCB (Printed Circuit Board)

The board base for physically supporting and wiring the surface-mounted and socketed components in most electronics. PCBs can be single layer for simple electronic devices. Printed circuit boards for complex hardware, such as computer graphics cards and motherboards, may have up to 12 layers.[2] Also known as a Printed Wiring Board (PWB) or electronic wiring board.

PCDH (Patient-Centered Data Home)

A cost-effective, scalable method of exchanging patient data among Health Information Exchanges (HIEs). A PCDH is based on triggering episode alerts, which notify providers a care event has occurred outside of the patient's "home" HIE, and confirms the availability and the specific location of the clinical data, enabling providers to initiate a simple query to access real-time information across state and regional lines and the care continuum. PCDH is an initiative of the Strategic Health Information Exchange Collaborative (SHIEC).[366]

PCDS (Patient Care Data Set)

A compilation of pre-coordinated terms used in patient records to record patients' problems, therapeutic goals, and care actions.[459]

PCMH (Patient-Centered Medical Home)

A model of the organization of primary care facilities that delivers the core functions of primary healthcare. The medical home encompasses five functions: (1) comprehensive care, (2) patient-centered, (3) coordinated care, (4) accessible services, and (5) quality and safety.[367]

PDC (Primary Domain Controller)

A service on a Windows® server that manages security for its local domain. Every domain has one PDC, which contains a database of usernames, passwords, and permissions. The PDC also provides a time service for the network and typically obtains the time from an edge router, which gets its time from the Internet.[565]

P

PDF (Portable Document Format)

A file format used to present and exchange documents reliably, independent of software, hardware, or operating system.[368]

PDF 417 (Portable Data File 417)

A two-dimensional (2D) stacked barcode symbology capable of encoding over a kilobyte of data per label. It is currently maintained by ISO/IEC. Large amounts of text and data can be stored securely and inexpensively when using the PDF417 symbology. The printed symbol consists of several linear rows of stacked codewords. Each codeword represents 1 of 929 possible values from one of three different clusters. A different cluster is chosen for each row, repeating after every three rows. The data are encoded using one of three compaction modes: Text compaction mode, Binary compaction mode, and Numeric compaction mode.[566]

PDMP (Prescription Drug Monitoring Program)

An electronic database that tracks controlled substance prescriptions, generally at the state level. PDMPs can provide practitioners and health authorities timely information about prescribing and patient behaviors.[80, 456]

PDP (Policy Decision Point)

The system entity that evaluates applicable policy and renders an authorization decision.[24]

Peer-to-Peer network

See **P2P**.

Penetration

A security event, or a combination of multiple security events, that constitutes a security incident in which an intruder gains, or attempts to gain, access to a system or system resource without having authorization to do so.[156]

PEP (Policy Enforcement Point)

The system entity that performs access control by making decision requests and enforcing authorization decisions.[24] *See* **ACS**.

Per seat license

A software license based on the number of users who have access to the software. The fee is paid per user, or "per seat," or per concurrent user, through negotiations with a vendor to allow a fixed number of copies of copyrighted software.[459] *See* **Site license**.

Perioperative Nursing Data Set

See **PNDS**.

Peripheral

Alternatively called an **auxiliary device**, a **peripheral** is a hardware input device or output device that gives a computer additional functionality. Peripheral devices, however, are not essential for the computer to perform its basic tasks; they are an enhancement to the user's experience.[335]

Permanent Virtual Circuit

See **PVC**.

Persistent data

Data that are stored on a permanent basis. Persistent data are stored in a database on disk, SSD, or magnetic tape.[146]

Person Identification Service

See **PIDS**.

Personal Computer

See **PC**.

Personal connected health

Relates to elements including, but not limited to, an individual's unique characteristics and needs as well as the ability to engage with health-related information and services. It encompasses individuals taking ownership of their own health through wellness and prevention. An important aspect of personal connected health is the enabling nature of technology to empower the person to make sustainable health behavior change by gaining visibility and insights into personal health information.[369]

Personal Health Management Tool

See **PHMT**.

Personal Health Record

See **PHR** and **ePHR**.

Personal Identification Number

See **PIN**.

Personal Identification Verification

See **PIV**.

Personal-Area Network

See **PAN**.

Pervasive computing

Pervasive computing, also called ubiquitous computing, is the growing trend of embedding computational capability (generally in the form of microprocessors) into everyday objects to make them effectively communicate and perform useful tasks in a way that minimizes the end user's need to interact with computers as computers. Pervasive computing devices are network-connected and constantly available. Unlike desktop computing, pervasive computing can occur with any device, at any time, in any place, and in any data format across any network and can hand tasks from one computer to another as, for example, a user moves from his car to his office. Pervasive computing devices have evolved to include laptops, notebooks, smartphones, tablets, wearable devices, and sensors (e.g., fleet management and pipeline components, lighting systems, and appliances). Often considered the successor to mobile computing, ubiquitous computing generally involves wireless communication and networking technologies, mobile devices, embedded systems, wearable computers, Radio Frequency ID (RFID) tags, middleweight, and software agents. Internet capabilities, voice recognition, and artificial intelligence are also considered ubiquitous computing. *See* **Ubiquitous computing**.[2]

Pharmacy informatics

The scientific field that focuses on medication-related data and knowledge within the continuum of healthcare systems, including its acquisition, storage, analysis, use, and dissemination, in the delivery of optimal medication-related patient care and health outcomes. Pharmacy informatics is a subset of health informatics that leverages both clinical expertise and knowledge about information technology to improve medication management processes and drug administration safety.[567]

Pharmacy Information System (PIS)

A system that provides pharmacy staff the necessary application environment to practice the profession of pharmacy, often includes the ordering, procurement, preparation, dispensing, and monitoring portions of the medication use process.[568]

Pharmacy management system

An application that provides support to the pharmacy department from an operational, clinical, and management perspective, helping to optimize patient safety, streamline workflow, and reduce operational costs.[459]

PHI (Protected Health Information)

Any individually identifiable health information, whether oral or recorded in any form or medium that is created or received by a healthcare provider, health plan, public health authority, employer, life insurer, school or university, or healthcare clearinghouse; and relates to the past, present, or future physical or mental health or condition of an individual; the provision of healthcare to an individual; or the past, present, or future payment for the provision of healthcare to an individual. Any data transmitted or maintained in any other form or medium by covered entities, including paper records, fax documents, and all oral communications or any other form (i.e., screen prints of eligibility information, printed e-mails that have identified individual's health information, claim, billing information, or hard copy of a birth or death certificate). Protected health information excludes school records that are subject to the Family Educational Rights and Privacy Act and employment records held in the Department of Homeland Security's role as an employer.[20] *See* **Individually Identifiable Health Information**.

PHIN (Public Health Information Network)

The Centers for Disease Control and Prevention (CDC) vision for advancing fully capable and interoperable information systems in the many organizations that participate in public health. PHIN is a national initiative to implement a multi-organizational business and technical architecture for public health information systems.[80]

PHIN-MS (Public Health Information Network-Messaging System)

A protocol for secure transmission of data, based on the ebXML model. Developed and supported by the Centers for Disease Control and Prevention (CDC), the protocol allows for rapid and secure messages to send sensitive health information over the Internet to other local, state, and federal organizations, as well as the CDC.[80]

Phishing

Deceptive computer-based means to trick individuals into disclosing sensitive personal information.[1]

PHMT (Personal Health Management Tool)

A set of functions that assist a consumer in managing his or her health status or healthcare.[459]

PHR (Personal Health Record)

1. An electronic Personal Health Record ("ePHR") is a universally accessible, layperson-comprehensible lifelong tool for managing relevant health information, promoting health maintenance, and assisting with chronic disease management via an interactive, common data set of electronic health information and e-health tools. The PHR is owned, managed, and shared by the individual or his or her legal proxy(s) and must be secure to protect the privacy and confidentiality of the health information it contains. It is not a legal record unless so defined and is subject to various legal limitations. **2.** Usually used when referring to the version of the health/medical record

P

owned by the consumer/patient. **3.** An electronic record of health-related information on an individual that conforms to nationally recognized interoperability standards and that can be drawn from multiple sources while being managed, shared, and controlled by the individual.[459]

Physical access control

An automated system that controls an individual's ability to access a physical location, such as a building, parking lot, office, or other designated physical space. A physical access control system requires validation of an individual's identity through some mechanism, such as a Personal Identification Number (PIN), card, biometric, or other token prior to providing access. It has the capability to assign different access privileges to different persons, depending on their roles and responsibilities in an organization.[1]

Physical layer

First layer in the OSI model. Defines the physical characteristics of a link between communicating devices, such as wireless transmission, cabling, cabling standards and types, connectors and types, network interface cards, and more.[52]

Physical safeguards

The physical measures, policies, and procedures to protect a covered entity's or business associate's electronic information system and related buildings and equipment from natural and environmental hazards and unauthorized intrusion.[459]

Physical security

The protection of personnel, hardware, software, networks, and data from physical actions and events that could cause serious loss or damage to an enterprise, agency, or institution. This includes protection from fire, flood, natural disasters, burglary, theft, vandalism, and terrorism.[2]

Picosecond

One trillionth of a second.[2]

Picture Archiving and Communication System

See **PACS**.

P

PIDS (Person Identification Service)

Specification defined by Object Management Group that organizes person ID management functionality to meet healthcare needs. PIDS is designed to support the assignment of IDs within a particular ID domain and the correlation of IDs among multiple ID domains. It supports the searching and matching of people, independent of a matching algorithm.[459]

Piggybacking

Unauthorized access to a wireless LAN. The usual purpose of piggybacking is to gain free network access but can slow down data transfer for legitimate network users.[2]

PIM (Platform Independent Model)

A model of a software or business system that is independent of the specific technological platform used to implement it. For example, HTML defines a model for hypertext that includes concepts such as title, headings, and paragraphs. This model is not linked to a specific operating system or web browser and is, therefore, being successfully implemented on a variety of different computing systems. The term is most frequently used in the context of model-driven architectures.[459]

PIN (Personal Identification Number)

Code used to authenticate or identify a user.[52]

PING (Packet Internet Groper)

Packet Internet or Inter-Network Groper is a basic Internet program that allows a user to test and verify if a particular destination IP address exists and can accept requests in computer network administration. The acronym was contrived to match the submariners' term for the sound of a returned sonar pulse. Ping is also used diagnostically to ensure that a host computer the user is trying to reach is operating. Any Operating System (OS) with networking capability, including most embedded network administration software, can use ping. PING sends an Internet Control Message Protocol (ICMP) echo request to the destination and waits for a reply. Used to test and debug a network as well as to see if a user is online.[2]

PIP (Policy Information Point)

Point that can provide external information to a policy decision point.[459] *See* **ACS**.

PIV (Personal Identification Verification)

A physical artifact (e.g., identity card and "smart" card) issued to an individual that contains stored identity credentials (e.g., photograph, cryptographic keys, and digitized fingerprint representation) so that the claimed identity of the cardholder can be verified against the stored credentials by another person (human readable and verifiable) or an automated process (computer readable and verifiable).[1]

PIX (Patient Identifier Cross-referencing)

Provides cross-referencing of patient identifiers from multiple patient identifier domains. These patient identifiers can then be used by identity consumer systems to correlate information about a single patient from sources that know the patient by different identifiers.[27] *See* **Profile**. Note: PIX is an Integrating the Healthcare Enterprise (IHE) Profile.

Pixel (Picture Element)

A word invented from *picture element*. The basic unit of programmable color on a computer display or in a computer image. Pixels are the smallest unit in a digital display. Up to millions of pixels make up an image or video on a device's screen. Each pixel comprises a subpixel that emits a Red, Green, and Blue (RGB) color, which displays at different intensities. The RGB color components make up the gamut of different colors that appear on a display or computer monitor. When referencing the resolution of a display, numbers like 1920 × 1080 refer to the number of pixels.[2]

PKC (Public Key Certificate)

X.509 Public Key Certificates (PKCs), which bind an identity and a public key; the identity may be used to support identity-based access control decisions after the client proves that it has access to the private key that corresponds to the public key contained in the PKC.[72]

P

PKI (Public Key Infrastructure)

1. Technology, facilities, people, operational procedures, and policy to support public key-based security mechanisms. It is an enabler for these encryption and digital signatures. **2.** Infrastructure used in the relation between a key holder and a relying party that allows a relying party to use a certificate relating to the key holder for at least one application using a public key-dependent security service and that includes a certification authority, a certificate data structure, means for the relying party to obtain current information on the revocation status of the certificate, a certification policy, and methods to validate the certification practice.[72]

Plain text

Any string (i.e., finite sequence of characters) that consists entirely of printable characters (i.e., human-readable characters) and, optionally, a very few specific types of control characters (e.g., characters indicating a tab or the start of a new line). Plain text usually refers to text that consists entirely of the ASCII printable characters and a few of its control characters. ASCII, an acronym for American standard code for information interchange, is based on the characters used to write the English language as it is used in the United States. It is the de facto standard for character encoding (i.e., representing characters by numbers) that is utilized by computers and communications equipment to represent text, and it (or some compatible extension of it) is used on most computers, including nearly all personal computers and workstations.[225]

Plan of care (also interdisciplinary plan of care)

A plan, based on data gathered during patient assessment, that identifies the participant's care needs, describes the strategy for providing services to meet those needs, documents treatment goals and objectives, outlines the criteria for terminating specified interventions, and documents the participant's progress in meeting goals and objectives. Patient-specific policies and procedures, protocols, clinical practice guidelines, clinical paths, care maps, or a combination thereof may guide the format of the plan in some organizations. The care plan may include care, treatment, habilitation, and rehabilitation.[459]

Platform Independent Model

See **PIM**.

P

Plenum cable

Cable designed specifically for use within a building's plenum space. Because the plenum space is used for air circulation, it is critical that anything used inside the plenum not impact air quality or increase the danger of fire. For these reasons, plenum spaces require cables that are plenum rated, meaning that they meet higher standards like being more resistant to fire and producing less smoke in the case of a fire.[569]

Plotter

A printer that interprets commands from a computer to make line drawings on paper with one or more automated pens. Unlike a regular printer, the plotter can draw continuous point-to-point lines directly from vector graphics files or commands.[2]

Plug-and-play

"PnP" is an automatic process that configures computer peripherals as soon as they are connected. The user does not need to manually install drivers or configure device settings, as those tasks are handled instead by the operating system. Plug-and-play is the standard behavior for connecting new devices to Windows, macOS, and Linux computers, as well as mobile devices and tablets.[570]

Plug-in

A plug-in is an element of a software program that can be added to provide support for specific features or functionality. Plug-ins are commonly used in Internet browsers but also can be utilized in numerous other types of applications.[52]

PMP (Point-to-Multipoint Communication)

A communications architecture that is accomplished through a distinct and specific form of one-to-many connections, offering several paths from one single location to various locations. PMP communication is commonly used in telecommunications. It is often used for establishing private enterprise connectivity to offices in remote locations, long-range wireless backhaul solutions for sites, and last-mile broadband access. Point-to-multipoint is generally abbreviated as PTMP, P2MP, or PMP.[52]

PNDS (Perioperative Nursing Data Set)

A standardized nursing vocabulary of nursing diagnoses, nursing interventions, and nurse-sensitive patient outcomes, which addresses the perioperative patient experience from preadmission to discharge.[5]

PNG (Portable Network Graphics)

A file format for image compression that, in time, is expected to replace the Graphics Interchange Format (GIF) that is widely used on today's Internet. Unlike GIF, which involves licensing or other legal considerations for its usage, the PNG format was developed by an Internet committee expressly to be patent-free.[2]

Point-of-care system

Hospital information system that includes bedside workstations or other devices for capturing and entering data at the locations where patients receive care.[571]

Point-of-Presence

See **POP**.

Point-to-Multipoint Communication

See **PMP**.

Point-to-Point Protocol

See **PPP**.

Point-to-Point Tunneling Protocol

See **PPTP**.

Policy

Overall intention and direction as formally expressed by management.[459]

Policy Decision Point

See **PDP**.

Policy enforcement point

See **PEP**.

Policy Information Point

See **PIP**.

POP (Point-of-Presence)

A point at which two or more different networks or communication devices build a connection with each other. POP mainly refers to an access point, location, or facility that connects to and helps other devices establish a connection with the Internet.[52] *See* **ISP**.

POP3 (Post Office Protocol)

The primary protocol behind e-mail communication. POP works through a supporting e-mail software client that integrates POP for connecting to the remote e-mail server and downloading e-mail messages to the recipient's computer. POP uses the TCP/IP protocol stack for network connection and works with Simple Mail Transfer Protocol (SMTP) for end-to-end e-mail communication, where POP pulls messages and SMTP pushes them to the server. As of 2012, Post Office Protocol is in its third version known as POP 3 and is commonly used in most e-mail client/server communication architecture.[52]

Portability

1. The capability of a program to be executed on various types of data processing systems with little or no modification and without converting the program to a different language. **2.** The ability of a program to run on systems with different architectures.[459]

Portable Document Format

See **PDF**.

Portable Network Graphics

See **PNG**.

P

Portable Open Systems Interface

See **POSIX**.

Portal

See **Web portal**.

Porting

Moving software and data files to other computer systems.[459]

POSIX (Portable Open Systems Interface)

IEEE standard for operating system interface and environment, including a command interpreter (or "shell"), and common utility programs to support application portability at the source code level. It is intended to be used by both application developers and system implementers.[371]

Post office protocol

See **POP3**.

Post-coordination

1. Describes representation of a concept using a combination of two or more codes. **2.** Using more than one concept from one or many formal systems, combined using mechanisms within or outside the formal systems.[77,114]

Postproduction

Part of the lifecycle of the product after the design has been completed and the medical device has been manufactured and released.[459]

PowerPC

Microprocessor developed by IBM, Apple, and Motorola that employs a Reduced Instruction Set Computing (RISC). The architecture is open standard.[2]

PPACA (Patient Protection and Affordable Care Act) (Public Law 111-148)

Legislation that focuses on provisions to expand healthcare coverage, control healthcare costs, and improve the healthcare delivery system.[459] *See* **ACA**.

PPP (Point-to-Point Protocol)

Method for transporting IP packets over a serial link between the user and the ISP. PPP establishes the session between the user's computer and the ISP using its own Link Control Protocol (LCP).[459]

PPTP (Point-to-Point Tunneling Protocol)

A protocol used to create a Virtual Private Network (VPN) over the Internet. Remote users can access their corporate networks via any ISP that supports PPTP on its servers.[459]

Practice management system

Term used to refer to a management system used to automate particular aspects of practice activities related to transactions and workflows, such as capturing patient demographics, scheduling and registration, and revenue cycle management.[3]

PRAM (Parameter RAM)

A battery-powered form of RAM where vital system information such as the date and time are stored. It also contains computer configuration information. Because PRAM is powered by an internal battery, the information is not lost when the computer powers off.[2]

Precision medicine

An emerging approach for disease treatment and prevention that takes into account individual variability in genes, environment, and lifestyle in striving to deliver the right treatment at the right time to the right person. The National Institutes of Health leads the All of Us Research Program, which is working to build a one million person research cohort to pioneer research on this approach. The research phases emphasize engaged research participants, responsible data sharing, and privacy protections.[459, 228]

Predicate migration

Steps taken to enable preexisting data retrieval predicates (including queries, standard reports, and decision support protocols) to be converted or utilized in a system using a mappable vocabulary.[77]

Predictive modeling

A commonly used statistical technique to predict future behavior. Predictive modeling solutions are a form of data-mining technology that works by analyzing historical and current data and generating a model to help predict future outcomes. In predictive modeling, data are collected, a statistical model is formulated, predictions are made, and the model is validated (or revised) as additional data become available.[68]

Preferred term

The term that is deemed to be the most clinically appropriate way of expressing a concept in a clinical record. Preferred term is one of the three types of terms that can be indicated by the description type field.[77]

Preparedness

Activities, programs, and systems developed and implemented prior to an incident that may be used to support and enhance mitigation of, response to, and recovery from disruptions, disasters, or emergencies.[87] Also known as readiness.

Prescribing system

An information system used in healthcare for processing the prescription of medication by a provider; such a system links the provider with pharmacies and others engaged in prescription of medication.[459] See **e-Prescribing**.

Prescription Drug Monitoring Program

See **PDMP**.

Presentation layer

Sixth layer of the Open Systems Interconnection (OSI) model. It is used to present data to the application layer (layer 7) in an accurate, well-defined, and standardized format.[52]

P

Prevention

Measures that enable an organization to avoid, preclude, or limit the impact of a disruption.[87]

Preventive action

Action to eliminate the cause of a potential nonconformity.[87]

PRG (Procedure-Related Group)

A classification system that groups patients based on the procedure rather than the diagnosis. This classification is based on the main procedures performed in the course of a patient's treatment. A potential benefit from this classification system includes incentives for the use of advanced technology. A drawback that currently exists in current models is that non-interventional procedures are still reimbursed on a per diem basis.[459]

Primary Domain Controller

See **PDC**.

Primary key

A key in a relational database that is unique for each record. It is a unique identifier. Primary keys typically appear as columns in relational database tables.[2]

Print server

A software application, network device, or computer that manages print requests from many different users by holding them in a queue until they can be printed. Print servers are used in both large enterprise and small office networks.[2]

Printed Circuit Board

See **PCB**.

Privacy

See **Health information privacy**.

P

Privacy consent policy identifier

An affinity domain-assigned Object Identifier (OID) that uniquely identifies the affinity domain, privacy consent policy. There is one unique OID for each privacy consent policy within the affinity domain.[459]

Privacy impact assessment

A Privacy Impact Assessment (PIA) is a method for identifying and assessing privacy risks throughout the development lifecycle of a program or system. These assessments state what Personally Identifiable Information (PII) is collected and explain how that information is maintained, protected, and shared. Regardless of where PII is stored, its privacy must be protected from data breaches and other cyberattacks. Information systems must have safeguards, such as PIAs, in place to protect data from privacy violations, especially in situations where privacy issues can be part of the cyber event.[2]

Privacy officer

Appointed by a covered entity to be responsible for developing and implementing policies and procedures for complying with the health information privacy requirements of the Health Insurance Portability and Accountability Act.[20]

Privacy rights

Specific actions that an individual can take, or request to be taken, with regard to the uses and disclosures of their information.[20]

Private key

A bit of code that is paired with a public key to set off algorithms for text encryption and decryption. It is created as part of public key cryptography during asymmetric-key encryption and used to decrypt and transform a message into a readable format.[52]

Privilege

The rights granted to a single user or group of users who operate a computer. Administrative privileges allow a user the right to make any and all changes to the computer, including setting up accounts for other users. User-level privileges are more restricted.[1]

Privileged information

Alternative term for confidential information.[4]

Problem-oriented medical record

Healthcare record in which all data may be linked to a list of health problems of an individual patient.[459]

Procedure-Related Group

See **PRG**.

Process

An instance of a program running in a computer. It is close in meaning to task, a term used in some operating systems. In Unix and some other operating systems, a process is started when a program is initiated (either by a user entering a shell command or by another program). Like a task, a process is a running program with which a particular set of data is associated so that the process can be kept track of. An application that is being shared by multiple users will generally have one process at some stage of execution for each user. A process can initiate a subprocess, which is called a *child* process (and the initiating process is sometimes referred to as its *parent*). A child process is a replica of the parent process and shares some of its resources but cannot exist if the parent is terminated. Processes can exchange information or synchronize their operation through several methods of Interprocess Communication (IPC). [2]

Process model

A number of tasks that have to be carried out and a set of conditions that determine the order of the tasks.[459]

Process standard

Standard that specifies requirements to be fulfilled by a process to establish fitness for purpose.[459]

Processor

The term *processor* has generally replaced the term central processing unit. *See* **CPU**.[459]

Product standard

Standard that specifies requirements to be fulfilled by a product or groups of products to establish fitness for purpose.[459]

Profile

A set of selected parameters that describes a particular implementation of a standard or standards.[459]

Program

A set of instructions that can be recognized by a computer system and used to carry out a set of processes.[2]

Program manager

The person ultimately responsible for the overall procurement, development, integration, modification, operation, and maintenance of an IT system.[1]

Programmable Read-Only Memory

See **PROM**.

Project Gemini

A joint initiative of HL7 and IHE to align efforts to achieve interoperability by leveraging the HL7 FHIR® standard and capitalizing on the individual strengths of the two standards development organizations. The initiative aims to create new robust, jointly owned specifications.[9]

Project management

A set of principles, methods, tools, and techniques for effective planning of work, thereby establishing a sound basis for effective scheduling, controlling, and preplanning in the implementation and management of programs and products.[459]

PROM (Programmable Read-Only Memory)

A computer memory chip that can be programmed once it is created. Once the PROM is programmed, the information written is permanent and cannot be erased or deleted.[335]

Promoting Interoperability Performance Category for Merit-based Incentive Payment System (MIPS) Eligible Clinicians

Performance category defined under the Medicare Access and CHIP Reauthorization Act of 2015 (MACRA) as part of the Quality Payment Program's (QPP) MIPS. This performance category focuses on interoperability, improving reporting flexibility, relieving burden, and placing an emphasis on measures that require the electronic exchange of health information between providers and patients. This may include sharing test results, visit summaries, and therapeutic plans with the patient and other facilities to coordinate care. This program replaces the Medicare EHR Incentive Program for eligible clinicians, commonly known as Meaningful Use.[372] *See* **QPP, MACRA,** and **MIPS**.

Proof of concept

A demonstration, the purpose of which is to verify that certain concepts or theories have the potential for real-world application.[52]

Proof of elapsed time

A blockchain network consensus mechanism algorithm that prevents high resource utilization and high energy consumption and keeps the process more efficient by following a fair lottery system. Each participating node in the network is required to wait for a randomly chosen time period, and the first one to complete the designated waiting time wins the new block. Each node in the blockchain network generates a random wait time and goes to sleep for that specified duration. The one to wake up first—that is, the one with the shortest wait time—commits a new block to the blockchain, broadcasting the necessary information to the whole peer network. The same process then repeats for the discovery of the next block.[18]

Proof of stake

In distributed ledger technology and cryptocurrency, the concept that a person can mine or validate block transactions according to how many coins he or she holds.[18]

Proof of work

A puzzle that is designed to take time to complete. In order to impede spammers, a proof-of-work algorithm has been suggested as a mandatory technique when sending e-mail. For example, if every e-mail message required just 30 seconds more to process, a compromised computer could never quickly unleash millions of messages. Cryptocurrency mining also uses a proof-of-work algorithm.[459, 18]

Protected Health Information

See **PHI**.

Protocol

A special set of rules using end points in a telecommunication connection for communication. Protocols exist at several levels.[459]

Protocol stack

A group of protocols that are running concurrently that are employed for the implementation of network protocol suite.[52]

Proximity

Refers to a technology used to provide physical access control. This technology uses a contactless interface with a card reader.[1]

Proxy server

A server that services the requests of its clients by forwarding those requests to other servers. Hardware security tool to help protect an organization against security breaches.[1]

P

Psychotherapy notes

Recorded in any medium by a healthcare provider who is a mental health professional, documenting or analyzing the contents of conversation during a private counseling session, or a group, joint, or family counseling session, when notes are separated from the rest of the individual's record.[20]

Public health agency

An agency that performs or conducts one or more of the following essential functions that characterize public health programs, services, or activities: (1) monitor health status to identify community health problems; (2) diagnose and investigate health problems and health hazards in the community; (3) inform, educate, and empower people about health issues; (4) mobilize community partnerships to identify and solve health problems; (5) develop policies and plans that support individual and community health efforts; (6) enforce laws and regulations that protect health and ensure safety; (7) link people to needed personal health services and ensure the provision of healthcare when otherwise unavailable; (8) ensure a competent public health and personal healthcare workforce; (9) evaluate effectiveness, accessibility, and quality of personal and population-based health services; and (10) research for new insights and innovation solutions to health problems.[572]

Public Health Information Network

See **PHIN**.

Public information

Any information, regardless of form or format, that an agency discloses, disseminates, or makes available to the public.[459]

Public key

An encryption key that can be made public or sent by ordinary means such as an e-mail message.[52]

Public Key Certificate

See **PKC**.

P

Public key cryptography

Sometimes referred to as asymmetric cryptography, it is a class of cryptographic protocols based on algorithms. This method of cryptography requires two separate keys, one that is private or secret, and one that is public. Public key cryptography uses a pair of keys to encrypt and decrypt data to protect it against unauthorized access or use. Network users receive a public and private key pair from certification authorities. If other users want to encrypt data, they get the intended recipient's public key from a public directory. This key is used to encrypt the message and to send it to the recipient. When the message arrives, the recipient decrypts it using a private key, to which no one else has access. The Rivest-Sharmir-Adleman (RSA) algorithm is the cryptography system that is used for public key cryptography, which is commonly used when sending secure, sensitive data over an insecure network like the Internet. The RSA algorithm is popular because it allows both public and private keys to encrypt messages, so their confidentiality and authenticity remain intact. Public key cryptography differs from "secret key cryptography," which uses the same key to encrypt and decrypt.[573]

Public Key Infrastructure

See **PKI**.

Publicly Available Specification

See **PAS**.

PULSE (Patient Unified Lookup System for Emergencies)

A nationwide health IT disaster response platform that can be deployed at the city, county, or state level to authenticate disaster healthcare volunteer providers. It allows disaster workers to query and view patient documents from all connected healthcare organizations.[435]

Push

Delivery of information on the web that is initiated by the information server rather than by the information user. The opposite of query.[2]

PVC (Permanent Virtual Circuit)

A connection that is permanently established between two or more nodes in frame relay and Asynchronous Transfer Mode (ATM)-based networks. It enables the creation of a logical connection on top of a physical connection between nodes that communicate frequently or continuously. AA point-to-point connection that is established ahead of time. A group of PVCs defined at the time of subscription to a particular service is known as a "virtual private network" (VPN).[52] *See* **SVC** and **VPN**.

Q

QA (Quality Assurance)

An ongoing planned and systematic effort to ensure confidence that processes and products meet established goals.[231]

QAPI (Quality Assessment Performance Improvement)

The coordinated application of two mutually reinforcing aspects of a quality management system: Quality Assurance (QA) and Performance Improvement (PI). QAPI takes a systematic, comprehensive, and data-driven approach to maintaining and improving safety and quality in nursing homes while involving all nursing home caregivers in practical and creative problem-solving.[26]

QASP (Quality Assurance Surveillance Plan)

The key government-developed surveillance process document, and applied to Performance-Based Service Contracting (PBSC). The QASP is used for managing contractor performance assessment by ensuring that systematic quality assurance methods validate that contractor quality control efforts are timely, effective, and are delivering the results specified in the contract or task order. The QASP directly corresponds to the performance objectives and standards (i.e., quality, quantity, and timeliness) specified in the Performance Work Statement (PWS).[373]

QC (Quality Control)

A procedure or set of procedures intended to ensure that a manufactured product or performed service adheres to a defined set of quality criteria or meets the requirements of the client or customer.[2]

QCDR (Qualified Clinical Data Registry)

An entity that collects clinical data from MIPS clinicians (both individual and groups) and submits it to CMS on their behalf for purposes of MIPS. The

DOI: 10.4324/9781003286028-17

QCDR reporting option is different from a qualified registry because it is not limited to measures within the Quality Payment Program.[26]

QDM (Quality Data Model)

An information model that defines concepts used in quality care and is intended to enable automation of EHR use.[179]

QE (Quality Entity)

The CMS Qualified Entity (QE) Program (also known as the Medicare Data Sharing for Performance Measurement Program) enables organizations to receive Medicare claims data under Parts A, B, and D for use in evaluating provider performance. Organizations approved as QEs are required to use the Medicare data to produce and publicly disseminate CMS-approved reports on provider performance.[26]

QHP (Qualified Health Plan)

An insurance plan that is certified by the Health Insurance Marketplace, provides essential health benefits, follows established limits on cost-sharing (like deductibles, copayments, and out-of-pocket maximum amounts), and meets other requirements under the Affordable Care Act. All qualified health plans meet the Affordable Care Act requirement for having health coverage, known as "minimum essential coverage." [521]

QI (Quality Improvement)

A systematic, formal approach to the analysis of practice performance and efforts to improve performance.[374]

QIDAM (Quality Improvement Domain Analysis Model)

Also known as HL7 Domain Analysis Model: Health Quality Improvement; a conceptual model for health data for use in the health quality domain. It harmonizes the requirements for patient data use in quality measurement and clinical decision support enabling a single model to be used in both aspects of quality improvement. This model will facilitate the development

Q

of unified knowledge representation standards such as structured formats for quality measures and clinical decision support knowledge artifacts.[9]

QIN/QIO (Quality Innovation Network— Quality Improvement Organizations)

Assist patients and families, providers, and communities to make care safer, support active engagement and self-management of chronic conditions, eliminate health disparities, promote best practices for healthy living, improve access to care, and make care affordable.[26]

QIO (Quality Improvement Organization)

A group of health quality experts, clinicians, and consumers organized to improve the quality of care delivered to people.[26]

QMF (Query Management Facility)

Ad-hoc query tool to extract data from some mainframe systems.[46]

QMR (Quick Medical Reference)

QMR is used to help diagnose adult diseases by providing access to information about the most common diseases seen by internists, including medical histories, symptoms, physical signs, and laboratory test results. QMR is a clinical diagnostic tool, which consists of descriptions of over 750 diseases. QMR is used by physicians in hospital and office practices. QMR is no longer being maintained or updated by the National Library of Medicine.[522]

QMS (Quality Management System)

A collection of business processes focused on consistently meeting customer requirements and enhancing their satisfaction. The QMS is aligned with an organization's purpose and strategic direction.[375]

QoS (Quality of Service)

1. A negotiated contract between a user and a network provider that renders some degree of reliable capacity in the shared network. **2.** A network's ability to achieve maximum bandwidth and deal with other network performance elements like latency, error rate, and uptime. Quality of service also involves controlling and managing network resources by setting priorities for specific types of data (video, audio, and files) on the network.[2,52]

Q

QP (Qualified Professional)

One who by possession of a recognized degree, certificate, or professional standing or who by extensive knowledge, training, and experience has successfully demonstrated his or her ability to solve or resolve problems relating to the subject matter, the work, or the project.[376]

QP (Qualifying APM participant)

Clinicians who participate in an Advanced Alternative Payment Model (APM) as a part of the Quality Payment Program (QPP) are considered Qualifying APM Participants.[26]

QPP (Quality Payment Program)

A quality incentive payment program implemented by the Centers for Medicare & Medicaid Services (CMS) as part of the Medicare Access and CHIP Reauthorization Act of 2015 (MACRA). QPP replaced the Sustainable Growth Rate (SGR) previously used to define payment for Medicare services. Clinicians have two tracks to choose from the Merit-based Incentive Payment System (MIPS) or the Advanced Alternative Payment Models track. QPP started on January 1, 2017.[26] *See* **MACRA, MIPS,** and **ACI**.

QPS (Quality Positioning System)

A web-based tool developed by the National Quality Forum (NQF) to help people select and use NQF-endorsed measures. It allows a user to search for NQF-endorsed measures in a number of ways: export search results and view types of measures. Using QPS, a user can find NQF-endorsed measures on particular topics, track and get reminders about measures that are important to them, provide feedback on measures, and see which measures others are using.[179]

QR codes (Quick Response codes)

High-density, two-dimensional bar codes that are readable by mobile phones and computer cameras with the correct software.[523]

Q

QRDA (Quality Reporting Data Architecture)

The data submission standard used for a variety of quality measurement and reporting initiatives. QRDA creates a standard method to report quality measure results in a structured, consistent format and can be used to exchange eCQM data between systems.[474]

QRUR (Quality and Resource Use Report)

Report that shows how payments under Medicare Part B Fee-For-Service (FFS) will be adjusted based on quality and cost.[26]

Qualified certificate

In public key infrastructure security information technology, a qualified certificate is used to describe a certificate with a certain qualified status within applicable governing law.[72]

Qualified Clinical Data Registry

See **QCDR**.

Qualified Health Plan

See **QHP**.

Qualified Professional

See **QP**.

Qualifying Participant

See **QP**.

Quality

The totality of features and other characteristics of a product or service that bear on its ability to satisfy stated or implied needs.[524]

Quality and Resource Use Report

See **QRUR**.

Q

Quality Assessment Performance Improvement

See **QAPI**.

Quality Assurance Surveillance Plan

See **QASP**.

Quality Control

See **QC**.

Quality Data Model

See **QDM**.

Quality design

Systematic approach to service design that identifies the key features needed or desired by both external and internal clients, creates design options for the desired features, and then selects the combination of options that will maximize satisfaction within available resources.[378]

Quality Entity

See **QE**.

Quality Improvement

See **QI**.

Quality Improvement Domain Analysis Model

See **QIDAM**.

Quality Improvement Organization

See **QIO**.

Quality indicator

An agreed-upon process for outcome measurement that is used to determine the level of quality achieved. A measurable variable, or characteristic, that can be used to determine the degree of adherence to a standard or achievement of quality goals.[525]

Quality Information and Clinical Knowledge

See **QUICK**.

Quality Innovation Network—Quality Improvement Organizations

See **QIN/QIO**.

Quality management

An ongoing effort to provide services that meet or exceed customer expectations through a structured, systematic process for creating organizational participation in planning and implementing quality improvements.[378]

Quality Management System

See **QMS**.

Quality measures

Mechanisms used to assign a quantity to the quality of care by comparison to a criterion.[526]

Quality monitoring

The collection and analysis of data for selected indicators that enable managers to determine whether key standards are being achieved as planned and are having the expected effect on the target population.[91]

Quality of care

Degrees to which healthcare services for individuals and populations increase the likelihood of desired health outcomes and are consistent with current professional knowledge. The National Academy of Medicine (formerly the Institute of Medicine) defines quality as having the following domains: effectiveness, efficiency, equity, patient centeredness, safety, and timeliness.[91]

Quality of Service
See **QoS**.

Quality Payment Program
See **QPP**.

Quality Positioning System
See **QPS**.

Quality Reporting Data Architecture
See **QRDA**.

Quantity
The extent, size, or sum of countable or measurable discrete events, objects, phenomenon expressed as a numerical value.[4]

Quantum Computing
Quantum computing is an area of research and development that focuses on how to use the unique properties of quantum mechanics to perform mathematical calculations faster and solve computational problems more efficiently than is currently possible with classical computers that use Boolean logic.[52]

Query
1. The process by which a web client requests specific information from a web server, based on a character string that is passed along. **2.** A request for information that results in the aggregation and retrieval of data.[39]

Query Management Facility
See **QMF**.

Queue
Defined as a linear data structure that is open at both ends, and the operations are performed in First In First Out (FIFO) order. We define a queue

Q

to be a list in which all additions to the list are made at one end and all deletions from the list are made at the other end. The element which is first pushed into the order, and the operation is first performed on that.[527]

Queuing services

A **message** refers to any data that are transferred between two applications. For example, *System A* may send a message to *System B* to perform a specific task, such as to send an e-mail. A **queue** refers to an order or line of these tasks that are waiting to be handled. A **messaging queuing service** is the system that pushes a message into a queue by providing an asynchronous communications protocol.[528]

QUICK (Quality Information and Clinical Knowledge)

The QICore model defines a set of HL7 FHIR® profiles that provide a physical implementation of the Quality Information and Clinical Knowledge (QUICK) logical model. The goal is to have a single logical data model (QUICK), as well as a single logical processing language (CQL), for CDS and clinical quality measurement (CQM).[9]

Quick response codes

See **QR codes**.

R

RA (Registration Authority)

1. Body responsible for assigning healthcare coding scheme designators and for maintaining the Register of Health Care Coding Schemes as described in a standard. **2.** Entity that is responsible for the identification and authentication of certificate subjects but that does not sign or issue certificates (i.e., an RA is delegated certain tasks on behalf of a CA).[459] *See* **CA**.

RAD (Rapid Application Development)

An Application Development (AD) approach that includes small teams—typically two to six people, but never more than 10—using Joint Application Development (JAD) and iterative-prototyping techniques to construct interactive systems of low to medium complexity within a timeframe of 60 to 120 days.[482]

Radio Frequency Identification

See **RFID**.

Radio frequency interference

Disruption of the normal functionality of a satellite due to the interference of radio astronomy. Radio frequency interference can disrupt and disturb the normal functioning of electronic and electrical devices, a subset of electromagnetic interference.[52] *See* **EMI**.

Radiology Information System

See **RIS**.

RAID (Redundant Array of Independent Disks)

A method of storing data on multiple hard disks. When disks are arranged in a RAID configuration, the computer sees them all as one large disk.

R

However, they operate much more efficiently than a single hard drive. Since the data are spread out over multiple disks, the reading and writing operations can take place on multiple disks at once, which can speed up hard-drive access time significantly.[2]

RAM (Random Access Memory)

1. Primary storage of data or program instructions that can directly access any randomly chosen location in the same amount of time. **2.** The data in RAM stay there only as long as your computer is running. When you turn the computer off, RAM loses its data.[2]

Random Access Memory

See **RAM**.

Ransomware

An ever-evolving form of malware designed to encrypt files on a device, rendering any files and the systems that rely on them unusable. Malicious actors then demand ransom in exchange for decryption. These resources are designed to help individuals and organizations prevent attacks that can severely impact business processes and leave organizations without the data they need to operate and deliver mission-critical services.[574,83]

Rapid Application Development

See **RAD**.

RAS (Remote Access Server)

A type of server that provides a suite of services to remotely connected users over a network or the Internet. It operates as a remote gateway or central server that connects remote users with an organization's internal Local Area Network (LAN). [52]

RBAC (Role-Based Access Control)

A method of regulating access to computer or network resources based on the roles of individual users within an enterprise. Roles are defined according to job competency, authority, and responsibility within the enterprise.[2]

R

RDBMS (Relational Database Management System)

A collection of programs and capabilities that enable IT teams and others to create, update, administer, and otherwise interact with a relational database. RDBMSes store data in the form of tables, with most commercial relational database management systems using Structured Query Language (SQL) to access the database. However, since SQL was invented after the initial development of the relational model, it is not necessary for RDBMS use. The RDBMS is the most popular database system among organizations across the world. It provides a dependable method of storing and retrieving large amounts of data while offering a combination of system performance and ease of implementation. RDBMS also includes functions that maintain the security, accuracy, integrity, and consistency of the data. *See* **DBMS**.[2]

RDF (Resource Description Framework)

A general framework for representing interconnected data on the web. RDF statements are used for describing and exchanging metadata, which enables standardized exchange of data based on relationships. RDF is used to integrate data from multiple sources. An example of this approach is a website that displays online catalog listings from a manufacturer and links products to reviews on different websites and to merchants selling the products. The semantic web is based on the use of the RDF framework to organize information based on meanings.[2]

Readiness

See **Preparedness**.

Read-Only Memory

See **ROM**.

Realm

A sphere of authority, expertise, or preference that influences the range of components required or the frequency with which they are used. A realm may be a nation, an organization, a professional discipline, a specialty, or an individual user.[77]

Real-Time Location System

See **RTLS**.

Real-time operating system

Operating system that guarantees a certain capability within a specific time constraint.[2]

REC (Regional Extension Center)

Organizations previously established by the Office of the National Coordinator (ONC) through the Health Information Technology for Economic and Clinical Health (HITECH) Act (enacted as part of the American Recovery and Reinvestment Act of 2009) to serve local communities by providing technical assistance, guidance, and information on best practices to support and accelerate healthcare providers' efforts to become meaningful users of certified Electronic Health Records (EHRs).[11]

Record

1. A database entry that may contain one or more variables. **2.** A collection of data items arranged for processing by a program. **3.** Document stating results achieved or providing evidence of activities performed.[73, 2, 87]

Records Management

See **RM**.

Recovery Point Objective

See **RPO**.

Recovery Time Objective

See **RTO**.

Redaction tools

Software used to edit content and, thereby, selectively and reliably remove information from documents or websites before sharing the remaining content with someone who is not authorized to see the entire original document.[482]

Reduced Instruction Set Computer

See **RISC**.

Redundant Array of Independent Disks

See **RAID**.

Reference architecture

Also known as enterprise architecture, it is a template or a set of documents. This template makes it easy for software architects and developers to address specific problems. For example, it could contain definitions for commonly used words, an **architecture blueprint** with elements and relationships, data models, communication standards, and recommended processes. The idea is to make the job easier for anyone investigating problems or implementing solutions in that domain. In short, enterprise architecture is a resource you can refer to while designing and implementing complex technology solutions.[575]

Reference Information Model

See **RIM**.

Reference model

An abstract framework for understanding significant relationships among the entities of some environments and for the development of consistent standards or specifications supporting that environment. It is based on a small number of unifying concepts and may be used as a basis for education and explaining standards to a non-specialist.[459]

Reference Model for Open Distributed Processing

See **RM-ODP**.

Reference terminology

A terminology in which each term has a formal computer-processable definition that supports meaning based retrieval and aggregation. SNOMED–CT is a reference terminology.[77]

R

Reference Terminology Model

See **RTM**.

Regional Extension Center

See **REC**.

Regional Health Information Organization

See **HIE**.

Registration Authority

See **RA**.

Registry

Directory-like system that focuses on managing data pertaining to one conceptual entity. In an EHR, registries store, maintain, and provide access to peripheral information not categorized as clinical in nature but required to operationalize an EHR. The primary purpose of a registry is to respond to searches using one or more predefined parameters in order to find and retrieve a unique occurrence of an entity.[459] *See* **Disease registry**.

Regression model

Provides a function that describes the relationship between one or more independent variables and a response, dependent, or target variable. Regression models predict the value of one variable based on one or more other variables. These models are powerful tools that allow predictions about past, present, or future events to be made with information about past or present events.[234]

Regression testing

1. The process of testing changes to computer programs to make sure that the older programming still works with the new changes. Regression testing is a normal part of the program development process. **2.** Repeated testing of an already tested program, after modification, to discover any defects introduced or uncovered as a result of the changes in the software being tested or in another related or unrelated software components.[2,]

Relational database

A collection of data items organized as a set of formally described tables from which data can be accessed or reassembled in many different ways without having to reorganize the database tables.[2]

Relational database management system

See **RDBMS**.

Relational online analytical processing

See **ROLAP**.

Relational model

A method of structuring data using relations, grid-like mathematical structures consisting of columns and rows. In this model, all data must be stored in relations with keys to order data or relate data to other relations.[2]

Relationship

A connection, association, or involvement between two or more items or concepts. An association between a source concept and a destination concept. The type of association is indicated by a reference to an attribute concept.[44,77]

Relative Value Unit

See **RVU**.

Release Of Information

See **ROI**.

Reliability

The probability that a product, system, or service will perform its intended function adequately for a specified period of time or will operate in a defined environment without failure.[381]

R

Relying party

1. An entity that relies on the validity of the binding of the subscriber's name to a public key to verify or establish the identity and status of an individual, role, or system or device; the integrity of a digitally signed message; the identity of the creator of a message; or confidential communications with the subscriber. **2.** An entity that relies upon the subscriber's authenticator(s) and credentials or a verifier's assertion of a claimant's identity, typically to process a transaction or grant access to information or a system. **3.** A party that depends on the validity of the digital signature process. **4.** Recipient of a certificate who acts in reliance on that certificate and/or digital signature verified using that certificate.[72]

Remote access

Remote access is the ability for an authorized person to access a computer or network from a geographical distance through a network connection. Remote access enables remote users to access files and other system resources on any devices or servers that are connected to the network at any time. This increases employee productivity and enables employees to better collaborate with colleagues around the world.[2]

Remote access software

A type of software that enables a local user to connect to and access a remote computer, server, or network. It enables connectivity of two or more computers/network nodes that are on separate networks and/or in different geographical locations.[52]

Remote hosting

A computer that resides in some distant location from which data are retrieved. It typically refers to a server in a private network or the public Internet. However, it can also refer to a user's PC in another location that is accessed over the Internet for file transfer or remote control operation.[459]

Remote network monitor

See **RMON**.

R

Remote patient monitoring (RPM)

A subcategory of homecare telehealth that allows patients to use mobile medical devices or technology to gather Patient-Generated Health Data (PGHD) and send it to healthcare professionals. The use of digital technologies to collect medical and other forms of health data from individuals in one location and electronically transmit that information securely to healthcare providers in a different location for assessment and recommendations.[2]

Removable media

See **Electronic media**.

Rendering

The process of generating a final digital product from a specific type of input. The term usually applies to graphics and video, but it can refer to audio as well.[73]

Repeater

A network device that retransmits a received signal with more power and to an extended geographical or topological network boundary than what would be possible with the original signal. Also known as a signal booster.[52]

Repetition Separator

Used in some data fields to separate multiple occurrences of a field. It is used only where specifically authorized in the descriptions of the relevant data fields.[9]

Replication

The process of copying data from one location to another.[2]

Repository

1. An implementation of a collection of information along with data access and control mechanisms, such as search, indexing, storage, retrieval, and security. **2.** A generic term for a storehouse of data. **3.** A database of

R

information about application software that includes authors, data elements, inputs, processes, outputs, and interrelationships. **4.** A database of digital certificate information. The repository is maintained by the Certificate Authority (CA) and is queried to find out if a certificate is valid, has expired, or has been revoked.[459] *See* **CA.**

Representational state transfer

See **REST**.

Repudiation

Act, intention, or threat of disowning or rejection of an agreement already accepted or agreed to.[4]

Request For Information

See **RFI**.

Request for proposal

See **RFP**.

Requirements

A set of needs, functions, and demands that need to be satisfied by a particular software implementation or specification.[459]

Resident virus

A type of computer virus that hides and stores itself within the computer memory, which then allows it to infect any file that is run by the computer, depending on the virus' programming.[52]

Residual risk

The risk that remains after efforts to identify and eliminate some or all types of risk have been made. Residual risk is important for several reasons. First to consider is that residual risk is the risk "left over" after security controls and process improvements have been applied. This means that residual risk is something organizations might need to live with based on the choices they have made regarding risk mitigation. Or they could opt to transfer the residual risk, for example, by purchasing insurance to offload the risk to an insurance company. Another reason residual risk consideration is important is for compliance and regulatory requirements: The International Organization for Standardization 27001 stipulates this risk calculation. Finally, residual risk is important to calculate for determining the appropriate types of security controls and processes that get priority over time.[2]

Resolution

The number of pixels (individual points of color) contained on a display monitor, expressed in terms of the number of pixels on the horizontal axis and the number on the vertical axis. The sharpness of the image on a display depends on the resolution and the size of the monitor. The higher the density, the sharper the display.[2]

Resource Description Framework

See **RDF**.

Response plan (or incident response plan)

The documented collection of procedures and information developed, compiled, and maintained in readiness for use in an emergency.[87]

Response team (or incident response team)

Group of individuals responsible for developing, executing, rehearsing, and maintaining the response plan, including the processes and procedures.[87] *See* **CERT**.

Response time

The time period between a terminal operator's completion of an inquiry and the receipt of a response. Response time includes the time taken to transmit the inquiry, process it by the computer, and transmit the response back to the terminal. Response time is frequently used as a measure of the performance of an interactive system.[138]

REST (Representational state transfer)

1. A style of software architecture for distributed systems such as the World Wide Web. REST has emerged as a predominant web service design model. REST facilitates the transaction between web servers by allowing loose coupling between different services. REST is less strongly typed than its counterpart, SOAP. The REST language is based on the use of nouns and verbs and has an emphasis on readability. Unlike SOAP, REST does not require XML parsing and does not require a message header to and from a service provider. This ultimately uses less bandwidth. **2.** Architectural style for developing web services. REST is popular due to its simplicity and the fact that it builds upon existing systems and features of the Internet's HTTP in order to achieve its objectives, as opposed to creating new standards, frameworks, and technologies.[2]

Retention

The continued storage of an organization's data for compliance, business, legal, or other reasons.[2]

Return On Investment

See **ROI**.

Revocation

The process of permanently ending the operational period of a certificate from a specified time forward. Generally, revocation is performed when a private key has been compromised. Revocation most often refers to the revocation of a digital security certificate.[52]

RFI (Request For Information)

A standard business process whose purpose is to collect written information about the capabilities of various suppliers. RFIs are intended to be written by customers and sent to potential suppliers. An RFI is typically the first and most broad series of requests intended to narrow down a list of potential vendor candidates.[2]

R

RFID (Radio Frequency Identification)

Refers to technologies that use wireless communication between an object (or tag) and an interrogating device (or reader) to automatically track and identify such objects. The tag transmission range is limited to several meters from the reader. A clear line of sight between the reader and tag is not necessarily required.[52]

RFP (Request For Proposal)

Document that solicits proposal, often made through a bidding process, by an agency or company interested in procurement of a commodity, service, or valuable asset to potential suppliers to submit business proposals.[2]

Rich Text Format

See **RTF**.

RIM (Reference Information Model)

A static model of health and healthcare information as viewed within the scope of HL7 standards development activities. It is the combined consensus view of information from the perspective of the HL7 working group and the HL7 international affiliates. The RIM is the ultimate source from which all HL7 Version 3.0 protocol specification standards draw their information-related content.[9]

Ring network

A Local Area Network (LAN) in which the nodes (workstations or other devices) are connected in a closed loop configuration.[2]

RIS (Radiology Information System)

1. A networked software system for managing medical imagery and associated data. An RIS is especially useful for tracking radiology imaging orders and billing information and is often used in conjunction with PACS and VNAs to manage image archives, record-keeping, and billing. **2.** A type of information system that is used to create, store, and manage radiological data and images of patients.[2,52] *See* **PACS**.

RISC (Reduced Instruction Set Computer)

A microprocessor that is designed to perform a smaller number of computer instruction types, so it can operate at a higher speed, performing more millions of instructions per second, or MIPS. Since each instruction type that a computer performs requires additional transistors and circuitry, a larger list or set of computer instructions tends to make the microprocessor more complicated and operate slower.[2]

Risk

1. Combination of the probability of an event and its consequences.
2. An activity or factor that may increase the likelihood of disease or harm.
3. Effect of uncertainty on objectives. A deviation from the expected—positive and/or negative. **4.** The expectation of loss. It is a function of the probability and the consequences of harm.[87,459] *See* **Residual risk**.

Risk analysis

Process to comprehend the nature of risk and to determine the level of risk.[87]

Risk assessment

1. Overall process of risk identification, risk analysis, and risk evaluation
2. A report that shows an organization's vulnerabilities and the estimated cost of recovery in the event of damage. It also summarizes defensive measures and associated costs based on the amount of risk the organization is willing to accept (the risk tolerance).[87,459]

Risk control

Process in which decisions are made and measures implemented by which risks are reduced to, or maintained within, specified levels.[18]

Risk estimation

1. Expressing duration, intensity, magnitude, and reach of the potential consequences of a risk in quantifiable or dollar value (monetary) terms.
2. Description of the probability that an organism exposed to a specific dose of substance will develop an adverse effect.[4]

R

Risk evaluation

Determination of risk management priorities through establishment of qualitative and/or quantitative relationships between benefits and associated risks.[4]

Risk management

1. The culture, processes, and structures that are directed toward the effective management of potential opportunities for adverse events. **2.** Coordinated activities to direct and control an organization with regard to risk. **3.** The optimal allocation of resources to arrive at a cost-effective investment in defensive measures within an organization. Risk management minimizes both risk and costs. **4.** Risk management in healthcare comprises the clinical and administrative systems, processes, and reports employed to detect, monitor, assess, mitigate, and prevent risks.[87,576]

Risk tolerance

Organization's readiness to bear the risk after risk treatments in order to achieve its objectives.[1,87] *See* **MTBF, MTTD,** and **MTTR**.

Risk treatment

Process of selection and implementation of measures to modify risk.[576,577]

RM (Records Management)

Technologies that enable organizations to enforce policies and rules for the retention and disposition of content required for documenting business transaction in addition to automating the management of their record-retention policies. These technologies, implemented with well-formulated and consistently enforced RM strategies and policies, form an essential part of the organization-wide lifecycle management of records. RM principles and technologies apply to both physical and electronic content.[2]

RM-ODP (Reference Model for Open Distributed Processing)

1. A reference model in computer science, which provides a co-coordinating framework for the standardization of Open Distributed Processing (ODP).

R

It supports distribution, interworking, platform and technology independence, and portability, together with an enterprise architecture framework for the specification of ODP systems. RM-ODP, also named ITU-T Rec. X.901-X.904 and ISO/IEC 10746, is a joint effort by the International Organization for Standardization (ISO), the International Electrotechnical Commission (IEC), and the Telecommunication Standardization Sector (ITU-T). **2.** An object modeling approach to describe distributed systems. Two structuring approaches are used to simplify the problems of design in large complex systems: five "viewpoints" provide different ways of describing the system. Each viewpoint is associated with a language, which can be used to describe systems from that viewpoint.[9]

RMON (Remote network monitor)

A standard specification that facilitates the monitoring of network operational activities through the use of remote devices known as monitors or probes. RMON assists network administrators with efficient network infrastructure control and management.[52]

Roadmap

A flexible technique that is widely used within industry to support strategic and long-range planning. The approach provides a structured (and often graphical) means for exploring and communicating the relationships between evolving and developing markets, products, and technologies over time. It is proposed that the roadmapping technique can help companies survive in turbulent environments by providing a focus for scanning the environment and a means of tracking the performance of individuals, including potentially disruptive technologies. Technology roadmaps are deceptively simple in terms of format, but their development poses significant challenges. In particular, the scope is generally broad, covering a number of complex conceptual and human interactions.[384] *See* **Transition plan**.

Robotics

A branch of engineering that involves the conception, design, manufacture, and operation of robots. This field overlaps with electronics, computer science, artificial intelligence, mechatronics, nanotechnology, and bioengineering.[2]

R

ROI (Release Of Information)

Formal process to request to release health information to other healthcare providers and authorized users, ensuring that the information is timely, accurate, complete, and confidential.[28]

ROI (Return On Investment)

A mathematical formula that investors can use to evaluate their investments and judge how well a particular investment has performed compared to others.[2]

ROLAP (Relational online analytical processing [OLAP])

A technical OLAP approach that analyzes data using multidimensional data models. The difference between ROLAP and other OLAPs is that it accesses data that are stored in a relational database rather than from a multidimensional database, which is the one most commonly used in other OLAPs. It can also generate SQL queries to perform calculations when an end user wishes to do so.[52] *See* **OLAP**.

Role

A collection of permissions in role-based access control, usually associated with a role or position within an organization.[72]

Role-Based Access Control

See **RBAC**.

ROM (Read-Only Memory)

Computer memory on which data have been prerecorded. Once data have been written onto a ROM chip, they cannot be removed and can only be read. Unlike main memory (RAM), ROM retains its contents even when the computer is turned off. ROM is referred to as being nonvolatile, whereas RAM is volatile. ROM contains the programming that allows a computer to start up or regenerate each time it is turned on. ROM also performs large input/output (I/O) tasks and protects programs or software instructions.[2]

R

Root directory

The top-level directory of a file system. All other directories and files are found under the root directory.[73] *See* **Directory**.

Router

1. A router connects networks. Based on its current understanding of the state of the network it is connected to, a router acts as a dispatcher as it decides which way to send each information packet. A router is located at any gateway (where one network meets another), including each point-of-presence on the Internet. **2.** A device that combines the functions of a switch, which forwards data by looking at a physical device address, and a router, which forwards packets by locating a next hop address. **3.** A device that provides connectivity between networks (e.g., between your internal network and the Internet). A router forwards data from one network to another and vice versa. Many routers also have built-in firewall capabilities.[2] *See* **Routing switch**.

Routing switch

Device that combines the functions of a switch, which forwards data by looking at a physical device address, and a router, which forwards packets by locating a next hop address.[2]

RPO (Recovery Point Objective)

The age of files that must be recovered from backup storage for normal operations to resume if a computer, system, or network goes down as a result of a hardware, program, or communications failure. It is an important consideration in disaster recovery planning.[2]

RSA

A public key encryption technology developed by RSA Data Security.[2]

RTF (Rich Text Format)

A text file format used by Microsoft® products, such as Word and Office. The format was developed by Microsoft for use in their products and for

R

cross-platform document interchange. RTF is readable by most word processors. RTF files support text style formatting as well as images within the text. RTF files can be converted into a different format by changing the formatting selection when saving the word document.[2]

RTLS (Real-Time Location System)

Provides actionable information regarding the location, status, and movement of equipment and people. Advanced RTLS search capabilities allow searching by specific location (floor, area, and room) or unique asset identifiers (department owner, type, manufacturer, model number, asset control number, or employee ID number). The detailed asset information and reporting capabilities of RTLS allow further analysis to support a variety of uses including equipment utilization data to identify inefficiencies that have required excess equipment inventory purchases, specific asset searches by manufacturer, or model number for retrieval of equipment subject. Real-Time Location Systems (RTLS) in healthcare are used to provide immediate or real-time tracking and management of medical equipment, staff, and patients within all types of patient care environments. While the locating systems differ from using location data captured by satellite trilateration, it can be thought of as a type of "indoor GPS" for hospitals. However, more so than just locating tagged assets, accurate locating technology that easily integrates with other Healthcare IT solutions enables facilities to improve workflow, reduce costs, and increase clinical quality.[39, 578]

RTM (Reference Terminology Model)

A set of concepts and relationships that provide a common reference point for comparisons and aggregation of data about the entire healthcare process recorded by multiple different individuals, systems, or institutions. A reference terminology is an ontology of concepts and the relationships linking them. An ontology is a collection of terms, similar to a dictionary or glossary, that is organized by meaning rather than alphabetically. A reference terminology can allow the concepts to be defined in a formal and computer-processable way. A network of meaning is created that is useful for computer representation and processing that allows a computer to answer basic questions. By creating computable definitions, a reference terminology supports reproducible transmission of patient data between information systems. It supports consistent and understandable coding of clinical concepts and so is a central feature for the function of computerized patient records.[236,579]

RTO (Recovery Time Objective)

The maximum tolerable length of time that a computer, system, network, or application can be down after a failure or disaster occurs. The RTO is a function of the extent to which the interruption disrupts normal operations and the amount of revenue lost per unit time because of the disaster. These factors, in turn, depend on the affected equipment and application(s). An RTO is measured in seconds, minutes, hours, or days. It is an important consideration in a Disaster Recovery Plan (DRP). [2] *See* **MTTD**.

Rule

A formal way of specifying a recommendation, directive, or strategy, expressed as "IF premise THEN conclusion" or "IF condition THEN action."[459]

Run chart

Used to study observed data for trends or patterns over a specified period of time and focus attention on vital changes in the process. The run chart is useful for tracking information and predicting trends or patterns. It can determine if a process has common cause or special cause variation.[459]

RVU (Relative Value Unit)

A comparable service measure used by hospitals to permit comparison of the amount of resource required to perform various services within a single department or between departments. It is determined by assigning weight to such factors as personnel time, level of skill, and sophistication of equipment required to render patient services. RVUs are a common method of physician bonus plans based partially on productivity.[459]

S

S/MIME (Secure Multipurpose Internet Mail Extensions)

A secure, encrypted method of sending e-mail.[2] *See* **MIME**.

SaaS (Software as a Service)

Software that is delivered and managed remotely by one or more providers.[138] Also known as on-demand software.

Safeguard

An approved security measure taken to protect computational resources by eliminating or reducing the risk to a system, which may include hardware and software mechanisms, policies, procedures, and physical controls.[1]

SAML (Security Assertion Markup Language)

An XML standard for exchanging security information about identity, authentication, and authorization data between security domains, that is, between an identity provider and a service provider.[2]

Sample

One or more parts taken, or to be taken from a system, and intended to provide information on that system or a subsystem, or to provide a basis for decision on either.[18]

SAN (Storage Area Network)

A high-speed special-purpose network (or sub-network) that interconnects different kinds of data storage devices with associated data servers on behalf of a larger network of users. Typically, a storage area network is part of the overall network of computing resources for an enterprise.[2]

DOI: 10.4324/9781003286028-19

Sanitization

Process to remove information from media such that recovery is not possible or feasible.[1]

SATA (Serial Advanced Technology Attachment [ATA])

De facto standard for internal PC storage, SATA is the evolutionary replacement for the Parallel ATA storage interface. A serial interface that can operate at speeds up to 6 Gb/s.[2]

SATAN (Security Administrator Tool for Analyzing Networks)

A tool to help systems administrators. It recognizes several common networking-related security problems and reports the problems without actually exploiting them.[386]

SBAR (Situation–Background–Assessment–Recommendation)

Institute for Healthcare Improvement (IHI) technique that provides a framework for communication between members of the healthcare team about a patient's condition.[387]

Scalability

The ability to support the required quality of service as load increases.[2]

Scanner

An electronic device which can capture images from physical items and convert them into digital formats that can be stored on a computer and viewed or modified with software applications.[52]

Scatter plot

A graphic display of data plotted along two dimensions that uses dots to represent the values obtained for two different variables.[388]

S

Scenario

Formal description of a class of business activities, including the semantics of business agreements, conventions, and information content.[459]

Scheduler

Software product that allows an enterprise to schedule and track computer batch tasks.[52]

Schema

An abstract representation of an object's characteristics and relationship to other objects. An XML schema represents the interrelationship between the attributes and elements of an XML object (e.g., a document or a portion of a document). To create a schema for a document, one would analyze its structure, defining each structural element as it is encountered (e.g., within a schema for a document describing a website, one would define a website element, a web page element, and other elements that describe possible content divisions within any page on that site). Just as in XML and HTML, elements are defined within a set of tags.[2,52,61]

Science of clinical informatics

The transformation of clinical data into information, then knowledge, which supports clinical decision-making. This transformation requires an understanding of how clinicians structure decision-making and what data are required to support this process.[459]

SCOS (Smartcard Operating System)

Organizes data on the integrated circuit chip into files and protects them from unauthorized access.[389]

Screen saver

An animated image that is displayed on the screen when no activity takes place for a specified period of time.[2]

S

Script

A type of code or program that consists of a set of instructions for another application or utility to use.[52]

SCRIPT standard

A standard published by NCPDP to facilitate the transfer of prescription data between pharmacies, prescribers, intermediaries, facilities, and payers. It supports transactions for new prescriptions, prescription changes, refill requests, prescription fill status notifications, cancellations, medication history, long-term care transactions, and prior authorization exchanges.[211]

SCRUM

An iterative and incremental framework for project management mainly deployed in agile software development. The scrum methodology emphasizes functional software, the flexibility to change along with emerging business realities, communication, and collaboration.[52]

SCSI (Small Computer System Interface)

Set of standards for physically connecting and transferring data between computers, storage, and peripheral devices. It is not common among consumer hardware devices but is still found in some business and enterprise servers.[200]

SCUI (Smartcard user interface)

A single common dialog box that lets the user specify or search for a smart card to connect to and use in an application.[533]

SDLC (Systems Development Lifecycle)

Model used in project management to describe the stages and tasks involved in each step of a project to write and deploy software. The process used by a systems analyst to develop an information system including requirements, validation, training, and user ownership through investigation, analysis, design, implementation, and maintenance.[2]

SDO (Standards Development Organization)

An organization dedicated to standardization in the field of information for health, and health information and communications technology to achieve compatibility and interoperability between independent systems and also to ensure compatibility of data for comparative statistical purposes (e.g., classifications) and to reduce duplication of effort and redundancies.[36]

SDoH (Social Determinants of Health)

Economic and social conditions and their distribution among the population that influence individual and group differences in health status. SDoH are health-promoting factors found in one's living and working conditions (such as the distribution of income, wealth, influence, and power) rather than individual risk factors (such as behavioral risk factors or genetics) that influence the risk of a disease or vulnerability to disease or injury.[534]

SDXC (Secure Digital Extended Capacity)

A flash memory card that resembles a Secure Digital (SD) card with greater storage capacity. SD and SDXC cards make storage portable among devices such as smartphones, eBooks, digital cameras, camcorders, music players, and computers.[2]

Searchable identifiers

Characteristics that uniquely identify an information object, support persistent access to that object, and support access to information about the object (i.e., metadata).[535]

Secondary data use

Use of data for additional purposes than the primary reason for their collection, adding value to this data.[2]

Secret key

Piece of information used to encrypt and decrypt messages.[52]

Section 508

Section of the U.S. Rehabilitation Act, which requires federal agencies to provide disabled people with easy access to electronic and information technology, provide for the development of technologies to aid the disabled, and help in providing more opportunities for disabled persons. Section 508 mandates that access to information technology for the disabled must equate with that offered to non-disabled individuals. Relative to disabled workers and others who suffer from disabilities, Section 508 enables them to perform electronic data retrieval and to more readily access information technology as a whole.[52]

Secure channel

Protected communication path that is designed to prevent third-party interception or corruption of signals flowing through it.[4]

Secure Digital Extended Capacity

See **SDXC**.

Secure Electronic Transmission

See **SET**.

Secure File Transport Protocol

See **SFTP**.

Secure MIME

See **S/MIME**.

Secure shell

See **SSH**.

Secure Socket Layer

See **SSL**.

Secure web server

A program that supports certain security protocols, typically SSL, to prevent eavesdropping on information transferred between a web server and a web browser. A server resistant to a determined attack over the Internet or from corporate insiders.[146]

Security

Measures and controls that ensure confidentiality, integrity, availability, and accountability of the information processed and stored by a computer.[1]

Security administrator

A member of the data system management team trained in data security matters, who manages, monitors, and administers security over one or more computer networks. This person is authorized to enforce the data security measures and to create a confidentiality/privacy-conscious working environment.[52]

Security architecture

A plan and set of principles for an administrative domain and its security domains that describe the security services that a system is required to provide to meet the needs of its users, the system elements required to implement the services, and the performance levels required in the elements to deal with the threat environment.[390]

Security Assertion Markup Language

See **SAML**.

Security audit

A systematic evaluation of the security of a company's information system by measuring how well it conforms to a set of established criteria. A thorough audit typically assesses the security of the system's physical configuration and environment, software, information handling processes, and user practices. Security audits are often used to determine regulatory compliance in the wake of legislation (such as HIPAA, the Sarbanes-Oxley Act, and the

S

California Security Breach Information Act) that specifies how organizations must deal with information.[2] See **Audit**.

Security clearance

An authorization that allows access to information that would otherwise be forbidden. Security clearances are commonly used in industry and government. When a security clearance is required for access to specific information, the information is said to be classified. Security clearances can be issued for individuals or for groups.[2]

Security compromise

An event that has resulted in an unauthorized person obtaining classified information.[391] See **Breach of security**.

Security control assessment

The testing and/or evaluation of the management, operational, and technical security controls in an information system to determine the extent to which the controls are implemented correctly, operating as intended, and producing the desired outcome with respect to meeting the security requirements for the system.[1]

Security incident

An occurrence that results in actual or potential jeopardy to the confidentiality, integrity, or availability of an information system or the information the system processes, stores, or transmits or that constitutes a violation or imminent threat of violation of security policies, security procedures, or acceptable use policies.[1] See **Incident**.

Security process

The series of activities that monitor, evaluate, test, certify, accredit, and maintain the system accreditation throughout the system lifecycle.[1]

Security requirements

Types and levels of protection necessary for equipment, data, information, applications, and facilities to meet security policy.[1]

Security service

A processing or communication service that is provided by a system to give a specific kind of protection to resources, where said resources may reside with said system or reside with other systems (e.g., an authentication service or a public key infrastructure-based document attribution and authentication service).[391]

Segment

A logical grouping of data fields. Segments of a message may be required or optional. They may occur only once in a message or they may be allowed to repeat. Each segment is identified by a unique character code known as the segment identifier.[9]

Semantic

Pertains to the meaning or interpretation of a word, sign, or other representation.[44]

Semantic correspondence

Relation on the conceptual level expressing semantic equivalence or similarity usable as a reference or mapping.[536]

Semantic interoperability

Provides for common underlying models and codification of the data, including the use of data elements with standardized definitions from publicly available value sets and coding vocabularies, providing shared understanding and meaning to the user ry.[53], *See* **Interoperability**.

Semantic link

A relational representation that connects two representations, supports interpretation and reasoning with other links, and facilitates predictive operations on representations.[537]

Semantic network

A formalism (often expressed graphically) for representing relational information, the arcs of the network representing the relationships, and the nodes of objects in the network.[2]

S

Semantic web

A project that intends to create a universal medium for information exchange by giving meaning, in a manner understandable by machines, to the content of documents on the web. The semantic web extends the ability of the web through the use of standards, markup languages, and related processing tools.[459]

Semantics

Refers to the ways that data and commands are presented. A linguistic concept separate from the concept of syntax, which is also often related to attributes of computer programming languages.[52]

Sensitivity label

A security level associated with the content of the information. Society has historically considered as sensitive that information which has a heightened potential for causing harm to the patient or data subject or to others, such as the subject's spouse, children, friends, or sexual partners.[459, 538]

Sequence

A task in a process is enabled after the completion of a preceding task in the same process.[165]

Serial ATA

See **SATA**.

Serial Line Internet Protocol

See **SLIP**.

Serial transmission

Sequential transmission of the signal elements of a group representing a character or other entity of data. The characters are transmitted in a sequence over a single line rather than simultaneously over two or more lines, as in parallel transmission.[146]

Server

A computer system in a network that is shared by multiple users. Servers come in all sizes from x86-based PCs to IBM mainframes. A server may have a keyboard, monitor, and mouse directly attached or one keyboard, monitor, and mouse may connect to any number of servers via a switch (see KVM switch). In datacenters with hundreds and thousands of servers residing in equipment racks, all access is via the network. Centralized network computer that provides an array of resources and services to network users. Also, a program that responds to a request from a client.[146]

Service

Discrete units of application logic that expose loosely coupled message-based interfaces suitable for being accessed across a network. [395]

Service event

The act of providing a health-related service. [395]

Service-Oriented Architecture

See **SOA**.

Session

A period of interaction. In computer science, a lasting connection using the session layer of a network protocol or a lasting connection between a user (or user agent) and a peer, typically a server. [52]

Session layer

Fifth layer of the Open Systems Interconnection (OSI) model. Provides file management needed to support intersystem communication through the use of synchronization and data stream checkpoints. Also responsible for the establishment, management, and termination of sessions.[393]

Session management

The process of securing multiple requests to a service from the same user or entity. A session is often initialized by authenticating a user or entity

S

with factors such as a password. Once the user is authenticated, subsequent requests authenticate the session as opposed to the user themself.[396]

SET (Secure Electronic Transmission)

A cryptographic protocol designed for ensuring the security of financial transactions over the Internet.[2]

Severity system

Expected likelihood of disease progression independent of treatment. Systems attempting to measure severity may use diagnostic codes, such as ICD, and/or additional clinical information.[238]

SFTP (Secure File Transfer Protocol)

Network protocol for accessing, transferring, and managing files on remote systems.[2]

SGML (Standard Generalized Markup Language)

A metalanguage in which one can define markup languages for documents. SGML should not be confused with the Geography Markup Language (GML) developed by the Open Geographic Information System (Open GIS) Consortium, CFML, or the Game Maker scripting language, GML. SGML provides a variety of markup syntaxes that can be used for many applications.[539]

Shared service

A dedicated unit of people, processes, and technologies that is structured as a centralized point of service and is focused on defined business functions.[2]

Shared space

A mechanism that provides storage of, and access to, data for users with bounded network space. Enterprise-shared space refers to a store of data that are accessible within or across security domains on the global information grid. A shared space provides virtual access to any number of data assets (catalogs, websites, registries, and document storage database). Any user, system, or application that posts data uses shared space.[459]

S

Shareware

Software that can be tried before purchase. It is distributed through online services and user groups.[73]

Shielded Twisted Pair

See **STP**.

Short Message Service

See **SMS**.

SIMM (Single In-line Memory Module)

A module containing one or several Random Access Memory (RAM) chips on a small circuit board with pins that connect to the computer motherboard.[2]

Simple Mail Transfer Protocol

See **SMTP**.

Simple merge

The convergence of two or more branches into a single subsequent branch such that each enablement of an incoming branch results in the thread of control being passed to the subsequent branch.[540]

Simple Network Monitoring Protocol

See **SNMP**.

Simplex

Communication channel/circuit that allows data transmission in one direction only.[39]

Simulation

Resembles a real-life situation that the learner might encounter; learners can engage in safe decision-making.[541]

S

Simulation exercise

Test performed under conditions as close as practicable to real-world conditions.[459]

Simultaneous peripheral operation online

See **SPOOL**.

Single In-line Memory Module

See **SIMM**.

Single sign-on

See **SSO**.

Site license

A fee for the usage of purchased, rights-protected work used by multiple users at a single location.[52] *See* **Per seat license**.

Situation–Background–Assessment–Recommendation

See **SBAR**.

SLIP (Serial Line Internet Protocol)

A TCP/IP protocol used for communication between two machines that are previously configured for communication with each other.[2]

Slow-scan video

A device that transmits and receives still pictures over a narrow telecommunications channel.[459]

Small data

Describes data use that relies on targeted data acquisition and data mining. It describes a shift in how businesses and other parties look at data use and is intended to be a counterpoint to the trend toward big data, which revolves around the idea that businesses can use massive amounts of acquired data to pinpoint customer behavior or drive business intelligence in key ways. By contrast, a small data approach involves acquiring specific data sets with less effort, which proponents believe to be a more efficient business practice. [52]

Smart contract

Computer code running on top of a blockchain that contains a set of rules under which participating parties agree to interact with each other. When the predefined rules are met, the agreement is automatically enforced. The smart contract facilitates, verifies, and enforces the negotiation or performance of an agreement or transaction. It is the simplest form of decentralized automation.[437]

Smartcard

An integrated circuit card that incorporates a processor unit. The processor may be used for security algorithms, data access, or other functions according to the nature and purpose of the card.[2]

Smartcard operating system

See **SCOS**.

Smartcard user interface

See **SCUI**.

Smartphone

A mobile telephone with an integrated computer and other features not originally associated with telephones, such as an operating system, web browsing, and the ability to run software applications.[2]

Smoke testing

In the context of software development is a series of test cases that are run before the commencement of more rigorous tests. The goal of smoke testing is to verify that an application's main features work properly. A smoke test suite can be automated or a combination of manual and automated testing. [52]

S

SMP (Symmetric multiprocessing)

A computing platform technology in which a single server uses multiple CPUs in a parallel fashion managed by a single operating system.[398]

SMS (Short Message Service)

Originally part of the Global System for Mobile Communications (GSM) standard developed by the European Telecommunications Standards Institute that enables a mobile device to send, receive, and display messages of up to 160 characters in Roman text and variations for non-Roman character sets. Messages received are stored in the network if the subscriber device is inactive and are relayed when it becomes active. Commonly known as text messaging on mobile devices.[459]

SMTP (Simple Mail Transfer Protocol)

Communication protocol used to transfer e-mail between systems and from one computer to another. E-mail software most commonly uses SMTP for sending mail and Post Office Protocol 3 (POP3) or Internet Message Access Protocol (IMAP) for receiving mail.[52]

SNA (Systems Network Architecture)

Data communication architecture developed by IBM® to specify common conventions for communication among IBM hardware and software products and platforms.[89]

Sniffer

Network tool that intercepts data flowing in a network. If computers are connected to a LAN that is not filtered or switched, the traffic can be broadcast to all computers contained in the same segment.[52]

SNMP (Simple Network Monitoring Protocol)

An application-layer protocol used to manage and monitor network devices and their functions. SNMP provides a common language for network devices to relay management information within single- and multivendor environments in a Local Area Network (LAN) or Wide Area Network (WAN).[2]

SNMP (System Network Management Protocol)

An application-layer protocol used to manage and monitor network devices and their functions. Provides a common language for network devices to relay management information within single and multivendor environments in a Local Area Network (LAN) or Wide Area Network (WAN).[2]

SNOMED–CT (Systematized nomenclature of medicine–clinical terms)

A controlled healthcare terminology developed by the College of American Pathologists in collaboration with the United Kingdom's National Health Service that is used for the purposes of health information exchange. SNOMED–CT includes comprehensive coverage of diseases, clinical findings, therapies, procedures, and outcomes.[77]

SOA (Service-Oriented Architecture)

A software development model for distributed application components that incorporates discovery, access control, data mapping, and security features. Its major functions include creating a broad architectural model that defines the goals of applications and the approaches that will help meet those goals. The second function is to define specific implementation specifications, usually linked to the formal Web Services Description Language (WSDL) and Simple Object Access Protocol (SOAP) specifications.[2]

SOAP (Simple Object Access Protocol)

A protocol that allows a program running in one kind of operating system to communicate with a program in the same or different kind of operating system by using HTTP and XML as the mechanisms for information exchange.[2]

Social Determinants of Health

See **SDoH**.

Social engineering

An attack vector that relies heavily on human interaction and often involves manipulating people into breaking normal security procedures in order to gain access to systems, networks, or physical locations.[2]

Social media fatigue

Refers to social media users' tendency to pull back from social media when they become overwhelmed with too many social media sites, too many friends and followers, and too much time spent online maintaining these connections. Boredom and concerns about online privacy are also linked to social media fatigue. May also be referred to as social networking fatigue or social media fatigue syndrome.[52]

Social media monitoring

A process of using social media channels to track, gather, and mine the information and data of certain individuals or groups, usually companies or organizations, to assess their reputation and discern how they are perceived online. Social media monitoring is also known as social media listening and social media measurement.[52]

Social network

1. A chain of individuals and their personal connections. Applications are used to make associations between individuals to further facilitate connections with other people. **2.** A website or platform that allows people with similar interests to come together and share information, photos, and videos.[52, 2]

Socket

One endpoint of a two-way communication link between two programs running on the network. It is bound to a port number so the TCP layer can identify the application that data are destined to be sent to.[459]

Soft copy

File maintained on disk in electronic storage format.[2]

Software

A set of instructions or programs instructing a computer to do specific tasks. Software is a generic term used to describe computer programs. Scripts, applications, programs, and a set of instructions are all terms often used to describe software.[52]

S

Software architecture

The structure or structures of the system, which comprise software components, the externally visible properties of those components, and the relationships among them.[399] See **Architecture**.

Software as a Service

See **SaaS**.

Software Asset Management

Software asset management (SAM) is the administration of processes, policies, and procedures that support the procurement, deployment, use, maintenance, and disposal of software applications within an organization. SAM is the part of IT asset management that seeks to ensure an organization complies with license agreements and does not overspend on software.[2]

SONET (Synchronous optical network)

American National Standard Institute (ANSI) standard for connecting high-speed, high-quality, digital fiber optic transmission systems. The international equivalent of SONET is synchronous digital hierarchy (SDH).[2] See **ATM** and **Frame relay**.

SOP (Standard Operating Procedure)

Established or prescribed methods to be followed for the performance of operations or situations.[2]

Source systems

Application systems where service encounter data are collected (e.g., laboratory information systems, pharmaceutical information systems, and immunization systems). These clinical data are extracted from the source system and transformed prior to being used in the electronic health record.[459] See **Feeder systems**.

SOW (Statement Of Work)

A document describing the scope and other relevant elements associated with the work to be done. It may be incorporated by reference in a contract or other instrument.[459]

Spam

Junk e-mail, unsolicited e-mail, or irrelevant social media or postings to a group, individual, or message board.[73]

SPD (Summary Plan Description)

Document that explains the product and services a subscriber purchased.[459]

Specification

An explicit statement of the required characteristics for an input used in the healthcare system. The requirements are usually related to supplies, equipment, systems, and physical structures used in the delivery of health services.[459]

Spider

See **Web crawler**.[7]

SPOOL (Simultaneous Peripheral Operation Online)

To read and store a computer document or task list, usually on a hard disk or larger storage medium, so that it can be printed or otherwise processed at a more convenient time (e.g., when a printer is finished printing its current document).[2]

Spooler

Service that buffers data for low-speed output devices.[2]

Spreadsheet

A software application that enables a user to save, sort, and manage data in an arranged form of rows and columns. A spreadsheet stores data in a tabular format as an electronic document. An electronic spreadsheet is based on and is similar to the paper-based accounting worksheet. A spreadsheet may also be called a worksheet.[52]

SQL (Structured Query Language)

A standard computer language for relational database management and data manipulation. SQL is used to query, insert, update, and modify data. The current standard SQL version is voluntary, vendor-compliant, and monitored by the American National Standards Institute (ANSI).[52]

SRAM (Static Random Access Memory)

A type of memory that holds data in static form as long as the memory has power. Unlike Dynamic RAM (DRAM), it does not need to be refreshed.[52]

SSH (Secure Shell)

Network protocol that provides administrators with a secure way to access a remote computer. It also refers to the suite of utilities that implement the protocol.[2]

SSL (Secure Socket Layer)

The standard security technology for establishing an encrypted link between a web server and a browser. This link ensures that all data passed between the web server and browsers remains private and integral. SSL is an industry standard and is used by millions of websites for the protection of their online transactions with their customers.[2] *See* **Socket** and **API**.

SSO (Single Sign-On)

A session and user authentication service that permits a user to use one set of login credentials (e.g., name and password) to access multiple applications.[2]

Standard

1. A prescribed set of rules, conditions, or requirements established by consensus and approved by a recognized body that provides, for common and repeated use, rules, guidelines, or characteristics for activities or their results aimed at the achievement of the optimum degree of order in a given context. **2.** A definition or format that has been approved by a recognized standards organization or is accepted as a de facto standard by the industry. Standards exist for programming languages, operating systems, data formats, communications protocols, and electrical interfaces.[401]

Standard Operating Procedure

See **SOP**.

Standardization

Activity of establishing, with regard to actual or potential problems, provisions for common and repeated use, aimed at the achievement of the optimum degree of order in a given content.[459]

Standardization of terminology

Official recognition of a terminology by an authoritative body.[543]

Standardized Generalized Markup Language

See **SGML**.

Standardized taxonomy

Use of common standardized definitions, criteria, terminology, and data elements for treatment processes, outcomes, data collection, and electronic transmission, with the goal of saving much time, effort, and misunderstanding in communicating these elements.[405]

Standards body

Entity that is recognized at the national, regional, or international level that has as a principle function, by virtue of statutes, for the preparation, approval, consensus, and adoption of standards that are made generally available.[542]

Standards Development Organization

See **SDO**.

Standing orders

Physicians' orders or protocols that allow patient care to be delivered by members of the care team, like medical assistants, therapists, and nurses. Orders are often based on national clinical guidelines but may be customized based on patient population or care environment.[403]

Star schema

The simplest form of a dimensional model in which data are organized into facts and dimensions. It is diagramed by surrounding each fact with its associated dimensions.[2] *See* **OLTP**.

Start of care

See **Admission date**.

Statement Of Work

See **SOW**.

Static audit tool

System scanner that looks for and reports weaknesses.[459]

Static Random Access Memory

See **SRAM**.

Stealth virus

A type of resident virus that attempts to evade detection by concealing its presence in infected files. To achieve this, the virus intercepts system calls, which examine the contents and attributes of infected files.[2]

Storage

The function of storing records for future retrieval and use.[2]

Storage Area Network

See **SAN**.

Store-and-forward

Transmission of static images or audio-video clips to a remote data storage device, from which they can be retrieved by a medical practitioner for review and consultation at any time, obviating the need for the simultaneous availability of the consulting parties and reducing transmission costs due to low bandwidth requirements.[52]

Storyboard

A panel or series of panels on which a set of sketches is arranged, depicting consecutively the important aspects of scene and action.[29]

S

STP (Shielded Twisted Pair)

Type of wiring used in some business installations. An outer covering or shield is added to the ordinary twisted pair wires, functioning as a ground.[2]

Streaming

A technique for delivering data used with audio and video in which the recipient is able to hear or see part of the file before the entire file is delivered. Involves a method for the recipient computer to be able to do a smooth delivery despite the uneven arrival of data.[66]

Stress testing

A type of performance testing focused on determining an application's robustness, availability, and reliability under extreme conditions. The goal of stress testing is to identify application issues that arise or become apparent only under extreme conditions. These conditions can include heavy loads, high concurrency, or limited computational resources.[52]

Structured analysis

A software engineering technique that uses graphical diagrams to develop and portray system specifications that are easily understood by users. These diagrams describe the steps that need to occur and the data required to meet the design function of a particular software. This type of analysis mainly focuses on logical systems and functions and aims to convert business requirements into computer programs and hardware specifications.[52]

Structured data

Coded, semantically interoperable data that are based on a reference information model. The consent directive may be captured as a scanned image, which is not semantically interoperable and would preclude the ability of the consent repository to analyze the data for conflicts with previously persisted consent directives.[2]

Structural interoperability

The structure or format of data exchange (i.e., the message format standards) where there is uniform movement of healthcare data from one system to another such that the clinical or operational purpose and meaning of the data are preserved and unaltered. Structural interoperability defines the syntax of the data exchange. It ensures that data exchanges between information technology systems can be interpreted at the data field level.[53] *See* **Interoperability**.

Subject field

Domain field of special knowledge.[75]

Subject Matter Expert

See **SME**.

Subject of care identifier

A unique number or code issued for the purpose of identifying a subject of healthcare.[241]

Subset

Represents groups of components that share specified characteristics that affect the way they are displayed or otherwise accessible within a particular realm, specialty, application, or context.[459]

Substitution

A method of cryptography based on the principle of replacing each letter in the message with another one. A cipher that replaces the characters of the original plain text. The characters retain their original position but are altered.[459]

SVC (Switched Virtual Circuit)

A temporary virtual circuit that is set up and used only as long as data are being transmitted. Once the communication between the two hosts is complete, the SVC disappears. In contrast, a Permanent Virtual Circuit (PVC) remains available at all times.[2]

S

Symmetric-key cryptography

An encryption system in which the sender and receiver of a message share a single, common key that is used to encrypt and decrypt the message. Symmetric-key systems are simpler and faster, but their main drawback is that both parties must exchange the key in a secure way.[39]

System

The combination of hardware and software which processes information for the customer.[2]

System administrator

A person who is responsible for managing a multi-user computing environment, such as a local area network. The responsibilities typically include installing and configuring system hardware and software, establishing and managing user accounts, upgrading software, and backup and recovery tasks.[2] Also known as sysadmin or systems administrator.

System analysis

The process of determining how a set of interconnected components whose individual characteristics are known will behave in response to a given input or a set of inputs. The process of observing systems for troubleshooting or development purposes. It is applied to information technology, where computer-based systems require defined analysis according to their makeup and design. Closely related to requirements analysis and operations research.[52]

System design

The process of defining the elements of a system, such as the architecture, modules, and components; the different interfaces of those components; and the data that goes through that system. It is meant to satisfy specific needs and requirements of a business or organization through the engineering of a coherent and well-running system. A specification of human factors, and hardware and software requirements, for an information system.[52]

S

System integration

1. The composition of a capability by assembling elements in a way that allows them to work together to achieve an intended purpose. **2.** The process of creating a complex information system that may include designing or building a customized architecture or application, integrating it with new or existing hardware, packaged and custom software, and communications.[2, 138] *See* **EAI**.

System integrator

An individual or business that builds computing systems for clients by combining hardware, software, networking, and storage products from multiple vendors.[2]

System Network Management Protocol

See **SNMP**.

System security

The result of all safeguards, including hardware, software, personnel policies, information practice policies, disaster preparedness, and oversight of these components.[52]

System of Record

The authoritative data source for a given data element or piece of information.[459]

System testing

Falling under the scope of black box testing, system testing is a phase in the software testing cycle where a total and integrated application/system is tested. The focus of the system testing is to evaluate the compliance of the entire system with respect to the specified requirements. System testing helps in approving and checking the business, functional, technical, and any non-functional requirements of the application concerning the architecture as a whole.[52]

Systematized nomenclature of medicine–clinical terms

See **SNOMED–CT**.

T

Table

Database object with a unique name and structured in columns and rows.[20]

TCO (Total Cost of Ownership)

A document that describes the cost of a project or initiative that usually includes hardware, software, development, and ongoing expenses.[20]

TCP/IP (Transmission Control Protocol/Internet Protocol)

1. Routable protocol required for Internet access. TCP portion is associated with data. IP is associated with source to destination packet delivery. **2.** A set of communication protocols encompassing media access, packet transport, session communications, file transfer, electronic mail, and terminal emulation. It is supported by a large number of hardware and software vendors and is the basis for Internet transactions.[20]

TDR (Time-Domain Reflectometry)

Identifies and measures errors related to aerial and underground cable and fiber optic wiring through the analysis of pulse reflection polarity. The TDR technique accurately detects errors and bugs in amplitude, frequencies, and other electrical signatures.[529]

Tebibyte: (TiB)

A unit of digital information storage used to denote the size of data. It is equivalent to 240, or 1,099,511,627,776, bytes and 1,024 gibibytes.

Technical specification

International Organization for Standardization (ISO) deliverable that addresses work still under technical development or where it is believed that there will be a future, but not immediate, possibility of agreement on an

DOI: 10.4324/9781003286028-20

International Standard. A Technical Specification is published for immediate use, but it also provides a means to obtain feedback. The aim is that it will eventually be transformed and republished as an International Standard.[530]

Technobabble

A broad, all-encompassing term for different kinds of terminology that rely on jargons, acronyms, made-up words, and other linguistic features to confuse listeners or to obfuscate an issue.[52]

TEFCA (Trusted Exchange Framework and Common Agreement)

In the 21st Century Cures Act (Cures Act), Congress identified the importance of interoperability and set out a path for the interoperable exchange of Electronic Health Information. Specifically, Congress directed ONC to "develop or support a trusted exchange framework, including a common agreement among health information networks nationally." The framework aims to outline a common set of principles for trusted exchange and the minimum terms and conditions for trusted exchange. This is designed to bridge the gap between providers' and patients' information systems and enable interoperability across disparate Health Information Networks (HINs). A draft framework was released in January 2018.[12]

Telehealth

A broad variety of technologies and tactics to deliver virtual medical, health, and education services. A collection of means to enhance care and education delivery. This term encompasses the concept of "telemedicine," which refers to traditional clinical diagnosis and monitoring delivered by technology. The term "telehealth" covers a wide range of diagnosis, management, education, and other related healthcare fields including, but not limited to, dentistry, counseling, physical and occupational therapy, home health, chronic disease monitoring and management, and consumer and professional education.[531]

Telemedicine

See **Telehealth**.

T

TELNET (TELecommunications NETwork)

A protocol used on the Internet or local area network to provide a bidirectional interactive text-oriented communication facility using a virtual terminal connection.[7]

Terabyte

Approximately one trillion bytes; unit of computer storage capacity.[2]

Terminal

1. A device that enables you to communicate with a computer. Generally, a combination of keyboard and display screen. Terminals are sometimes divided into three classes based on how much processing power they contain intelligent terminal, a stand-alone device that contains main memory and a CPU; smart terminal, contains some processing power but not as much as an intelligent terminal; and dumb terminal, has no processing capabilities. It relies entirely on the computer's processor. **2.** In networking, a terminal is a personal computer or workstation connected to a mainframe.[39] *See* **Workstation**.

Terminal server

A hardware device or server that provides terminals (PCs, printers, and other devices) with a common connection point to a local or wide area network.[2]

Terminal window

For local or remote execution of a program, it is a window in a graphical interface that is used to display a command line.[146]

Terminology

A system of words used to name things in a particular discipline.[29]

TFTP (Trivial File Transfer Protocol)

An Internet software utility for transferring files that are simpler to use than the File Transfer Protocol (FTP). TFTP uses the User Datagram Protocol (UDP) rather than the Transmission Control Protocol (TCP).[2]

T

TGE (Token Generation Event)

See **ICO**.

Thesaurus

The vocabulary of a controlled indexing language, formally organized so that the a priori relationships between concepts (e.g., broader and narrower) are made explicit.[406]

Thin client/dumb terminal

A networked computer with few locally stored programs and a heavy dependence on network resources. It may have very limited resources of its own, perhaps operating without auxiliary drives, CD-R/W/DVD drives, or even software applications.[52]

Third-Party Administrator

See **TPA**.

Thread

A collection of any number of online posts defined by a title. A thread is a component of an Internet forum.[20,459]

Threat

1. Any circumstance or event with the potential to adversely impact organizational operations (including mission, functions, image, or reputation), organizational assets, or individuals through an information system via unauthorized access, destruction, disclosure, modification of information, and/or denial of service. Also, the potential for a threat source to successfully exploit a particular information system vulnerability.[1]

Threshold

Minimum or maximum value (established for an attribute, characteristic, or parameter) that serves as a benchmark for comparison or guidance, and any breach of which may call for a complete review of the situation or the redesign of a system.[4]

T

TIFF (Tagged Image File Format)

A standard file format that is largely used in the publishing and printing industry. The extensible feature of this format allows storage of multiple bit-map images having different pixel depths, which makes it advantageous for image storage needs.[52]

Tightly coupling

A coupling technique in which hardware and software components are highly dependent on each other. It is used to refer to the state/intent of interconnectivity between two or more computing instances in an integrated system.[52]

Time bomb

A malicious program that is programmed to "detonate" at a specific time and release a virus onto the computer system or network.[39] *See* **Logic bomb**.

Time-Domain Reflectometer

See **TDR**.

TKIP (Temporal Key Integrity Protocol)

A wireless network security protocol of the Institute of Electrical and Electronics Engineers (IEEE) 802.11. TKIP encryption is more robust than Wired Equivalent Privacy (WEP), which was the first Wi-Fi security protocol, or WPA2 protocol.[52]

TLS (Transport Layer Security)

A protocol that provides privacy and data integrity between two communicating applications. It is used for Web browsers and other applications that require data to be securely exchanged over a network, such as file transfers, VPN connections, instant messaging, and voice over IP.[2]

TOC

See **Transitions Of Care**.

T

Token

An object that represents something else, such as another object (either physical or virtual), or an abstract concept. In computer science, there are a number of types of tokens. A programming token is the basic component of source code. Characters are categorized as one of five classes of tokens that describe their functions (constants, identifiers, operators, reserved words, and separators) in accordance with the rules of the programming language. A security token is a physical device, such as a special smart card, that together with something that a user knows, such as a PIN, will enable authorized access to a computer system or network.[2]

Top-level concept

A concept that is directly related to the Root Concept by a single relationship of the Relationship Type.[407]

Topology

The arrangement of a network, including its nodes and connecting lines. There are two ways of defining network geometry: the physical topology and the logical (or signal) topology.[2]

Total Cost of Ownership

See **TCO**.

Touch screen

A computer display screen that is also an input device. The screens are sensitive to pressure; a user interacts with the computer by touching pictures or words on the screen.[2]

TPA (Third-Party Administrator)

An organization that administers group insurance policies for an employer. This organization works with the employer as well as the insurer to communicate information between the two, as well as processing claims and determining eligibility.[4]

T

Traceroute

A network diagnostic tool used to track the pathway taken by a packet on an IP network from source to destination. Traceroute also records the time taken for each hop the packet makes during its route to the destination. Traceroute uses Internet Control Message Protocol (ICMP) echo packets with variable Time To Live (TTL) values.[52]

Trading partner agreement

1. An agreement that may include various terms of trade, such as duties, responsibilities, and liabilities, including delivery and receipt of goods and services. This is meant to provide additional security for each party to prevent disputes since the terms of trade have been outlined and agreed upon. **2.** As defined in HIPAA, an agreement related to the exchange of information in electronic transactions, whether the agreement is distinct or part of a larger agreement, between each party to the agreement.[4, 55]

Train the trainer

A model used to describe, much as the name would imply, training potential instructors or less experienced instructors on the best ways to deliver training materials to others.[408]

Transaction

1. Under HIPAA, the exchange of information between two parties to carry out clinical, financial, and administrative activities related to healthcare. **2.** An exchange of information between actors. For each transaction, the technical framework describes how to use an established standard, such as HL7, DICOM, or W3C.[113, 27]

Transaction standard

A standard specifying the format of messages being sent from or received by a system rather than how the information is stored in the system.[113]

Transactional data

Information recorded from transactions. A transaction, in this context, is a sequence of information exchange and related work (such as database updating) that is treated as a unit for the purposes of satisfying a request. Transactional data can be financial, logistical, or work-related, involving everything from a purchase order to shipping status to employee hours worked to insurance costs and claims.[2]

Transition plan

A set of techniques to address all aspects of transitioning to a new environment. The key aspects of change that must be addressed are managerial (M), operational (O), social (S), and technical (T).[428]

Transitions of care

The movement of a patient from one setting of care (hospital, ambulatory primary care practice, ambulatory specialty care practice, long-term care, home health, or rehabilitation facility) to another.[26]

Transmission

The process of sending digital or analog data over a communication medium to one or more computing, network, communication, or electronic devices. It enables the transfer and communication of devices in a point-to-point, point-to-multipoint, and multipoint-to-multipoint environment. Data transmission is also known as digital transmission or digital communications.[52]

Transmission confidentiality

Process to ensure that information in transit is not disclosed to unauthorized individuals, entities, or processes.[459] *See* **Confidentiality**.

Transmission Control Protocol/Internet Protocol

See **TCP/IP**.

Transmission integrity

Process to guard against improper information modification or destruction while in transit.[532] *See* **Integrity**.

T

Transparent background

An image file that has one color assigned to be "transparent" so that the assigned color will be replaced by the browser's background color, whatever it may be.[2] *See* **GIF**.

Transport layer

Fourth layer of the Open System Interconnection (OSI) model responsible for end-to-end communication over a network. It provides logical communication between application processes running on different hosts within a layered architecture of protocols and other network components. The transport layer is also responsible for the management of error correction, and providing quality and reliability to the end user. This layer enables the host to send and receive error-corrected data, packets, or messages over a network and is the network component that allows multiplexing.[52]

Transport Layer Security

See **TLS**.

Trap doors

Provides an undocumented method of gaining access to an application, operating system, or online service. Programmers write trapdoors into programs for a variety of reasons. Left in place, trapdoors can facilitate a range of activities, from benign troubleshooting to illegal access.[410] *See* **Backdoor**.

Trial implementation supplement

A specification candidate for addition to an IHE Domain Technical Framework (e.g., a new profile) that is issued for early implementation by any interested party. The authoring technical committee expects developers' feedback.[120]

Trigger event

An event that causes the system to initiate a response.[1]

T

Trivial File Transfer Protocol
See **TFTP**.

Trojan horse
A computer program that appears to have a useful function but also has a hidden and potentially malicious function that evades security mechanisms, sometimes by exploiting legitimate authorizations of a system entity that invokes the program.[1] *See* **Malware**.

Trunk
A communications line or link designed to carry multiple signals simultaneously to provide network access between two points. Trunks typically connect switching centers in a communications system.[2]

Trust anchor
Acts as an intermediary between users and certificate authorities, reviewing and approving certificate requests.[9]

Trusted Exchange Framework and Common Agreement
See **TEFCA**.

Tunneling
See **Virtual private network**.[57]

Tutorial
A program that provides step-by-step information for presenting a concept or learning unit.[4]

Twisted-pair cable
A type of cable made by putting two separate insulated wires together in a twisted pattern and running them parallel to each other. This type of cable is widely used in different kinds of data and voice infrastructures.[52]

U

UART (Universal Asynchronous Receiver Transmitter)

The microchip with programming that controls a computer's interface to its attached serial devices.[2]

Uberveillance

Uberveillance is a term used to describe intensive surveillance processes only developed in the 21st century. At its most basic level, uberveillance refers to the most comprehensive surveillance possible at a given moment in time. This involves the use of cutting-edge surveillance technology.[52]

Ubiquitous computing

The growing trend toward embedding microprocessors in everyday objects so they can communicate information. The words pervasive and ubiquitous mean "existing everywhere." Ubiquitous computing devices are completely connected and constantly available and are also known as Ubicomp. *See* **Pervasive computing**.[2]

UDDI (Universal Description, Discover, and Integration)

A web-based distributed directory that enables businesses to list themselves on the Internet and discover each other, similar to a traditional phone book's yellow and white pages.[39]

UDI (Unique Device Identifier)

A unique numeric or alphanumeric code that consists of two parts: a Device Identifier (DI), a mandatory, fixed portion of a UDI that identifies the labeler and the specific version or model of a device, and a Production Identifier (PI), a conditional, variable portion of a UDI that identifies one or more of the following when included on the label of

DOI: 10.4324/9781003286028-21

U

a device: the lot or batch number within which a device was manufactured; the serial number of a specific device; the expiration date of a specific device; the date a specific device was manufactured; and the distinct identification code required by §1271.290(c) for a human cell, tissue, or cellular and tissue-based product (HCT/P) regulated as a device.[41]

UDP (User Datagram Protocol)

Part of the Internet Protocol suite used by programs running on different computers on a network. UDP is used to send short messages called datagrams, but overall, it is an unreliable connectionless protocol. An OSI transport layer protocol. This protocol contrasts with TCP.[52]

UI (User Interface)

Term to describe everything designed into an information device with which a person may interact. This can include display screens, keyboards, a mouse, and the appearance of a desktop. It is also the way in which a user interacts with an application or a website.[2]

UID (Unique Identifier)

A numeric or alphanumeric string that is associated with a single entity within a given system, making it possible to access and interact with that entity.[2]

UM (Utilization Management)

The evaluation of the necessity, appropriateness, and efficiency of the use of healthcare services, procedures, and facilities.[412]

UMDNS (Universal Medical Device Nomenclature System)

The purpose of UMDNS is to facilitate identifying, processing, filing, storing, retrieving, transferring, and communicating data about medical devices. The nomenclature is used in applications ranging from hospital inventory and work order controls to national agency medical device regulatory systems and from e-Commerce and procurement to medical device databases.[248]

UML (Unified Modeling Language)

A language for specifying, visualizing, constructing, and documenting the artifacts of software systems. UML is a standard notation for the modeling of real-world objects.[293]

UMLS (Unified Medical Language System)

The National Library of Medicine (NLM) produces the Unified Medical Language System® (UMLS®) to facilitate the development of computer systems that behave as if they "understand" the meaning of the language of biomedicine and health. As part of the UMLS, NLM produces and distributes the UMLS Knowledge Sources (databases) and associated software tools (programs) for use by system developers in building or enhancing electronic information systems that create, process, retrieve, integrate, and/or aggregate biomedical and health data and information, as well as in informatics research.[269]

UMS (Unified Messaging System)

The handling of voice, fax, and regular text messages as objects in a single mailbox that a user can access either with a regular e-mail client or by telephone.[2]

UNC (Universal Naming Convention)

Text-based method to identify the path to a remote device, server, directory, or file. Implemented as \\computername\sharename\directoryname\ filename.[2]

Underuse

Refers to the failure to provide a healthcare service when it would have produced a favorable outcome for a patient. Standard examples include failures to provide appropriate preventive services to eligible patients (e.g., Pap smears, flu shots for elderly patients, and screening for hypertension) and proven medications for chronic illnesses (e.g., steroid inhalers for asthmatics, aspirin, beta-blockers, and lipid-lowering agents for patients who have suffered a recent myocardial infarction).[413]

U

Unicode

A standard character set that represents most of the characters used in the world using a 16-bit encoding. Unicode can be encoded in using UTF-8 (USC Transformation Format) to more efficiently store the most common ASCII characters.[414]

Unified Messaging System

See **UMS**.

Unified Modeling Language

See **UML**.

Uniform data standards

Methods, protocols, or terminologies agreed to by an industry to allow disparate information systems to operate successfully with one another.[43]

Uniform Resource Locator

See **URL**.

Uninterruptible Power Supply

See **UPS**.

Unique Device Identifier

See **UDI**.

Unique Identifier

See **UID**.

Unique Patient Identifier

See **UPI**.

U

Unit testing

A software development process in which the smallest testable parts of an application, called units, are individually and independently scrutinized for proper operation. Unit testing is often automated, but it can also be done manually.[2]

Universal Asynchronous Receiver Transmitter

See **UART**.

Universal Health Coverage (UHC)

UHC means that all individuals and communities receive the health services they need without suffering financial hardship. It includes the full spectrum of essential, quality health services, from health promotion to prevention, treatment, rehabilitation, and palliative care across the life course.[444]

Universal identifier

See **UPI**.

Universal Medical Device Nomenclature System

See **UMDNS**.

Universal Naming Convention

See **UNC**.

Universal Serial Bus

See **USB**.

Unstructured data

Represents any data that do not have a recognizable structure. These data are unorganized and raw and can be non-textual or textual. Unstructured data may also be identified as loosely structured data, wherein the data sources include a structure, but not all data in a data set follow the same structure.[52]

U

UPI (Unique Patient Identifier)

1. The identity of an individual consists of a set of personal characters by which that individual can be recognized. Identification is the proof of one's identity. Identifier verifies the sameness of one's identity. Patient identifier is the value assigned to an individual to facilitate positive identification of that individual for healthcare purposes. Unique patient identifier is the value permanently assigned to an individual for identification purposes and is unique across the entire national healthcare system. Unique patient identifier is not shared with any other individual. **2.** A form of identification and access control that identifies humans by their characteristics or traits. Biometric identifiers (or biometric authentication) are the distinctive, measurable characteristics used to label and describe individuals. Two categories of biometric identifiers include physiological and behavioral characteristics.[7]

UPS (Uninterruptible Power Supply)

Device that keeps a computer running by protecting against power outages, power surges, and power sags by maintaining constant power via battery. Provides the opportunity for a graceful shutdown in a commercial power-out condition.[2]

URI (Uniform Resource Identifier)

A sequence of characters that identifies a logical or physical resource. URL is an example of a type of URI.[2]

URL (Uniform Resource Locator)

The method to locate a resource on the web. It contains the name of the protocol to be used to access the resource and the resource name.[2]

URL Rewriting

The process of modifying Uniform Resource Locators (URLs) for various purposes. The URL as a "web address" is a string that, when entered into the browser bar field, directs the browser to move to a given site and page. Changing the URL can help with user access and site visibility; it can also be used by hackers to redirect users without their knowledge or "trap" them in a certain site.[52]

U

Usability

The effectiveness, efficiency, and satisfaction with which specified users achieve specified goals in particular environments. Effectiveness refers to the accuracy and completeness with which specified users can achieve specified goals in particular environments.[90]

Usability testing

Evaluating a product or service by testing it with representative users. Typically, during a test, participants will try to complete typical tasks while observers watch, listen, and take notes. The goal is to identify any usability problems, collect qualitative and quantitative data, and determine the participant's satisfaction with the product.[251]

USB (Universal Serial Bus)

A plug-and-play interface between a computer and peripheral devices, such as media players, keyboards, digital cameras, and printers. It can also support electrical power. It enables the operating system to spontaneously configure and discover a new peripheral device without having to restart the computer.[2, 52]

USCDI (U.S. Core Data for Interoperability)

Outlined by the Office of the National Coordinator for Health Information Technology (ONC) as part of the effort to establish the Trusted Exchange Framework and Common Agreement (TEFCA), USCDI is a common set of data classes that are required for interoperable exchange. USCDI lists data classes and associated standards and outlines a process to review and update these data classes with additional data classes for future versions of the document. This document incorporates and expands on the Common Clinical Data Set (CCDS). *See* **TEFCA** and **CCDS**.[12]

U.S. Core Data for Interoperability

See **USCDI**.

U

Use

With respect to individually identifiable health information, the sharing, employment, application, utilization, examination, or analysis of information within the entity that maintains such information.[261]

Use case

A methodology used in system analysis to identify, clarify, and organize system requirements. The use case is made up of a set of possible sequences of interactions between systems and users in a particular environment and related to a particular goal. It consists of a group of elements (e.g., classes and interfaces) that can be used together in a way that will have an effect larger than the sum of the separate elements combined. The use case should contain all system activities that have significance to the users. A use case can be thought of as a collection of possible scenarios related to a particular goal; indeed, the use case and goal are sometimes considered to be synonymous.[2]

User Acceptance Testing (UAT)

UAT is an important phase of the software development process that verifies whether a product or software is fit for the purpose it was built for in the first place—namely, that it fulfills business requirements and provides a good User Experience (UX) for end users. Typically done after functional tests have been completed, this involves testing the system or service with real users—or representatives of the target user group—in a controlled environment. This allows the developers to observe how the users interact with the system and identify any issues or areas for improvement.[52]

User authentication

See **Authentication**.

User Datagram Protocol

See **UDP**.

User experience

A person's perceptions and responses that result from the use and/or anticipated use of a product, system, or service. User experience includes all the

U

users' emotions, beliefs, preferences, perceptions, physical and psychological responses, behaviors, and accomplishments that occur before, during, and after use. User experience is a consequence of brand image, presentation, functionality, system performance, interactive behavior, and assistive capabilities of the interactive system; the user's internal and physical state resulting from prior experiences, attitudes, skills, and personality; and the context of use. Usability, when interpreted from the perspective of the users' personal goals, can include the kind of perceptual and emotional aspects typically associated with user experience. Usability criteria can be used to assess aspects of user experience.[90]

User Flow

The description of a set of tasks that a user must do to complete some process. In IT and on the Web, professionals might analyze user flows to try to make websites or technologies more user-friendly and to understand the goals of the user as well as the goals of the company or other party that the Web project serves.[52]

User Interface

See **UI**.

User-friendly

Refers to anything that makes it easier for individuals to use a computer.[39]

User permissions

The authorization given to users that enables them to access specific resources on the network, such as data files, applications, printers, and scanners. Permissions also designate the type of access, such as read-only or read/write privileges.[150]

User profile

1. Information about an individual user. **2.** The preferences and current desktop configuration of a user's machine.[150]

USHIK (United States Health Information Knowledgebase)

Was a metadata registry of healthcare-related data elements from Standard Development Organizations supported by the Agency for Healthcare Research and Quality (AHRQ). This site is archived [252]

Utilization Management

See **UM**.

UTP (Unshielded Twisted Pair)

A popular type of cable that consists of two unshielded wires twisted around each other. Due to its low cost, UTP cabling is used extensively for Local Area Networks (LANs) and telephone connections. UTP cabling does not offer as high bandwidth or as good protection from interference as coaxial or fiber optic cables, but it is less expensive and easier to work with.[39]

V

Validation

Process of demonstrating that a system under consideration meets the specifications of that system. Confirmation that requirements for a specific intended use or application have been fulfilled.[1]

Value-Added Network

See **VAN**.

Value-Based Payment

See **VBC**.

Value stream

The specific activities within a supply chain required to design, order, and provide a specific product or service.[142]

Value Stream Mapping

See **VSM**.

VAN (Value-Added Network)

A hosted service used for sharing received, stored, and forwarded messages. A VAN may also add audit data and modify data for automatic error detection, correction, or conversion between communication protocols.[52]

Vanilla

In information technology, an adjective meaning plain or basic. The original, uncustomized version of a product is sometimes referred to as the vanilla version.[2]

DOI: 10.4324/9781003286028-22

V

Vaporware

Refers to a technology or product for which a tech company may pre-announce development but it never actually hits the market. Because many of these announcements are never backed up by an actual product release or are officially canceled, vaporware alludes to their spectral nature and the fact that they essentially vanish into thin air before consumers get to see them.[52]

Variance analysis

Process aimed at computing differences between actual and budgeted or targeted levels of performance and identification of their causes.[4]

VAX (Virtual Address Extension)

An established line of mid-range server computers from the Digital Equipment Corporation (DEC, now a part of Hewlett-Packard).[2]

VBC (Value-Based Care)

A healthcare delivery model in which providers, including hospitals and physicians, are paid based on patient health outcomes. Under value-based care agreements, providers are rewarded for helping patients improve their health, reduce the effects and incidence of chronic disease, and live healthier lives in an evidence-based way. Value-based care differs from a fee-for-service approach, in which providers are paid based on the number of healthcare services they deliver. The "value" in value-based healthcare is derived from measuring health outcomes against the cost of delivering those outcomes.[415]

VBID (Value-Based Insurance Design)

Promotes patients' use of high-value care options by changing the cost-sharing the consumers must pay for different care options. Under a VBID approach, treatments that provide high clinical value have reduced or no cost-sharing (out-of-pocket costs like copays), to make sure they are affordable for patients. In some situations, health plans may have higher cost-sharing for services that offer little or no added clinical benefit, compared to their added cost.[416]

VBP (Value-Based Payment)

See **VM**.

VDT (View, Download, Transmit)

Activity previously listed as part of the CMS Meaningful Use Stage 2 core measures. View refers to the patient (or authorized representative) accessing their health information online. Download refers to ambulatory or inpatient summaries (as applicable to the EHR technology setting for which certification is onsortium requested) in human-readable format or formatted according to the standard adopted with minimum information requirements. Transmit refers to third-party access to the downloaded ambulatory and inpatient summaries.[26]

Vendor

A company that provides products and/or services.[135]

Verification confirmation

Process used to determine whether the product or functionality fulfills the intended use and user requirements.[194]

Vertical scalability

The addition of resources to a single system node, such as a single computer or network station, which often results in additional CPUs or memory. Vertical scalability provides more shared resources for the operating system and applications.[52]

Veterans Health Information Systems Technology Architecture

See **VistA**.

Video RAM or Video Random Access Memory

See **VRAM**.

V

Viral

A buzzword used to describe any content or media that becomes widely shared through social networks and online. The concept of "going viral" extends to many mediums, including videos, photos, games, articles, or even advertisements.

Virtual Address Extension

See **VAX**.

Virtual appliance

A virtual machine image file consisting of a preconfigured operating system environment and a single application.[2]

Virtual community

A community of people sharing common interests, ideas, and feelings over the Internet of collaborative networks.[2]

Virtual CPU

A physical central processing unit that is assigned to a virtual machine. Also known as a virtual processor.[2]

Virtual Data Room

A Virtual Data Room (VDR) is a secure, online repository for data and documents pertinent to business, legal transactions, or proceedings. The VDR uses a central server and an extranet connection, which is an Internet connection with very controlled access. This Internet connection uses a secure log-on supplied by the appropriate overseeing vendor or authority responsible for disabling or enabling the secure log-on at any time.[52]

Virtual hospital

1. A format for providing healthcare in a central location that relies on the components of telemedicine and high-tech communications devices to connect it to a regional hospital where a greater range of expertise is available.

2. Model in which caregivers are able to provide care to patients, regardless of where the patient is located.[123,417]

Virtual Machine
See **VM**.

Virtual machine monitor
See **Hypervisor**.

Virtual Private Network
See **VPN**.

Virtual reality
The computer-generated simulation of a three-dimensional image or environment that can be interacted with in a seemingly real or physical way by a person using special electronic equipment, such as a helmet with a screen inside or gloves fitted with sensors.[52]

Virtual Reality Modeling Language
See **VRML**.

Virtual SAN appliance
See **VSA**.

Virtual server farm
A networking environment that employs multiple application and infrastructure servers running on two or more physical servers using a server virtualization program such as VMware or Microsoft Virtual Server®.[2]

Virtual to Virtual (V2V)
A term that refers to the migration of an Operating System (OS), application programs, and data from a virtual machine or disk partition to another virtual machine or disk partition. The target can be a single system or multiple

systems. To streamline the operation, part or all of the migration can be carried out automatically by means of specialized programs known as migration tools.[2]

Virtualization

The creation of a virtual (rather than actual) version of something, such as an operating system, a server, a storage device, or network resources. Virtualization can be viewed as part of an overall trend in enterprise IT that includes autonomic computing, a scenario in which the IT environment will be able to manage itself based on perceived activity, and utility computing, in which computer processing power is seen as a utility that clients can pay for only as needed. The usual goal of virtualization is to centralize administrative tasks while improving scalability and workloads.[2]

Virtualization software

Virtualization software acts as a layer between a computer's primary OS and the virtual OS. It allows the virtual system to access the computer's hardware, such as the RAM, CPU, and video card, just like the primary OS. This is different than emulation, which actually translates each command into a form that the system's processor can understand. Since Apple and Windows® computers now both use the "x86" processor architecture, it is possible to run both OSes on the same machine via virtualization rather than emulation.[73]

Virtualization sprawl

A term used to describe a scenario when the number of virtual machines on a network reaches a point where they can no longer be handled by the administrator effectively.[52]

Virus

Software used to infect a computer. After the virus code is written, it is buried within an existing program. Once that program is executed, the virus code is activated and attaches copies of itself to other programs in the computer and other computers in the network. Infected programs continue to propagate the virus, which is how it spreads. A virus cannot run by itself; it requires that its host program be run to make the virus active.[150,1]

V

Virus hoax

An e-mail that provides a warning about a virus, worm, or some other disaster and urges recipients to forward the message. Hoax e-mails are often sent from what appears to be a reliable source, which can make determining whether to heed their message difficult for recipients. Although such hoaxes are usually benign, they suggest that recipients delete important files from their computers or download an infected attachment.[52]

Virus signature

A string of characters or numbers that makes up the signature that anti-virus programs are designed to detect. One signature may contain several virus signatures, which are algorithms or hashes that uniquely identify a specific virus. A large number of viruses may share a single signature, allowing a virus scanner to detect viruses it has never seen before.[52]

Vishing (voice or VoIP phishing)

An electronic fraud tactic in which individuals are tricked into revealing critical financial or personal information to unauthorized entities. Vishing works like phishing but does not always occur over the Internet and is carried out using voice technology. A vishing attack can be conducted by voice e-mail, VoIP (voice over IP), landline, or cellular telephone.[2] *See* **Social engineering**.

VISN (Veterans Integrated Service Network)

VA's Veterans Health Administration is divided into 21 areas called VISNs. VISNs are regional systems of care working together to better meet local healthcare needs and provide greater access to care.[418,419]

VistA (Veterans Health Information Systems Technology Architecture)

A Health Information Technology (HIT) system created and used by the Veterans Health Administration (VHA) of the U.S. Department of Veterans Affairs (VA) in serving America's veterans through the provision of exceptional-quality healthcare that enhances our veterans' health and well-being.[255]

V

VM (Value Modifier)

Before the enactment of the Quality Payment Program, the Value Modifier previously measured the quality and cost of care provided to people with Medicare under the Medicare Physician Fee Schedule (PFS). The Value Modifier is an adjustment made on a per claim basis to Medicare payments for items and services under the Medicare PFS. It is applied at the Taxpayer Identification Number (TIN) level to doctors billing under the TIN. It determines the amount of Medicare payments to physicians based on their performance on specified quality and cost measures. The program rewards quality performance and lower costs.[26]

VM (Virtual Machine)

1. The name given to various programming language interpreters. **2.** One instance of an operating system along with one or more applications running in an isolated partition within the computer. It enables different operating systems to run in the same computer at the same time. Virtual Machines (VMs) are also widely used to run multiple instances of the same operating system, each running the same set or a different set of applications. Each virtual machine functions as if it owned the entire computer. The operating systems in each VM partition are called "guest operating systems," and they communicate with the hardware via the hypervisor control program. *See* **Hypervisor**.[150]

VMR (Virtual Medical Record)

A data model for representing the data that are analyzed and/or produced by Clinical Decision Support (CDS) engines. The term VMR has historically been used in the CDS community to refer to a simplified representation of the clinical record that is suitable and safe for a CDS knowledge engineer to directly manipulate in order to derive patient-specific assessments and recommendations. Historically, the challenge has been that different organizations used different VMRs. The purpose of the VMR effort is to define a standard VMR that can be used across CDS implementations. Moreover, due to the intended use of the VMR, a primary goal is a simple and intuitive representation of data that are easy and safe for a typical CDS knowledge engineer to understand, use, and implement.[9]

V

Voice ID (voice authentication)

A type of user authentication that uses voice print biometrics. It relies on the fact that vocal characteristics, like fingerprints and the patterns of people's irises, are unique for each individual.[2]

Voice over Internet Protocol

See **VoIP**.

Voice Recognition

Computer analysis of the human voice, especially for the purposes of interpreting words and phrases or identifying an individual voice.[107]

Voice response system

See **VRS**.

Voice Response Unit

See **VRU**.

VoIP (Voice over Internet Protocol)

1. A technology that allows telephone calls using an Internet connection instead of a regular (or analog) phone line. Some services using VoIP may only allow you to call other people using the same service but others may allow you to call anyone who has a telephone number—including local, long distance, mobile, and international numbers. **2.** Refers to the use of the Internet Protocol (IP) to transfer voice communications in much the same way that web pages and e-mail are transferred. Each piece of voice data is digitized into chunks and then sent across the Internet (in the case of public VoIP) to a destination server where the chunks are reassembled. This process happens in real time so that two or more people can carry on a conversation.[257,258]

Volume testing

Also known as load testing, it evaluates system performance with predefined load levels. Load testing measures how long it takes a system to perform various program tasks and functions under normal or predetermined conditions.[259]

VPN (Virtual Private Network)

A network that is constructed using public wires—usually the Internet—to connect remote users or regional offices to a company's private, internal network. A VPN secures the private network, using encryption and other security mechanisms to ensure that only authorized users can access the network and that the data cannot be intercepted. This type of network is designed to provide a secure, encrypted tunnel in which to transmit the data between the remote user and the company network.[39]

VRAM (Video RAM or Video Random Access Memory)

Refers to any type of random access memory used to store image data for computer display. VRAM is a type of buffer between a computer processor and the display.[2]

VRML (Virtual Reality Modeling Language)

An open-standard programming language created to design three-dimensional (3-D) and web-based models, textures, and illusions. VRML is used to illustrate 3-D objects, buildings, landscapes, or other items requiring 3-D structure and is very similar to Hypertext Markup Language (HTML). VRML also uses textual representation to define 3-D illusion presentation methods.[52]

VRS (Voice Response System)

Specialized technologies designed for providing callers with verbal and faxed answers to inquiries without assistance from a person. They provide account information, fulfill requests for mailable items, prescreen callers for script customization, interact with host systems (read and write), and produce reports.[142]

VRU (Voice Response Unit)

An automated telephone answering system consisting of hardware and software that allows the caller to navigate through a series of prerecorded

V

messages and use a menu of options through the buttons on a touch-tone telephone or through voice recognition.[142]

VSA (Virtual SAN Appliance)

Also called a Virtual Storage Appliance (VSA), it is a software bundle that allows a storage manager to turn the unused storage capacity in his or her network's virtual servers into a Storage Area Network (SAN). The SAN provides a pool of shared storage that can be accessed by the virtual servers as needed.[2]

VSM (Value Stream Mapping)

A lean manufacturing or lean enterprise technique used to document, analyze, and improve the flow of information or materials required to produce a product or service. Through value stream mapping, a hypothetical hospital is able to identify and eliminate waste, making its processes more efficient and profitable.[148]

Vulnerability

A cybersecurity term that refers to a flaw in a system that can leave it open to attack. A vulnerability may also refer to any type of weakness in a computer system itself, in a set of procedures, or in anything that leaves information security exposed to a threat.[52]

Vulnerability assessment

1. Systematic examination of an information system or product to determine the adequacy of security measures, identify security deficiencies, provide data from which to predict the effectiveness of proposed security measures, and confirm the adequacy of such measures after implementation. **2.** The process of identifying and quantifying vulnerabilities and prioritizing (or ranking) the vulnerabilities in a system.[1,87]

WAN (Wide Area Network)

A computer network that spans a relatively large geographical area and consists of two or more local area networks. Often connected through public networks, such as phone systems, but can also be connected through lease lines or satellites.[39] *See* **LAN, MAN**, and **WLAN**.

WAP (Wireless Application Protocol)

A secure specification that allows users to access information instantly via handheld wireless devices such as mobile phones, pagers, two-way radios, smartphones, and communicators.[39]

Warez

Warez refers to freely distributed copyrighted materials considered to violate copyright law. Warez pertains to releases of unauthorized duplicates by organized groups.[52]

Warm data

Warm data is a term for data that get analyzed on a fairly frequent basis but are not constantly in play or in motion. By contrast, hot data are data that are used very frequently and data that administrators perceive to be always changing. Handling requirements for warm data can be less stringent than those for hot data because of the lower amount of activity that takes place around warm data sets.

Warm standby

Warm standby is a redundancy method that involves having one system running in the background of the identical primary system. The data are regularly mirrored to the secondary server. Therefore, at times, the primary and secondary systems do contain different data or different data versions.[52]

W

WASP (Wireless Application Service Provider)

Provides the same service of a regular application service provider but to wireless clients. WASPs are typically used in enterprises to connect a mobile workforce to company data, including e-mail, Internet access, CRM, ERP, and company financials.[39]

WAV or WAVE (Waveform audio format [.wav])

An audio file format standard for storing an audio bitstream.[39]

Waveform audio format (.wav)

See **WAV** or **WAVE**.

Wavelet

A mathematical function useful in digital signal processing and image compression. Wavelet compression works by analyzing an image and converting it into a set of mathematical expressions that can then be decoded by the receiver.[2]

WCF (Windows Communication Foundation)

A technology for developing applications based on Service-Oriented Architecture (SOA). WCF is implemented using a set of classes placed on top of the. NET Common Language Runtime (CLR). It addresses the problem of interoperability using. NET for distributed applications.[52]

Wearable technology

Technology worn in clothing or accessories that records and reports information about behaviors such as physical activity or sleep patterns. This technology aims to educate and motivate individuals toward better habits and better health. Also known as Wearables.[260]

Web Analytics

The process of analyzing the behavior of visitors to a website. The use of web analytics is said to enable a business to attract more visitors, retain or attract new customers for goods or services, or to increase the dollar volume each customer spends.[2]

W

Web content management

Web Content Management (WCM) is an application for creating, storing, managing, and publishing web page content, which may be in the form of text, audio, graphics, video, etc. The WCM may also organize, index, or otherwise present data uniquely for specific site visitors.[52]

Web crawler

An Internet bot that helps in web indexing. They "crawl" one page at a time through a website until all pages have been indexed. Web crawlers help in collecting information about a website and the links related to them and also help in validating the HTML code and hyperlinks. A web crawler is also known as a web spider, an automatic indexer, or simply a crawler.[52]

Web portal

1. A website or service that offers a broad array of resources and services, such as e-mail, forums, search engines, and online shopping malls. The first web portals were online services, such as AOL, which provided access to the web. **2.** An enterprise portal is a web-based interface for users of enterprise applications. Enterprise portals also provide access to enterprise information such as corporate databases, applications (including web applications), and systems. **3.** Web portals come in two types: internal and external. Internal portals are designed to provide services within an organization, while external portals serve as a starting point for browsing the web.[39,73]

Webmaster

An individual who manages and ensures that a website effectively and efficiently meets its deliverables.[39]

Web server

1. A program that uses HTTP (Hypertext Transfer Protocol) to serve the files that form web pages to users in response to their requests, which are forwarded by their computers' HTTP clients. Dedicated computers and appliances may be referred to as web servers as well. The process is an example of the client/server model. All computers that host websites must have web server programs.[2] *See* **HTTP** and **HTTPS**.

W

Web services

A standardized way of integrating Web-based applications using the XML, SOAP, WSDL, and UDDI open standards over an Internet protocol backbone.[39] Services that are made available from a business's web server for web users or other web-connected programs. Web services range from such major services as storage management and Customer Relationship Management (CRM) down to more limited services.[2]

Web Services Description Language

See **WSDL**.

Web stack

The collection of software required for web development. At a minimum, a web stack contains an Operating System (OS), a programming language, database software, and a web server.[2]

WEP (Wired Equivalent Privacy)

A security protocol for Wireless Local Area Networks (WLANs) defined in the 802.11b standard. WEP is designed to provide the same level of security as that of a wired LAN. LANs are inherently more secure than WLANs because LANs are somewhat protected by the physicalities of their structure, having some or all part of the network inside a building that can be protected from unauthorized access. This has been replaced by WPA.[39]

Wet signature

Created when a person physically marks a document. Ink on paper signature.[262]

Whitelist

A whitelist is a list of entities approved for authorized access or privileged membership to enter a specific area in the computing world. These entities could include electronic groups or organizations, privileged websites, or even e-mail addresses.[52]

W

WHOIS

A query and response protocol that is widely used for querying databases that store the registered users or assignees of an Internet resource, such as a domain name, an IP address block, or an autonomous system, but is also used for a wider range of other information.[7]

WI (Web Interface)

1. The interaction between a user and software running on a web server. The user interface is the web browser and the web page it downloaded and rendered. *See* **Web server**. **2.** A programming connection to the web. *See* **Web services** and **API**.[150]

Wide Area Network

See **WAN**.

Wide SCSI (Wide Small Computer System Interface)

A 20–40 Mbps high-speed interface for connecting devices to the computer bus.[52]

Wide Small Computer System Interface

See **Wide SCSI**.

Widget

A broad term that can refer to either any GUI (graphical user interface) element or a tiny application that can display information and/or interact with the user. A widget can be as rudimentary as a button, scroll bar, label, dialog box, or check box; or it can be something slightly more sophisticated like a search box, tiny map, clock, visitor counter, or unit converter.[52]

Wi-Fi

A wireless networking technology that uses radio waves to provide high-speed network and Internet connections. The Wi-Fi Alliance, the organization that owns the Wi-Fi (registered trademark) term, specifically defines Wi-Fi as "wireless Local Area Network (WLAN) products that are based on the Institute of Electrical and Electronics Engineers' (IEEE) 802.11 standards."

W

Initially, Wi-Fi was used in place of only the 2.4GHz 802.11b standard, but the Wi-Fi Alliance has expanded the generic use of the Wi-Fi term to include any type of network or WLAN product based on any of the 802.11 standards, including 802.11b, 802.11a, dual-band, and others, in an attempt to stop confusion about wireless LAN interoperability.[39]

Wi-Fi Protected Access

See **WPA**.

Wiki

Piece of server software that allows users to freely create and edit web page content using any web browser.[29]

Wildcard

A character (usually * or ?) that can stand for one or more unknown characters during a search and cause the search results to yield all files within a general description or type of software.[2]

Window

A separate viewing area on a computer display screen in a system that allows multiple viewing areas as part of a Graphical User Interface (GUI).[2]

Windows Communication Foundation

See **WCF**.

Wiper

Malware whose goal is to completely destroy or erase all data from the targeted computer or network.[420]

Wired Equivalent Privacy

See **WEP**.

Wireless Application Protocol

See **WAP**.

W

Wireless Application Service Provider

See **WASP**.

Wireless Local Area Network

See **WLAN**.

Wireless technology

An encompassing term that describes numerous communication technologies that rely on a wireless signal to send data rather than using a physical medium (often a wire). In wireless transmission, the medium used is the air, through electromagnetic, radio, and microwave signals. The term communication here means communication not only between people but between devices and other technologies as well.[52]

Wirth's Law

Wirth's Law is a famous quote from Niklaus Wirth, a Swiss computer scientist. In 1995, he proposed an adage that "Software is getting slower more rapidly than hardware is getting faster."

WLAN (Wireless Local Area Network)

Also referred to as LAWN. A type of local area network that uses high-frequency radio waves rather than wires to communicate between nodes. *See* **Wi-Fi**.[39]

Workflow

Progression of steps (tasks, events, and interactions) that comprises a work process, involves two or more persons, and creates or adds value to the organization's activities. In a sequential workflow, each step is dependent on occurrence of the previous step; in a parallel workflow, two or more steps can occur concurrently.[4]

Workflow management

1. An approach that allows for the definition and control of business processes that span applications. **2.** Automated events or processes—a workflow approach that enables automated tasks (e.g., the automation of steps in a marketing campaign or a sales process) to be performed.[142]

Workstation

1. A computer (and often the surrounding area) that has been configured to perform a certain set of tasks, such as processing orders, recording notes, audio recording, or video production. **2.** Workstations generally come with a large, high-resolution graphics screen, large amounts of RAM, access shared network resources, and run local applications. Most workstations also have a mass storage device such as a disk drive, but a special type of workstation, called a diskless workstation, comes without a disk drive. The most common operating systems for workstations are Unix and Windows® NT.[52, 39]

Workstation on Wheels

See **WOW**. *See also* **COW**.

World Wide Web

See **WWW**.

WORM (Write Once, Read Many times)

1. An optical disk technology that allows you to write data onto a disk just once. After that, the data are permanent and can be read any number of times. **2.** A program or algorithm that replicates itself over a computer network and usually performs malicious actions, such as using up the computer's resources and possibly shutting the system down.[39] *See* **Virus**.

WOW (Workstation On Wheels)

Mobile computer stations that can easily be transported between patients and around the hospital. Also known as mobile workstations.[421]

WPA (Wi-Fi-Protected Access)

A security scheme for wireless networks developed by the networking industry in response to the shortcomings of Wired Equivalent Privacy (WEP). WPA uses Temporal Key Integrity Protocol (TKIP) encryption and provides built-in authentication, giving security comparable to VPN tunneling with

WEP, with the benefit of easier administration and use. The current version of these protocols is WPA3.[8, 150]

Write back

A storage method in which data are written into the cache every time a change occurs but is written into the corresponding location in main memory only at specified intervals or under certain conditions.[2]

Write Once, Read Many Times

See **WORM**.

WSDL (Web Services Description Language)

An XML-formatted language used to describe a web service's capabilities as collections of communication end points capable of exchanging messages. WSDL is an integral part of UDDI, an XML-based worldwide business registry. WSDL is the language that UDDI uses. WSDL was developed jointly by Microsoft and IBM.[39]

WWW (World Wide Web)

The web, or World Wide Web, is basically a system of Internet servers that support specially formatted documents. The documents are formatted in a markup language called HTML (HyperText Markup Language) that supports links to other documents, as well as graphics, audio, and video files.[39]

WYSIWYG (What You See Is What You Get)

Some early systems yielded a screen image that was unlike a printed document or file. This term is used to confirm that the system presents a screen image that matches the prints on paper. Pronounced "wizzy-wig."[2]

WYSIWYP (What You See Is What You Print)

Pronounced wizzy-whip, this refers to the ability of a computer system to print colors exactly as they appear on a monitor. WYSIWYP printing requires a special program, called a Color Management System (CMS), to calibrate the monitor and printer.[39] Interactive whiteboard display in which multiple computer users in different geographical locations can write or draw while others watch. They are often used in teleconferencing.[2]

X

X.25

1. Standard protocol for packet-switched Wide Area Network (WAN) communication developed by the International Telecommunication Union-Telecommunication (ITU-T) Standard Sector. **2**. Interface between Data Terminal Equipment (DTE) and Data Circuit-terminating Equipment (DCE) for terminals operating in packet mode and connected to public data networks by a dedicated circuit.[263]

X12 Standard (ASC X12)

Chartered by the American National Standards Institute (ANSI), ASC X12 develops and maintains EDI (Electronic Data Interchange) and CICA (Context Inspired Component Architecture) standards along with XML schemas which drive business processes globally. The ASC X12 organization develops and maintains EDI standards that facilitate electronic interchange relating to business transactions such as order placement and processing, shipping and receiving information, invoicing, payment and cash application data, and data to and from entities involved in finance, insurance, transportation, supply chains, and state and federal governments. Committee members jointly develop and promote EDI standards that streamline business transactions, using a common, uniform business language.[264] *See* **EDI**.

Xenodochial

Xenodochial describes something that is friendly to strangers. In IT, this has a more specific meaning of being intuitive or easy to understand.[52]

XDS (Cross-enterprise Document Sharing)

Focused on providing a standards-based specification for managing the sharing of documents that healthcare enterprises (anywhere from a private physician to a clinic to Health Information Exchange (HIE), to an acute care

DOI: 10.4324/9781003286028-24

inpatient facility) have decided to explicitly share. This contributes to the foundation of a shared electronic health record.[27] *See* **Profile**. Note: XDS is Integrating the Healthcare Enterprise (IHE) Profile.

XML (Extensible Markup Language)

1. General-purpose markup language for creating special-purpose markup languages. It is a simplified subset of standard generalized markup language capable of describing many different kinds of data. Its primary purpose is to facilitate the sharing of data across different systems, particularly systems connected via the Internet. **2.** Describes a class of data objects, called XML documents, and partially describes the behavior of computer programs that process them. XML is an application profile or restricted form of SGML, the Standard Generalized Markup Language (ISO 8879). By construction, XML documents conform to SGML documents.[7] Extensible Markup Language, a specification developed by the W3C. XML is a pared-down version of SGML (Standard Generalized Markup Language) (ISO 8879), designed especially for web documents. It allows designers to create their own customized tags, enabling the definition, transmission, validation, and interpretation of data between applications and between organizations.[39]

XSL (Extensible Stylesheet Language)

A standard developed by the World Wide Web Consortium defining a language for transforming and formatting XML (eXtensible Markup Language) documents. An XSL stylesheet is written in XML and consists of instructions for tree transformation and formatting. The tree transformations describe how each XML tag relates to other data, and the formatting instructions describe how to output the various types of data.[2]

Y

Yobibyte

A unit of digital information storage used to denote the size of data. It is equivalent to 2^{80}, or 1,208,925,819,614,629,174,706,176, bytes and equal to 1,024 zebibytes.[52]

Yottabyte

A unit of digital information storage used to denote the size of data. It is equivalent to a quadrillion gigabytes, 1,000 zettabytes, or 1,000,000,000,000,000,000,000,000 bytes.[52]

Yoyo Mode

A situation wherein a computer or a similar device seems stuck in a loop— turning on briefly, then turning off again. The idea is that the rapid restart and shut-off patterns can be compared to the down and up cycles of a yoyo.[52]

DOI: 10.4324/9781003286028-25

Z

Zenware

A term used to describe the complexity of software as judged by the user by analyzing the User Interface (UI). Software that is simple to use often has a non-cluttered user interface that allows the user to accomplish navigation tasks with a minimal number of clicks and distractions.[52]

Zero-Configuration Network

A zero-configuration network is an IP network that is configured without using any manual configuration or configuration servers. This setup allows someone without networking expertise to connect computers, printers, and other network devices and receive automatic network functionality. Automatic functions include allocating IP addresses, translating between domain names and IP addresses, and locating services such as printing without employing a directory service.[52]

Zero-day attack

Exploitation by a malicious actor of a vulnerability that is unknown to the manufacturer.[48]

Zero-day threat

A zero-day threat is a threat that exploits an unknown computer security vulnerability. The term is derived from the age of the exploit, which takes place before or on the first (or "zeroth") day of a developer's awareness of the exploit or bug. This means that there is no known security fix because developers are oblivious to the vulnerability or threat.[52]

Zero Latency Enterprise

See **ZLE**.

Z

Zero Trust (ZT)

A data-centric cybersecurity strategy for enterprise computing that assumes no end user, computing device, web service, or network connection can be trusted—even when an access request originates from within the organization's own network perimeter. The Zero Trust model has evolved to take into account distributed computing and an ever-expanding attack surface. Unlike a Single Sign-On (SSO) strategy that allows users to log in once and access multiple network services without re-entering authentication factors, Zero Trust requires authentication factors to be verified—and re-verified—each time a network resource is requested.[52]

ZigBee

A specification for a suite of high-level communication protocols using small, low-power digital radios based on an IEEE 802 standard for personal-area networks.[265]

Zip or zipping

A popular data compression format. Files that have been compressed with the ZIP format are called ZIP files and usually end with a. ZIP extension.[39]

ZLE (Zero Latency Enterprise)

The immediate exchange of information across geographical, technical, and organizational boundaries so that all departments, customers, and related parties can work together in real time.[142]

Zombie cookie

A zombie cookie is an HTTP cookie that returns to life automatically after being deleted by the user. Zombie cookies are recreated using a technology called Quantcast, which creates Flash cookies to trace users on the Internet. The Flash cookies are then used to recreate browser cookies, becoming zombie cookies that never die.[52]

Zombie process

A process in its terminated state. Usually occurring in a program with parent-child functions, the process occurs after a child function has finished execution and sends an exit status to its parent function. Until the parent function receives and acknowledges the message, the child function is in a zombie state, meaning it has executed but not exited.[39]

Zombie network

A zombie network is a network or collection of compromised computers or hosts that are connected to the Internet. A compromised computer becomes a zombie that is wirelessly controlled through standards-based networking protocols like HTTP and Internet Relay Chat (IRC).[52]

Appendix A: Healthcare Information Technology Organizations

AAHAM (American Association of Healthcare Administrative Management)

National membership association that represents a broad-based constituency of healthcare professionals in the revenue cycle, reimbursement, registration, admitting, medical records, data management, and patient relations. *www.aaham.org*

AAHC (Association of Academic Health Centers)

Nonprofit organization to improve the healthcare system by mobilizing and enhancing the strengths and resources of the academic health centers. *www.aahcdc.org*

AAMI (Association for Advancement of Medical Instrumentation)

A unique alliance of over 6,000 members united by the common goal of increasing the understanding and beneficial use of medical instrumentation. *www.aami.org*

ABMGG (American Board of Medical Genetics and Genomics)

Physician/PhD certification organization to qualify and examine medical genetic and subspecialty candidates who successfully meet certification requirements.
www.abmgg.org

AcademyHealth

National organization serving the fields of health services and policy research and the professionals who produce and use this important work.
www.academyhealth.org

ACHE (American College of Healthcare Executives)

Membership organization for healthcare executives who lead hospitals, healthcare systems, and other healthcare organizations.
www.ache.org

ACM (Association for Computing Machinery)

Professional organization of computing professionals. The special interest group (SIGHIT) emphasizes the computing and information science-related aspects of health informatics.
www.acm.org

ACT (The App Association)

Advocacy organization for small and mid-size application developers and information technology firms.
www.actonline.org

AdvaMed (Advanced Medical Technology Association)

Membership organization open to medical technology firms worldwide.
www.advamed.org

AEHADA (Association for Executives in Healthcare Applications, Data and Analytics)

An association launched to provide an education and networking platform to healthcare's senior IT applications leaders.
http://aehia.org/

AEHIS (Association for Executives in Healthcare Information Security) (ion Security)

An association launched to provide an education and networking platform to healthcare's senior IT security leaders.
http://aehis.org/

AEHIT (Association for Executives in Healthcare Information Technology)

An association launched to provide an education and networking platform to healthcare's senior IT technology leaders.
http://aehit.org/

AHA (American Hospital Association)

Membership organization for hospitals, healthcare systems, pre-acute/post-acute patient care facilities, and hospital-affiliated educational programs (e.g., hospital school of nursing and program in health administration).
www.aha.org

AHDI (Association for Healthcare Documentation Integrity)

Membership organization for individuals enrolled in a medical transcription program, individual professionals working or involved in healthcare documentation and data capture, healthcare delivery facilities, companies or manufacturers that employ healthcare documentation specialists or provide services or products to the profession, and educational facilities that train medical transcriptionists.
www.ahdionline.org

AHIMA (American Health Information Management Association)

Membership organization for health information management (HIM) professionals interested in promoting the business and clinical uses of electronic and paper-based medical information.
www.ahima.org

AHRQ (Agency for Healthcare Research and Quality)

Federal agency within the Department of Health and Human Services focused on the national mission to improve the quality, safety, efficiency, and effectiveness of healthcare for Americans.
www.ahrq.gov

AIM (Association for Automatic Identification and Mobility)

An international trade association representing automatic identification, data capture, and mobility technology solution providers.
www.aimglobal.org

Alliance HPSR (Alliance for Health Policy and Systems Research)

International partnership hosted by the World Health Organization to promote health policy and systems research in developing countries.
https://ahpsr.who.int/

AMDIS (Association of Medical Directors of Information Systems)

Membership organization for medical directors of information systems.
www.amdis.org

AMIA (American Medical Informatics Association)

Membership organization open to individuals interested in biomedical and health informatics. AMIA focuses on transforming healthcare through trusted science, education, and the practice of informatics.
www.amia.org

ANCC (American Nurses Credentialing Center)

Nursing certification organization to qualify and examine nurse candidates who have successfully completed an accredited program and meet certification requirements. There is a certification for Nursing Informatics. *www.nursingworld.org/ancc*

ANI (Alliance for Nursing Informatics)

Membership organization of nursing informatics associations and groups. *www.allianceni.org*

ANIA (American Nursing Informatics Association)

Membership organization to advance the field of nursing informatics. *www.ania.org*

ANSI (American National Standards Institute)

National voice of the U.S. standards and conformity assessment system, the American National Standards Institute is a membership organization for government agencies, organizations, companies, academic and international bodies, and individuals. *www.ansi.org*

API (Association for Pathology Informatics)

Membership organization for individuals, trainees (e.g., residents, fellows, students, and post-docs), teaching institutions, commercial entities, and other organizations interested in pathology informatics. *www.pathologyinformatics.org*

ASC X12 (Accredited Standards Committee X12)

Membership organization chartered by the American National Standards Institute (ANSI) to support business and technical professionals in a cross-industry forum to enhance business processes with consensus-based, interoperable, syntax-neutral data exchange standards. *www.x12.org*

ASTM International (American Society for Testing and Materials)

Membership organization chartered by ASTM under the American National Standards Institute (ANSI) to support the development of test methods, specifications, guides, and practice standards that support industries and governments worldwide.
www.astm.org

ATA (American Telemedicine Association)

Membership is open to all individuals and organizations interested in providing distance healthcare through technology.
www.americantelemed.org

AUPHA (Association of University Programs in Health Administration)

Membership organization of healthcare management/administration education programs in North America that includes non-academic institutions and individuals inside and outside the United States.
www.aupha.org

BRI (Blockchain Research Institute)

Conducts studies on the impact of blockchain technology on business, government, and society.
www.blockchainresearchinstitute.org

Carequality

A public-private, multi-stakeholder collaborative from across the healthcare ecosystem that uses a consensus-based process to enable seamless connectivity across all participating networks. Carequality is a collaborative project under the Sequoia Project.
www.sequoiaproject.org/carequality

CARIN Alliance (Creating Access to Real-time Information Now through Consumer-Directed Exchange)

A bi-partisan, multi-sector alliance convened to unite industry leaders in advancing the adoption of consumer-directed exchange across the United States.
www.carinalliance.*com*

CCC (Computing Community Consortium)

Cooperative consortium formed by the Computing Research Association (CRA) and the U.S. National Science Foundation, CCC is broadly inclusive and is open to any computing researcher who wishes to become involved.
www.cra.*org/ccc*

CCHIIM (Commission on Certification for Health Informatics and Information Management)

Certification organization focused on establishing, implementing, and enforcing standards and procedures for the certification and recertification of health informatics and information management (HIIM) professionals.
www.ahima.*org/certification*

CDISC (Clinical Data Interchange Standards Consortium)

Membership organization open to any organization of any size interested in information system interoperability to improve medical research and related areas of healthcare.
www.cdisc.*org*

CEN (European Committee for Standardization)

Membership includes the 27 European Union National Standards Bodies (NSBs), Croatia, the Former Yugoslav Republic of Macedonia, Turkey, and three countries of the European Free Trade Association (Iceland, Norway, and Switzerland).
CEN-CENELEC Management Centre
www.cen.*eu*

Center for Medical Interoperability

A 501(c)(3) cooperative research and development lab founded by health systems to simplify and advance data sharing among medical technologies and systems.
www.medicalinteroperability.org

Chamber of Digital Commerce

Our mission is to promote the acceptance and use of digital assets and blockchain technologies. Through education, advocacy, and working closely with policymakers, regulatory agencies, and industry, our goal is to develop an environment that fosters innovation, jobs, and investment. The *World's Leading Blockchain & Digital Asset Trade Association*
https://digitalchamber.org

CHI (Canada Health Infoway)

Organization accountable to Canada's 14 federal, provincial, and territorial governments represented by their Deputy Ministers of Health to foster the development and adoption of information technology to transform healthcare in Canada.
www.infoway-inforoute.ca/en/

CHI (Center for Healthcare Innovation)

Organization encouraging and enabling meaningful and executable innovation that aims to address existing and ensuing healthcare dynamics through communication, education, training, symposia, reports, and research.
www.chisite.org

CHIME (College of Healthcare Information Management Executives)

Membership open to CIOs and senior IT leaders at healthcare-related organizations.
www.chimecentral.org

CHT (Center for Health and Technology)

Private, academic research organization working to advance innovation in telehealth and connected healthcare.
https://health.ucdavis.edu/cht/

CIAQ (Center for Innovation Access & Quality)

Organization promoting the creation and implementation of innovative approaches to improving quality care in safety net systems.
www.ciaqsf.org

CIHI (Canadian Institute for Health Information)

An independent, not-for-profit organization that provides essential data and analysis on Canada's health system and the health of Canadians.
www.cihi.ca

CIHR (Canadian Institutes of Health Research)

Agency responsible for funding health research in Canada.
www.cihr-irsc.gc.ca

Clinical Research Forum

Provide leadership to the national clinical and translational research enterprise and promote understanding and support for clinical research and its impact on health and healthcare.
www.clinicalresearchforum.org

CLSI (Clinical and Laboratory Standards Institute)

Membership organization for IVD manufacturers and suppliers, LIS/HIS companies, pharmaceutical and biotechnology companies, consulting firms, professional societies, trade associations, and government agencies.
www.clsi.org

CMS (Centers for Medicare & Medicaid Services)

Federal agency within the Department of Health and Human Services focused on the national mission to improve the quality, safety, efficiency, and effectiveness of healthcare for Americans.
www.cms.gov

CNC (Center for Nursing Classification and Clinical Effectiveness)

Academia research center at the University of Iowa School of Nursing that facilitates the development of Nursing Interventions Classification (NIC) and Nursing Outcomes Classification (NOC).
www.nursing.uiowa.edu/center-for-nursing-classification-and-clinical-effectiveness

CommonWell Health Alliance

Membership is open to all organizations that share CommonWell's vision that health IT must be inherently interoperable, including health IT suppliers, healthcare providers, and other health-focused organizations such as nonprofit and for-profit institutes.
www.commonwellalliance.org/

CompTIA (The Computing Technology Industry Association Trade Association)

Nonprofit education and certification association for IT professionals and companies inside and outside the United States.
www.comptia.org

DAMA (Data Management Association International)

Chapter-based, as well as global, membership organization for those who engage in information and data management.
www.dama.org

DARPA (Defense Advanced Research Projects Agency)

U.S. Military research agency that invests in breakthrough technologies for national security.
www.darpa.mil

DICOM (Digital Imaging and Communications in Medicine)

Membership organization chartered by Digital Imaging and Communications in Medicine (DICOM) under the American National Standards Institute (ANSI) to develop health information standards.
http://dicom.nema.org/

Digital Bridge

Partnership that establishes effective bidirectional data exchange between healthcare and public health. It creates a forum for key stakeholders in healthcare, public health, and health IT to address information-sharing challenges.
www.digitalbridge.us

Digital Health Canada

Connects, inspires, and educates digital health professionals, creating the future of health in Canada.
https://digitalhealthcanada.com

DirectTrust

DirectTrust is a collaborative nonprofit association of health IT and healthcare provider organizations to support secure, interoperable health information exchange via the direct message protocols.
www.directtrust.org

DoD (Department of Defense) (Health Affairs)

U.S. Military department responsible for the health benefits and healthcare operations of those entrusted to our care.
http://prhome.defense.gov/HA

ECRI Institute

A nonprofit organization dedicated to bringing the discipline of applied scientific research to discover which medical procedures, devices, drugs, and processes are best, all to enable you to improve patient care.
www.ecri.org

eHealth Exchange

A network of exchange partners who securely share clinical information over the Internet across the United States using a standardized approach. eHealth Exchange is part of the Sequoia Project.
www.sequoiaproject.org/ehealth-exchange/

eHI (eHealth Initiative)

Independent, nonprofit organization whose mission is to drive improvements in the quality, safety, and efficiency of healthcare through information technology.
www.ehidc.org

EHNAC (Electronic Healthcare Network Accreditation Commission)

A voluntary, self-governing standards development organization established to develop standard criteria and accredit organizations that electronically exchange healthcare data.
www.ehnac.org

EHRA (Electronic Health Record Association)

A trade association of Electronic Health Record (EHR) companies within HIMSS addressing national efforts to create interoperable EHRs in hospital and ambulatory care settings. The EHR Association operates on the premise that the rapid, widespread adoption of EHRs will help improve the quality of patient care as well as the productivity and sustainability of the healthcare system.
www.ehra.org

Ethereum Foundation

Promotes and supports the Ethereum platform and base layer research, development, and education to bring decentralized protocols and tools to the world that empower developers to produce next-generation decentralized applications and build a more globally accessible, more free, and trustworthy Internet.
www.ethereum.org/foundation

ETSI (European Telecommunications Standards Institute)

Membership organization for individuals, nonprofit associations, universities, public research bodies, governmental organizations, and observers interested in globally applicable standards for Information and Communications Technologies (ICT), including fixed, mobile, radio, converged, broadcast, and Internet technologies.
www.etsi.org

EUnetHTA (European Network for Health Technology Assessment)

Organization supporting collaboration between European Health Technology Applications.
www.eunethta.eu

FCC (Federal Communications Commission)

An independent U.S. government agency directly responsible to Congress charged with regulating interstate and international communications by radio, television, wire, satellite, and cable.
www.fcc.gov

FDA (U.S. Food and Drug Administration)

Federal agency responsible for protecting the public health by ensuring the safety, efficacy, and security of human and veterinary drugs, biological products, medical devices, our nation's food supply, cosmetics, and products that emit radiation.
www.fda.gov

GBA (Government Blockchain Association)

An International Professional Association and a U.S.-based nonprofit, membership organization that consists of individuals and organizations that are interested in promoting blockchain-related solutions to government requirements.
www.gbaglobal.org

HBMA (Healthcare Business Management Association)

A nonprofit professional trade association focused on the revenue cycle management industry in the United States.
www.hbma.org

HC3 (Health Care Cloud Coalition)

Not-for-profit group of stakeholders representing cloud computing, tele-communication, digital health, and healthcare companies in the healthcare sector.
www.hcccoalition.org

HDAA (Healthcare Data and Analytics Association)

Forum where healthcare organizations planning or engaged in data ware-housing and analytics can share ideas and lessons learned.
www.hdwa.org

Health 2.0

Health 2.0 promotes, showcases, and catalyzes new technologies in health-care. Through a worldwide series of conferences, code-a-thons, and prize challenges, we bring together the best minds, resources, and technology for compelling panels, discussions, and product demonstrations, and more.
https://health2conf.com/

Healthbox

A HIMSS Innovation Company, Healthbox is a healthcare advisory firm that leading organizations trust with innovation and digital strategy development and execution.
https://healthbox.com/

HEN World Health Organization (Health Evidence Network)

Network of organizations and institutions promoting the use of evidence in health policy or health technology assessment.
www.euro.who.int/en/data-and-evidence/evidence-informed-policymaking/ health-evidence-network-hen

HFES (Human Factors and Ergonomics Society)

Association representing human factors/ergonomics professionals. Members include psychologists and other scientists, designers, and engineers, all of whom have a common interest in designing systems and equipment to be safe and effective for the people who operate and maintain them.
www.hfes.org

HFMA (Healthcare Financial Management Association)

Membership organization for healthcare financial management executives and leaders.
www.hfma.org

HIBCC (Health Industry Business Communications Council)

An industry-sponsored and supported nonprofit organization. As an ANSI-accredited organization, its primary function is to facilitate electronic communications by developing appropriate standards for information exchange among all healthcare trading partners.
www.hibcc.org

HIMSS (Healthcare Information and Management Systems Society)

HIMSS is a global adviser and thought leader supporting the transformation of health through the application of information and technology.
www.himss.org

HL7 (Health Level Seven)

A not-for-profit, ANSI-accredited standards-developing organization dedicated to providing a comprehensive framework and related standards for the exchange, integration, sharing, and retrieval of electronic health information that supports clinical practice and the management, delivery, and evaluation of health services.
www.hl7.org

HLC (Healthcare Leadership Council)

A coalition of chief executives from all disciplines within the healthcare system.
www.hlc.org

HMD (Health and Medicine Division of the National Academies)

A division of the National Academies of Sciences, Engineering and Medicine, whose aim is to help those in government and the private sector make informed health decisions by providing evidence. Previously referred to as the Institute of Medicine of the National Academies (IOM).
www.nationalacademies.org/hmd

HTA (Health Technology Alliance)

The HTA provides a forum for the productive exchange of ideas and the identification of challenges and solutions common to the use and support of medical and information technologies in all care delivery settings.
www.healthtechnologyalliance.org

HTAi (Health Technology Assessment International)

Membership organization embracing all stakeholders, including researchers, agencies, policymakers, industry, academia, health service providers, and patients/consumers interested in the field of scientific research, to inform policy and clinical decision-making around the introduction and diffusion of health technologies.
www.htai.org

IAPP (International Association of Privacy Professionals)

Membership organization for privacy professionals, corporations, government agencies, and nonprofit groups from around the world.
https://iapp.org/

IBIA (International Biometrics and Identity Association)

The leading international trade group representing the identification technology industry. IBIA advances the adoption and responsible use of

technologies for managing human identity to enhance security, privacy, productivity, and convenience for individuals, organizations, and governments. To effectively carry out its mission, IBIA focuses on three core activities: advocacy, connections, and education.
www.ibia.org

ICCBBA (International Council for Commonality in Blood Bank Automation)

Registration and licensing organization for the ISBT 128 global standard for the identification, labeling, and information processing of human blood, cell, tissue, and organ products across international borders and disparate healthcare systems.
www.iccbba.org

IDESG (Identity Ecosystem Steering Group)

A voluntary, public-private partnership dedicated to redefining how people and organizations identify themselves online by fostering the creation of privacy-enhancing trusted digital identities.
www.idesg.org

IEC (International Electrotechnical Commission)

A not-for-profit, nongovernmental organization. Members are national committees and their appointed experts and delegates coming from industry, government bodies, associations, and academia to participate in technical and conformity assessments.
www.iec.ch

IEEE (Institute of Electrical and Electronics Engineers)

Membership organization for individuals and students who are contributing or working in a technology or engineering field.
www.ieee.org

IEFT (Internet Engineering Task Force)

An open international community of network designers, operators, vendors, and researchers concerned with the evolution of the Internet architecture

and the smooth operation of the Internet. Membership is open to any interested individual.
www.ietf.org

IHA (Intelligent Health Association)

Nonprofit organization with the mission to raise the level of awareness through educational programs, empower the health community with vendor-neutral information, and encourage the adoption and implementation of technology.
www.ihassociation.org

IHE International (Integrating the Healthcare Enterprise)

A nonprofit organization that promotes the coordinated use of established standards such as DICOM and HL7 to address specific clinical needs in support of optimal patient care.
www.ihe.net

IMIA (International Medical Informatics Association)

Membership is limited to organizations, societies, and corporations interested in promoting informatics in healthcare.
www.imia.org

INAHTA (International Network of Agencies for Health Technology Assessment)

An organization of non-profit-making organizations producing health technology assessments and linked to regional or national governments.
www.inahta.org

INCITS (InterNational Committee for Information Technology Standards)

Membership is open to organizations directly and materially affected by standardization in the field of Information and Communications Technologies (ICT), encompassing storage, processing, transfer, display, management, organization, and retrieval of information.
www.incits.org

Institute for e-Health Policy

Nonprofit organization providing research and educational opportunities for public and private sector stakeholders—two key constituents that make and are most directly impacted by e-health policy decisions.
www.e-healthpolicy.org

ISACA (previously known as the Information Systems Audit and Control Association)

Nonprofit, global association engaging in the development, adoption, and use of globally accepted, industry-leading knowledge and practices for information systems. ISACA now goes by its acronym only.
www.isaca.org

(ISC)² (International Information Systems Security Certification Consortium)

An international, nonprofit membership association for information security leaders.
www.isc2.org

ISO (International Organization for Standardization)

A network of national standards bodies that develop and publish International Standards. The national standards bodies represent ISO in their country.
www.iso.org

ISSA (Information Systems Security Association)

Volunteer organization for information security professionals and practitioners.
www.issa.org

ITAC (Information Technology Association of Canada) Technation

A membership organization of for-profit companies with a presence in Canada, for whom the provision of information technology products or services is a significant component of revenue and of strategic importance,

or one which increases the efficiency of electronic markets by facilitating the meeting and interaction of buyers and sellers over the Internet.
https://technationcanada.ca/en/

ITIF (Information Technology and Innovation Foundation)

An independent, nonpartisan research and educational institute focusing on the intersection of technological innovation and public policy.
www.itif.org

ITU (International Telecommunication Union)

Membership organization representing a cross-section of the global Information and Communication Technologies (ICT) sector along with leading research and development (R&D) institutions and academia. ITU is the United Nations specialized agency for ICT.
www.itu.int

The Joint Commission

Accreditation organization to support performance improvement in healthcare organizations.
www.jointcommission.org

JPHIT (Joint Public Health Informatics Taskforce)

Coalition of nine national associations that help U.S. governmental agencies build modern information systems across a spectrum of public health programs.
www.jphit.org

Kantara Initiative

Organization providing strategic vision and real-world innovation for the digital identity transformation. Developing initiatives including: Identity Relationship Management, User Managed Access, Identities of Things, and Minimum Viable Consent Receipt. Kantara Initiative connects a global, open, and transparent leadership community.
www.kantarainitiative.org

Leapfrog Group

Voluntary program aimed at mobilizing employer purchasing power to alert America's health industry that big leaps in healthcare safety, quality, and customer value will be recognized and rewarded.
www.leapfroggroup.org

Linux Foundation

Supports the creation of sustainable open-source ecosystems by providing financial and intellectual resources, infrastructure, services, events, and training.
www.linuxfoundation.org

LOINC (Logical Observation Identifiers Names and Codes)

LOINC is a database and universal standard for identifying medical laboratory observations developed and maintained by the Regenstrief Institute, an international nonprofit medical research organization associated with Indiana University. The scope of the LOINC effort includes laboratory and other clinical observations.
www.loinc.org

MassChallenge HealthTech

MassChallenge strengthens the global innovation ecosystem by accelerating high-potential startups across all industries, from anywhere in the world.
https://masschallenge.org/programs-healthtech

MDISS (Medical Device Innovation, Safety and Security Consortium)

Nonprofit professional organization committed to advancing quality healthcare with a focus on the safety and security of medical devices. Serves providers, payers, manufacturers, universities, government agencies, technology companies, individuals, patients, patient advocates, and associations.
https://mdiss.org/

MITA (Medical Imaging and Technology Alliance)

The leading organization and collective voice of medical imaging equipment manufacturers, innovators, and product developers, a division of the National Electrical Manufacturers Association (NEMA).
www.medicalimaging.org

MLA (Medical Library Association)

Membership organization for individuals with an interest in the health sciences information field.
www.mlanet.org

MTPPI (Medical Technology & Practice Patterns Institute)

A nonprofit organization conducting research on the clinical and economic implications of healthcare technologies. MTPPI research is directed toward the formulation and implementation of local and national healthcare policies.
www.mtppi.org

NAHDO (National Association of Health Data Organizations)

A national, not-for-profit membership organization dedicated to improving healthcare through the collection, analysis, dissemination, public availability, and use of health data.
www.nahdo.org

NANDA International

NANDA International is an organization focused on the development and use of nursing's standardized terminology to ensure patient safety through evidence-based care, thereby improving the healthcare of all people.
www.nanda.org

NAPHSIS (National Association for Public Health Statistics and Information Systems)

Membership association of state vital records and public health statistics offices in the United States.
www.naphsis.org

NASCIO (National Association of State Chief Information Officers)

Membership organization of state chief information and information technology executives from the states, territories, and the District of Columbia. Leading advocate for technology policy at all levels of government. Other public sector and nonprofit organizations may join.
www.nascio.org

NATE (National Association for Trusted Exchange)

Nonprofit association bringing the expertise of its membership and other stakeholders together to find common solutions that optimize the appropriate exchange of health information for greater gains in adoption and outcomes.
www.nate-trust.org

NCHS (National Center for Health Statistics)

Centers for Disease Control and Prevention (CDC) center for statistical information.
www.cdc.gov/nchs

NCSA (National Cyber Security Alliance)

Organization building strong public/private partnerships to create and implement broad-reaching education and awareness efforts to empower users at home, work, and school with the information they need to keep themselves, their organizations, their systems, and their sensitive information safe and secure online and encourage a culture of cybersecurity.
www.staysafeonline.org

NEHI (Network for Excellence in Health Innovation)

Dedicated to identifying innovations that improve the quality and lower the costs of healthcare. NEHI's network of nearly 100 healthcare organizations is a hotbed for consensus solutions that cut across traditional silos and drive policy change.
www.nehi-us.org/

NHIC (National Health Information Center)

A health information referral service sponsored by the Office of Disease Prevention and Health Promotion, Office of Public Health and Science, Office of the Secretary, and the U.S. Department of Health and Human Services (HHS). NHIC links people to organizations that provide reliable health information.
www.health.gov/nhic

NH-ISAC (National Health Information Sharing and Analysis Center)

A trusted community of critical infrastructure owners and operators within the Health Care and Public Health sector (HPH).
https://h-isac.org/

NHIT (National Health IT Collaborative for the Underserved)

Nonprofit organization working to ensure that underserved populations are not left behind as health information technologies are developed and employed.
www.nhit.org/

NIC (National Interoperability Collaborative)

An initiative with the Stewards of Change Institute (SOCI) and AcademyHealth to increase collaboration among sectors that impact health and well-being by improving information sharing, interoperability, and use of technology.
https://nic-us.org/

NIH (National Institutes of Health)

A part of the U.S. Department of Health and Human Services, NIH is the nation's medical research agency.
www.nih.gov

NIST (National Institute of Standards and Technology)

Federal agency responsible for advancing measurement science, standards, and technology to improve quality of life.
www.nist.gov

NITRD (Networking and Information Technology Research and Development Program)

National program that provides a framework in which many federal agencies coordinate networking and information technology research and development efforts. Operates under the aegis of the NITRD Subcommittee of the National Science and Technology Council's (NSTC) Committee on Technology.
www.nitrd.gov/

NLM (National Library of Medicine)

NLM is the world's largest medical library. The library collects materials in all areas of biomedicine and healthcare, as well as works on biomedical aspects of technology, the humanities, and the physical, life, and social sciences. The collections stand at more than 9 million items—books, journals, technical reports, manuscripts, microfilms, photographs, and images. NLM is a national resource for all U.S. health science libraries through a National Network of Libraries of Medicine®.
www.nlm.nih.gov

NQF (National Quality Forum)

Private sector standard setting organization whose efforts center on the evaluation and endorsement of standardized performance measurement.
www.qualityforum.org

NSF (National Science Foundation)

An independent federal agency funding approximately 20 percent of all federally supported basic research conducted by America's colleges and universities. In many fields, such as mathematics, computer science, and the social sciences, NSF is the major source of federal backing.
www.nsf.gov

NTCA—The Rural Broadband Association

Association representing independent, community-based telecommunications companies that are leading innovation in rural and small-town America.
www.ntca.org/

NUBC (National Uniform Billing Committee)

Goal is to achieve administrative simplification as outlined in HIPAA. Membership includes national provider and payer organizations. Recently, the NUBC increased its membership to include the public health sector as well as the electronic standard development organization. NUBC maintains the integrity of the UB-92 data set.
www.nubc.org/

OASIS (Advancing Open Standards for the Information Society)

Open membership to ensure that all those affected by open standards have a voice in their creation.
www.oasis-open.org

OMG (Object Management Group)

An international, open-membership, not-for-profit computer industry consortium of government agencies, small and large information technology users, vendors, and research institutions. Any organization may join OMG and participate in the standards-setting process. OMG Task Forces develop enterprise integration standards for a wide range of technologies.
www.omg.org

ONC (Office of the National Coordinator for Health Information Technology)

The Office of the National Coordinator for Health Information Technology is the principal federal entity charged with coordination of nationwide efforts to implement and use the most advanced health information technology and the electronic exchange of health information. ONC is organizationally located within the Office of the Secretary for the U.S. Department of Health and Human Services.
www.healthit.gov

Patient Safety Movement

Nonprofit organization working to confront the large-scale problem of more than 200,000 preventable patient deaths in U.S. hospitals each year by providing actionable ideas and innovations that can transform the process of care, dramatically improve patient safety, and help eliminate patient preventable deaths.
https://psmf.org/

Patientory Association

The Patientory Association is a global nonprofit healthcare member organization that connects healthcare industry adopters of disruptive healthcare technologies. The PTOYMatrix storage network improves data integrity and reduces transactional and operational costs. This system eliminates the friction of third-party intermediaries in managing healthcare data. $PTOY is a digital cryptocurrency that drives the PTOYMatrix's value in private health data and cybersecurity.
https://ptoy.org/

PCH Alliance (Personal Connected Health Alliance)

A nonprofit organization formed by HIMSS that believes that health is personal and extends beyond healthcare. The Alliance mobilizes a coalition of stakeholders to realize the full potential of personal connected health.
www.pchalliance.org

PCORI (Patient-Centered Outcomes Research Institute)

An independent nonprofit, nongovernmental organization located in Washington, DC, authorized by Congress in 2010, focused on improving the quality and relevance of evidence available to help patients, caregivers, clinicians, employers, insurers, and policymakers make informed health decisions.
www.pcori.org

Pharmacy HIT (Health Information Technology) Collaborative

Formed by nine pharmacy professional associations representing over 250,000 members, the Pharmacy HIT Collaborative's vision and mission is

for the U.S. healthcare system to be supported by the integration of pharmacists for the provision of quality patient care.
www.pharmacyhit.org

PHI (Public Health Institute)

An independent, nonprofit organization that partners with foundations, federal and state agencies, and other nonprofit organizations to support a diverse array of research products and public health interventions.
www.phi.org

PHII (Public Health Informatics Institute)

A program of the Task Force for Global Health at the Centers for Disease Control and Prevention that works to improve health outcomes worldwide by transforming health practitioners' ability to apply information effectively. The Institute works with public health organizations, both domestically and internationally, through a variety of projects funded by government agencies and private foundations.
www.phii.org

PMI (Project Management Institute)

Individual membership is open to anyone interested in project management.
www.pmi.org

Regenstrief Institute

An internationally recognized informatics and healthcare research organization. It is closely affiliated with the Indiana University School of Medicine, Roudebush VA Medical Center, and Wishard Health Services to improve health through research that enhances the quality and cost-effectiveness of healthcare.
www.regenstrief.org

Scottsdale Institute

A not-for-profit membership organization of prominent healthcare systems whose goal is to support members as they move forward to achieve clinical integration and transformation through information technology.
www.scottsdaleinstitute.org

The Sequoia Project

An independent, nonprofit, 501c3, public-private collaborative chartered to advance the implementation of secure, interoperable nationwide health information exchange.
www.sequoiaproject.org

SHIEC (Strategic Health Information Exchange Collaborative)

A national collaborative representing health information exchanges (HIEs) representing 60 HIEs, which collectively cover more than 200 million people across the United States.
https://healthix.org/strategic-health-information-exchange-collaborative-shiec/

SHS (Society for Health Systems)

Membership association for productivity and efficiency professionals specializing in industrial engineering, healthcare, ergonomics, and other related professions.
www.iise.org/shs/

SIIM (Society for Imaging Informatics in Medicine)

Membership open to anyone with an interest in the vital and growing field of medical imaging informatics and image management.
www.siim.org

SIMGHOSTS

Nonprofit organization dedicated to supporting individuals and institutions operating medical simulation technology and spaces through hands-on training events, online resources, and professional development.
www.simghosts.org

SNOMED International

A not-for-profit organization that owns, administers, and develops SNOMED–CT, a clinical terminology created by a range of healthcare specialists to support clinical decision-making and analytics in software programs.
www.snomed.org

Springboard Enterprises

Nonprofit network of innovators, investors, and influencers who are dedicated to building high-growth technology-oriented companies led by women.
www.sb.co

TIGER Initiative (Technology Informatics Guiding Education Reform)

An initiative focused on education reform and interprofessional community development to maximize the integration of technology and informatics into seamless practice, education, and research resource development.
www.himss.org/professional-development/tiger-initiative

W3C (World Wide Web Consortium)

An international community where member organizations, full-time staff, and the public work together to develop Web standards. The W3C mission is to lead the World Wide Web to its full potential by developing protocols and guidelines that ensure the long-term growth of the Web.
www.w3.org

WEDI (Workgroup for Electronic Data Interchange)

Membership organization actively seeking membership from all key parties in healthcare to ensure broad representation from throughout the healthcare community, including individuals, providers, health plans, hybrid organizations (formerly mixed provider/health plan), government organizations, standards organizations, vendors, not-for-profit, and affiliates/regional entities.
www.wedi.org

Appendix B: Healthcare IT-Related Credentials

*All information current as of 09/01/23

Certifications, Degrees, Professional Fellowships, Honors Designations

I. Certifications

Credential	Full Name	Organization Acronym	Organization Full Name
a-IPC	Associate-Infection Prevention & Control	CBIC	Certification Board of Infection Control and Epidemiology
ACCNS-AG	CNS Wellness Through Acute Care (Adult/Gero)	AACN	American Association of Critical-Care Nurses
ACCNS-N	CNS Wellness Through Acute Care (Neonatal)	AACN	American Association of Critical-Care Nurses
ACCNS-P	CNS Wellness Through Acute Care (Pediatric)	AACN	American Association of Critical-Care Nurses
ACHPN	Advanced Certified Hospice & Palliative Nurse	HPCC	Hospice & Palliative Care Credentialing Center
ACNP-BC	Acute Care Nurse Practitioner	ANCC	American Nurses Credentialing Center

(Continued)

(Continued)

Credential	Full Name	Organization Acronym	Organization Full Name
ACNPC-AG	(Adult-Gerontology) Acute Care Nurse Practitioner	AACN	American Association of Critical-Care Nurses
ACRP-CP	ACRP Certified Professional	ACRP	Association of Clinical Research Professionals
ACRP-MDP	ACRP Medical Device Professional	ACRP	Association of Clinical Research Professionals
ACRP-PM	ACRP Project Manager	ACRP	Association of Clinical Research Professionals
AFN-BC*	Advanced Forensic Nursing Certification	ANCC	American Nurses Credentialing Center
ACNS-BC	Adult Health Clinical Nurse Specialist	ANCC	American Nurses Credentialing Center
AGACNP-BC	Adult-Gerontology Acute Care Nurse Practitioner	ANCC	American Nurses Credentialing Center
AGCNS-BC	Adult-Gerontology Clinical Nurse Specialist	ANCC	American Nurses Credentialing Center
AGNP	Adult-Gerontology Primary Care Nurse Practitioner	AANPCP	American Academy of Nurse Practitioners Certification Program
AGPCNP-BC	Adult-Gerontology Primary Care Nurse Practitioner	ANCC	American Nurses Credentialing Center
AHN-BC	Advanced Holistic Nurse, Board certified	AHNCC	American Holistic Nurses Credentialing Corporation
AHPP	Agile Hybrid Project Pro	PMI	Project Management Institute
AMB-BC*	Ambulatory Care Nursing Certification	ANCC	American Nurses Credentialing Center
AM-MC	Agile Metrics Micro Credential	PMI	Project Management Institute

Credential	Full Name	Organization Acronym	Organization Full Name
ANP-BC	Adult Nurse Practitioner, Board Certified	ANCC	American Nurses Credentialing Center
AOCN	Advanced Oncology Certified Nurse	ONCC	Oncology Nursing Certification Corporation
AOCNP	Advanced Oncology Certified Nurse Practitioner	ONCC	Oncology Nursing Certification Corporation
AOCNS	Advanced Oncology Certified Clinical Nurse Specialist	ONCC	Oncology Nursing Certification Corporation
APHN-BC	Advanced Practice Holistic Nurse, Board Certified	AHNCC	American Holistic Nurses Credentialing Corporation
APHSW-C	Advanced Palliative Hospice Social Worker-Certified	HPCC	Hospice & Palliative Care Credentialing Center
BB	Technologist in Blood Banking	ASCP BOC	American Society for Clinical Pathology Board of Certification
BC	Board Certified	ANCC	American Nurses Credentialing Center
BC-ADM	Board Certified Advanced Diabetes Management	ADCES	Association of Diabetes Care & Education Specialists
BEPC	Built Environment Project Communications Pro	PMI	Project Management Institute
BETI	Built Environment Technology & Innovation Pro	PMI	Project Management Institute
BMTCN	Blood & Marrow Transplant Certified Nurse	ONCC	Oncology Nursing Certification Corporation

(Continued)

(Continued)

Credential	Full Name	Organization Acronym	Organization Full Name
CAHIMS	Certified Associate in Healthcare Information and Management Systems	HIMSS	Healthcare Information and Management Systems Society
CAPM	Certified Associate in Project Management	PMI	Project Management Institute
CBCN	Certified Breast Cancer Nurse	ONCC	Oncology Nursing Certification Corporation
CC	Certified in Cybersecurity	$(ISC)^2$	International Information Systems Security Certification Consortium
CCA	Certified Coding Associate	AHIMA	American Health Information Management Association
CCC-A	Certificate of Clinical Competence, Audiology	ASHA	American Speech-Language-Hearing Association
CCC-SLP	Certificate of Clinical Competence, Speech-Language Pathology	ASHA	American Speech-Language-Hearing Association
CCHT	Certified Clinical Hemodialysis Technician	NNCC	Nephrology Nursing Certification Commission
CCHT-A	Certified Clinical Hemodialysis Technician, Advanced	NNCC	Nephrology Nursing Certification Commission
CCM	Certified Case Manager	CCMC	Commission for Case Manager Certification
CCMHC	Certified Clinical Mental Health Counselor	NBCC	National Board for Certified Counselors
CCRA	Certified Clinical Research Associate	ACRP	Association of Clinical Research Professionals

Credential	Full Name	Organization Acronym	Organization Full Name
CCRC	Certified Clinical Research Coordinator	ACRP	Association of Clinical Research Professionals
CCRN	Critical Care Registered Nurse (Adult, Pediatric, Neonatal)	AACN	American Association of Critical-Care Nurses
CCRN-E	TeleICU Acute/Critical Care Nursing (Adult)	AACN	American Association of Critical-Care Nurses
CCRN-K	Acute/Critical Care Knowledge Professional (Adult, Pediatric, Neonatal)	AACN	American Association of Critical-Care Nurses
CCS	Certified Coding Specialist	AHIMA	American Health Information Management Association
CCSP	Certified Cloud Security Professional	(ISC)^2	International Information Systems Security Certification Consortium
CCS-P	Certified Coding Specialist, Physician-Based	AHIMA	American Health Information Management Association
CDBA	Citizen Developer Business Architect	PMI	Project Management Institute
CDCES	Certified Diabetes Care & Education Specialist	ADCES	American Association of Diabetes Educators
CDIP	Certified Documentation Integrity Practitioner	AHIMA	American Health Information Management Association
CDIP	Certified DICOM Integration Professional	PARCA	PACS Administrators Registry and Certification Association

(Continued)

(Continued)

Credential	Full Name	Organization Acronym	Organization Full Name
CDMS	Certified Disability Management Specialist	CCMC	Commission for Case Manager Certification
CDN	Certified Dialysis Nurse	NNCC	Nephrology Nursing Certification Commission
CD-LPN/ CD-LVN	Certified Dialysis LPN Certified Dialysis LV<	NNCC	Nephrology Nursing Certification Commission
CD-P	Citizen Developer Practitioner	PMI	Project Management Institute
CDPSE	Certified Data Privacy Solutions Engineer	ISACA	Information Systems Audit and Control Association
CEMC	Certified Evaluation & Management Coder	AAPC	American Academy of Professional Coders
CERT	Community Emergency Response Team	FEMA	Federal Emergency Management Agency
CGEIT	Certified in the Governance of Enterprise IT	ISACA	Information Systems Audit and Control Association
CGRC	Governance Risk & Compliance Certification	(ISC)^2	International Information Systems Security Certification Consortium
CGRN	Certified Gastroenterology Registered Nurse	ABCGN	American Board of Certification for Gastroenterology Nurses
CHC	Certified Health Care Constructor	AHA-CC	American Hospital Association Credentialing Center
CHCIO	Certified Healthcare CIO	CHIME	College of Healthcare Information Management Executives

Credential	Full Name	Organization Acronym	Organization Full Name
CHDA	Certified Health Data Analyst	AHIMA	American Health Information Management Association
CHESP	Certified Health Care Environmental Services Professional (CHESP)	AHA-CC	American Hospital Association Credentialing Center
CHFM	Certified Healthcare Facility Manager	AHA-CC	American Hospital Association Credentialing Center
CHFP	Certified Healthcare Financial Professional	HFMA	Healthcare Financial Management Association
CHISL	Certified Healthcare Information Security Leader	CHIME	College of Healthcare Information Management Executives
CHPN	Certified Hospice and Palliative Care Nurse	HPCC	Hospice and Palliative Care Credentialing Center
CHPPN	Certified Hospice and Palliative Care Pediatric Nurse	HPCC	Hospice and Palliative Care Credentialing Center
CHPS	Certified in Healthcare Privacy and Security	AHIMA	American Health Information Management Association
CIC	Certified Inpatient Coder	AAPC	American Academy of Professional Coders
CIC	Certification in Infection Control	CBIC	Certification Board of Infection Control and Epidemiology
CIIP	Certified Imaging Informatics Professional	SIIM	Society for Imaging Informatics in Medicine

(Continued)

(Continued)

Credential	Full Name	Organization Acronym	Organization Full Name
CISA	Certified Information Systems Auditor	ISACA	Information Systems Audit and Control Association
CISM	Certified Information Security Manager	ISACA	Information Systems Audit and Control Association
CISSP	Certified Information Systems Security Professional	(ISC)^2	International Information Systems Security Certification Consortium
CISSP-ISSAP	Information Systems Security Architecture Professional	(ISC)^2	International Information Systems Security Certification Consortium
CISSP-ISSEP	Information Systems Security Engineering Professional	(ISC)^2	International Information Systems Security Certification Consortium
CISSP-ISSMP	Information Systems Security Management Professional	(ISC)^2	International Information Systems Security Certification Consortium
CRCR	Certified Revenue Cycle Representative	HFMA	Healthcare Financial Management Association
CSSBB	Certified Lean Six Sigma Black Belt	ASQ	American Society for Quality
CSSGB	Certified Lean Six Sigma Green Belt	ASQ	American Society for Quality
CSSLP	Certified Secure Software Lifecycle Professional	(ISC)^2	International Information Systems Security Certification Consortium
CM	Certified Midwife	AMCB	American Midwifery Certification Board

Credential	Full Name	Organization Acronym	Organization Full Name
CMA	Certified Management Accountant	IMA	Institute of Management Accountants
CMDA	Certified Medical Device Auditor	ASQ	American Society for Quality
CMGT-BC*	Nursing Case Management Certification	ANCC	American Nurses Credentialing Center
CMAS	Certified Medical Audit Specialist	CCMA	Council for Certification of Medical Auditors, Inc.
CMC	Cardiac Medicine, Adult	AACN	American Association of Critical-Care Nurses
CMRP	Certified Materials & Resources Professional (CMRP)	AHA-CC	American Hospital Association Credentialing Center
CNM	Certified Nurse Midwife	AMCB	American Midwifery Certification Board
CNN	Certified Nephrology Nurse	NNCC	Nephrology Nursing Certification Commission
CNN-NP	Certified Nephrology Nurse-Nurse Practitioner	NNCC	Nephrology Nursing Certification Commission
COC	Certified Outpatient Code	AAPC	American Academy of Professional Coders
COTA	Certified Occupational Therapy Assistant	NBCOT	National Board for Certification in Occupational Therapy
CPA	Certified Public Accountant	AICPA	American Institute of Certified Public Accountants
CPAS	Certified PACS Associate	PARCA	PACS Administrators Registry and Certification Association

(Continued)

(Continued)

Credential	Full Name	Organization Acronym	Organization Full Name
CPC	Certified Professional Coder	AAPC	American Academy of Professional Coders
CPDHTS	Certified Professional in Digital Health Transformation Strategy	HIMSS	Healthcare Information and Management Systems Society
CPHIMS	Certified Professional in Healthcare Information and Management Systems	HIMSS	Healthcare Information and Management Systems Society
CPHIMS-CA	Certified Professional in Healthcare Information and Management Systems, Canada	HIMSS	Healthcare Information and Management Systems Society
CPHON	Certified Pediatric Hematology Oncology Nurse	ONCC	Oncology Nursing Certification Corporation
CPHQ	Certified Professional in Healthcare Quality	NAHQ	National Association for Healthcare Quality
CPHRM	Certified Professional in Health Care Risk Management	AHA-CC	American Hospital Association Credentialing Center
CPLC	Certified in Perinatal Loss Care	HPCC	Hospice & Palliative Care Credentialing Center
CPhT	Certified Pharmacy Technician	PTCB	Pharmacy Technician Certification Board
CPhT-Adv	Advanced Certified Pharmacy Technician	PTCB	Pharmacy Technician Certification Board
CPNP-PC	Certified Pediatric Nurse Practitioner, Primary Care	PNCB	Pediatric Nurse Certification Board
CPNP-AC	Certified Pediatric Nurse Practitioner, Acute Care	PNCB	Pediatric Nursing Certification Board

Credential	Full Name	Organization Acronym	Organization Full Name
CPSA	Certified PACS System Analyst	PARCA	PACS Administrators Registry and Certification Association
CRC	Certified Risk Adjustment Coder	AAPC	American Academy of Professional Coders
CRISC	Certified in Risk & Information System Control	ISACA	Information Systems Audit and Control Association
CRNA	Certified Registered Nurse Anesthetist	AANA	American Association of Nurse Anesthesiology
CRNFA	Certified Registered Nurse First Assistant	NASC	National Assistant at Surgery Certification
CRT	Certified Respiratory Therapist	NBRC	National Board for Respiratory Care
CSC	Cardiac Surgery, Adult	AACN	American Association of Critical Care Nurses
CSCA	Certified in Strategy & Competitive Analysis	IMA	Institute of Management Accountants
CSP	Certified Specialty Pharmacist	SPCB	Specialty Pharmacy Certification Board
CT	Cytologist	ASCP BOC	American Society for Clinical Pathology Board of Certification
CV-BC*	Cardiac Vascular Nursing Certification	ANCC	American Nurses Credentialing Center
DAC	Discipline Agile Coach	PMI	Project Management Institute
DASM	Discipline Agile Scrum Master	PMI	Project Management Institute
DASSM	Discipline Agile Senior Scrum Master	PMI	Project Management Institute

(Continued)

(Continued)

Credential	Full Name	Organization Acronym	Organization Full Name
DAVSC	Discipline Agile Value Stream Consultant	PMI	Project Management Institute
ENP	Emergency Nurse Practitioner	AANPCB	American Academy of Nurse Practitioners Certification Program
FACHE	Fellow of the American College of Healthcare Executives	ACHE	American College of Healthcare Executives
FNP	Family Nurse Practitioner	AANPCP	American Academy of Nurse Practitioners Certification Program
FNP-BC	Family Nurse Practitioner	ANCC	American Nurses Credentialing Center
GERO-BC*	Gerontological Nursing Certification	ANCC	American Nurses Credentialing Center
HN-BC	Holistic Nurse, Board Certified	AHNCC	American Holistic Nurses Credentialing Corporation
HNB-BC	Holistic Nurse Baccalaureate, Board Certified	AHNCC	American Holistic Nurses Credentialing Corporation
MECH	Mechanic Evaluation and Certification for Health Care	AHA-CC	American Hospital Association Credentialing Center
LTC-CIP	Long-Term Care Certification in Infection Prevention	CBIC	Certification Board of Infection Control and Epidemiology
MED-SURG-BC*	Medical-Surgical Nursing Certification	ANCC	American Nurses Credentialing Center
MT (AAB)	Medical Technologist	ABOR	American Association of Bioanalysts Board of Registry
NE-BC*	Nurse Executive Certification	ANCC	American Nurses Credentialing Center
NEA-BC*	Nurse Executive Advanced Certification	ANCC	American Nurses Credentialing Center

Credential	Full Name	Organization Acronym	Organization Full Name
NHDP-BC*	National Healthcare Disaster Certification (Interprofessional)	ANCC	American Nurses Credentialing Center
NNP-BC	Neonatal Nurse Practitioner, Board Certified	NCC	National Certification Corporation
NPD-BC*	Nursing Professional Development Certification	AACN	American Nurses Credentialing Center
OTF	Organizational Transformation Foundation	PMI	Project Management Institute
OTI	Organizational Transformation Implementation	PMI	Project Management Institute
OTO	Organizational Transformation Orchestration	PMI	Project Management Institute
OTR	Occupational Therapist Registered	NBCOT	National Board for Certification in Occupational Therapy
PA-C	Physician Assistant, Certified	NCCPA	National Commission on the Certification of Physician Assistants
PED-BC*	Pediatric Nursing Certification	ANCC	American Nurses Credentialing Center
PCCN	Progressive Care Nursing, Adult	AACN	American Association of Critical-Care Nurses
PCCN-K	Progressive Care Knowledge Professional, Adult	AACN	American Association of Critical-Care Nurses
PCNS-BC	Pediatric Clinical Nurse Specialist	ANCC	American Nurses Credentialing Center
PfMP	Portfolio Management Professional	PMI	Project Management Institute

(Continued)

(Continued)

Credential	Full Name	Organization Acronym	Organization Full Name
PgMP	Program Management Professional	PMI	Project Management Institute
PHCNS-BC	Public/Community Health Clinical Nurse Specialist	ANCC	American Nurses Credentialing Center
PMGT-BC*	Pain Management Certification	ANCC	American Nurses Credentialing Center
PMH-BC*	Psychiatric-Mental Health Nursing Certification	ANCC	American Nurses Credentialing Center
PMHCNS-BC	Adult Psychiatric-Mental Health Clinical Nurse Specialist, Board Certified	ANCC	American Nurses Credentialing Center
PMHCNS-BC	Psychiatric-Mental Health Clinical Nurse Specialist	ANCC	American Nurses Credentialing Center
PMHNP-BC	Psychiatric-Mental Health Nurse Practitioner	ANCC	American Nurses Credentialing Center
PMHS	Pediatric Primary Care Mental Health Specialist	PNCB	Pediatric Nursing Certification Board
PMI-ACP	PMI-Agile Certified Practitioner	PMI	Project Management Institute
PMI-CP	Construction Professional in Built Environment Projects	PMI	Project Management Institute
PMI-PBA	PMI Professional in Business Analysis	PMI	Project Management Institute
PMI-RMP	PMI Risk Management Professional	PMI	Project Management Institute
PMI-SP	PMI Scheduling Professional	PMI	Project Management Institute
PMP	Project Management Professional	PMI	Project Management Institute
RNAS-C	Registered Nurse Assistant At Surgery-Certified	NASC	National Assistant at Surgery Certification

Credential	Full Name	Organization Acronym	Organization Full Name
RN-BC*	Registered Nurse, Board Certified, Informatics	ANCC	American Nurses Credentialing Center
SANE-A	Sexual Assault Nurse Examiner, Adult/Adolescent	IAFN	International Association of Forensic Nurses
SANE-P	Sexual Assault Nurse Examiner, Pediatric	IAFN	International Association of Forensic Nurses
SNP-BC	School Nurse Practitioner	ANCC	American Nurses Credentialing Center
SSCP	Systems Security Certified Practitioner	(ISC)^2	International Information Systems Security Certification Consortium

* Denotes a Specialty Certification

II. Degrees

Designation	Full Name
AA	Associate of Arts
AAA	Associate of Applied Arts
AAB	Associate of Applied Business
AAS	Associate of Applied Science
AAS (R)	Associate of Applied Sciences in Radiography
AAS/ADN	Associate of Applied Science/Associate Degree Nursing
AAT	Associate in Applied Technology, Associate of Arts in Teaching
AB	Associate of Business
ABA	Associate of Business Administration
ABS	Associate in Business Science
ADN	Associate Degree in Nursing
AHS	Associate of Health Science
AIM	Applied Information Management

(Continued)

(Continued)

Designation	Full Name
ALA	Associate of Liberal Arts
AOT	Associate in Occupational Technology
APT	Associate in Physical Therapy
ARM	Associate in Risk Management
AS, ASc	Associate of Science
ASCIS	Associate of Science in Computer Information Systems
ASCNT	Associate of Science in Computer Network Technology
ASDH	Associate of Science in Dental Hygiene
ASMA	Associate of Science in Medical Assisting
ASN	Associate of Science in Nursing
ASPT	Associate of Science in Physical Therapy
ASR	Associate of Science in Radiography
ASW	Associate Clinical Social Worker
AT	Associate of Technology
ATR	Art Therapist Registered
AuD	Doctor of Audiology
AyD	Doctor of Ayurvedic Medicine
B Comm	Bachelor of Commerce
BA	Bachelor of Arts
BABA	Bachelor of Arts of Business Administration
BAC	Baccalaureate Addictions Counselor
BAE, BAEd	Bachelor of Arts in Education
BAS	Bachelor of Applied Science
BBA	Bachelor in Healthcare or Business Administration
BBE	Bachelor of Biosystems Engineering
BD	Bachelor of Divinity
BDS	Bachelor of Dental Surgery
BDSc	Bachelor of Dental Science

Designation	Full Name
BE	Bachelor of Education
BHS	Bachelor of Health Science
BHSA	Bachelor of Health Service Administration
BLD	Bioanalyst Laboratory Director
BMT	Bachelor of Medical Technology
BN	Bachelor of Nursing
BOT	Bachelor of Occupational Therapy
BPH	Bachelor of Public Health
BPharm	Bachelor of Pharmacy
BPHS	Bachelor of Professional Health Science
BPod	Bachelor of Podiatry
BPT	Bachelor of Physical Therapy
BS, BSc	Bachelor of Science
BSBA	Bachelor of Science in Business Administration
BSBME	Bachelor of Science in Biomedical Engineering
BScN, BSN	Bachelor of Science in Nursing
BSCS	Bachelor of Science in Computer Science
BSEd	Bachelor of Science in Education
BSHCA	Bachelor of Science in Healthcare Administration
BSMicr	Bachelor of Science in Microbiology
BSPT	Bachelor of Science in Physical Therapy
BSRT	Bachelor of Science in Radiography
BSSW	Bachelor of Science in Social Work
BSW	Bachelor of Social Work
BSwE	Bachelor of Software Engineering
BTh, ThB	Bachelor of Theology
BVSC	Bachelor of Veterinary Science
CCC	Certificate of Clinical Competency
D	Diploma

(Continued)

(Continued)

Designation	Full Name
DA	Doctor of Arts
DAOM	Doctor of Acupuncture and Oriental Medicine
DBA	Doctor of Business Administration
DC	Doctor of Chiropractic
DCH	Doctor of Clinical Hypnotherapy
DCL	Doctor of Cannon Law, Doctor of Civil Law
DCLS	Doctor of Clinical Lab Science
DD	Doctor of Divinity
DDM	Doctor of Dental Medicine
DDS	Doctor of Dental Surgery
DEd	Doctor of Education
DHM	Doctor of Homeopathic Medicine
DIS	Doctor of Information Security
DM	Doctor of Management, Doctor of Music
DMA	Doctor of Musical Arts
DMD	Doctor of Dental Medicine, Doctor of Medical Dentistry
DMin	Doctor of Ministry
DMT	Doctor of Medical Technology
DNE	Doctor of Nursing Education
DNP	Doctor of Nursing Practice
DNS, DNSc, DSN, DScN	Doctor of Nursing Science
DO	Doctor of Ostheopathy
DOS	Doctor of Ocular Science, Doctor of Optical Science
DOT	Doctor of Occupational Therapy
DP	Doctor of Podiatry
DPH, DrPH	Doctor of Public Health
DPhC	Doctor of Pharmaceutical Chemistry
DPM	Doctor of Podiatric Medicine

Designation	Full Name
DPT	Doctor of Physical Therapy
DrPH	Doctor of Public Health
DS, DSc, ScD, SD	Doctor of Science
DSC	Doctor of Surgical Chiropody
DScD	Doctor of Science in Dentistry
DScPT	Doctor of Science in Physical Therapy
DSCS	Doctorate of Science in Computer Science
DSP	Doctor of Surgical Podiatry
DSSc	Doctor of Social Science
DSTh, STD	Doctor of Sacred Theology
DSW	Doctor of Social Welfare, Doctor of Social Work
DTh, ThD	Doctor of Theology
DVM	Doctor of Veterinary Medicine
EdD	Doctor of Education
EdS	Education Specialist
JD	Doctor of Laws, Doctor of Jurisprudence, Juris Doctor
LAC, LicAc	Licensed Acupuncturist
LACMH	Licensed Associate Counselor of Mental Health
LCPC	Licensed Clinical Professional Counselor
LCSW	Licensed Clinical Social Worker
LD	Licensed Dietician
LDTC	Learning Disabilities Teacher Consultant
LLB	Bachelor of Laws
LLD	Doctor of Laws
LLM	Master of Laws
LMFC	Licensed Marriage Family Counselor
LMFT	Licensed Marriage/Family Therapist
LPC	Licensed Professional Counselor

(Continued)

(Continued)

Designation	Full Name
LPN	Licensed Practical Nurse
LSW	Licensed Social Worker
LVN	Licensed Vocational Nurse
MA	Master of Arts
MAC	Master of Acupuncture, Master Addictions Counselor
MAEd	Master of Arts in Education
MAGD	Master of Academy of General Dentistry
MAcOM	Master of Acupuncture and Oriental Medicine
MAT	Master of Arts in Teaching
MBA	Master of Business Administration
MC	Master of Counseling
MCAT	Master of Creative Arts in Therapy
MCD	Master of Communication Disorders
MCS	Master of Computer Science
MD	Doctor of Medicine
MDiv	Master of Divinity
MDS	Master of Dental Surgery, Master of Dental Science
MEd	Master of Education
MFT	Marriage and Family Therapist, Master of Family Therapy
MHA	Master of Health Administration
MHS	Master of Health Science, Masters in Human Services
MHSA	Master of Health Services Administration
MISM	Master of Information Systems Management
MN	Master of Nursing
MNA	Master of Nurse Anesthesia
MNS	Master of Nutrition Science
MP	Master of Psychotherapy
MPAS	Master of Physician Assistant Science

Designation	Full Name
MPH	Master of Public Health
MPharm	Master of Pharmacy
MRad	Master of Radiology
MRC	Master of Rehabilitation Counseling
MS/MSc	Master of Science
MSBME	Master of Science in Biomedical Engineering
MSBMS	Master of Science in Basic Medical Sciences
MSC	Master of Science in Counseling
MSCIS	Master of Science in Computer Information Systems
MSCS	Master of Science in Computer Science
MSD	Master of Science in Dentistry
MSFS	Master of Science in Forensic Science
MSHA	Master of Science in Health Administration
MSHI	Master of Science in Health Informatics
MSIS	Master of Science in Information Systems
MSN	Master of Science in Nursing
MSOT	Master of Science in Occupational Therapy
MSPAS	Master of Science in Physician Assistant Studies
MSPH	Master of Science in Public Health
MSRD	Master of Science Registered Dietician
MSS	Master of Social Science, Master of Social Service
MSSE	Master of Science in Software Engineering
MSSLP	Master of Science in Speech Language Pathology
MSW	Master of Social Work
MSwE	Master of Software Engineering
MTh	Master of Theology
MusD, DMus	Doctor of Music
ND	Doctor of Naturopathy
OD	Doctor of Optometry

(Continued)

(Continued)

Designation	Full Name
OT, OTR	Occupational Therapist, Occupational Therapist Registered
PharmD	Doctor of Pharmacy
PhB	Bachelor of Philosophy
PhD	Doctor of Philosophy
PsyD	Doctor of Psychology
PsyM	Master of Psychology
PT	Physical Therapist, Physiotherapist
PTA	Physical Therapy Assistant
RD	Registered Dietician
RDA	Registered Dental Assistant
RDH	Registered Dental Hygienist
RDN	Registered Dietician Nutritionist
RMA	Registered Medical Assistant
RN	Registered Nurse
RNA	Registered Nursing Assistant
RNBSN	Registered Nurse Bachelor of Science Nursing
RNC	Registered Nurse Certified
RNMSN	Registered Nurse Master of Science Nursing
RPh	Registered Pharmacist
RRA	Registered Radiology Assistant
RRT	Registered Respiratory Therapist, Registered Radiologic Technologist
RT	Registered Technologist, Radiological Technologist, Respiratory Therapist
SLP	Speech Language Pathologist
SScD	Doctor of Social Science
STB	Bachelor of Sacred Theology

III. Professional Fellowships/Honors Designations

Designation	Full Name
FAAFP	Fellow of the American Academy of Family Physicians
FAAN	Fellow of the American Academy of Nursing
FACC	Fellow of the American College of Cardiology
FACEP	Fellow of the American College of Emergency Physicians
FACHE	Fellow of the American College of Healthcare Executives
FACMI	Fellow of the American College of Medical Informatics
FACMPE	Fellow of the American College of Medical Practice Executives
FACP	Fellow of the American College of Physicians
FAMIA	Fellow of the American Medical Informatics Association
FASCP	Fellow of the American Society of Clinical Pathologists
FCAP	Fellow of the College of American Pathologists
FCHIME	Fellow of the College of Healthcare Information Management Executives
FHAPI	Honorary Fellow, Association for Pathology Informatics
FHFMA	Fellow of the Healthcare Financial Management Association
FHIMSS	Fellow of the Healthcare Information and Management Systems Society
FIAHSI	Fellow of the International Academy of Health Sciences Informatics
FIEEE	Fellow of the Institute of Electrical and Electronics Engineers
FNLM	Friends of the National Library of Medicine
LCHIME	Lifetime College of Healthcare Information Management Executives
LFHIMSS	Life Member and Fellow of the Healthcare Information and Management Systems Society
SHIMSS	Senior Member of the Healthcare Information and Management Systems Society
SMIEEE	Senior Member of the Institute of Electrical and Electronics Engineers

Acronyms

A

AA	Attribute Authority
AAA	Authentication, Authorization, and Accounting
ABAC	Attribute-Based Access Control
ABC	Activity-Based Costing
ABC codes	Alternative billing codes
ACA	Affordable Care Act
ACB	Authorized Certification Body (see ATCB)
ACDF	Access Control Decision Function
ACG	Ambulatory Care Group
ACI	Access Control Information
ACID	Atomicity, Consistency, Isolation, and Durability
ACK	General Acknowledgment Message
ACL	Access Control List
ACO	Accountable Care Organization
AD	Active Directory
AD	Addendum
ADE	Adverse Drug Event
ADG	Ambulatory Diagnostic Group
ADPAC	Automated Data Processing Application Coordinator
ADR	ADT Response message
ADR	Adverse Drug Reaction
ADSL	Asymmetric Digital Subscriber Line
ADT	Admission, Discharge, and Transfer
AE	Adverse Event/Adverse Experience
AE Title	Application Entity Title
AEF	Access Control Enforcement Function

AHC	Academic Health Center
AHT	Average Handling Time/Average Handle Time
AI	Artificial Intelligence
AIDC	Automatic Identification and Data Capture
AIMS	Anesthesia Information Management System
AIS	Automated Information System
ALOS	Average Length of Stay
ALU	Arithmetic Logic Unit
AMR	Ambulatory Medical Record
ANN	Artificial Neuron Network
APACHE	Acute Physiology and Chronic Health Evaluation
APC	Ambulatory Payment Class
APG	Ambulatory Patient Group
API	Application Program Interface
APMs	Alternative Payment Model
APT	Advanced Persistent Threat
ARI	Access to Radiology Information
ARP	Address Resolution Protocol
ARRA	American Recovery and Reinvestment Act of 2009
ASA	Average Speed of Answer
ASCII	American Standard Code for Information Interchange
ASN	Abstract Syntax Notation
ASO	Administrative Services Only
ASP	Active Server Pages
ATCB	Authorized Testing and Certification Body
ATM	Asynchronous Transfer Mode
AUC	Appropriate Use Criteria
AUI	Attachment Unit Interface
AUP	Acceptable Use Policy
AVR	Analysis, Visualization, and Reporting

B

B2B	Business-to-business
B2B2C	Business-to-business-to-consumer
B2C	Business-to-consumer
BA	Business Associate
BAN	Body Area Network

BASIC	Beginner's All-purpose Symbolic Instruction Code
BAT	Filename Extension for a Batch File
BCMA	Bar Code Medication Administration
BCP	Business Continuity Plan
BEC	Business e-mail Compromise
BH	Behavioral Health
BHOM	Behavioral Health Outcome Management
BIA	Business Impact Analysis
BIOS	Basic Input Output System
BLE	Bluetooth Low Energy
BPA	Blanket Purchasing Agreement
BPM	Business Process Management
BPS	Bits Per Second
BRE	Business Rules Engine
BRFSS	Behavioral Risk Factor Surveillance System
BTRIS	Biomedical Translational Research Information System
BYOC	Bring Your Own Cloud
BYOD	Bring Your Own Device

C

CA	Certificate Authority
CA	Corrective Action
CAD	Computer-Aided Detection
CAH	Critical-Access Hospital
CAL	Computer-Assisted Learning
CAP	Common Alerting Protocol
CAP	Corrective Action Plan
CASE	Computer-Assisted Software Engineering
CAT	Computerized Axial Tomography
CATH	Cardiac Catheterization Workflow
CBL	Computer-Based Learning
CC	Chief Complaint
CCC	Clinical Care Classification
CCD	Continuity of Care Document
C-CDA	Consolidated Clinical Document Architecture
CCDS	Common Clinical Data Set
CCO	Chief Compliance Officer

CCM	Chronic Care Management
CCMM	Continuity of Care Maturity Model
CCO	Chief Compliance Officer
CCR	Continuity of Care Record
CD	Committee Draft
CD	Compact Disk
CDA	Clinical Document Architecture
CDMA	Code Division Multiple Access
CDPD	Cellular Digital Packet Data
CDR	Clinical Data Repository/Clinical Data Registry
CD-ROM	Compact Disk, read-only memory
CDS	Clinical Decision Support
CDS	Core Data Services
CDSS	Clinical Decision Support System
CDT	Current Dental Terminology
CDW	Clinical Data Warehouse
CE	Coded Element
CEHRT	Certified EHR Technology
CEN	European Committee for Standardization
CERT	Computer Emergency Response Team
CF	Conditional Formatting/Coded Formatted Element
CGI	Common Gateway Interface
CHAP	Challenge Handshake Authentication Protocol
CHG	Charge Posting
CHIP	Children's Health Insurance Program
C-HOBIC	Canadian Health Outcomes for Better Information and Care
CHPL	Certified Health IT Product List
CHV	Consumer Health Vocabulary initiative
CIA	Confidentiality/Integrity/Availability
CIO	Chief Informatics Officer
CIO	Chief Information Officer
CIS	Clinical Information System
CISC	Complex Instruction Set Computer processor
CM	Composite Message/Composite Data Type
CMD	Command
CMET	Common Message Element Type
CMIO	Chief Medical Informatics Officer
CMIO	Chief Medical Information Officer
CMYK	Cyan, Magenta, Yellow, and Black

CNCL	Canceled
CNIO	Chief Nursing Informatics Officer
CNIO	Chief Nursing Information Officer
COAS	Clinical Observations Access Service
COB	Close of Business
COB	Coordination of Benefits
CORBA	Common Object Request Broker Architecture
COW	Computer-On-Wheels
CP	Certificate Policy
CPC	Comprehensive Primary Care Initiative
CPC+	Comprehensive Primary Care Plus Initiative
CPOE	Computerized Practitioner Order Entry
CPR	Computer-based Patient Record
CPRS	Computer-based Patient Record System
CPS	Certification Practices Statement
CPT	Current Procedural Terminology
CPU	Central Processing Unit
CQL	Clinical Quality Language
CQM	Clinical Quality Measure
CRA	Countermeasure Response Administration
CRM	Customer Relationship Management
CRUD	Create, Read, Update, and Delete
CSIRT	Computer Security Incident Response Team
CSMA/CD	Carrier Sense Multiple Access with Collision Detection
CSO	Chief Security Officer
CSU/DSU	Channel Sharing Unit/Data Service Unit
CT	Consistent Time
CTI	Computer Telephony Integration
CTIO	Chief Technology Innovation Officer
CTO	Chief Technology Officer
CTS	Common Terminology Services
CU	Control Unit
CUI	Concept Unique Identifier
CVE	Common Vulnerabilities and Exposures
CVS	Concurrent Versions System
CWE	Coded with Exceptions
CWE	Common Weakness Enumeration
CxO	Corporate executives or C-level or C-Suite
CY	Calendar Year

D

DaaS	Data as a Service
DAF	Data Access Framework
DAG	Directed Acyclic Graph
DApp	Decentralized Application
DAM	Domain Analysis Model
DBA	Database Administrator
DBMS	Database Management System
DCM	Detailed Clinical Models
DCM	Dynamic Case Management
DDI	Design, Develop, Implement
DDL	Data Definition Language
DEEDS	Data Elements for Emergency Department Systems
DFD	Data Flow Diagram
DHCP	Data Host Configuration Protocol
DI	Diagnostic imaging
DICOM	Digital Imaging and Communications in Medicine
DLC	Data Link Control
DLL	Dynamic Link Library
DLT	Distributed Ledger Technology
DMA	Direct Memory Access
DME	Durable Medical Equipment
DML	Data Manipulation Language
DNS	Domain Name Server
DNSSEC	Domain Name System Security Extension
DOS	Disk Operating System
DPI	Dots Per square Inch
DRAM	Dynamic Random Access Memory
DRG	Diagnosis Related Group
DS4P	Data Segmentation for Privacy
DSA	Digital Signature Algorithm
DSG	Document Digital Signature
DSL	Digital Subscriber Line
DSL	Domain-Specific Language
DSLAM	Digital Subscriber Line Access Multiplexer
DSM	Diagnostic and Statistical Manual of Mental Disorders
DSML	Directory Services Markup Language
DSMO	Designated Standard Maintenance Organization

DSRIP	Delivery System Reform Incentive Payment
DSSS	Direct Sequence Spread Spectrum
DSTU	Draft Standard for Trial Use
DSU	Data Service Unit
DSU/CSU	Data Service Unit/Channel Service Unit
DT	Date data type (YYYY-MM-DD)
DTD	Document Type Definition
DTE	Data Terminal Equipment
DTR	Data Terminal Ready
DTR	Draft Technical Report
DUA	Data Use Agreement
DVD	Digital Video Disk or Digital Versatile Disk

E

e-[text] or e-text	Electronic text
E-1	European digital signal
EAI	Enterprise Application Integration
EAP	Extensible Authentication Protocol
EAV	Entity-Attribute-Value
EBB	Eligibility-Based Billing
EBCDIC	Extended Binary Coded Decimal Interchange Code
EC	Eligible Clinician
EC	Electronic COMMERCE
ECN	Explicit Congestion Notifier
eCQI	Electronic Clinical Quality Improvement
eCQM	Electronic Clinical Quality Measures
e-Commerce	Electronic Commerce
ED	Encapsulated Data
ED	Evidence Documents
EDC	Electronic Data Capture System
EDDS	Electronic Document Digital Storage
EDI	Electronic Data Interchange
EDI gateway	Electronic Data Interchange Gateway
EED	Early Event Detection
EDXL	Emergency Data Exchange Language

EDXL–HAVE	Emergency Data Exchange Language–Hospital Availability Exchange
EEPROM	Electronically Erasable Programmable Read-Only Memory
E-GOV	The "E-Government Act of 2002"
EHR	Electronic Health Record
EIDE	Enhanced or Extended Integrated Drive Electronics
EIN	Employer Identification Number
EIP	Enterprise Information Portal
EIS	Enterprise Information System
eLTSS	Electronic Long-Term Care Support Services
eMAR	Electronic Medication Administration Record
EMC	Electronic Media Claims
EMI	Electromagnetic Interference
EMPI	Enterprise Master Patient Index
EMR	Electronic Medical Record
EMRAM	Electronic Medical Record Adoption Model
EMSEC	Emanations Security
EN	European Standard
ENP	European Nursing Care Pathways
EOA	Enhanced Oversight Accountability Rule
EOB	Explanation of Benefits
EOP	Explanation of Payment
ePA	Electronic Prior Authorization
EPCS	Electronic Prescriptions for Controlled Substances
ePHI	Electronic Protected Health Information
ePHR	Electronic Personal Health Record
ERA	Electronic Remittance Advice
ERD	Entity Relationship Diagram
ERDA	Emergency Respond Data Architecture
ERISA	Employee Retirement Income and Security Act of 1975
ERP	Enterprise Resource Planning
ESS	Executive Support System
ETL	Extraction, Transformation, Loading
EUA	Enterprise User Authentication
EULA	End-User License Agreement
Extended ASCII	Extended American Standard Code for Information Interchange

F

FACA	Federal Advisory Committee Act
FAQ	Frequently Asked Questions
FAR	False Acceptance Rate
FCoE	Fiber Channel over Ethernet
FDDI	Fiber-Distributed Data Interface
FFP	Federal Financial Participation
FFS	Fee-for-Service
FHIR	Fast Healthcare Interoperability Resources
FIFO	First In, First Out
FIPS	Federal Information Processing Standard
FISMA	Federal Information Security Management Act
FQDN	Fully Qualified Domain Name
FQHC	Federally Qualified Health Center
FTP	File Transfer Protocol

G

GB	Gigabyte
GBps	Gigabits per second
GDPR	General Data Protection Regulation
GELLO	Guideline Expression Language, Object Oriented
GIF	Graphics Interchange Format
GIG	Global Information Grid
GIGO	Garbage In, Garbage Out
GSM	Global System for Mobile communications
GUDID	Global Unique Device Identification Database
GUI	Graphical User Interface
GUID	Global Unique Identifier

H

HAN	Health Alert Network
HCPCS	Healthcare Common System Coding System
hData	A specification for exchanging electronic health data
HEDIS	Healthcare Effectiveness Data and Information Set

HIE	Health Information Exchange
HIEx	Health Insurance Exchange
HIO	Health Information Organization
HIPAA	Health Insurance Portability and Accountability Act of 1996
HIS	Health Information System
HISP	Health Information Service Provider
HIT	Health Information Technology
HITECH Act	Health Information Technology for Economic and Clinical Health Act
HITAC	Health Information Technology Advisory Committee
HL7	Health Level Seven
HQMF	Health Quality Measure Format
HTML	Hypertext Markup Language
HTTP	Hypertext Transfer Protocol
HTTPS	HTTP Secure
HUD	Heads-Up Display
Hz	Hertz

I

I/O	Input/Output Device
IAM	Identity Access Management
ICC	Integrated Circuit Chip
ICD	International Classification of Diseases
ICIDH	International Classification of Impairments, Disability, and Health
ICMP	Internet Control Message Protocol
ICO	Initial coin Offering
ICR	Intelligent Call Routing
ICR	Intelligent Character Recognition
ICU	Intensive Care Unit
IDM	Identity Digital Management
IDMS	Identity Management System
IDN	Integrated Delivery Network
IDR	Intelligent Document Recognition
IDS	Integrated Delivery System

IGP	Interior Gateway Protocol
IHE	Integrating the Healthcare Enterprise
IIF	Information in Identifiable Form
IIS	Immunization Information Systems
IIS	Internet Information Systems
IKE	Internet Key Exchange
ILD	Injection Laser Diode
iOS	iPhone Operating System
IoT	Internet of Things
IP	Internet Protocol
IPA	Independent Practice Association
IPsec	Internet Protocol Security
IPX/SPX	Internetwork Packet Exchange/Sequence Packet Exchange
IRC	Internet Relay Chat
IrDA	Infrared Data Association
IRM	Information Resource Management
IRQ	Interrupt Request Line
ISA	Interoperability Standards Advisory
ISDN	Integrated Service Digital Network
ISO/TC 215	International Organization for Standardization (ISO) Technical Committee for Health Informatics
ISP	Internet Service Provider
ITMRA	Information Technology Management Reform Act
IVR	Interactive Voice Response

J

JAD	Joint Application Development
JCR	Joint Commission Resources
JFS	Journaling File System
JPEG	Joint Photographic Experts Group
JSON	JavaScript Object Notation
JTC	Joint Technical Committee

K

KAS	Clinical Decision Support (CDS) Knowledge Artifact Specification
KB	Kilobyte
Kbps	Kilobits per second
KHz	Kilohertz

L

LAN	Learning and Action Network
LAN	Local Area Network
LASA	Look Alike/Sound Alike
LAT	Local Area Transport
LDA	Latent Dirichlet Allocation
LDAP	Lightweight Directory Access Protocol
LIFO	Last In, First Out
LIP	Licensed Independent Practitioner
LIS	Laboratory Information System
LLC	Logical Link Control
LOE	Level of Effort
LOI	Letter of Intent
LOINC	Logical Observation Identifiers Names and Codes
LOTO	Lock Out/Tag Out
LPDR	Longitudinal Patient Disease Registries
LQS	Lexicon Query Service
LRI	Lab Results Interface
LSC	Life Safety Code
LTC	Long-Term Care
LTCF	Long-Term Care Facility
LTPAC	Long-Term and Post-Acute Care
LTSS	Long-Term Services and Support
LU	Logical Unit
LUN	Logical Unit Number
LVT	Low-Volume Threshold
LWBS	Left without Being Seen

M

MAC	Mandatory Access Control
MAC	Message Authentication Code
MAC address	Media Access Control Address
MACRA	Medicare Access and CHIP Reauthorization Act 2015
MAN	Metropolitan-Area Network
MAO	Maximum Acceptable/Allowable Outage
MAU	Media Access Unit
Mb	Megabit
MBDS	Minimum Basic Data Set
Mbps	Megabits per second
MDA	Model-Driven Architecture
MDI	Medical Device Interface
MDI-X port	Medium-Dependent Interface crossover
MDM	Master Data Management
MDM	Medical Document Management Message
MDM	Mobile Device Management
MDS	Minimum Data Set
MedDRA	Medical Dictionary for Regulatory Activities
MEDS	Minimum Emergency Data Set
MeSH	Medical Subject Heading
mHealth	Mobile Health
MHz	Megahertz
MIB	Medical Information BUS
MIME	Multipurpose Internet Mail Extensions
MIPS	Merit-based Incentive Payment System
MIS	Management Information System
MITA	Medicaid Information Technology Architecture
MLM	Medical Logic Model
MMIS	Medicaid Management Information System
MOLAP	Multidimensional Online Analytical Processing
MOU	Memorandum of Understanding
MPEG	Motion Picture Expert Group
MPI	Master Patient Index
MPP	Massively Parallel Processing
MSA	Master Services Agreement

MSAU	Multiple Station Access Unit
MSO	Management Service Organizations
MTBF	Mean Time Between Failures
MTTD	Mean Time to Diagnose
MTTR	Mean Time to Repair
MU	Meaningful Use
MUX	Multiplexer, MultipleXer, or MultipleXor

N

NAC	Network Access Control/Network Admission Control
NAS	Network Attached Storage
NAT	Network Address Translation
NCPDP	National Council for Prescription Drug Programs
NDC	National Drug Code
NDIS	Network Driver Interface Specification
NEDSS	National Electronic Disease Surveillance System
NEMSIS	National Emergency Medical System (EMS) Information System
NFS	Network File System
NHRIC	National Health-Related Items Code
NIC	Network Interface Card
NIC	Nursing Intervention Classification
NLP	Natural Language Processing
NMB	National Member Body
NMDS	Nursing Minimum Data Set
NMMDS	Nursing Management Minimum Data Set
NOC	Network Operation Center
NOC	Nursing Outcome Classification
NOI	Notice of Intent
NPF	National Provider File
NPI	National Provider Identifier
NSF	National Standard Format
NSP	Network Service Provider
NSSN	National Standards System Network
NUMA	Nonuniform Memory Architecture
NWIP	New Work Item Proposal

O

OASIS	Outcome and Assessment Information Set
OAuth	Open Authorization
OC	Optical Carrier
OCR	Optical Character Recognition
OCSP	Online Certificate Status Protocol
ODA	Open Document Architecture
ODBC	Open Database Connectivity
ODS	Operational Data Store
OEID	Other Entity Identifier
OID	Object Identifier
OLAP	Online Analytical Processing
OLE	Object Linking and Embedding
OLTP	Online Transaction Processing
OM	Outbreak Management
OOA	Out of Area
OON	Out of Network
OOP	Object-Oriented Programming
OOP	Out of Pocket
ORB	Object Request Broker
OS	Operating System
OSI	Open Systems Interconnection
OWL	Web Ontology Language

P

P2P	Peer-to-Peer
PACS	Picture Archiving and Communication Systems
PAN	Personal-Area Network
PAP	Password Authentication Protocol
PAS	Publicly Available Specification
PC	Personal Computer
PCB	Printed Circuit Board
PCDH	Patient-Centered Data Home™
PCDS	Patient Care Data Set
PCMH	Patient-Centered Medical home
PCP	Primary Care Provider

PDC	Primary Domain Controller
PDF	Portable Document Format
PDMP	Prescription Drug Monitoring Program
PDP	Policy Decision Point
PEP	Policy Enforcement Point
PHI	Protected Health Information
PHIN	Public Health Information Network
PHIN-MS	Public Health Information Network-Messaging System
PHMT	Personal Health Management Tool
PHR	Personal Health Record
PIDS	Person Identification Service
PIM	Platform Independent Model
PIN	Personal Identification Number
PING	Packet Internet Groper
PIP	Policy Information Point
PIV	Personal Identification Verification
PIX	Patient Identifier Cross-referencing
PKC	Public Key Certificate
PKI	Public Key Infrastructure
PMP	Point-to-Multipoint Communication
PNDS	Perioperative Nursing Data Set
PNG	Portable Network Graphics
POP3	Post Office Protocol
POP	Point-of-Presence
POSIX	Portable Open Systems Interface
PPACA	Patient Protection and Affordable Care Act
PPO	Preferred Provider Organization
PPP	Point-to-Point Protocol
PPTP	Point-to-Point Tunneling Protocol
PRAM	Parameter RAM
PRG	Procedure-Related Group
PROM	Programmable Read-Only Memory
PULSE	Patient Unified Lookup System for Emergencies
PVBM	Physician Value-Based Modifier
PVC	Permanent Virtual Circuit

Q

QA	Quality Assurance
QAPI	Quality Assessment Performance Improvement
QASP	Quality Assurance Surveillance Plan
QC	Quality Control
QCDR	Qualified Clinical Data Registry
QDM	Quality Data Model
QE	Quality Entity
QHP	Qualified Health Plan
QI	Quality Improvement
QIDAM	Quality Improvement Domain Analysis Model
QIIO	Quality Improvement and Innovation Organization
QIN/QIO	Quality Innovation Network—Quality Improvement Organizations
QIO	Quality Improvement Organization
QMF	Query Management Facility
QMR	Quick Medical Reference
QMRT	Quality Measures Reporting Tool
QMS	Quality Management System
QoS	Quality of Service
QP	Qualified Professional
QP	Qualifying APM Participant
QPP	Quality Payment Program
QPS	Quality Positioning System
QR codes	Quick Response Codes
QRDA	Quality Reporting Data Architecture
QRUR	Quality and Resource Use Report
QUICK	Quality Information and Clinical Knowledge

R

RA	Registration Authority
RAD	Rapid Application Development
RAID	Redundant Array of Independent Disks
RAM	Random Access Memory
RAS	Remote Access Server
RBAC	Role-Based Access Control

RDBMS	Relational Database Management System
RDF	Resource Description Framework
REC	Regional Extension Center
REST	Representational State Transfer
RFI	Request for Information
RFID	Radio frequency Identification
RFP	Request for Proposal
RGB	Red, Green, Blue color model
RHIO	Regional Health Information Organization
RIM	Reference Information Model
RIS	Radiology Information System
RISC	Reduced Instruction Set Computer
RM	Records Management
RMI	Remote Method Invocation
RM-ODP	Reference Model for Open Distributed Processing
RMON	Remote Network Monitor
ROI	Release of Information
ROI	Return on Investment
ROLAP	Relational Online Analytical Processing
ROM	Read-Only Memory
RPO	Recovery Point Objective
RTF	Rich Text Format
RTLS	Real-Time Location Service
RTM	Reference Terminology Model
RTO	Recovery Time Objective
RVU	Relative Value Unit

S

S/MIME	Secure MIME
SaaS	Software as a Service
SAML	Security Assertion Markup Language
SAN	Storage area Network
SATA	Serial Advanced Technology Application
SATAN	Security Administrator Tool for Analyzing Networks
SBAR	Situation–Background–Assessment–Recommendation

SCOS	Smartcard Operating System
SCSI	Small Computer System Interface
SCUI	Smartcard User Interface
SDLC	System Development Lifecycle
SDO	Standards Development Organization
SDoH	Social Determinants of Health
SDXC	Secure Digital Extended Capacity
SEC	Security
SET	Secure Electronic Transmission
SFTP	Secure File Transport Protocol
SGML	Standardized Generalized Markup Language
SIG	Special Interest Group
SIMM	Single In-line Memory Module
SLIP	Serial line Internet Protocol
SME	Subject Matter Expert
SMP	Symmetric Multiprocessing
SMS	Short Message Service
SMTP	Simple Mail Transfer Protocol
SNA	System Network Architecture
SNMP	Simple Network Monitoring Protocol
SNMP	System Network Management Protocol
SNOMED–CT	Systematized Nomenclature of Medicine–Clinical Terms
SOA	Service-Oriented Architecture
SOAP	Simple Object Access Protocol
SONET	Synchronous Optical Network
SOP	Standard Operating Procedure
SOW	Statement of Work
SPD	Summary Plan Description
SPOOL	Simultaneous Peripheral Operation Online
SQL	Structured Query Language
SRAM	Static Random Access Memory
SSH	Secure Shell
SSL	Secure Socket Layer
SSO	Single Sign-On
STP	Shielded Twisted Pair
SVC	Switched Virtual Circuit

T

TC	Technical Committee
TCO	Total Cost of Ownership
TCP/IP	Transmission Control Protocol/Internet Protocol
TDR	Time-Domain Reflectometer
TELNET	TELecommunications NETwork
TFTP	Trivial File Transfer Protocol
TGE	Token Generation Event
TIFF	Tagged Image File Format
TKIP	Temporal Key Integrity Protocol
TLS	Transport Layer Security
TOC	Transitions of Care
TPA	Third-Party Administrator

U

UART	Universal Asynchronous Receiver Transmitter
UDDI	Universal Description, Discover, and Integration
UDI	Unique Device Identifier
UDP	User Datagram Protocol
UI	User Interface
UID	Unique Identifier
UM	Utilization Management
UMDNS	Universal Medical Device Nomenclature System
UML	Unified Modeling Language
UMLS	Unified Medical Language System
UMS	Unified Messaging System
UNC	Universal Naming Convention
UPI	Unique Patient Identifier
UPS	Uninterruptible Power Supply
URI	Uniform Resource Identifier
URL	Uniform Resource Locator
USB	Universal Serial Bus
USCDI	U.S. Core Data for Interoperability
USHIK	United States Health Information Knowledgebase
UTP	Unshielded Twisted Pair

V

VAN	Value-Added Network
VAX	Virtual Address Extension
VBC	Value-Based Care
VBID	Value-Based Insurance Design
VBP	Value-Based Payment
VDT	View, Download, Transmit
VISN	Veterans Integrated Service Network
VistA	Veterans Health Information Systems Technology Architecture
VM	Value Modifier
VM	Virtual Machine
VMR	Virtual Machine Record
VoIP	Voice over Internet Protocol
VPN	Virtual Private Network
VRAM	Video RAM or Video Random Access Memory
VRML	Virtual Reality Modeling Language
VRS	Voice Response System
VRU	Voice Response Unit
VSA	Virtual SAN Appliance
VSM	Value Stream Mapping

W

WAN	Wide Area Network
WAP	Wireless Application Protocol
WASP	Wireless Application Service Provider
WAV or WAVE	Waveform Audio format (.wav)
WCF	Windows Communication Foundation
WEP	Wired Equivalent Privacy
WG	Work Group
WI	Web Interface
Wide SCSI	Wide Small Computer System Interface
WLAN	Wireless Local Area Network
WORM	Write Once, Read Many Times

WOW	Workstation on Wheels
WPA	Wi-Fi Protected Access
WSDL	Web Services Description Language
WWW	World Wide Web
WYSIWYG	What You See Is What You Get
WYSIWYP	What You See Is What You Print

X

XDS	Cross-enterprise Document Sharing
XML	Extensible Markup Language
XSL	Extensible Stylesheet Language

Z

ZLE	Zero Latency Enterprise

References

(All references, URL's & DOI's are
current as of November 2023.)

1. National Institute of Standards and Technology. (2023). Computer Security Resource Center. Retrieved from: https://csrc.nist.gov/glossary.
2. TechTarget. (2023). Retrieved from: whatis.techtarget.com.
3. American Medical Association. (2023). How to select a practice management system. Retrieved from: www.ama-assn.org/practice-management/how-select-practice-management-system.
4. Business Dictionary. (2023). Retrieved from: www.businessdictionary.com.
5. American Nursing Association. (2022). *Nursing Informatics: Scope and Standards of Practice* (3rd ed.). Silver Springs, MD: American Nurses Association.
6. Connet. (2023). IT terminology: Dictionary of information technology. Retrieved from: www.consp.com/it-information-technology-terminology-dictionary.
7. Wikipedia. (2023). Retrieved from: www.wikipedia.org.
8. Howe, D. (1985–2023). The Free Online Dictionary of Computing (FOLDOC). Retrieved from: http://foldoc.org/.
9. Health Level Seven (HL7). (2023). Retrieved from: www.hl7.org/.
10. HIMSS Analytics. (2023). Digital health transformation maturity models. Retrieved from: www.himss.org/what-we-do-solutions/digital-health-transformation/maturity-models.
11. Office of the National Coordinator for Health Information Technology (ONC). (2023). Retrieved from: http://healthit.gov/.
12. Office of the National Coordinator for Health Information Technology (ONC). (2023). Long term and post acute care. Retrieved from: www.healthit.gov/topic/health-it-health-care-settings/long-term-and-post-acute-care.
13. EGNYTE. (2023). What is data compliance? Retrieved from: www.egnyte.com/guides/governance/data-compliance.
14. Sadaoki, F. (2007). False acceptance rate. Retrieved from: www.sciencedirect.com/topics/computer-science/false-acceptance-rate.

15. Health Level 7. (2023). Order message definitions: ORM-general order message. Retrieved from: www.hl7.eu/HL7v2x/v231/std231/CH4.html#Heading13.
16. IT Law Wiki. (2023). Retrieved from: https://itlaw.fandom.com/wiki/ Exceeds_authorized_access.
17. Department of Health and Human Services. (2023). National Committee on Vital and Health Statistics (NCVHS). Retrieved from: www.ncvhs.hhs.gov.
18. Investopedia.com. (2023). Retrieved from: www.investopedia.com.
19. American National Standards Institute (ANSI). (2021). Electronic data interchange primer for CEOS. Retrieved from: https://ansi.org/standards-news/ member-updates/2021/09/9-24-21-x12-publishes-electronic-data-interchange-primer-for-ceos.
20. HIPAA.com. (2009). The definition of protected health information. Retrieved from: www.hipaa.com/2009/05/11/ the-definition-of-protected-health-information/.
21. CloudPatterns. (2023). Learn & master cloud computing with cloud patterns. Retrieved from: www.cloudpatterns.org/.
22. Acreditation Commission for Health Care (ACHC). (2023). Retrieved from: https://achc.org.
23. Health Care Services Corporation. (2023). HCSC interoperability solutions. Retrieved from: https://interoperability.hcsc.com/s/.
24. ISO/TS 22600-3. (2023). HealthCare Information Privilege Management & Access Control P-3 (terms only). Retrieved from: www.iso.org.
25. Tungal, A.T. (2023). What is access control? The essential cybersecurity practice. Retrieved from: www.upguard.com/blog/access-control.
26. Centers for Medicare & Medicaid Services (CMS). (2023). Retrieved from: www.cms.gov/regulations-and-guidance/legislation/ehrincentiveprograms/ certification.
27. Integrating the Healthcare Enterprise. (2023). Retrieved from: www.ihe.net.
28. Amatayakul, M. (2023). United under HIPAA: A comparison of arrangements and agreements (HIPAA on the Job): Organized healthcare arrangement. American Health Information Management Association (AHIMA). Retrieved from: https://bok.ahima.org/doc?oid=60011.
29. *Merriam Webster Dictionary*. (2023). Retrieved from: www.merriam-webster.com.
30. Microsoft.com. (2022). About domain specific languages. Retrieved from: https://learn.microsoft.com/en-us/visualstudio/modeling/ about-domain-specific-languages?view=vs-2022.
31. United States Department of Veterans Affairs. (2023). VHA National Center for Patient Safety (NCPS). Retrieved from: www.patientsafety.va.gov/.
32. United States Department of Health and Human Services. (2023). Office of Disease Prevent and Health Promotion. Retrieved from: https://health.gov/.
33. Stack Exchange. (2023). What is a background process? Retrieved from: http:// unix.stackexchange.com/questions/82934/what-is-a-background-process.

34. European Commission, Eurostat, Collaboration in Research and Methodology for Official Statistics. (2023). What are normative documents? Retrieved from: https://cros-legacy.ec.europa.eu/content/what-are-normative-documents_en.
35. United States Department of Health and Human Services. (2023). Retrieved from: www.hhs.gov.
36. International Organization for Standardization (ISO). (2023).1, ch. de la Voie-Creuse CP 56 CH-1211 Geneva 20, Switzerland. Retrieved from: www.iso.org.
37. Vistapedia. (2023). Retrieved from: www.vistapedia.com/index.php/Main_Page.
38. Venes, D. (2021). *Taber's Cyclopedic Medical Dictionary* (24th ed.). New York: F.A. Davis Company.
39. Webopedia. (2023). Retrieved from: www.webopedia.com.
40. Sengstack, P., & Boicey, C. (2015) *Mastering Informatics: A Healthcare Handbook for Success*. Indianapolis, IN: Sigma Theta Tau International.
41. Unique Device Identification System. (n/d). Retrieved from: www.fda.gov/medical-devices/device-advice-comprehensive-regulatory-assistance/unique-device-identification-system-udi-system.
42. Lucas, H.C. (1975). *Why Information Systems Fail*. New York: Columbia University Press.
43. HealthIT.Gov. (n/d). Clinical decision support. Retrieved from: www.healthit.gov/topic/safety/clinical-decision-support.
44. Random House Unabridged Dictionary. (2023). Retrieved from: www.dictionary.com/.
45. Pfleeger, C., & Pfleeger, S. (2023). *Security in Computing* (6th ed.). Boston, MA: Addison-Wesley Professional.
46. CIGNA. Electronic claims/EDI. (2023). Retrieved from: www.cigna.com/search?query=electronic+claim.
47. Douglas, J.R., & Ritter, M.J. (2011). Implementation of an Anesthesia Information Management System (AIMS). *The Ochsner Journal, 11*(2), 102–114. Retrieved from: www.ncbi.nlm.nih.gov/pmc/articles/PMC3119212/.
48. Mastrian, K.G., & McGonigle, D. (2017). *Informatics for Health Professionals*. Burlington, MA: Jones & Bartlett Learning.
49. Organization for Economic Cooperation and Development (OECD). (2023). OECD iLibrary. Retrieved from: www.oecd-ilibrary.org/.
50. University of Missouri. (2023). Feeder systems. Retrieved from: https://bppm.missouri.edu/policy/feeder-systems/.
51. Freiler, L. (2019). Test strategy: Alpha vs. Beta testing. Retrieved from: www.centercode.com/blog/2011/01/alpha-vs-beta-testing/.
52. Techopedia. (2023). Dictionary. Retrieved from: www.techopedia.com/dictionary.
53. Healthcare Information and Management Systems Society (HIMSS). (2023) What is interoperability? Retrieved from: www.himss.org/resources/interoperability-healthcare.
54. Health Smart Ancillary Care Services. Retrieved from: www.anci-care.com/about2.html.

55. Cornell School of Law, Legal Information Institute. (2004). Electronic Code of Federal Regulations (e-CFR); Title 45—Public Welfare; SUBTITLE A—Department of Health and Human Services; SUBCHAPTER C—ADMINISTRATIVE DATA STANDARDS AND RELATED REQUIREMENTS; PART 160—GENERAL ADMINISTRATIVE REQUIREMENTS; Subpart A—General Provisions; § 160.103 Definitions. Trading partner agreement. Retrieved from: www.law.cornell.edu/definitions/index.php?width=840&height=800&iframe=true&def_id=60f3fd377fde12f8784c85ef7ba22469&term_occur=999&term_src=Title:45:Chapter:A:Subchapter:C:Part:162:Subpart:I:162.915.

56. Encyclopedia.com, Free Online Encyclopedia. (2023). Retrieved from: www.encyclopedia.com.

57. SSL.com. (2021). What is a certificate authority? Retrieved from: www.ssl.com/faqs/what-is-a-certificate-authority/.

58. Mumtaz, H., Ejaz, M.K., Tayyab, M., Vohra, L.I., Sapkota, S., Hasan, M., & Saqib, M. (2023). APACHE scoring as an indicator of mortality rate in ICU patients: A cohort study. *Annals of Medicine and Surgery, 85*(3), 416–421. https://doi.org/10.1097/MS9.0000000000000264.

59. University of British Columbia, Vancouver Campus. (2023). What is the digital tatoo project? Retrieved from: https://digitaltattoo.ubc.ca/.

60. Farlex. (2023). The Free Dictionary. (2023). Retrieved from: http://encyclopedia2.thefreedictionary.com/.

61. World Wide Web Consortium (W3C). (2023). Web ontology language overview. Retrieved from: www.w3.org/TR/owl-features/.

62. OpenEHR International. (2023). The future of health & care is open. Retrieved from: https://openehr.org/.

63. ISO/IS #13606–1. (2023). Electronic health record communication—Part 1: Reference model. Retrieved from: www.iso.org/search.html?q=ISO%2FIS%2013606&hPP=10&idx=all_en&p=0#13606.

64. Federal CIO Council. Retrieved from: www.cio.gov/resources.

65. Coiera E. (2015). *Guide to Health Informatics* (3rd ed.). Chicago, IL: CRC Press.

66. Sewell, J., These, L., & Sanborn Miller, K. (2024). *Informatics & Nursing: Opportunities & Challenges* (7th North American ed.). New York, NY: LWW.

67. U.S. Department of Veterans Affairs. (2023). Pharmacy benefits management services. Retrieved from: www.pbm.va.gov/.

68. Gartner. (2023). Glossary: Clinical data repository. Retrieved from: www.gartner.com/en/information-technology/glossary/cdr-clinical-data-repository.

69. TechDifferences. (2018). Differences between analog and digital signal. Retrieved from: https://techdifferences.com/difference-between-analog-and-digital-signal.html.

70. Goossen, W.T.F. (2014). Detailed clinical models: Representing knowledge, data and semantics in healthcare information technology. *Healthcare Informatics Research, 20*(3), 163–172. http://doi.org/10.4258/hir.2014.20.3.163.

71. Saldanha, T. (2019). *Why Digital Transformations Fail: The Surprising Disciplines of How to Take Off and Stay Ahead.* New York: Berrett-Koehler Publishers.
72. National Institute of Standards and Technology. (2023). Computer Security Resources Center, Glossary. Retrieved from: https://csrc.nist.gov/glossary.
73. TechTerms.com. (2023). The computer dictionary. Retrieved from: www.tech-terms.com.
74. Inclusive Engineering Consortium. (2023). Retrieved from: www.iec.org.
75. ISO/TS 17117 (revision). (2023). Criteria for the categorization and evaluation of terminological systems (terms only). Retrieved from: www.iso.org.
76. ISO/IS #17115. (2023). Vocabulary for terminological systems (terms only). Retrieved from: www.iso.org.
77. SNOMED. International Health Terminology Standards Development Organization (IHTSDO). (2023). Gammeltory 4, 1.1457 Copenhagen K, Denmark. Retrieved from: www.ihtsdo.org.
78. Bright Hub. (2022). Information security concepts: Authenticity. Retrieved from: www.brighthub.com/computing/smb-security/articles/31234/#this-post-is-part-of-the-series-information-security-concepts.
79. HIPAA Survival Guide.Com. (2023). HIPAA survival guide: Get help with HIPAA compliance. Retrieved from: www.hipaasurvivalguide.com/.
80. CDC Centers for Disease Control. (2023). Retrieved from: www.cdc.gov.
81. Patients Rights Council. (2013). Advance directives: Definitions. Retrieved from: www.patientsrightscouncil.org/site/advance-directives-definitions/.
82. Open Source Initiative. (2023). Retrieved from: https://opensource.org/faq.
83. Federal Bureau of Investigation. (2016). Incidents of ransomware on the rise. Retrieved from: www.fbi.gov/news/stories/incidents-of-ransomware-on-the-rise.
84. Tech Target. (2023). What is beta testing? Retrieved from: www.techtarget.com/whatis/definition/beta-test.
85. American Medical Association. (2022). What is behavioral health? Retrieved from: www.ama-assn.org/delivering-care/public-health/what-behavioral-health.
86. American Medical Informatics Association (AMIA). (2023). What is informatics? Retrieved from: https://amia.org/about-amia/why-informatics/informatics-research-and-practice.
87. ANSI/ASIS SPC.1–2009. (2023). Organizational resilience: Security preparedness, and continuity management systems. Retrieved from: www.ansi.org.
88. Office of the National Coordinator for Health Information Technology. (2023). Certified health IT product list. Retrieved from: https://chpl.healthit.gov/#/search.
89. IBM. (2023). Retrieved from: www.ibm.com.
90. ISO 9241–11: 2018. (2018). Ergonomics of human-system interaction – Part 11: Usability: Definitions and concepts. Retrieved from: www.iso.org/standard/63500.html.
91. Castellino, R.A. (2005). Computer Aided Detection (CAD): An overview. *Cancer Imaging,* 5(1), 17–19. https://doi.org/10.1102/1470-7330.2005.0018.
92. American Hospital Association. (2023). Retrieved from: www.aha.org.

93. Federal Emergency Management Agency. (2023). Retrieved from: www.fema. gov/.
94. Agency for Healthcare Research and Quality (AHRQ). (2023). Retrieved from: www.ahrq.gov.
95. Health Insurance Terms Glossary. Joint Learning Network. (2023). Retrieved from: www.jointlearningnetwork.org/technical-initiatives/information-technology/glossary.
96. Medicine Net. (2023). Retrieved from: www.medicinenet.com.
97. Vocabulary.com. (2023). Retrieved from: www.vocabulary.com/.
98. Quia.com. (2023). Software testing support. Retrieved from: www.quia.com/jg/1181678list.html.
99. USAID ASSIST Project. (2023). Cause and affect analysis. Retrieved from: www.usaidassist.org/resources/cause-and-effect-analysis.
100. Hansche, S. (2005). *Official (ISC)² Guide to the CISSP-ISSEP CBK*. Boca Raton, FL: Taylor and Francis Group, LLC.
101. HCA Healthcare. (2023). Clinical care classification system. Retrieved from: https://careclassification.org/.
102. Reachhealth.org. (2023). UDS (Uniform Data System) definitions. Retrieved from: https://reachhealth.org/wp-content/uploads/2011/10/UDS-Definitions.pdf.
103. Kibbe, D.C., Phillips, R.L., & Green, L.A. (2004). The continuity of care record. *American Family Physician, 70*(7), 1220–1223. Retrieved from: www.aafp.org/pubs/afp/issues/2004/1001/p1220.html.
104. Karami, M., Rahimi, A., & Shahmirzadi, A.H. (2017). Clinical data warehouse: An effective tool to create intelligence in disease management. *Health Care Management, 36*(4), 380–384. Retrieved from: https://pubmed.ncbi.nlm.nih.gov/28938242/.
105. European Committee for Standardization. (n/d). What is CEN? Retrieved from: www.cencenelec.eu/about-cen/.
106. Carnegie Mellon University. (2023). Software engineering institute. Retrieved from: www.sei.cmu.edu/about/divisions/cert/index.cfm.
107. Tech Targt. (2023). What is BIOS? Retrieved from: www.techtarget.com/whatis/definition/BIOS-basic-input-output-system.
108. Microsoft. (2023). Microsoft 365 help and learning. Office Support. Retrieved from: https://support.microsoft.com/en-us/microsoft-365?ui=en-us&rs=en-us&ad=us.
109. Federal Communications Commission (FCC). (2023). Glossary of telecommunications terms. Retrieved from: www.fcc.gov/general/glossary-telecommunications-terms.
110. Public Health Development and Social Cognition. (2020). Retrieved from: https://phdsc.org/.
111. Rosenbloom, S.T., Miller, R.A., & Johnson, K.B., et al. (2008). A model for evaluating interface terminologies. *JAMIA, 15*(1), 65–76.
112. Big Data Insights. (2023). Hadoop: What it is and why it matters. Retrieved from: www.sas.com/en_us/insights/big-data/hadoop.html.

113. National Institute for Standards Technology (NIST). (2023). Retrieved from: www.nist.gov/healthcare/index.cfm.

114. Clinical Observation Access Service Specification. (2001). Clinical Observation Access Service. Retrieved from: www.omg.org/spec/COAS/1.0/PDF.

115. Ohio Laws and Administrative Rules: Legislative Service Commission. (2007). Administrative Code: 5101:   3: Ohio works first: Federal work participation rates. Retrieved from: https://codes.ohio.gov/ohio-administrative-code/rule-5101:1-3-01.

116. Sembritzki, J. (2002). Your medical history all on a smartcard. *ISO Bulletin.* Retrieved from: www.iso.org.

117. Centers for Medicare & Medicaid Services (CMS). (2023). Administrative simplification: Code set basics. Retrieved from: www.cms.gov/files/document/code-sets.pdf.

118. Renner, S.A. (2001) A "community of interest" approach to data interoperability. MITRE Corporation. Retrieved from: www.mitre.org/sites/default/files/pdf/renner_community.pdf.

119. The Free Dictionary: Medical Dictionary. (2023). Retrieved from: http://medical-dictionary.thefreedictionary.com/.

120. ISO/TR 28380-1. (2023). IHE Global Standards Adoption—Part 1 The Process (terms only). Retrieved from: www.iso.org.

121. ISO/IEC 27011. (2018). ISO/IEC 27011:2016/ITU-T X.1051 Information technology—Security techniques: Code of practice for information security controls based on ISO/IEC 27002 for telecommunications organisations (2nd ed.). Retrieved from: www.iso27001security.com/html/27011.html.

122. Organization for Economic Co-operation and Development. (2023). Retrieved from: www.oecd.org/.

123. Tasq.ai. (2023). What is convergence. Retrieved from: www.tasq.ai/glossary/converge/.

124. Scott-Clark Medical. (2020). 5 Key benefits of a Computer on Wheels (COW) in healthcare & hospitals. Retrieved from: www.scott-clark.com/blog/key-benefits-computer-wheels-healthcare-hospitals/.

125. Government Technology. (2023). Retrieved from: www.govtech.com/.

126. Caristix. (2023). HL7 Definition, v 2. Retrieved from: https://hl7-definition.caristix.com/v2/HL7v2.5.1/DataTypes/CWE.

127. ISO 18308: 2011. (2017). Health informatics—Requirements for an electronic health record architecture. Retrieved from: www.iso.org/standard/52823.html.

128. National Institute of Standards and Technology. Computer Security Resource Center. (2023). Glossary. Retrieved from: https://csrc.nist.gov/glossary?index=A.

129. Reference.com. (2020). What is data capture? Retrieved from: www.reference.com/world-view/data-capture-c3571dbc36b1021?ueid=699B3C7A-2054-4499-A93C-6A4499843E11.

130. Cowen, P.S., & Moorhead, S. (2014). *Current Issues in Nursing.* St. Louis: Elsevier Health Sciences.

131. Cambridge Dictionary. (2023). Retrieved from: https://dictionary.cambridge.org/us/.

132. McGonigle, D., & Mastrain, K. (2022). *Nursing Informatics and the Foundation of Knowledge* (5th ed.). Boston, MA: Jones and Bartlett Publishing.

133. IT Law Wiki. (2023). Retrieved from: http://itlaw.wikia.com/wiki/.

134. Confluence HL7. (2023). Argonaut project home. Retrieved from: https://confluence.hl7.org/display/AP.

135. Hayes, A. (2023). American Recovery and Reinvestment Act (ARRA): Objectives and FAQs. Retrieved from: www.investopedia.com/terms/a/american-recovery-and-reinvestment-act.asp.

136. Richesson, R.L., & Krischer, J. (2007). Data standards in clinical research: Gaps, overlaps, challenges and future directions. *JAMIA*, *14*(6), 687–696.

137. Signal.Co. (2020). Tag management 101. Retrieved from: https://signal.co/resources/tag-management-101/.

138. Gartner Group. (2023). Retrieved from: www.gartner.com/it-glossary.

139. Obitko, M. (2007). Description logics. Retrieved from: www.obitko.com/tutorials/ontologies-semantic-web/description-logics.html.

140. Diagnostic Imaging. (2023), Medicine Plus. US National Library of Medicine. Retrieved from: www.nlm.nih.gov/medlineplus/diagnosticimaging.html.

141. NIST. (2023). Retrieved from: https://xlinux.nist.gov/dads//HTML/dictionary.html.

142. Information Technology Laboratory. National Institute of Standards and Technology. (2013). Digital signature standard. Retrieved from: https://csrc.nist.gov/pubs/fips/186/upd1/final.

143. Workgroup for Electronic Data Interchange (WEDI). (2023). Retrieved from: www.wedi.org/about-us/.

144. Agrawal, A. (2020). Value stream mapping. Retrieved from: www.isixsigma.com.

145. Thomas Jefferson University, Asano-Gonnella Center for Research in Medical Education & Health Care. (2023). Disease staging. Retrieved from: www.jefferson.edu/academics/colleges-schools-institutes/skmc/research/research-medical-education/disease-staging.html.

146. PC Magazine. (2023). Retrieved from: www.pcmag.com/encyclopedia.

147. American Psychiatric Association. (2022). *Diagnostic and Statistical Manual of Mental Disorders, Text Revision Dsm-5-tr* (5th ed.). Washington, DC: American Psychiatric Association Publishing.

148. National Information Standards Organization. (2023). NISO draft standards-specific ontology standard now open for public comments. Retrieved from: www.niso.org/press-releases/niso-draft-standards-specific-ontology-standard-now-open-public-comments.

149. Institute for Telecommunication Sciences. (2023). Federal Standard 1037C. Retrieved from: https://its.ntia.gov/publications/details.aspx?pub=2381.

150. US Department of Transportation. (2023). Deployment resources. Retrieved from: www.standards.its.dot.gov/DeploymentResources/BriefStroll.

151. Geraghty, S. (2017). An overview of average speed of answer in the call center. Retrieved from: www.talkdesk.com/blog/an-overview-of-average-speed-of-answer-in-the-call-center/.

152. New World Encyclopedia. (2023). eCommerce. Retrieved from: www.newworldencyclopedia.org.

153. Oasis Open. (2023). Retrieved from: www.oasis-open.org/org/.

154. United States House of Representatives. (2023). Retrieved from: www.house.gov/.

155. Westland, J. (2022). How to conduct a gap analysis: Definition, steps, & example. Retrieved from: www.projectmanager.com/blog/gap-analysis-project-management.

156. National Institute of Standards and Technology, Computer Security Resource Center. (n/d). Global information grid. Retrieved from: https://csrc.nist.gov/glossary/term/global_information_grid.

157. United States General Services Administration. (2023). Blanket purchase agreements. Retrieved from: www.gsa.gov/buy-through-us/purchasing-programs/gsa-multiple-award-schedule/schedule-features/blanket-purchase-agreements.

158. Hauenstein, L., Gao, T., Sze, T.W., Crawford, D., Alm, A., & White, D. (2006). A cross-functional service-oriented architecture to support real-time information exchange in emergency medical response. *Conference Proceedings of the IEEE Engineering, Medicine, Biology and Society*, Suppl: 6478–6481.

159. Masic, I., Miokovic, M., & Muhamedagic, B. (2008). Evidence based medicine – New approaches and challenges. *Acta Informatica Medica, 16*(4), 219–225. http://doi.org/10.5455/aim.2008.16.219-225.

160. Mulyar, N., Van der Aalst, W.M.P., & Peleg, M. (2007). A pattern-based analysis of clinical computer–interpretable guideline modeling languages. *JAMIA, 14*(6), 781–797.

161. Van der Aalst, W.M.P., Hofstede, A.H.M., Russell, N. et al.Control Flow Patterns. (2003, 2006). Retrieved from: www.workflowpatterns.com/patterns/control/.

162. How Stuff Works. (2023). Retrieved from: https://computer.howstuffworks.com/.

163. Ram, M.S. (2003). Film-less radiology—A future perspective. *Medical Journal, Armed Forces India, 59*(3), 187–188. https://doi.org/10.1016/S0377-1237(03)80002-3.

164. National Institutue of Standards and Technology. (2022). Retrieved from: https://csrc.nist.gov/glossary/term/federal_information_processing_standard.

165. Federal Information Processing Standards Publications (FIPS PUBS). (2023). Retrieved from: www.nist.gov/itl/fips.cfm.

166. Linktionary. (2023). Retrieved from: www.linktionary.com. Note: The site is no longer being updated.

167. Pyca/Cryptography. (2023). Recipes. Retrieved from: https://cryptography.io/en/latest/ Available at: https://cryptography.io/en/latest/.

168. Health Level Seven International. (2023). HL7 Version 3 Standard: GELLO, A Common Expression Language, Release 2. Retrieved from: www.hl7.org/implement/standards/product_brief.cfm?product_id=5.

169. National Human Genome Research Institute. (2023) Genetics versus genomics fact sheet. Retrieved from: www.genome.gov/about-genomics/fact-sheets/Genetics-vs-Genomics.

170. HashTags.org. (2023). What is a (#) Hashtag? Retrieved from: www.hashtags. org/how-to/history/what-is-a-hashtag/.

171. Hubspot. (2023). Retrieved from: https://blog.hubspot.com/.

172. Kulikowski, C.A., Shortliffe, E.H., Currie, L.M., Elkin, P.L., Hunter, L.E., Johnson, T.R., & Williamson, J.J. (2012). AMIA Board white paper: Definition of biomedical informatics and specification of core competencies for graduate education in the discipline. *JAMIA, 19*(6), 931–938. http://doi.org/10.1136/amiajnl-2012-001053.

173. National Association of County and City Health Officials (NACCHO). (2014). Statement of policy: Biosurveillance. Retrieved from: www.naccho.org/uploads/downloadable-resources/06-02-Biosurveillance.pdf.

174. Apple Computer. (2023). Health kit. Retrieved from: https://developer.apple.com/design/human-interface-guidelines/healthkit.

175. Lisk Foundation. (2023). Blockchain basics. Retrieved from: https://lisk.com/learn/about-web3/what-is-a-blockchain.

176. National Committee for Quality Assurance (NCQA). (2023). HEDIS and Performance Measurement. Retrieved from: www.ncqa.org/hedis/.

177. FQHC Associates. (n/d). What is an FQHC? Retrieved from: https://www.fqhc.org/what-is-an-fqhc.

178. Health Resources and Services Administration. (2023). Data warehouse. Retrieved from: https://data.hrsa.gov/.

179. National Quality Forum. (2023). Retrieved from: www.qualityforum.org.

180. National Institutes of Health. (2023). Office of Biomedical Translational Research Informatics. Retrieved from: https://btris.nih.gov/.

181. World Health Organization. (2016). Transitions of care. Retrieved from: www.who.int/publications/i/item/9789241511599.

182. International Council of Nurses (ICN). (2023). Retrieved from: www.icn.ch.

183. Advisory Board. (2023). C-Suite cheat sheet: Integrated delivery networks. Retrieved from: www.advisory.com/topics/purchased-services/2013/10/integrated-delivery-network#.

184. Mancini, J. (2016). What is intelligent document recognition and how does it work? Retrieved from: https://info.aiim.org/aiim-blog/what-the-heck-is-intelligent-document-recognition.

185. SSL.com. (2023). SSL.com Knowledge Base. Retrieved from: www.ssl.com/info/.

186. Columbia University. Department of Biomedical Informatics. (2023). Retrieved from: www.dbmi.columbia.edu/.

187. HIT Consultant. (2023). Health IT interoperability: News, policy, analysis, insights. Retrieved from: https://hitconsultant.net/tag/health-it-interoperability/.

188. Hartmann, J. (2023). What is Class and Object in Java OOPS? Learn with example. Retrieved from: www.guru99.com/java-oops-class-objects.html#what-is-class-in-java.

189. Hovenga, E.J.S., & Mantas, J. (2004). *Global Health Informatics Education*. Washington, DC: IOS Press.

190. Substance Abuse and Mental Health Services Administration. (2023). Retrieved from: www.samhsa.gov/.

191. IEEE Standards Association. (2023). Retrieved from: https://standards.ieee.org/findstds/standard/1012-2012.html.

192. Office of Technology Assessment. (1993). *Making Government Work: Electronic Delivery of Federal Services*. Washington, DC: Diane Publishing Co.

193. Elsevier and Mosby. (2013). *Mosby's Dental Dictionary* (3rd ed.). New York: Elsevier, Inc.

194. National Library of Medicine. (2023). National Information Center on Health Services Research and Health Care Technology (NICHSR). Retrieved from: www.nlm.nih.gov/hsrph.html.

195. ICCBA. (2023). What is ISBT 128? Retrieved from: https://iccbba.org/.

196. American Academy of Family Physicians. (2023). Independent Physician Associations (IPAs) definition. Retrieved from: www.aafp.org/about/policies/all/independent-physician-associations.html.

197. DAU. (2023). Glossary of defense acquisition acronyms and terms. Retrieved from: www.dau.edu/glossary?combine=&title=.

198. JSON.org. (1999). Introducing JSON. Retrieved from: www.json.org/json-en.html.

199. Arnold S. (ed.). (2008). *Guide to the Wireless Medical Practice: Finding the Right Connections for Healthcare*. Chicago, IL: HIMSS.

200. Fisher, T. (2023). Small Computer System Interface (SCSI). Retrieved from: www.lifewire.com/small-computer-system-interface-scsi-2626002.

201. Abdelhak, M., Grostick, S., & Hanken, M. (2015). *Health Information: Management of a Strategic Resource* (5th ed.). St. Louis, MO: Elsevier Inc.

202. Tomsho, G. (2019). *Guide to Networking Essentials (8th* ed.). Boston, MA: Cengage Learning.

203. Logical Observation Identifiers Names and Codes (LOINC). (2023). Retrieved from: www.loinc.org.

204. Woolf, S.H., Grol, R., Hutchinson, A., Eccles, M., & Grimshaw, J. (1999). Potential benefits, limitations, and harms of clinical guidelines. *BMJ, 318*(7182), 527–530.

205. Rhapsody. (2023). HL7 resources. Retrieved from: https://rhapsody.health/type/hl7-resources/.

206. American Academy of Pediatrics. (2023). Medical home. Retrieved from: www.aap.org/en/practice-management/medical-home.

207. Deloitte LLP. (2023). Deloitte Center for Health Solutions. Retrieved from: https://www2.deloitte.com/us/en/insights/research-centers/center-for-health-solutions.html?icid=nav2_center-for-health-solutions.

208. Saba, V., & McCormick, K. (2021). *Essentials of Nursing Informatics* (7th ed.). New York, NY: McGraw-Hill Medical.

209. Chron. (2021). Definition of Master Services Agreement. Retrieved from: https://smallbusiness.chron.com/definition-master-services-agreement-40141.html.

210. Madden, S. (2016). Understanding Management Services Organizations (MSOs). Retrieved from: www.physicianspractice.com/practice-models/understanding-management-services-organizations-msos.
211. National Council on Prescription Drug Programs (NCPDP). (2023). Retrieved from: www.ncpdp.org.
212. NEMSIS.org. (2023). National Emergency Medical Services Information System (NEMSIS). Retrieved from: www.nemsis.org.
213. University of Iowa College for Nursing Centers. (2018). NIC overview. Retrieved from: www.nursing.uiowa.edu/cncce/nursing-interventions-classification-overview.
214. The OMAHA System. (2023). Retrieved from: www.omahasystem.org/.
215. Healthcare.gov. (2023). Medicaid and CHIP. Retrieved from: www.healthcare.gov/medicaid-chip/childrens-health-insurance-program/.
216. Ortiz, A., Lario, F., & Ros, L. (1999). Enterprise integration-business processes integrated management: A proposal for a methodology to develop enterprise integration programs. *Computers in Industry, 40*(2–3), 155–171.
217. SPARC. (2023). Open access. Retrieved from: https://sparcopen.org/open-access//.
218. Hickey, J., & Brosnan, C. (2016). *Evaluation of Health Care Quality for DNPs* (2nd ed.). New York, NY: Springer Publishing Company.
219. Glover, E. (2022). What is cognitive computing? Retrieved from: https://builtin.com/artificial-intelligence/cognitive-computing.
220. Digital Preservation Workshop. (2023). Common services. Retrieved from: https://dpworkshop.org/dpm-eng/foundation/oais/services.html.
221. eHealth Ontario. (n/d). Health Information Access Layer. Retrieved from: www.ehealthblueprint.com/en/documentation/chapter/health-information-access-layer-hial.
222. Data Conversion Organization. (2023). Data structure and compatibility. Retrieved from: https://data-conversion.org/data-structure-and-compatibility/.
223. Lehpamer, H. (2012). *RFID Design Principles* (2nd ed.). Norwood, MA: Artech House.
224. Eck, D. (2022) Introduction to Programming Using Java, Version 9.0, Java FX Edition. Retrieved from: https://math.hws.edu/javanotes/index.html.
225. The Linux Information Project. (2023). Plain text. Retrieved from: www.linfo.org/plain_text.html.
226. Joint Commission (formerly Joint Commission on Accreditation of Healthcare Organizations). (2023). Retrieved from: www.jointcommission.org.
227. Kaiser Family Foundation. (2023). Retrieved from: www.kff.org/.
228. National Institutes of Health. (2023). All of Us Research Program. Retrieved from: https://allofus.nih.gov/.
229. Institute for Safe Medication Practices (ISMP). (2023). ISMP list of confused drug names. Retrieved from: www.ismp.org/news/updated-ismp-list-often-confused-drug-names-now-available.
230. Australian Government. (2023). Office of the Australian Information Commissioner. Retrieved from: www.oaic.gov.au/.

231. Information Systems Audit and Control Association. (2019). *CISA Review Manual* (27th ed.). Schaumberg, IL: ISACA.

232. Dammann, O. (2018). Data, information, evidence, and knowledge: A proposal for health informatics and data science. *Online Journal of Public Health Informatics, 10*(3), e224. Retrieved from: www.ncbi.nlm.nih.gov/pmc/articles/PMC6435353/.

233. Hasman, A., & Sosa, M. (1994 January 1). Education and training of health informatics in Europe. *Technol Health Care, 2*(1), 61–70. https://doi.org/10.3233/THC-1994-2107. PMID: 25273808.

234. IMSL by Perforce. (2021). What is a regression model? Retrieved from: www.imsl.com/blog/what-is-regression-model.

235. Stanford University. RISC architecture. Retrieved from: https://cs.stanford.edu/people/eroberts/courses/soco/projects/risc/whatis/index.html.

236. Andison, M., & Moss, J. (2007). What nurses do: Use of the ISO reference terminology model for nursing action as a framework for analyzing MICU nursing practice patterns. *AMIA Annual Symposium Proceedings 2007*, 21–25. Retrieved from: www.ncbi.nlm.nih.gov/pmc/articles/PMC2942066/.

237. The Serial ATA International Organization (SATA). Developers. Retrieved from: https://sata-io.org./.

238. MD Clarity. (2023). Severity of illness (SOI). Retrieved from: www.mdclarity.com/glossary/severity-of-illness-soi.

239. Department of Defense. (2003). DoD net-centric data strategy. Retrieved from: https://dodcio.defense.gov/Portals/0/documents/Net-Centric-Data-Strategy-2003-05–092.pdf.

240. National Institute of Standards and Technology. (2023) Conformity assessment basics. Retrieved from: www.nist.gov/standardsgov/conformity-assessment-basics.

241. ISO. (2023). ISO/ TS 22220. Identification of subjects of health care (terms only). Retrieved from: www.iso.org/standard/59755.html.

242. MITRE Corporation. (2023). Focus area: Health. Retrieved from: www.mitre.org/focus-areas/health.

243. Pattichis, C.S., & Panayides, A.S. (2019). Connected health. Retrieved from: www.frontiersin.org/articles/10.3389/fdgth.2019.00001/full.

244. National Institute of Standards and Technology (NIST). (2023). Overview of conformance testing. Retrieved from: www.nist.gov/itl/ssd/information-systems-group/overview-conformance-testing.

245. ECRI Institute. (2023). About ECRI. Retrieved from: www.ecri.org.

246. Heath, S. (2018). What is the role of connected health in patient engagement? Retrieved from: https://patientengagementhit.com/news/what-is-the-role-of-connected-health-in-patient-engagement.

247. International Organisation for Standardization (ISO). Health sector. Retrieved from: www.iso.org/sectors/health.

248. Virothaisakun, J. (2023). User acceptance testing versus usability testing . . . What's the dif? Retrieved from: https://digital.gov/2014/10/06/user-acceptance-testing-versus-usability-testing-whats-the-dif/.

249. United States Health Information Knowledgebase. (2014). Archived at: https://web.archive.org/web/20010801203020/.

250. Oxford Reference. (2023). Retrieved from: www.oxfordreference.com/.

251. Personal Connected Health Alliance. (2017). Continua design guidelines. Retrieved from: www.pchalliance.org/continua-design-guidelines.

252. US Department of Veterans Affairs. (2020). VistA evolution program plan. Retrieved from: www.data.va.gov/dataset/VistA-Evolution-Program-Plan/nswa-7nyb.

253. CORBA.org. (2023). Retrieved from: www.corba.org/history_of_corba.htm.

254. Dalhio, H.S., & Singh, J. (2010). VoIP signal processing in digital domain. *IUP Journal of Electrical & Electronics Engineering, 3*(4), 38–43.

255. Infolific. (n/d) Definition of VOIP. Retrieved from: https://infolific.com/technology/definitions/internet-dictionary/voip/.

256. Goodbole, N.S. (2004). *Software Quality Assurance: Principles and Practice.* Pangbourne, UK: Alpha Science Intl Ltd. p. 288.

257. Patel, M., Asch, D., & Volpp, K. Wearable devices as facilitators, not drivers, of health behavior change. *Journal of the American Medical Association, 313*(5). Retrieved from: http://jama.jamanetwork.com/article.aspx?articleid=2089651.

258. U.S. Department of Health and Human Services. Research. (2023). Health information privacy. Retrieved from: www.hhs.gov/hipaa/for-professionals/special-topics/research/index.html.

259. Laserfiche. (2023). What's the difference between wet, digital and electronic signatures? Retrieved from: www.laserfiche.com/resources/blog/whats-the-difference-between-wet-digital-and-electronic-signatures/.

260. International Telecommunications Union. (1996). X.25: Interface between Data Terminal Equipment (DTE) and Data Circuit-Terminating Equipment (DCE) for terminals operating in the packet mode and connected to public data networks by dedicated circuit. Retrieved from: www.itu.int/rec/T-REC-X.25-199610-I/en.

261. X12. (2023). About X12. Retrieved from: https://x12.org/about/about-x12.

262. Connectivity Standards Alliance (CSA). (2022). Zigbee FAQ. Retrieved from: https://csa-iot.org/all-solutions/zigbee/zigbee-faq/.

263. U.S. Department of Treasury. (2023). Certificate policies. Retrieved from: https://pki.treas.gov/cert_policies.htm.

264. Ameerican Medical Association. (2023). Retrieved from: www.ama-assn.org/.

265. Javvin Technologies. (2007). Network Dictionary. Retrieved from: https://books.google.com/books?id=On_Hh23IXDUC&printsec=frontcover&source=gbs_ge_summary_r&cad=0#v=onepage&q&f=false.

266. National Library of Medicine. (2023). Unified medical language system (UMLS) glossary. Retrieved from: www.nlm.nih.gov/research/umls/new_users/glossary.html.

267. Blockchainhub Berlin. (2018). Decentralized applications – dApps. Retrieved from: https://blockchainhub.net/decentralized-applications-dapps/.

268. Medium.com. (2018). The year of DApps. Retrieved from: https://medium.com/the-mission/2018-the-year-of-dapps-dbe108860bcb.

269. Onetrust. (2023). Complete guide to General Data Protection Regulation (GDPR). Retrieved from: www.onetrust.com/blog/gdpr-compliance/.

270. Your Dictionary. (2023). Retrieved from: www.yourdictionary.com.

271. Shortliffe, E., Cimino, J.J., & Chiang, M.F. (2021). *Biomedical Informatics: Computer Applications in Health Care and Biomedicine* (5th ed.). New York, NY: Spring Science and Business Media.

272. Design Develop Implement. (2021). Retrieved from: https://ddiprogram.org/.

273. Karris, S. (2009). *Networks: Design and Management.* Fremont, CA: Orchard Publications.

274. IBM. (2023). What is deep learning? Retrieved from: www.ibm.com/topics/deep-learning.

275. Juniper Networks. (2023). Juniper TechLibrary. Retrieved from: www.juniper.net/us/en/search.html.

276. Computed Radiography vs. Digital Radiography. (2018). JPI Healthcare Solutions. Retrieved from: www.jpihealthcare.com/computed-radiography-cr-and-digital-radiography-dr-which-should-you-choose/.

277. Bioverge. (2018). The present and future of digital therapeutics. Retrieved from: https://bioverge.medium.com/the-present-and-future-of-digital-therapeutics-954c121fdf20.

278. Bauerle, N. (2023). What is a distributed ledger? Retrieved from: www.coindesk.com/information/what-is-a-distributed-ledger/.

279. CDISC. (2023). Domain information model. Retrieved from: www.cdisc.org./standards/domain-information-module.

280. TechnologyUK. (2023). Welcome. Retrieved from: www.technologyuk.net.

281. Medicaid and CHIP Payment and Access Commission (MACPAC). (2023). Commonly used acronyms and abbreviations. Retrieved from: www.macpac.gov/reference-materials/reference-guide-to-federal-medicaid-statute-and-regulations/macpac-acronyms-list/.

282. Simple Trials. (2023). What is EDC? Retrieved from: www.simpletrials.com/what-is-edc.

283. Government Publishing Office. (2002). Public Law 107–347 – E-Government Act of 2002. Retrieved from: www.gpo.gov/fdsys/pkg/PLAW-107publ347/content-detail.html.

284. IGI Global. (2023). What is information infrastructure? Retrieved from: www.igi-global.com/dictionary/information-infrastructure/14415.

285. Davis, L., Watts, R., & Haskins, J. (2022). Electronic signature: An instant, convenient and green way to sign documents. Retrieved from: www.forbes.com/advisor/business/electronic-signature/.

286. DIN. (2023). European standards. Retrieved from: www.din.de/en/din-and-our-partners/din-in-europe/european-standards.

287. CoverMyMeds. (2023). Retrieved from: www.covermymeds.com/main/.

288. Practice Fusion. (2023). Retrieved from: www.practicefusion.com.

289. Porterfield, A., Engelbert, K., & Coustasse, A. (2014). Electronic prescribing: Improving the efficiency and accuracy of prescribing in the ambulatory care

setting. *Perspectives in Health Information Management,* 11(Spring), 1g.

290. Lucidchart. (2023), What is an entity relationship diagram (ERD)? Retrieved from: www.lucidchart.com/pages/er-diagrams.

291. Ethereum. (2023). Welcome to ethereum. Retrieved from: https://ethereum.org/.

292. Hawkins, R.C. (2005). The evidence based medicine approach to diagnostic testing: Practicalities and limitations. *Clinical Biochemistry Review, 26*(2), 7–18. Retrieved from: www.ncbi.nlm.nih.gov/pubmed/16278748.

293. Thammasak, R., & Shi, J.J. (2005). *A Project-Oriented Data Warehouse for construction. Automation in Construction.* New York, NY: Elsevier.

294. IBM. (2021). Building a dimensional data model 14.1 Retrieved from: www.ibm.com/docs/en/informix-servers/14.10?topic=model-building-dimensional-data.

295. Monegro, J. (2016). Fat protocols. Retrieved from: www.usv.com/blog/fat-protocols.

296. Federal Register. (2023). Fedeal financial participation. Retrieved from: www.federalregister.gov/documents/2022/12/05/2022-26390/federal-financial-partici-pation-in-state-assistance-expenditures-federal-matching-shares-for.

297. RP Photonics, The Company. (2023). Encyclopedia. Retrieved from: www.rp-photonics.com/encyclopedia_a.html.

298. Salesforce. (2023). Field level security. Retrieved from: https://help.salesforce.com/s/articleView?id=sf.admin_fls.htm&type=5.

299. Cohen, T.A., & Patel, V.L. (2023). *Intelligent Systems in Medicine and Health: The Role of AI. (Cognitive Informatics in Biomedicine and Healthcare.)* New York, NY: Springer.

300. GANTT.com. (2023). What is a Gantt Chart? Retrieved from: www.gantt.com.

301. WhatIsMyIPAdress.com? (2023). What is a gateway and what does it do? Retrieved from: https://whatismyipaddress.com/gateway.

302. GDPR.EU. (2023). What is GDPR, the EU's new data protection law? Retrieved from: https://gdpr.eu/what-is-gdpr/.

303. Grid Computing Info Centre. (n/d). Frequently asked questions. Retrieved from: www.gridcomputing.com.

304. GS1 US. (2023). Authentic barcodes powered by GS1 standards. Retrieved from: www.gs1us.org/.

305. GUID.one. (n/d). What is a GUID? (Globally Unique Identifier.). Retrieved from: http://guid.one/guid.

306. Gantt, W.A.H. (2021). *Healthcare Cybersecurity.* New York, NY: American Bar Association.

307. The SSL Store. (2021). What is a hash function in cryptography? A beginner's guide. Retrieved from: www.thesslstore.com/blog/what-is-a-hash-function-in-cryptography-a-beginners-guide/.

308. Trend Micro Incorporated. (2023). Definition. Retrieved from: www.trendmicro.com/vinfo/us/security/definition/a.

309. Curie, C. (2016). Study design for assessing effectiveness, efficiency and acceptability of services including measures of structure, process, service quality, and outcome of health care. Retrieved from: www.healthknowledge.org.uk/public-health-textbook/research-methods/1c-health-care-evaluation-health-care-assessment.

310. Wolfram MathWorld. (2023). Hexadecimal. Retrieved from: https://mathworld.wolfram.com/Hexadecimal.html.

311. HealthInsurance.org. (2023). The state of your health insurance marketplace. Retrieved from: www.healthinsurance.org/state-health-insurance-exchanges/.

312. Secure Technology Alliance. (2023). Benefits of smart cards versus magnetic stripe cards for healthcare applications. Retrieved from: www.securetechalliance.org/publications-benefits-of-smart-cards-versus-magnetic-stripe-cards-for-healthcare-applications/.

313. Hyperledger Foundation. (2023). Recorded videos. Retrieved from: www.hyperledger.org/learn/webinars.

314. Secure Technology Alliance. (2022). Smart Card Primer. Retrieved from: www.securetechalliance.org/smart-cards-intro-primer/.

315. Hyperledger Foundation. (2018). An introduction to hyperledger. Retrieved from: https://8112310.fs1.hubspotusercontent-na1.net/hubfs/8112310/Hyperledger/Offers/HL_Whitepaper_IntroductiontoHyperledger.pdf.

316. Clifton, C. (2009). Individually identifiable data. In: Liu, L., & Özsu, M.T. (eds) *Encyclopedia of Database Systems*. Boston, MA: Springer. https://doi.org/10.1007/978-0-387-39940-9_1390.

317. Diffen. (2023). Data vs. Information. Retrieved from: www.diffen.com/difference/Data_vs_Information.

318. Encyclopaedia Britannica. (2023). Information system. Retrieved from: www.britannica.com/search?query=information+system.

319. Butts, D., Strilesky, M., & Fadel, M. (2014). The 7 components of a clinical integration network. Retrieved from: www.beckershospitalreview.com/hospital-physician-relationships/the-7-components-of-a-clinical-integration-network.html.

320. Bires, S., & McMurray, M. (2019). Clinically integrated networks: Guidelines and common barriers for establishment. Retrieved from: www.medicaleconomics.com/view/clinically-integrated-networks-guidelines-and-common-barriers-establishment.

321. McKenzie, C. (2021). Interpreted vs. compiled languages: What's the difference? Retrieved from: www.theserverside.com/answer/Interpreted-vs-compiled-languages-Whats-the-difference.

322. Nivedita, S., Padmini, R., Shanmugam, R. (2012). TCP/IP: The internet layer protocol. Retrieved from: www.informit.com/articles/article.aspx?p=29578&seqNum=5.

323. Parr, B. (2011). IPv4 & IPv6: A short guide. Retrieved from: https://mashable.com/2011/02/03/ipv4-ipv6-guide/#ibtu68q9uOq9.

324. IEEE Standards Association. (2023). Standards health informatics. Retrieved from: https://standards.ieee.org/search/?q=standards%20health%20informatics.

325. Federation of American Scientists. (2022). JASON defense advisory panel reports. Retrieved from: https://irp.fas.org/agency/dod/jason/.

326. The Joint Commission. (2023). Joint Commission Resources. Retrieved from: www.jcrinc.com.

327. Atlassian. (2023) JIRA. Retrieved from: www.atlassian.com/software/jira.

328. What is DBMS. Com. (2023). Joins. Retrieved from: http://whatisdbms.com/what-is-join-and-its-types-in-dbms/.

329. Online Learning Institute. (2023). My accounting course: What is a ledger? Retrieved from: www.myaccountingcourse.com/accounting-dictionary/ledger.

330. Sugumaran, V. (2014) *Recent Advances in Intelligent Technologies and Information Systems*. Hershey, PA: IGI Global.

331. Kulshrestha, R. (2019). A beginner's guide to Latent Dirichlet Allocation (LDA). Towards data science. Retrieved from: https://towardsdatascience.com/latent-dirichlet-allocation-lda-9d1cd064ffa2.

332. Project Management Knowledge. (2023). Level of Effort (LOE). Retrieved from: https://project-management-knowledge.com/definitions/l/level-of-effort-loe/.

333. Stutman, H. (2010). A longitudinal medical record is key to clinical decision support. Retrieved from: https://healthexec.com/topics/health-it/medical-records/longitudinal-medical-record-key-clinical-decision-support.

334. Computer Hope. (2023). Computer terms, dictionary and glossary. Retrieved from: www.computerhope.com/jargon.htm.

335. Occupational Safety & Health Administration (OSHA). (2023). Control of hazardous energy Lockout/Tagout. Retrieved from: www.osha.gov/control-hazardous-energy/concepts.

336. Gliklich, R.E., Dreyer, N.A., Leavy, M.B. (eds). (2014). *Registries for Evaluating Patient Outcomes: A User's Guide* [Internet] (3rd ed.). Rockville, MD: Agency for Healthcare Research and Quality. Retrieved from: www.ncbi.nlm.nih.gov/books/NBK208643/.

337. McSweeney-Feld, M.H., & Molinari, C.A. (2023). *Dimensions of Long-Term Care Management: An Introduction* (3rd ed.). Chicago, IL: American College of Healthcare Executives.

338. National Institutue on Aging. (2023). What is long term care? Retrieved from: www.nia.nih.gov/health/what-long-term-care.

339. Stankeviciute, G. (2020). Understanding machine readable zone. Retrieved from: www.idenfy.com/blog/machine-readable-zone/.

340. Secureframe. (2023). What is continuous compliance and how to achieve it. Retrieved from: https://secureframe.com/hub/grc/continuous-compliance.

341. Network Encyclopedia. (2024). Retrieved from: https://networkencyclopedia.com/.

342. Grober, E.D., & Bohnen, J.M.A. (2005). Defining medical error. *Canadian Journal of Surgery, 48*(1), 39–44.

343. Saranummi, N. (2005). *Regional Health Economies and ICT Services: The PICNIC Services*. Washington, DC: IOS Press.

344. Ingram, D. (2019). What is a management information system? Retrieved from: http://smallbusiness.chron.com/management-information-system-2104.html.

345. The Moving Picture Experts Group. (2020). MPEG. Retrieved from: https://mpeg.chiariglione.org.

346. Gliklich R.E., Dreyer, N.A., & Leavy M.B. (eds). (2014). *Registries for Evaluating Patient Outcomes: A User's Guide* [Internet] (3rd ed.). Rockville, MD: Agency for Healthcare Research and Quality. Retrieved from: www.ncbi.nlm.nih.gov/books/NBK208618/.

347. Hersh, W.R. (2022). *Health Informatics: Practical Guide* (8th ed.). Washington, DC: Lulu.com.

348. Castr.com. (2023). Unicast vs. Multicast vs. Broadcast. What's the difference? Retrieved from: https://castr.com/blog/unicast-vs-multicast-vs-broadcast/.

349. WebsiteBuilders.com. (2023). The interactive glossary: Defining the net. Retrieved from: https://websitebuilders.com/how-to/glossary/.

350. McCarthy, D.B., Propp, K., Cohen, A., Sabharwal, R., Schachter, A.A., & Rein, A.L. (2014). Learning from health information exchange technical architecture and implementation in seven beacon communities. *EGEMS, 2*(1), 1060. http://doi.org/10.13063/2327-9214.1060.

351. Riak.com. (2023). NoSQL databases. Retrieved from: https://riak.com/resources/nosql-databases/.

352. Yegulalp, S. (2017) What is NoSQL? NoSQL databases explained. Retrieved from: www.infoworld.com/article/3240644/nosql/what-is-nosql-nosql-data-bases-explained.html.

353. Academy of Nutrition and Dietetics. (2019). Position of the academy of nutrition and dietetics: Nutrition informatics. *Journal of the Academy of Nutrition and Dietetics, 119*(8), 1375–1382. https://doi.org/10.1016/j.jand.2019.06.004.

354. Jessin, A. (2014). How to configure OCSP stapling on APACHE and Nginx. Retrieved from: www.digitalocean.com/community/tutorials/how-to-configure-ocsp-stapling-on-apache-and-nginx.

355. ISO. (2023). What is ODA?" Retrieved from: https://xml.coverpages.org/odan-ovl0.html.

356. Military Health System and Defense Health Agency. (2023). Health plan identifier (HPID) and other entity identifier (OEID). Retrieved from: www.health.mil/Military-Health-Topics/Technology/HIPAA-TCSI/HIPAA-Transactions-Code-Sets-Identifiers/Identifiers/Health-Plan-Identifier-and-Other-Entity-Identifier.

357. Jermey, J., & Browne, G. (2004). *Website Indexing: Enhancing Access to Information within Websites*. Adelaide, South Australia: Auslib Press.

358. HealthInsurance.Org. (2023). Out of network: Out of plan. Retrieved from: www.healthinsurance.org/glossary/out-of-network-out-of-plan/.

359. User Interface. (2023). HN computing. Scottish Qualifications Authority. Retrieved from: www.sqa.org.uk/e-learning/COS101CD/page_04.htm.

360. Handy, L.R. (2023). *Health Informatics: An Interprofessional Approach* (3rd ed.). New York: Elsevier.

361. Information Resources Management Association. (2016). *Public Health and Welfare: Concepts, Methodologies, Tools and Applications*. Hershey, PA: IGI Global.

362. Benson, T., & Grieve, G. (2021). *Principles of Health Interoperability: FHIR, HL7 and SNOMED CT (Health Information Technology Standards)* (4th ed.). New York: Springer.

363. Yeoman, G., Furlong, P., & Seres, M., et al. (2017) Defining patient centricity with patients for patients and caregivers: A collaborative endeavor. *BMJ Innovations.* Published Online First: https://doi.org/10.1136/bmjinnov-2016-000157.

364. Fong, D. (2018) *Patient-centric Technology Improves Access, Efficiency and Quality of Care.* Wolters Kluwer. Retrieved from: www.wolterskluwercdi.com/blog/patient-centric-technology/.

365. Strategic Health Information Exchange Collaborative (SHIEC). (2023). Patient Centered Data Home. Retrieved from: www.iheusa.org/sites/iheusa/files/IHE_Connectathon_PCDH_February%2017%202018.pdf.

366. Agency for Healthcare Research and Quality. U.S. Department of Health & Human Services. (2021). Defining the PCMH. Retrieved from: https://pcmh.ahrq.gov/page/defining-pcmh.

367. Adobe. (2023). What does pdf mean? Retrieved from: www.adobe.com/acrobat/about-adobe-pdf.html/.

368. HIMSS and Personal Connected Health Alliance. (2017). What is personal connected health? Retrieved from: www.pchalliance.org/sites/pchalliance/files/PCHA_Defining_Personal_Connected_Health.pdf.

369. European Commission. (2021). ICT Standards for Procurement. Retrieved from: https://joinup.ec.europa.eu/collection/ict-standards-procurement/interoperability-and-portability.

370. IEEE. (2016). Standard for Information Technology—Portable Operating System Interface (POSIX(TM)) Base Specifications, Issue 7," in IEEE Std 1003.1, 2016 Edition (incorporates IEEE Std 1003.1–2008, IEEE Std 1003.1–2008/Cor 1–2013, and IEEE Std 1003.1–2008/Cor 2–2016), vol., no., pp. 1–3957, 30 Sept. 2016. https://doi.org/10.1109/IEEESTD.2016.7582338. Retrieved from: https://ieeexplore.ieee.org/document/7582338.

371. Centers for Medicare and Medicaid Services (CMS). (2023). Quality payment program. Retrieved from: https://qpp.cms.gov/mips/traditional-mips.

372. Defense Acquisition University (DAU). (2023). Quality Assurance Surveillance Plan (QASP). Retrieved from: www.dau.edu/glossary/quality-assurance-surveillance-plan.

373. American Academy of Family Physicians (AAFP). (2023). Basics of quality improvement. Retrieved from: www.aafp.org/practice-management/improvement/basics.html.

374. ISO 9001: 2015. Quality management systems – Requirements. Retrieved from: www.iso.org.

375. Regulations. Occupational Safety and Health Administration (OSHA). Retrieved from: www.osha.gov/pls/oshaweb/owadisp.show_document?p_table=STANDARDS&p_id=10618.

376. Peters, D.H., El-Saharty, S., Siadat, B., Janovsky, K., & Vujicic, M. (2013). *Improving Health Service Delivery in Developing Countries: From Evidence to Action.* Washington, DC: World Bank Publications. https://doi.org/10.1596/978-0-8213-7888-5.
377. International Standards Organization. (2015). Quality management principles. Retrieved from: www.iso.org/publication/PUB100080.html.
378. NHS Digital. (2023). Terminology and classifications. Retrieved from: https://digital.nhs.uk/services/terminology-and-classifications.
379. Magnuson, J.A., & Dixon, B.E. (eds). (2021). *Public Health Informatics and Information Systems* (3rd ed.). New York, NY: Springer.
380. ASQ-Excellance through Quality. (2023). What is reliability? Retrieved from: https://asq.org/quality-resources/reliability.
381. Center for Connected Health Policy. (2023). Remote patient monitoring. Retrieved from: www.cchpca.org/topic/remote-patient-monitoring/.
382. Braunstein, M. (2022). *Health Informatics on FHIR: How HL7's API is Transforming Healthcare* (2nd ed.). New York, NY: Springer.
383. Phaal, R., Farrukh, C., & Probert, D. (2004). Technology roadmapping—A planning framework for evolution and revolution. *Technological Forecasting and Social Change,* 71(1–2), 5–26. https://doi.org/10.1016/S0040-1625%2803%2900072-6.
384. Rolstadas, A. (2012). *Computer-Aided Production Management.* New York, NY: Springer.
385. Porcupine. (1995). What SATAN is. Retrieved from: www.porcupine.org/satan/summary.html.
386. Institute for Healthcare Improvement. (2023). SBAR: Situation-Background-Assessment-Recommendation. Retrieved from: www.ihi.org/Topics/SBARCommunicationTechnique/Pages/default.aspx.
387. Yi, M. (2021). What is a Scatter Plot? Retrieved from: https://chartio.com/learn/dashboards-and-charts/what-is-a-scatter-plot/.
388. Mayes, K., & Markantonakis, K. (2017). *Smart Cards, Tokens, Security and Applications* (2nd ed.). Switzerland: Springer-Verlag.
389. Cohen, F. (2010). *Fast SOA: The Way to Use Native XML Technology to Achieve Service Oriented Architecture Governance, Scalability and Performance.* New York, NY: Morgan Kaufmann Publishers.
390. Hughes, A. (2017). Definition of security compromise. Retrieved from: https://bizfluent.com/about-6567858-definition-security-compromise.html.
391. Hornun-Prahauser, V., Behrendt, W., & Benari, M. (n/d). Developing further the concept of ePortfolio with the use of semantic web technologies. Retrieved from: http://citeseerx.ist.psu.edu/viewdoc/download?doi=. https://doi.org/10.1.1.83.8494&rep=rep1&type=pdf.
392. Geeks for Geeks.com. (2023). Session Layer in OSI model. Retrieved from: www.geeksforgeeks.org/session-layer-in-osi-model/.
393. Tomsho, G. (2020). *Guide to Operating Systems* (6th ed.). Boston, MA: Cengage Learning.
394. Cao, L. (2015). *Metasynthetic Computing and Engineering of Complex Systems.* London: Springer.

395. Spacey, J. (2023). What is session management? Retrieved from: https://simpli-cable.com/IT/session-management.

396. Friedman, C.P. Wyatt, J.C., & Ash, J.S. (2022). *Evaluation Methods in Biomedical and Health Informatics* (3rd ed.). New York, NY: Springer.

397. Matlis, J. (2000). Symmetrical multiprocessing. Retrieved from: www.computer-world.com/article/2588624/symmetrical--multiprocessing.html.

398. Bass, L., Clements, P., & Kazman, R. (2021). *Software Architecture in Practice* (4th ed.). New York, NY: Addison-Wesley Professional.

399. Certified Software Testing Professional. (2023). Software testing support. Retrieved from: www.quia.com/jg/1181678list.html.

400. ISO. (2016). ISO/IEC guide 2: 2004 standardization and related activities—General vocabulary. ISO. Retrieved from: www.iso.org/standard/39976.html.

401. Rognehaugh, R. (1998). *The Managed Health Care Dictionary*. Burlington, MA: Jones & Bartlett Learning.

402. UCSF Center for Excellence in Primary Care. (2023). Retrieved from: https://cepc.ucsf.edu/standing-orders.

403. Garfinkel, S., & Spafford, G. (2011). *Web Security, Privacy & Commerce: Security for Users, Administrators and ISP's*. Sebastopol, CA: O'Reilly Media, Inc.

404. Shiri, A. (2012). Powering search: The role of thesauri in new information environments. *Journal of the Association for Information Science and Technology, 65*(5), 1085–1088. https://doi.org/10.1002/asi.23157.

405. SNOMED Glossary. (2023). Top-level concept. Retrieved from: https://conflu-ence.ihtsdotools.org/display/DOCGLOSS/top+level+concept.

406. eLeap LMS. (2023). The concept of train-the-trainer. Retrieved from: www.eleapsoftware.com/exploring-the-train-the-trainer-model-the-what-why-and-hows/.

407. Kiel, J. (2000). *Information Technology for the Practicing Physician*. New York, NY: Springer-Verlag.

408. Dunning, D. (2023). What is a computer trapdoor?" Retrieved from: www.tech-walla.com/articles/what-is-a-computer-trapdoor.

409. Gray B.H., & Field M.J. (eds). (1989). *Controlling Costs and Changing Patient Care? The Role of Utilization Management*. Washington, DC: National Academies Press (US). Retrieved from: www.ncbi.nlm.nih.gov/books/NBK234995/.

410. Croskerry, P., & Cosby, K. (2009). *Patient Safety in Emergency Medicine*. Philadelphia, PA: Lippincott Williams & Wilkins.

411. Unicode. (2023). Frequently asked questions. Retrieved from: http://unicode.org/faq/utf_bom.html.

412. NEJM Catalyst. (2018). What is value-based healthcare? Retrieved from: https://catalyst.nejm.org/what-is-value-based-healthcare/.

413. CMS. (2023). Medicare advantage Value Based Insurance Design (VBID). Retrieved from: https://innovation.cms.gov/innovation-models/vbid.

414. Intermountain Healthcare. (2018). Intermountain Healthcare Opens New Hospital – Without a Building or Walls. Retrieved from: https://intermountainhealthcare.org/news/2018/02/intermountain-healthcare-opens-new-hospital-without-a-building-or-walls/.
415. Association for Healthcare Volunteer Resource Professionals (AHVRP). (2023). Veterans Integrated Service Network (VISN). Retrieved from: www.ahvrp.org/about/visn.shtml.
416. U.S. Department of Veterans Affairs. (2023). Veterans Health Administration. Retrieved from: www.va.gov/health/aboutVHA.asp.
417. Palmer, D. (2018). What is malware? Everything you need to know about viruses, Trojans and malicious software. Retrieved from: www.zdnet.com/article/what-is-malware-everything-you-need-to-know-about-viruses-trojans-and-malicious-software/.
418. AddonData.com. (2017). Benefits of Workstations on Wheels in Healthcare. Retrieved from: www.addondata.com/2017/09/benefits-of-workstations-on-wheels-in-healthcare/.
419. Chapple, M., Littlejohn Shinder, D., & Tittel, E. (2002). *TICSA Training Guide*. Indianapolis, IN: Pearson IT Certification.
420. NIST Computer Security Resource Center. (2023). Access Control Policy and Implementation Guides. Retrieved from: https://csrc.nist.gov/Projects/Access-Control-Policy-and-Implementation-Guides.
421. Public Welfare – Accounting of disclosures of protected health information. 45 CFR 164.528 (2011).
422. Miller, D., & Mancuso, P. (2008). *MCITP 70–623 Exam Cram: Supporting and Troubleshooting Applications on a Windows Vista Client for Consumer Support Technicians*. Indianapolis, IN: Pearson IT Certification.
423. Federal Bureau of Investigation. (2017). Public Service Announcement: Business Email Compromise. Retrieved from: www.ic3.gov/media/2017/170504.aspx.
424. Internal Revenue Service. (2014). Notice 2014–21. Retrieved from: www.irs.gov/pub/irs-drop/n-14-21.pdf.
425. ProjectManagment.com. (2006). Transition planning. Retrieved from: www.projectmanagement.com/wikis/233094/Transition-Planning.
426. MITRE. (2023). Common attack pattern enumeration and classification. Retrieved from: https://capec.mitre.org/index.html.
427. American College of Physicians. (2023). Chronic care management toolkit. Retrieved from: www.acponline.org/system/files/documents/running_practice/payment_coding/medicare/chronic_care_management_toolkit.pdf. S.
428. Kessler, K. (2015). Enhanced ABAP development with Core Data Services (CDS). Retrieved from: https://sapinsider.wispubs.com/Assets/Articles/2015/October/SPI-enhanced-ABAP-development-with-Core-Data-Services.
429. Fiks, A.G. (2011). Designing computerized decision support that works for clinicians and families. *Current Problems in Pediatric and Adolescent Health Care, 41*(3), 60–88. http://doi.org/10.1016/j.cppeds.2010.10.006.

430. ISO/IEC 15417: 2007 (2007). Information technology -Automatic identification and data capture techniques—Code 128 bar code symbology specification. Retrieved from: www.iso.org.

431. Data Linkage Services of Western Australia. (2023). What is data linkage? Retrieved from: www.datalinkageservices.health.wa.gov.au/glossary/.

432. Indiana University IT Support Center Knowledge Base. (2019). About daemons in Unix. Retrieved from: https://kb.iu.edu/d/aiau.

433. Thake, M. (2018). What is DAG? Distributed ledger technology. Retrieved from: https://medium.com/nakamo-to/what-is-dag-distributed-ledger-technology-8b182a858e19.

434. Sequoia Project. (2023). Patient unified lookup system for emergencies. Retrieved from: https://sequoiaproject.org/pulse/.

435. Blockchain Hub Berlin. (2018). Smart contracts. Retrieved from: https://blockchainhub.net/smart-contracts/.

436. MassChallenge HealthTech. (2018). A digital health collaborative. Retrieved from: https://medium.com/@MassChallengeHT/a-digital-health-collaborative-a4f633dc9118.

437. Provost, P., Johns, M., & Palmer, S. (2018) Procuring interoperability: Achieving high-quality, connected, and person-centered care. Retrieved from: https://nam.edu/wp-content/uploads/2018/10/Procuring-Interoperability_web.pdf.

438. Olavsrud, T., & Fruhlinger, J. (2023). What is business intelligence? Transforming data into business insights. Retrieved from: www.cio.com/article/272364/business-intelligence-definition-and-solutions.html.

439. Medtrainer.com. (2023). Chief Compliance Officer. Retrieved from: https://medtrainer.com/compliance-corner/chief-compliance-officer/.

440. Dental Claim Support. (2023), CDT codes: Current dental terminology explained. Retrieved from: www.dentalclaimsupport.com/blog/cdt-codes-current-dental-terminology.

444. WHO. (2023). Universal Health Coverage. Retrieved from: www.who.int/news-room/fact-sheets/detail/universal-health-coverage-(uhc).

445. Institute for Healthcare Improvement. (2023). Failure Modes and Effects Analysis Tools (FMEA). Retrieved from: www.ihi.org/resources/pages/tools/failuremodesandeffectsanalysistool.aspx.

446. ECQI Resource Center. (2022). Harmonization. Retrieved from: https://ecqi.healthit.gov/glossary/harmonization.

447. Centers for Medicare & Medicaid Services (CMS). (2023). HCPCS general information. Retrieved from: www.cms.gov/medicare/coding/medhcpcsgeninfo.

448. Infowerks. (2020). What is a health information system? Retrieved from: https://infowerks.com/health-information-system/.

449. Health Resources & Services Administration. (2022). Health literacy. Retrieved www.hrsa.gov/about/organization/bureaus/ohe/health-literacy/index.html.

450. National Library of Medicine. (2022). Health literacy. Retrieved from: www.ncbi.nlm.nih.gov/books/NBK216035/.

451. US Department of Health and Human Services, Office of Disease Prevention and Health Promotion. (2023). Healthcare Effectiveness Data and Information Set (HEDIS). Retrieved from: https://health.gov/healthy-people/objectives-and-data/data-sources-and-methods/data-sources/healthcare-effectiveness-data-and-information-set-hedis.

452. HealthIT.gov. (n/d). Health information exchange. Retrieved from: www.healthit.gov/topic/health-it-and-health-information-exchange-basics/health-information-exchange.

453. Talking Health Tech. (2020). Health Information Service Provider (HISP). Retrieved from: www.talkinghealthtech.com/glossary/health-information-service-provider-hisp.

454. US Department of Health and Human Services. (2023). Health information technology. Retrieved from: www.hhs.gov/hipaa/for-professionals/special-topics/health-information-technology/index.html.

455. The HIPAA Journal. (2023). What is the HITECH Act? Retrieved from: www.hipaajournal.com/what-is-the-hitech-act/.

456. Office of the National Coordinator for Health Information Technology. ECQI Resource Center. (2023). HQMF-Health Quality Measure Format. Retrieved from: https://ecqi.healthit.gov/hqmf.

457. Cloud Academy. (2023). What is a hypervisor? Video. Retrieved from: https://cloudacademy.com/course/introduction-to-virtualization-technologies/paravirtualization-full-virtualization-1/?gclid=EAIaIQobChMI6bierOv6_wIVARSzAB2TdwHNEAAYAiAAEgJvTvD_BwE&hsa_acc=5890858304&hsa_ad=651406236896&hsa_cam=12050150150&hsa_grp=115060577886&hsa_kw=&hsa_mt=&hsa_net=adwords&hsa_src=s&hsa_tgt=dsa-19959388920&hsa_ver=3&utm_campaign=&utm_medium=ppc&utm_source=adwords&utm_term=.

458. Talking Health Tech. (2021). Clinical Information System (CIS). Retrieved from: www.talkinghealthtech.com/glossary/clinical-information-system-cis.

459. HIMSS. (2019). *HIMSS Dictionary of Health Information and Technology Terms, Acronyms, and Organizations* (5th ed.). Boca Raton, FL: CRC Press, Taylor & Francis Group.

460. Miller, R.S., Mitchell, K., Myslinski, R., & Rising, J. (2019). Chapter 1: Health information technology (HIT) and patient registries. In (Gliklich RE, Leavy MB, Dreyer NA, eds), *Tools and Technologies for Registry Interoperability, Registries for Evaluating Patient Outcomes: A User's Guide* (3rd ed.). Addendum 2 [Internet].

461. Green, G. (1978). What is a clinical algorithm? *Clinical Pediatrics, 17*(5), 457. Retrieved from: https://doi.org/10.1177/000992287801700512.

462. American Medical Informatics Association (AMIA). (n/d). Clinical informatics subspecialty. Retrieved from: https://amia.org/careers-certifications/clinical-informatics-subspecialty.

463. Russler, D. (2009). Clinical observation. In: Liu, L., & Özsu, M.T. (eds) *Encyclopedia of Database Systems*. Boston, MA: Springer. https://doi.org/10.1007/978-0-387-39940-9_61.

464. Rotter, T., Baatenburg de Jong, R., Lacko, S.E., Ronellenfitsch, U., & Kinsman, L. (2019). Clinical pathways as a quality strategy. In: Busse, R., Klazinga, N., & Panteli D., et al., (eds) *Improving Healthcare Quality in Europe: Characteristics, Effectiveness and Implementation of Different Strategies* [Internet]. Health Policy Series, No. 53. Copenhagen (Denmark): European Observatory on Health Systems and Policies.

465. American Academy of Osteopathic Surgeons. (n/d). Performance measures frequently asked questions: What is a clinical performance measure? Retrieved from: www.aaos.org/globalassets/quality-and-practice-resources/quality-perfor-mance-measures-resouces/pm-faqs_3-6-172.pdf.

466. Centers for Medicare & Medicaid Services (CMS). (2023). Retrieved from: www.cms.gov/medicare/coordination-of-benefits-and-recovery/coordination-of-benefits-and-recovery-overview/coordination-of-benefits/coordination-of-benefits. Last accessed July 2023.

467. Arihant, J. (2023). Different types of coding schemes to rep-resent data. Retrieved from: www.geeksforgeeks.org/different-types-of-coding-schemes-to-represent-data.

468. Zito, P. (2017). Smart Buildings Academy: What is a communica-tions bus? Retrieved from: https://blog.smartbuildingsacademy.com/what-is-a-communications-bus.

469. Padamker, P. (2023). Types of communication network. Retrieved from: www.educba.com/types-of-communication-network/.

470. Data Manafement Wiki. Comparability. (2023). Retrieved from: https://dataman-agement.wiki/data_quality_dimension/comparability_over_populations.

471. Forbes, L. (2021). Computer-assisted coding. Retrieved from: https://mcuser-content.com/95c4af0da811aedf405eeb692/files/65735c74-4544-60c9-3cb4-74531d23fc23/Computer_Assisted_Coding_Blog_1_.pdf.

472. International Standards Organization. (2007). ISO860:2007(en) Terminology work—Harmonization of concepts and terms. Retrieved from: www.iso.org/obp/ui/#iso:std:iso:860:ed-3:v1:en.

473. Landau, P. (2023). Cost-benefit analysis for projects: Finding the cost benefit ratio. Retrieved from: www.projectmanager.com/blog/cost-benefit-analysis-for-projects-a-step-by-step-guide.

474. ECQI Resource Center. (2022). Clinical quality language. Retrieved from: https://ecqi.healthit.gov/cql.

475. Pearson, S.D., Fisher, D.G., & Lee, T.H. (1995), Critical pathways as a strat-egy for improving care: Problems and potential. *Annals of Internal Medicine*. Retrieved from: https://doi.org/10.7326/0003-4819-123-12-199512150-00008.

476. Spirion. (2023). Data classification guide. Retrieved from: www.spirion.com/data-classification/#:~:text=is%20data%20classification.-,What%20is%20data%20classification%3F,compliance%20regulations%20that%20protect%20them.

477. Nord VPN Cybersecurity Glossary. (2023). Data diddling. Retrieved from: https://nordvpn.com/cybersecurity/glossary/data-diddling/.

478. Noah. (2023). Analyst answers: What is a data object? Definition, types, & examples. Retrieved from: https://analystanswers.com/what-is-a-data-object-definition-types-examples/.

479. Express Analytics. (2023). What is data processing? Retrieved from: www.expressanalytics.com/blog/data-processing-steps-types/.

480. Arbor Matrix Admin. (2021). The basics of clinical data registries. Retrieved from: www.arbormetrix.com/blog/clinical-data-registry-basics/.

481. Informatica. (2023). What is data validation? Retrieved from: www.informatica.com/services-and-training/glossary-of-terms/data-validation-definition.html.

482. Gartner Glossary: Data Warehouse. (2023). Retrieved from: www.gartner.com/en/information-technology/glossary/data-warehouse.

483. SolarWinds.com. (2023). Database schema definition. Retrieved from: www.solarwinds.com/resources/it-glossary/database-schema.

484. Pollock, D.A., Adams, D.L., Bernardo, L.M., Bradley, V., Brandt, M.D., Davis, T.E., Garrision, H.G., Iseke, R.M., Johnson, S., Kaufmann, C.R., Kidd, P., Leon-Chisen, N., MacLean, S., Manton, A., McClain, P.W., Michelso, E.A., Pickett, D., Rosen, R.A., Schwartz, R.J., Smith, M., Snyder, J.A., &Wright, J.L. (1998). Data elements for emergency department systems, release 1.0 (DEEDS): A summary report. DEEDS Writing Committee. *Journal of Emergency Nursing, 24*(1), 35–44. https://doi.org/10.1016/s0099-1767(98)90168-4.

485. IBM. (2023). Default routes. Retrieved from: www.ibm.com/docs/en/i/7.3?topic=concepts-default-routes.

486. Gartner Glossary: Clinical Data Repository. (2023). Retrieved from: www.gartner.com/en/information-technology/glossary/cdr-clinical-data-repository.

487. Infoscipedia. (2023). What is descriptor? Retrieved from: www.igi-global.com/dictionary/using-global-shape-descriptors-content/7294.

488. Lowgren, J., & Stilterman, E. (2007). *Thoughtful Interaction Design: A Design Perspective on Information Technology.* Boston, MA: The MIT Press.

489. Federal Agencies Digital Guidelines Initiatives. (2023). Glossary: Derivative file. Retrieved from: www.digitizationguidelines.gov/term.php?term=derivativefile#:~:text=Term%3A%20Derivative%20file&text=Definition%3A,parts%20of%20an%20archival%20collection.

490. Sonnier, P. (2017). The story of digital health. Retrieved from: http://storyofdigitalhealth.com/videos/.

491. Canberra Health Literacy Hub. (2022). What is digital health literacy? Digital health literacy. Retrieved from: https://cbrhl.org.au/what-is-health-literacy/digital-health-literacy/.

492. Office of the National Coordinator. (2023). HealthIT.gov. Direct basics: Q & A for providers. Retrieved from: www.healthit.gov/sites/default/files/directbasicsforprovidersqa_05092014.pdf.

493. Healthcare.gov. (2023). Durable Medical Equipment (DME). Retrieved from: www.healthcare.gov/glossary/durable-medical-quipment-dme/.

494. Centers for Medicare & Medicaid Services (CMS). (2023). Design and development of the Diagnosis Related Group (DRG). Retrieved from: www.cms.gov/icd10m/version37-fullcode-cms/fullcode_cms/Design_and_development_of_the_Diagnosis_Related_Group_(DRGs).pdf.

495. Centers for Medicare & Medicaid Services. (2022). Standard-setting and related organizations. Retrieved from: www.cms.gov/regulations-and-guidance/administrative-simplification/hipaa-aca/standardssettingandrelatedorganizations.
496. Bednarz, P. (2020). Entity-Attribute-Value (EAV) database model. Retrieved from: https://pbedn.github.io/post/2020-05-25-entity-attribute-value/.
497. CIO Wiki. (2022). Enterprise Information System (EIS). Retrieved from: https://cio-wiki.org/wiki/Enterprise_Information_System_(EIS).
498. Cornell Law School, Legal Information Institute. (2023). Electronic Code of Federal Regulations (e-CFR) Title 45—Public Welfare. SUBTITLE A—Department of Health and Human Services. SUBCHAPTER C—ADMINISTRATIVE DATA STANDARDS AND RELATED REQUIREMENTS. PART 160—GENERAL ADMINISTRATIVE REQUIREMENTS. Subpart A—General Provisions. § 160.103 Definitions. Retrieved from: www.law.cornell.edu/cfr/text/45/160.103.
499. Glossaria.net. (2023). EN46000. Retrieved from: www.glossaria.net/en/quality/en-46000.
500. CIO.gov. (2023). Clinger-Cohen Act of 1996. Retrieved from: www.cio.gov/handbook/it-laws/clinger-cohen-act/.
501. Centers for Medicare & Medicaid Services (CMS). (2023). E-prescribing. Retrieved from: www.cms.gov/medicare/e-health/eprescribing.
502. 9000 Store. (2023). What is error proofing? Retrieved from: https://the9000store.com/articles/what-is-error-proofing/.
503. Dunaway, J. (2023). What is a data interchange format? Retrieved from: www.easytechjunkie.com/what-is-a-data-interchange-format.htm.
504. Babuchandran, S. (2021). Software extensibility: Definition, attributes and techniques. Retrieved from: www.peerspot.com/articles/software-extensibility-definition-attributes-and-techniques.
505. Center for Medicare and Medicaid Services. (n/d). Health care payment learning and action network. Retrieved from: https://innovation.cms.gov/innovation-models/health-care-payment-learning-and-action-network.
506. Center for Medicare and Medicaid Services. (2021). Life safety code & Health Care Facilities Code (HCFC). Retrieved from: www.cms.gov/medicare/provider-enrollment-and-certification/guidanceforlawsandregulations/lsc.
507. Centers for Disease Control and Prevention (CDC), National Center for Health Statistics. (2023). International Classification of Diseases, Tenth Revision (ICD-10). Retrieved from: www.cdc.gov/nchs/icd/icd10.htm.
508. World Health Organization (WHO). (2023). International Classification of Functioning, disability and health (ICF). Retrieved from: www.who.int/standards/classifications/international-classification-of-functioning-disability-and-health.
509. Kumar, V., & Bhardwaj, A. (2018). Identity management systems: A comparative analysis. *International Journal of Strategic Decision Sciences (IJSDS)*, *9*(1), 63–78. https://doi.org/10.4018/IJSDS.2018010105.

510. DelFiol, G., Huser, V., Strasberg, H.R., Maviglia, S.M., Curtis, C., & Cimino, J. (2012). Implementations of the HL7 context-aware knowledge retrieval ("Infobutton") standard: Challenges, strengths, limitations, and uptake. *Journal of Biomedical Informatics, 45*(4), 726–735.

511. Goodwin, N. (2016). Understanding integrated care. *International Journal of Integrated Care, 16*(4). https://doi.org/10.5334/ijic.2530.

512. Windows Security Encyclopedia. (2023). Interactive services detection. Retrieved from: www.windows-security.org/windows-service/interactive-services-detection.

513. Chief Information Officer Council. (2023). Clinger-Cohen Act of 1996. Retrieved from: www.cio.gov/handbook/it-laws/clinger-cohen-act/.

514. Robinson, L.A. (2017). An Introduction to OASIS: Outcome and assessment information set. Retrieved from: www.relias.com/blog/an-introduction-to-oasis-outcome-and-assessment-information-set.

515. Social Security Administration. (2023). Definition of objective medical evidence. Retrieved from: https://secure.ssa.gov/poms.nsf/lnx/0424503010.

516. Gruber, T. (2008). Ontology. In: L. Liu, & M. Tamer Özsu (eds) *Entry in the Encyclopedia of Database Systems*. Springer-Verlag, 2009. Retrieved from: https://tomgruber.org/writing/definition-of-ontology.

517. Doherty, E. (2023). What is object-oriented programming? OOP explained in depth. Retrieved from: www.educative.io/blog/object-oriented-programming.

518. Jason, C. (2020). What is a national patient identifier and why is it important? Retrieved from: https://ehrintelligence.com/news/what-is-a-national-patient-identifier-and-why-is-it-important.

519. HealthIT.Gov. (n/d). Health insurance information. Retrieved from: www.healthit.gov/isa/uscdi-data/payer-identifier.

520. Live Action. (2019). Network architecture primer. Retrieved from: www.liveaction.com/blog/network-architecture/.

521. Healthcare.gov. (2023). Qualified Health Plan (QHP). Retrieved from: www.healthcare.gov/glossary/qualified-health-plan/.

522. National Library of Medicine. (2001). Quick Medical Reference-synopsis (QMR). Retrieved from: www.nlm.nih.gov/research/umls/sourcereleasedocs/current/QMR/index.html.

523. Digital.gov. (2023). Introduction to QR codes. Retrieved from: https://digital.gov/resources/introduction-to-qr-codes/.

524. CQI/IRCA. (2023). What is quality? Retrieved from: www.quality.org/what-quality.

525. Agency for Healthcare Research and Quality (AHRQ). (2023). AHRQ Quality indicators. Retrieved from: https://qualityindicators.ahrq.gov/.

526. Center for Medicare and Medicaid Services, Measures Management System. (2023). Quality measure FAQs. Retrieved from: https://mmshub.cms.gov/about-quality/new-to-measures/what-is-a-measure.

527. Geeks for Geeks. (2023). Queue data structure. Retrieved from: www.geeksforgeeks.org/queue-data-structure/.

528. Mule Soft. (2023). What is a messaging queuing service? Retrieved from: www.mulesoft.com/resources/cloudhub/what-is-a-messaging-queuing-service.

529. HV Technologies, Inc. The basics of time-domain reflectometry-tdrtime-domin. Retrieved from: https://hvtechnologies.com/the-basics-of-time-domain-reflectometry-tdr/.

530. SyncResource. (2023). Defining an ISO Technical Specification (TS). Retrieved from: https://sync-resource.com/blog/iso-technical-specification/.

531. Mayo Clinic Staff. (2023). Telehealth: Technology meets health care. Retrieved from: www.mayoclinic.org/healthy-lifestyle/consumer-health/in-depth/telehealth/art-20044878.

532. NIST Special Publication 800–53, SC: System and Communications Protection. (2023). SC-8: Transmission confidentiality and integrity. Retrieved from: https://csf.tools/reference/nist-sp-800-53/r5/sc/sc-8/.

533. Microsoft.com. (2021). Smart card user interface. Retrieved from: https://learn.microsoft.com/en-us/windows/win32/secauthn/smart-card-user-interface.

534. US Department of Health and Human Services, Office of Disease Prevention and Health Promotion. (2023). Social determinants of health. Retrieved from: https://health.gov/healthypeople/priority-areas/social-determinants-health.

535. Ex Libris. (2023). Configuring searchable user identifiers. Retrieved from: https://knowledge.exlibrisgroup.com/Alma/Product_Documentation/010Alma_Online_Help_(English)/050Administration/040Configuring_User_Management/110Linking_Users_in_Collaborative_Networks.

536. IGI Global. (2023). What is semantic correspondence? Retrieved from: www.igi-global.com/dictionary/semantic-alignment-business-standards-legacy/34584 www.igi-global.com/dictionary/information-infrastructure/14415.

537. Zhuge, H. (2016). "The emerging structures" in *Multi-Dimensional Summarization in Cyber-Physical Society*. New York: Elsevier.

538. CodeTwo.com. (2021). What is a sensitivity label? Retrieved from: www.code-two.com/admins-blog/sensitivity-labels-office-365/#definition.

539. Geeks for Geeks.com. (2023). What is SGML? Retrieved from: www.geeksforgeeks.org/what-is-sgml/.

540. National Institute of Standards and Technology. (2023). Simple merge. Retrieved from: https://xlinux.nist.gov/dads/HTML/simplemerge.html.

541. TWI, Ltd. (2023). What is simulation? What does it mean? (Definition and Examples). Retrieved from: www.twi-global.com/technical-knowledge/faqs/faq-what-is-simulation.

542. National Institute of Standards and Technology, Office of the Director/Chief of Staff. (2023). National standards bodies. Retrieved from: www.nist.gov/iaao/national-standards-bodies.

543. Healthcare Information and Management Systems Society (HIMSS). (2023). Terminology standards. Retrieved from: www.himss.org/terminology-standards.

544. Centers for Medicare & Medicaid Services (CMS). (2023). Retrieved from: www.cms.gov/medicare/quality/value-based-programs/chip-reauthorization-act.

545. Kaspersky.com. (2023). What is malicious code? Retrieved from: www.kaspersky.com/resource-center/definitions/malicious-code.

546. Giardino, A.P., & DeJesus, O. (2022). Managed care. Retrieved from: www.ncbi.nlm.nih.gov/books/NBK564410/.

547. BCM Institute, BCMpedia. (2023). Maximum acceptable outage. Retrieved from: www.bcmpedia.org/wiki/Maximum_Acceptable_Outage_(MAO).

548. Centers for Medicare & Medicaid Services. (2023). Minimum data set 3.0 public reports. Retrieved from: www.cms.gov/data-research/computer-data-systems/minimum-data-sets-3.0-public-reports.

549. International Council for Harmonisation of Technical Requirements for Pharmaceuticals for Human Use (ICH)/. (2023). Welcome to the ICH MedDRA website. Retrieved from: www.meddra.org/how-to-use/support-documentation/english/welcome.

550. United States Food & Drug Administration (FDA). (2023). How to determine if your product is a medical device. Retrieved from: www.fda.gov/medical-devices/classify-your-medical-device/how-determine-if-your-product-medical-device.

551. Primary Care Collaborative. (2023). Defining the medical home. Retrieved from: https://thepcc.org/content/defining-medical-home.

552. National Coordinating Council for Medication Error Reporting and Prevention (NCCMERP). (2023). About medication errors: What is a medication error? Retrieved from: www.nccmerp.org/about-medication-errors.

553. National Library of Medicine. (2023). MeSH. Retrieved from: www.ncbi.nlm.nih.gov/mesh/.

554. National Library of Medicine. (2023). Unified Medical Language System® (UMLS®): Metathesaurus. Retrieved from: www.nlm.nih.gov/research/umls/knowledge_sources/metathesaurus/index.html.

555. IEEE Standards Association. (2023). Retrieved from: https://standards.ieee.org/ieee/11073-10101/5034/.

556. Medicaid.gov. (2023). Medicaid information technology architecture. Retrieved from: www.medicaid.gov/medicaid/data-systems/medicaid-information-technology-architecture/index.html.

557. Tardi, C. (2023). What is Moore's law and is it still true? Retrieved from: www.investopedia.com/terms/m/mooreslaw.asp.

558. Moore's Law.org. (2023). Moore's law. Retrieved from: www.mooreslaw.org/.

559. MPAI Community. (2022). Why MPAI? Retrieved from: https://mpai.community/why-mpai/.

560. Office of the National Coordinator for Health Information Technology (ONC). (2023). Frequently asked questions. Retrieved from: www.healthit.gov/faq/what-meaningful-use.

561. Endace. (2023). A complete guide to packet sniffing. Retrieved from: www.endace.com/learn/what-is-packet-sniffing.

562. Talking HealthTech. (2020). Patient Administration Systems (PAS). Retrieved from: www.talkinghealthtech.com/glossary/patient-administration-systems-pas.

563. Nursing Guide. (2015). The patient classification system. Retrieved from: www.nursingguide.ph/category-career-guides/the-patient-classification-system.

564. Talking HealthTech. (2020). Patient Administration Systems (PAS). Retrieved from: www.talkinghealthtech.com/glossary/patient-portals.

565. Network Encyclopedia. (2023). Primary domain controller. Retrieved from: https://networkencyclopedia.com/primary-domain-controller-pdc/.

566. Neodynamic. (2023). PDF 417 barcode. Retrieved from: www.neodynamic.com/barcodes/PDF417-Barcode.aspx.

567. Cortes, D., Leung, J., Ryl, A., & Lieu, J. Pharmacy informatics: Where medication use and technology meet. *The Canadian Journal of Hospital Pharmacy*, 72(4), 320–326. www.ncbi.nlm.nih.gov/pmc/articles/PMC6699873/.

568. Hardy, Chad. (2008). Chapter 4: Pharmacy information systems. In: Dimitru, D. (ed) *The Pharmacy Informatics Primer*. The Woodlands Texas: American Society of Hospital Pharmacists.

569. Lanier, C. (2023). What is plenum? What is plenum cable? Retrieved from: www.gammaelectronics.net/what-is-plenum-what-is-plenum-cable/.

570. TechTerms.com. (2023). Plug and play. Retrieved from: https://techterms.com/definition/plug_and_play.

571. Shortliffe, E.H., Cimino, J.J., & Chiang, M.F. (2021). *Biomedical Informatics: Computer Applications in Health Care and Biomedicine* (5th ed.). New York, NY: Springer.

572. Centers for Disease Control and Prevention (CDC). (2023). Original essential public health services framework. Retrieved from: www.cdc.gov/publichealth-gateway/publichealthservices/originalessentialhealthservices.html.

573. Fortra Digital Guardian. (2023). What is public key cryptography? Retrieved from: www.digitalguardian.com/blog/what-public-key-cryptography.

574. CISA.gov. (2023). Stop ransomware: Resources. Retrieved from: www.cisa.gov/stopransomware/resources.

575. Rathnam, L. (2022). What is reference architecture? Retrieved from: https://techgenix.com/reference-architecture-guide/.

576. NEJM Catalyst. (2018). What is risk management in healthcare? Retrieved from: https://catalyst.nejm.org/doi/full/10.1056/CAT.18.0197.

577. European Union Agency for Cybersecurity (ENISA). (2023). Risk treatment. Retrieved from: www.enisa.europa.eu/topics/risk-management/current-risk/risk-management-inventory/rm-process/risk-treatment.

578. Centrak. (2023). What is RTLS in healthcare? Retrieved from: https://centrak.com/resources/blog/rtls-for-hospitals.

579. Imel, M., & Campbell, J.R. (2003). Mapping from a clinical terminology to a classification. Retrieved from: https://library.ahima.org/doc?oid=61537.

Printed in the United States
by Baker & Taylor Publisher Services